'Guilty Women,' Foreign Policy,
in Inter-War Britain

Also by Julie V. Gottlieb

FEMININE FASCISM
Women in Britain's Fascist Movement, 1923–1945

THE CULTURE OF FASCISM
Visions of the Far Right in Britain (*edited with Thomas P. Linehan*)

MAKING REPUTATIONS
Power, Persuasion and the Individual in Modern British Politics (*edited with Richard Toye*)

THE AFTERMATH OF SUFFRAGE
Women, Gender and Politics in Britain, 1918–1945 (*edited with Richard Toye*)

'Guilty Women,' Foreign Policy, and Appeasement in Inter-War Britain

Julie V. Gottlieb
Senior Lecturer in Modern History, University of Sheffield, UK

First published 2015 by
PALGRAVE MACMILLAN

Palgrave Macmillan in the UK is an imprint of Macmillan Publishers Limited, registered in England, company number 785998, of Houndmills, Basingstoke, Hampshire RG21 6XS.

Palgrave Macmillan in the US is a division of St Martin's Press LLC, 175 Fifth Avenue, New York, NY 10010.

Palgrave Macmillan is the global academic imprint of the above companies and has companies and representatives throughout the world.

Palgrave® and Macmillan® are registered trademarks in the United States, the United Kingdom, Europe and other countries.

ISBN 978-0-230-30430-7   ISBN 978-1-137-31660-8 (eBook)
DOI 10.1007/978-1-137-31660-8

This book is printed on paper suitable for recycling and made from fully managed and sustained forest sources. Logging, pulping and manufacturing processes are expected to conform to the environmental regulations of the country of origin.

A catalogue record for this book is available from the British Library.

A catalog record for this book is available from the Library of Congress.

Typeset by MPS Limited, Chennai, India.

Contents

List of Illustrations

Acknowledgements

As befits a book with such a judicial-sounding title, I begin with a small confession. The first thing I read when I open a book are the acknowledgments. This must have something to do with the fact that the writing of the dedications is as close as most academic writers will ever get to performing an Oscar acceptance speech. For my part, what draws me to the front piece first is that it offers a potted, albeit ramekin-sized, autobiography of the author, and a bildungsroman of the book. So here it goes, a short account of my 'guilty women years.'

First, I would like to thank the following for making my journeys through archives and libraries straightforward and rewarding, and for permission to quote from collections: Keelan Carr for permission to quote from, and Jeremy McIlwaine for guiding me through, the Conservative Party Archive; Guy Baxter and Caroline Benson at the Nancy Astor Collection, University of Reading, with special thanks for permission to reproduce images; Susan Worall, Director, Neville Chamberlain Papers, Cadbury Archive Centre, University of Birmingham, for permission to reproduce images, and for the help of the special collections team who were always most courteous and informative; the University of Kent Cartoon archive and Solo Syndication for permission to publish cartoons by David Low; and the staff at the Special Collections, University of Liverpool, for the use of a photo portrait and for access to this rich archive. Extracts from the works of Sir Winston Churchill are reproduced with permission of Curtis Brown, London, on behalf of the Estate of Winston S. Churchill. Extracts from the Mass-Observation Archive are reproduced with permission of the Curtis Brown Group Ltd, and on behalf of the Trustees of the Mass-Observation Archive. I am also grateful to librarians and archivists at the Labour History Research Centre, Manchester; the Women's Library, London; Jacky Hodgson at the Special Collections, and Clare Scott, University of Sheffield Library; the John Rylands Library, University of Manchester, and the Manchester Central Library; the British Library; the National Archive, Kew; the Churchill Archive Centre, Churchill College, Cambridge; the Vera Brittain Collection, McMasters University; and the Catherine Marshall Collection, Cumbria Record Office. Further, I thank the Department of History and the University of Sheffield for kindly subsidizing research travel and conference attendance, contributing towards copyright fees, and for providing me with periods of study leave; the British Academy for a small research grant; and the University of Paris-Diderot for inviting me on two separate occasions as a visiting professor—in fact, the last edits were completed in Paris in the springtime, when it unseasonably drizzled.

I am fortunate to be surrounded by some wonderful people who have taken a close interest in the book as it has developed. Richard Toye–who, as it happens, brought Baxter's *Guilty Women* (1941) to my attention in the first place–has always most generously taken time out from his own hyper-productive writing schedule to read the manuscript in its entirety. I am very grateful to those who have read draft chapters and shared their insights. Adrian Bingham, Clarisse Berthezène, Susan Grayzel, Matthew Hendley, David Hudson, Martin Pugh, June Purvis, and Matthew Stibbe, thank you all for putting me through my paces. The two anonymous readers of the proposal and the manuscript commissioned by Palgrave provided invaluable constructive criticism that has made this, I hope, a better book. In various vibrant research networks, at conferences, seminars, and in more informal opportunities for the exchange of ideas, many others have posed searching questions that have helped me sharpen my arguments, while no one but myself, of course, bears responsibility for any errors herein of fact, form, or judgement. The longer it takes for a monograph to be written, the lengthier such a list of names will inevitably be, and here is mine: Stuart Ball, Peter Clarke, Nigel Copsey, Krista Cowman, Ian Kershaw, Peter Marsh, Helen McCarthy, Susan Pedersen, Paul Readman, Ingrid Sharpe, Dan Stone, Pat Thane, Philippe Vervaecke, Mary Vincent, and Philip Williamson. Then there are those with whom I have been able to share the trials and travails of the writing process, friends and confidants Julia Hillner, Natalie Zacek, Julia and Nick Mansfield, Glyn Redworth, Akos Farkas and Maria Palla, Maiken Umbach, Karen Harvey, Judith Szapor, Florence Binard, Michel Prum, and Peter Gottlieb (it helps to have a brother who is both a writer and a best friend). It is a privilege too to be a member of an intellectually energizing and ambitious Department of History, and I have appreciated my colleagues' and my students' interest in my research and their incisive comments. The editorial team at Palgrave, especially Jenny McCall, Clare Mence, Angharad Bishop, and Emily Russell, have been highly efficient and supportive throughout.

This book was written during a period in my life where I experienced the greatest joy, the birth of my two amazing children, but also the deepest sadness, the passing of my brilliant parents. Writing about crisis, both political and emotional, coincided for me with the process of bereavement, with the added resonance that the turbulent times of which I write are precisely those when my parents were born. Their leave-no-stone-unturned work ethic and the high value they always placed on creative and intellectual striving is their most generous legacy, and I can only hope that this book honours their memory. My late mother inspires me every day, on a very personal level but also in my scholarly choices, and I believe she would have approved of my cultural approach to political history. At an earlier stage of this project my father, a great wordsmith, suggested that I use 'the appeasettes' as the book's title, and although I have not followed this paternal guidance to the letter,

I am channelling his voice each time I permit myself some stylistic whimsy or include a pun.

And many people have helped alleviate my own guilty feelings that unavoidably arise as part of the struggle to achieve the work/life balance. It really does take a village, and I want to express my gratitude to those 'super-women' who have nurtured and cared for our children (and for me), starting with my unfailingly giving and accommodating mother-in-law Janette, my small but tight-knit family in Canada, and Karen, Christina, Fannie, Reka, and Sophie, as well as a circle of treasured friends. The greatest support and most heart-felt encouragement has come, unstintingly, from Julian, and it is with love and affection that I dedicate this book to him, and to Benjamin and Elizabeth.

List of Abbreviations

ARP	Air Raid Precautions
BBC	British Broadcasting Corporation
BIPO	British Institute of Public Opinion
BU	British Union of Fascists and National Socialists (from 1936)
BUF	British Union of Fascists
CPGB	Communist Party of Great Britain
CSL	Citizens Service League
CWA	Conservative Women's Association
ERI	Equal Rights International
FIR	Feminist International Relations
GIR	Gender and International Relations
IAW	International Alliance of Women
ICW	International Council of Women
ILP	Independent Labour Party
IPC	International Peace Campaign
IWSA	International Women's Suffrage Alliance
LCC	London County Council
LNU	League of Nations Union
LSI	Labour and Socialist International
M-O	Mass-Observation
NCW	National Council of Women
NMDL	National Men's Defence League
NUSEC	National Union of Societies for Equal Citizenship
NUWSS	National Union of Women's Suffrage Societies
ODC	Open Door Council
ODI	Open Door International
PPU	Peace Pledge Union
SPG	Six Point Group
VAD	Volunteer Aid Detachment
WATS	Women's Auxiliary Territorial Service

WGE	Women's Guild of Empire
WI	Women's Institutes
WIL	Women's International League (British Section)
WILPF	Women's International League of Peace and Freedom
WNLF	Women's National Liberal Federation
WPC	Women's Peace Crusade
WSPU	Women's Social and Political Union
WUO	Women's Unionist Organisation
WVS	Women's Voluntary Service
WWCAWF	Women's World Committee against War and Fascism

Introduction—Guilty Women? Gendering Appeasement

In the year after the 'Men of Munich' were exposed in 'Cato's' *Guilty Men* (1940), an indictment of the National Government's foreign policy, British journalist and propagandist Richard Baxter provided something of a sequel in the form of *Guilty Women* (1941). Red-covered and printed on war-rationed newsprint, this little-known book marvelled at the public ignorance about women's nefarious influence on Anglo–German relations, their fomenting of wartime demoralization, and the threat a dangerous minority of British and German women posed as Fifth Columnists capable of undermining the war effort.[1] As the Blitz was raining down on British cities, Baxter unleashed his own attack on women for their part in Britain's diplomatic fumbling of the late 1930s, and their even greater share of responsibility for placing the nation in a state of material and psychological unreadiness for the Second World War. While much of Baxter's evidence would not stand the test of time or the scrutiny of historians, it is still significant that a dissident voice emerged in British anti-Nazi propaganda that presented women as something other than victims of the Nazi patriarchal regime or as the innocent casualties of war, and, furthermore, that raised the question of British women's part in the failed and, for many, the ignominious policy of appeasing the dictators.

Guilty Women was an odd and incongruous tract, simultaneously staunchly anti-fascist and anti-woman. Baxter began by saying that "possibly never in the history of Europe has the influence of women been so marked, both openly and *sub rosa*, in political life as during the past ten years. Few realise that much of the suffering now being endured is due to that influence."[2] He relied on essentialist constructions of women's nature that rang with Victorian condescension and, ironically, resounded with a woman-hating streak analogous to Nazi misogyny: women have a false sense of their own power and a will to dominate; their vanity is easily flattered; they are liable to indulge in scheming and plotting; and most politically engaged women are frustrated spinsters. His accusations could not jar more with the concurrent and coherently articulated feminist anti-fascist discourse. Indeed, one

1

of the keynotes in British anti-fascist literature of the 1930s was to conflate women with the victims of Nazism—as the 'weaker sex' they were figured as a persecuted 'minority' whose suffering was akin to that of Jews, democrats, political and religious dissidents, artists and intellectuals.[3]

Baxter deviated from this line, casting women as perpetrators, and thus anticipating a vigorous debate within German historiography over whether Nazi 'Aryan' women should be classed as the victims or the perpetrators of the genocidal regime.[4] For his part Baxter was driven by the desire to reveal actual or potential traitors among the female population, those he characterizes as "warped, mentally confused creatures who can never see any good in their own country or their country's policy."[5] He included among this group of women fellow travellers of both the Left and the Right, scandalous figures like Press Baron Lord Rothermere's ill-advised choice to serve as his European emissary and fixer Viennese-born Princess Stephanie Hohenlohe[6] and the notorious Unity Mitford,[7] as well as those women seduced by the machismo of authoritarian personalities. But what is particularly interesting is that Baxter was also suspicious of the well-intentioned British female politician whom he regarded as easily deceived by the overtures to peace directed at her by the conniving and intriguingly attractive foreign male. He mocked the "heroines making dramatic sacrifices for a cause which they hold to be dear,"[8] and he also cast suspicion on British women collectively, and as a species distinct from the whitewashed patriotic British male. Of British women, Baxter remarked that although they "happily ... enjoy a far greater degree of political freedom than women in Nazi Germany or in occupied countries," and although "the average British woman is a loyalist who places honour and the nation's welfare far above her personal ambitions," as a type she is nonetheless susceptible to the "love of participation in intrigue" that is "part of her make-up."[9] According to this logic, the unwittingly guilty women were pacifists and supporters of appeasement, disarmament, and no more war, and he surmised that there were two distinct types of guilty women, "those who were consciously guilty and those who did not realise until almost too late that they were being used as the tools of the Nazis. The 'unconsciously guilty' women in this country by far outnumbered those who were conscious of their guilt."[10] Hardly a British woman in politics or in the population at large escaped the tar of Baxter's brush, and of the latter category the only one with an iron-clad alibi of anti-fascist resistance was Labour's forceful critic of appeasement, 'Red' Ellen Wilkinson.

My research began as an investigation of Baxter's sensational allegations, and from the start I set out to contextualize his misogynist rant from the perspectives of British inter-war political, gender, and cultural history. While I have titled this book 'Guilty Women,' the reader should be persuaded that those two loaded words are followed by an implied interrogation mark. Nor do I share Baxter's shocking judgement or his lack of compassion for women's (and men's) forebodings of the war to come. I use the title not to pass a verdict on women but rather because women's culpability and certainly their complicity with the appeasers ran as a motif through the national and provincial press, as well as through the public and private musings of politicians on all sides of the visceral controversies over British foreign policy. In the domestic fallout of the international crisis we also see women grappling with feelings of remorse and shame, and, as my research demonstrates, highly susceptible to the affective disorders caused by the 'war of nerves.'

Yet, and taking into account its tabloid tone of paranoid fantasy and the fact that it is replete with unsubstantiated charges against named and many unnamed women, it is surprising that Baxter's provocative booklet received so little notice, then and since. In contrast, Cato's *Guilty Men* is considered a literary classic and it is still acknowledged as the keystone of appeasement historiography.[11] Why the very different reception and recognition of these two quazi-allegorical, scapegoating, wartime propaganda page-turners?

The most ready explanation is that women, guilty or otherwise, have hardly featured in the history of appeasement. Appeasement is the term given to the British and French governments' reactive policy of making political and territorial concessions to Nazi Germany in order to avoid war. The Munich Crisis represented the climax of this policy as Prime Minister Neville Chamberlain was the first 'shuttle diplomat' and inventor of "modern summitry,"[12] flying to see German Chancellor Adolf Hitler on three occasions to try to avert war over the Sudetenland, the region of the young democracy of Czechoslovakia with a large German minority. Chamberlain met Hitler at Berchtesgaden on 15 September; at Godesberg on 22–23 September; and at the Four Powers conference together with French Prime Minister Daladier and Italian Duce, Mussolini, on 29–30 September where the Munich Agreement was signed. Whole populations were on the edge of their seats as the nail-biting diplomatic drama unfolded, and the crisis was experienced intellectually, morally, emotionally, and very tangibly by everyone from royalty down to the man and the woman on the street. The Munich narrative was framed by Chamberlain, its screenwriter cum leading man, as part didactic children's story and part Shakespearian history play. Before boarding the plane for Munich the PM recited his childhood mantra 'if at once you do not succeed, try, try, try again,' and then quoted Hotspur in *Henry V*: 'out of this nettle, danger, we pluck this flower, safety.' The crowds obliged by playing their part in this historic *mis en scene*, and when Chamberlain returned from Munich, the *Daily Mail* reporter "saw hundreds of ordinary Englishmen and women lose all sense of reserve, and pour out the emotions they had hidden for weeks so that you felt a strange grip at the throat."[13] Too often, however, this story has been told as a male-centred history from above, with the people and certainly with the women left out.[14]

The reason for this male-centrism is not a paucity of sources, and it will soon become apparent that Richard Baxter was not a lone voice as he aired his anxieties and laid into the female of the species for giving free reign to their maternal and irenic instincts as war seemed imminent. Indeed, women were repeatedly represented as the Prime Minister's firmest supporters, and as the "best friends of Mr Chamberlain's policy."[15] The larger half of the electorate since the passage of the equal franchise in 1928, women voters were homogenized as a bloc, and, as such, they were reckoned to be underwriting the National Government's foreign policy at the ballot box. Newspapers declared that "Women can Make Premier Change his Policy,"[16] and in the post-Munich by-elections National Conservative candidates pressed "home at women's meetings ... the debt of gratitude women of the country owe to Mr Chamberlain for saving their homes and families by his Munich intervention."[17] BIPO polls, British Gallup, showed that Chamberlain was much more popular with women voters.[18] At the weathervane Oxford City by-election in October, 1938, Mass-Observation forecast A.D. Lindsay's (Independent Progressive) defeat because, whereas men felt "we ought to have stood up to [Hitler] before," the "general feeling of women: Anything for peace. Chamberlain did his best. He's a good gent."[19] An epigram circulated in the early months of 1939 to the effect that "in these days of fewer babies, the hand that has ceased to rock the cradle has begun to rule the world,"[20] as women's putative abnegation of their biological roles in favour of realizing their citizenship had changed the world for the worse.

Coming from the other side of the political spectrum, but nonetheless reaching a compatible conclusion, Michael Harmsworth, son of the proprietor of the *Daily Mail*, was convinced that "the women's vote will go against all anti-Chamberlain war-mongers."[21] Tory propaganda relied on these assumptions, and Conservative MP, *Daily Express* editor, and staunch appeaser Beverley Baxter entreated the women of Britain to "realise their responsibility to the nation" by playing their part in the campaign for 'Peace and Preparedness.' They could do this by making contact with the women of Germany and Italy, and he pondered: "If only the women could prevent the bombers from taking off—not by standing in masses around the aeroplanes, but by creating a world peace movement of the homes!" He felt that "our Government can be criticised for much that it has failed to do, but when Mr Chamberlain stood in no man's land and said 'They shall not die!' he gave expression to the agony and the hopes of women throughout the world."[22] Munich had been a women's peace.

There was just as much consternation about elite women surreptitiously pulling the strings in Anglo–German relations, including political hostesses, sisters, wives, and daughters of great men, the Cliveden Set, and the handful of women MPs. All these female influences on the most male-identified branch of policy—defence and war-making[23]—were deemed undue influence. Furthermore, women's incursions into international relations and diplomacy, however popular the movement was to democratize and feminize its practices after the First World War,[24] were identified as symptomatic of Britain's national and imperial decline. Career diplomat and Edenite

National Labour MP Harold Nicolson saw a direct causality between women's political emancipation and national decline as driven by the aversion to war. Weeks after the Munich Agreement had been signed, he told an audience of women that:

> a great body of women rendered nationally immobile by fear without resolution must be regarded as a dead-weight, a restrictive influence on national policy. With a majority population clamouring for peace at any price, what, we may wonder, can any Government do but clinch a bad bargain and snatch a peace that is momentarily presentable but as poisonous behind its exterior as Snow White's apple?[25]

Reified British womanhood, flesh-and-blood women, and even Disneyfied fairy tale characters who dominated the box office during those apprehensive months were far more invested and embedded in the appeasement debate than historians have hitherto recognized.

Of course the thirties was a decade of crisis, both domestic and foreign, and both political and personal. In 1939, that great literary eulogizer of Edwardian England, E.M. Forster, encapsulated the 'tragic' decade he had just lived through: "this decade has lasted long enough and the Crisis in particular has become a habit, indeed almost a joke."[26] The coalition National Government—formed in 1931 to deal with the economic crisis and re-elected at the 1935 General Election, with a majority of members from the Conservative Party and a sprinkling of National Labour and National Liberal MPs—lurched from crisis to crisis. Battles between democracy and dictatorship and between civilization and barbarism raged in Italy, Manchuria, Germany, Abyssinia, Spain, Austria, Czechoslovakia, and throughout East and Central Europe. Crisis by crisis the League of Nations and the system of collective security failed to bring increasingly emboldened expansionist powers to heel.

Yet for the vast majority of the British people, the experience of these catastrophes was vicarious. The brutality of dictatorship, loss of liberty, the persecution of minorities and dissidents, and the horrific consequences of mechanized aerial warfare were mediated through politicians and diplomats, journalists and broadcasters, tourists and travel writers, and refugees and émigrés. Mass-Observation, launched in 1937 in order to educate and empower public opinion and demystify modern propaganda, quickly diagnosed a kind of crisis fatigue within the population at large: "At the present stage of Western civilisation changes are taking place with such rapidity that there is a sense of a continuous crisis."[27] Few lives were left untouched by these crises and the Munich Crisis in particular, whether female or male, young and old, urbanites and rural, rich and poor, and conservative, progressive, or revolutionary. All were gripped by the sense of emergency, as in one instance after another the diplomatic impasse was experienced as a very personal and emotional shock. For example, Mass-Observer Mrs I. Blackwell was ill with worry during so-called Crisis Week in late September, 1938, but she confessed that "[o]nce war seemed a certainty, I lost my worry and began to feel quite an exhilaration in all the bustle and hurry, the anti-aircraft guns, searchlights, trenches, gas masks, queues."[28] Many others lived these days as did Mrs E.A. Russell, "in an agony of suspense,"[29] and she was overwhelmed with gratitude for the Prime Minister as the Man of Peace. Those most moved where those who had suffered in war, like May Yale from Chiswick, "a wife of a soldier disabled in the last war" and a "mother to-day," who felt she must thank the PM's wife "from the bottom of my heart for Mr Chamberlain's great bravery and ultimate success."[30] In the build up to the Crisis Virginia Woolf noted: "Odd this new public anxiety: how it compares with private: how it blinds: but too stupid to write."[31] It all had extra resonance for Woolf as these days when the whole world waited in suspense to know if it would be war or peace coincided with the arrival of reviews of her feminist-pacifist-anti-fascist *Three Guineas*. She regarded Friday 30 September as a day of reprieve from "having our noses rubbed in death," and it was, all in all, "a very fine day."[32] Only two days after the Munich Agreement, Woolf confessed how "other emotions rapidly chase each other ... peace seems dull. Solid."[33] It was soon apparent that the Munich Agreement did little to resolve things in either international relations or internal relations, and the months to follow—the 11 months that proved to be the countdown to war—were "a confused and inglorious period. Immediate sense of relief was followed by a feeling of humiliated anger, and then by a purblind apathy."[34] There can be little doubt that this crisis cycle was profoundly affecting. However, too much of the history is written as if the most dramatic events, the intractable strategic, moral, and emotional dilemmas, weighed on only a small cast of guilty men.

Over the course of 75 years, the debate over British foreign policy has maintained a dialectical momentum, starting with those who blew the whistle on the Guilty Men, moving on to the revisionists, followed by the counter-revisionists and more recently taken on by the post-revisionists. They have contested the rectitude of judgement and the legacies of British Prime Minister Neville Chamberlain and his fellow architects of appeasement, the prophecy of the Churchillian anti-appeasers, and the institutional, diplomatic, military, economic, and political constraints on foreign policy. The scholarship has been boundless, and appeasement has been one of the most ravenously picked over documentary carcasses in modern British history, international history, and International Relations (IR). The original polemic has been reignited at intervals by eminent historians asserting their controversial claims, like A.J.P. Taylor turning all previous assumptions about Nazi intentionality about the war on their head, Gilbert and Gott reasserting the moral failures of British policy, or John Charmley's attempted rehabilitation of Neville Chamberlain's reputation.[35] Further, appeasement has consistently served as 'useable history.' The subject has attracted ever new 'old news hounds' to the pack on each occasion a languishing world power prevaricates over military intervention on foreign soil. As Rasmussen has suggested, the history of the Munich lesson is more illuminating as a window onto contemporary strategic and political interests than the lessons being drawn from the 1938 Munich fiasco.[36]

Reconsideration and new activity has also been spurred by the release of official and private documents. In 1945 only a selection of official documents were released, and much of the most revealing records were under the 50-year rule. But in 1967 the Public Records Act lowered the closed period of public archives to 30 years, and later other documents were released before the 30 year closure period had elapsed. From 1975, access to Chamberlain's private papers at the University of Birmingham reinvigorated the discussion, and political biography remains one of the most prevalent framing devices in appeasement scholarship. There was another shift in the narrative account as new source material again became available during the 1980s. In the last few years the digitization of archives and newspaper collections has made certain types of research more efficient. Overall, we have an embarrassment of scholarly riches in the quantity and quality of empirical studies, as well as in historiographical surveys themselves. Helpfully, works of synthesis and instructive exercises in self-reflexivity have captured the state of the art of appeasement scholarship at various points in time.[37]

Even as much of the documentary material is now widely accessible, it is unlikely that we will get to the point where there is nothing left to unmask, unpick, and unpack. As Adams explains, "because of the fundamental issues about the nature of men and nations which this story raises, and because we know all too well what followed, appeasement will always be controversial—it will always be studied, and books will always be written about it."[38] That being said, with few exceptions the Munich Crisis has been examined through a narrow range of conceptual frameworks and the praxis of high politics and diplomatic history, international history, and IR. Within these traditions, scholars have been reliant on quite similar source bases: official records, diplomatic papers, the papers of 'Great men,' newspapers, intelligence reports, and top-down, media-constructed public opinion.

But different sources tell different stories, and new approaches write alternative histories. Rather than delving deeper into well-drudged furrows, this study charts new ground by gendering the international crisis, and by offering a people's history of the 'People's Crisis'—to coin a phrase—that preceded the 'People's War.' The seemingly exhaustive appeasement scholarship rests on essentially non-gendered premises, and, similarly, attempts to integrate social and cultural perspectives have been few. But before we assume that the entrenched positions in the scholarship might act as barriers to innovative approaches and repel intrusions into well-rehearsed polemics, veteran appeasement scholar Sidney Aster has assured us that "appeasement studies retain their capacity to raise new questions and open new areas of investigation." In particular, Aster has noted that the "exploration of women's/gender studies has focused new light into the debates about foreign policy in 1930s Britain," admitting too that "this has not always been greeted with the enthusiasm it deserves for raising a new agenda." In addition, it is encouraging that Aster is open to cultural approaches that embrace the role of ethnicity, race, gender, and religion, and the search for the *mentalite* of appeasement, regarding these as "new avenues to understanding the roots of policy making and international history."[39] A number of studies have followed their own paths. These include Finney's re-reading of the historiography of appeasement as another way of locating the seismic shifts in national identity; Stone's history of ideas approach to British interpretations of Nazism before the war; McLouglin's discursive analysis of the aural history of the crisis; and Hucker's investigation of British and French politicians' and journalists' rendering of the *vox populi*.[40] Overy's darkly-lit panorama of the inter-war years does a marvellous job of evoking a paradoxical national mood in which "dread of war and certainty of war cohabited in unnatural union,"[41] while for Gardiner the thirties came to a close with "a scenic ride to catastrophe."[42] These alternative mappings of appeasement are of newer vintage, and Pedersen's pioneering biography of Eleanor Rathbone, Britain's arch resolute woman anti-appeaser; Pennybacker's re-reading of the 1930s at the nexus of race, anti-imperialism, anti-fascism, and anti-appeasement; and Susan Grayzel's cultural and gendered history of the expectations and representations of modern warfare on the domestic front have each poured new wine into new bottles.[43]

Just as much of the classical historiography of appeasement has been insensitive to gender difference and cultural factors, women's historians have averted their gaze from what, at face value, appears to be an androcentric realm of formal diplomacy, government foreign policy, and the study of 'chaps and maps.'[44] It bears mentioning that female academics have been in a small minority among scholars of appeasement, as the attitudes of male exclusivity that blocked women from the consular service, the Foreign Office, and Chamberlain's Cabinet in the interwar years have cast a long shadow. Elizabeth Wiskemann, who was both witness and historian; American academic Margaret George, author of *The Warped Vision: British Foreign Policy, 1933–1939* (1965); and the prolific international historian Zara Steiner are among the few women scholars to have treated the subject. I do not wish to be biologically determinist and get entangled into debates about identity politics—it is not required that a female historian be a women's historian, or that a man be discouraged from writing women's history. Nonetheless, we cannot help but mind the gender gap! This pattern can be seen in cognate areas of the discipline, and far fewer women are historians of high politics, and high politics has been one area of study where scholars have too often depreciated gender analysis. Back in 2000, Pedersen highlighted the regrettable dearth of scholarly endeavour at the intersection of modern British women's and political history, and it is gratifying to note that since then there has been something of a boom in gendered studies of politics and of women in politics.[45] Indeed, in pointing to the "role of gender in the signification and articulation of relationships of power, gender history has opened new paths of inquiry in political history."[46]

The winds of change have also blown over from other disciplines. As chartered in Chapter 1, women's history has taken the 'international turn,' with a cross-fertilization of inspiration and ideas between FIR (Feminist International Relations), GIR (Gender and International Relations), and history.[47] Promising as these developments have been, the resulting studies of the inter-war period have tended to focus on women working within women's and feminist international, transnational, and peace organizations, and motivated by Leftist and progressive ideologies of feminist internationalism. What has yet to be attempted is a history from below of women's responses to international issues and a gendered reading of its accompanying discourse. Correspondingly, feminist scholars have not taken much of an interest in those they might regard as 'guilty women,' women who did little credit to the numerically diminished but spiritually determined interwar women's movement. For example, while women organized by the Conservative party and Tory women voters outstripped their counterparts in the Liberal and Labour parties—and exponentially outnumber women active in a range of post-suffrage feminist organizations—Right-wing women are hardly represented in the secondary literature. In short, women who have been held responsible for betraying the promise of sexual emancipation have always received less attention and little retrospective celebration.

Therefore, what this study sets out to do is connect the scholarship of appeasement and women's history, and thereby reengage those working in these fields. It brings into relationship two of the most vexing questions in the historiography of inter-war Britain, two questions that have not hitherto been converged. How did women's new citizenship status reshape British politics in the post-suffrage years, and, did Britain follow a reasonable course in foreign policy in response to the rise of the dictators? In other words, how did the post-enfranchisement gender order shape British foreign policy? In order to be able to answer these intertwined questions we need, on the one hand, a gendered history of the British experience of the international crisis. Such an approach must be sensitive to the ways in which appeasement became identified as a feminine policy; the manner that anti-appeasers used gendered language to feminize their opponents; and the representations of Chamberlain as effeminate and meek in physique as in resolve next to the domineering masculinity of the increasingly aggressive and territorially greedy fascist dictators. Shifting to this gender paradigm also requires the re-reading of canonical appeasement sources, thereby providing a necessary corrective to the male-identified Great Man/Guilty Man narrative of appeasement.

On the other hand, we need to reclaim and resituate women in the history of the international crisis of the 1930s. This requires an empirical reorientation to sources where women live, breath, think, emote, and record their experiences for their own satisfaction, their sanity, and for posterity. While it would be reductive to suggest that there was a quintessentially feminine pathway through the stormy debates over Britain's foreign entanglements in these years, there were nonetheless a number of confluences that brought women together and differentiated their engagement with foreign affairs from that of their male counterparts. In dozens of gender segregated organizations, from feminist pressure groups to the Conservative Women's Association, women mobilized and framed their thoughts as women to agitate for peace; women understood the special vulnerability of the 'weaker sex' under dictatorship; women celebrated the achievements of the Men of Munich in granting a reprieve to their husbands and sons; and women eventually, many grudgingly, prepared for a total war in which there was no longer any distinction between civilians—mainly women and children—and combatants.

Chapter 1 provides the wider chronological context in which to understand women's involvement and agency in international affairs. During the First World War the women's movement organized internationally, and throughout the 1920s and well into the 1930s women activists were dedicated to educating women in international affairs, and mobilizing other women as the world's 'natural' pacifists. The optimistic faith in women's power to remake the world was severely shaken by the triumph of National Socialism in Germany, and Chapter 2 tours the battle grounds in 'women's war on fascism.' Both at home and abroad British women identified their own reasons to resist fascism, and while no one organization united them, the discursive charge of feminist anti-fascism was powerful, codifying women's anti-Nazi war aims well before war was a reality.

From feminists we move on to women in mainstream and malestream politics. Chapter 3 begins by pondering the meaning of the poorly timed and ill-advised visit by Gertrud Scholtz-Klink, the Nazi women's leader, to London in March 1939. Significantly, this visit has hardly been noted in the classical narrative of appeasement. Was it the culmination of women's desperate desire for the maintenance of peace in the face of rapidly deteriorating international relations, a glaring diplomatic *faux pas*, or both? Chapters 3 and 4 identify the women who emerged as protagonists (and antagonists) in the 'Guilty Men' saga, assessing the political choices, the influence, and the representations of the women of the Chamberlain family (wife, sisters, and sister-in-law), Lady Nancy Astor as reluctant leader of the 'Cliveden Set,' Lady Londonderry as equal partner with her husband in fostering Anglo–German friendship, as well as those prominent women who sided with Chamberlain's appeasement policy as it seemed to offer the best possibility for peace.

Neville Chamberlain had a special relationship and a certain rapport and ease of communication with women. This was in evidence at local, party, national, and international levels, and Chapter 5 investigates the ways in which women in the Conservative party underwrote and undergirded appeasement. It places the status and representations of women within the context of the gendered culture and power dynamics of the party, understanding how the new premium placed upon the marshalling and political education of women was the party's response to women's still new electoral strength. Relying on the patchy records of the Conservative Women's Associations, and supplemented by regional and national newspapers, and personal recollections, it considers Conservative women MPs and those in leadership positions within the party structure, as well as the activities and attitudes of women at grass roots. That appeasement became a female-identified policy, a policy that was seen to satisfy the women of the world, can be traced back to support at the base line of the Tory party.

The next trio of chapters reveal how 'ordinary' women experienced the Munich Crisis, both by considering how British womanhood was represented by media elites and opinion-formers, and by listening to women speaking for themselves. Chapter 6 focuses on representational and what I have termed 'impressive' evidence. In newspapers, opinion polls, and the internal imaginaries of protagonists in foreign policy debates, the public was feminized, and men feared the force of newly enfranchised, terror-ridden mothers and wives. Attempts to democratize international relations were met with some scepticism by the traditional elite, and former Undersecretary of State for Foreign Affairs, Robert Vansittart regretted the fact that "foreign policy got tangled up with vote-catching, which was most easily practised by prophesying smooth things."[48]

However, the narrative changes when we allow women to represent themselves, and Chapter 7 draws on two rich source bases to gauge the nature and the fluctuations in women's public opinion, and to illustrate the real and perceived gender differentials in attitudes to foreign policy and to war. It makes extensive use of the Mass-Observation archive, and especially the diaries kept by women Mass-Observers during the Crisis. It considers these private sentiments about public events alongside a treasure trove of intimate sentiments that women shared with Neville and Anne Chamberlain in 1938 and 1939 in the so-called 'Crisis Letters,' exposing qualitative differences in the ways in which women reached out to political leaders and the nature of the confessions they shared.

Sexual schism was also very apparent in voting and political behaviour. Especially when opinion polling was in its infancy, elections and by-elections were regarded as the most reliable measures of public sentiment. Chapter 8 examines gendered patterns in voting behaviour and in support for appeasement through an examination of the series of by-elections in the autumn and winter of 1938 and 1939. Together these by-elections were seen as a referendum on the Munich Agreement. Ironically, while women voters as a bloc were presumed to support appeasement, a psephological analysis exposes a much more nuanced picture. What was consistent, however, was the construction and the constriction of women's citizenship, and the implications, not always very subtle, that women were exercising a dangerous and undue influence on politics in general, and on foreign policy more specifically.

Finally, Chapter 9 turns its attention to the women in Churchill's orbit, women who made common cause with the arch anti-appeaser in passionate opposition to Chamberlain's direction of British foreign policy. They were an even looser grouping than the feminist anti-fascists, Chamberlain's 'crisis women,' or the shadowy Cliveden cabal with its female figurehead, Nancy Astor. Cassandra-figures Violet Bonham-Carter, Eleanor Rathbone, the Duchess of Atholl, Baffy Dugdale, Ellen Wilkinson, and Shiela Grant Duff would be vindicated by history, but they have hardly fared better than the 'women of Munich' in the transmitted appeasement metanarrative. Undoubtedly, coming to a close with an examination of the women Churchillians serves as a vigorous riposte to Richard Baxter's cynical allegations—in a reversal of the guilty woman construct, the women anti-appeasers keenly felt and were motivated by their shame and guilt at the betrayals of worthy allies.

A gendered history of appeasement lays bare some deep cleavages between men and women as the ubiquitous sense of peril in the countdown to war strained both the most intimate personal ties, and the relationship between men and women of the nation writ large. Fear of the cataclysm to come was conflated with fear of women, culminating in mistrust of women's collective and sexual power. This kind of suspicion was given literary form in Baxter's *Guilty Women* and powerful visual expression in the now iconic propaganda poster of 1942, 'Keep mum—she's not so dumb!'[49] By the end of the 1930s the endemic sex war and an ever fiercer political competition between the sexes had migrated from the domestic to the international arena.

1
British Women and the Three Encounters: International, European, and Fascist

Women's political status and the political relationships between the sexes were transformed between the two world wars. Not only did women become British citizens with the vote if they were over 30 in 1918 and on equal terms with men in 1928, but the politically motivated among them seized every opportunity for women to exercise influence in international affairs and through international bodies. Much hope was invested in women to heal a world profoundly wounded by a war of annihilation, to reform the culture of international relations, to democratize diplomacy, to educate the next generation to abhor war, and to remake the world in their own feminine image and as an alternative to male aggression. The tone was set during the war. In April 1915 radical women from 12 countries, belligerent and neutral, met at The Hague for a congress that is widely regarded as the inauguration of feminist pacifist internationalism. Its British Committee held its first congress in London that October at which it ratified its manifesto. The document articulated the maternalist anti-militarist principles that were to underpin women's aspirations in international politics post-war: "Since women are in a special sense the custodians of life, we are determined that we will no longer consent to political social conditions involving the reckless destruction of life either in peace or in war." Supposedly biologically pre-destined to be the world's natural pacifists, women now demanded for themselves that they "be given a share in deciding the conditions which influence and determine war and peace, in the home, the school, the church, the industrial order, and the State."[1] Emerging from The Hague congress, the Women's International League of Peace and Freedom (WILPF)[2] and its national Women's International League (WIL) branches sought to "create a habit of international thinking as one of the surest preventatives of war," while its educational work was geared towards "emphasizing the international significance of the problems with which women are most concerned, and encouraging their sense of comradeship with women in other nations."[3] The deceptively simple equation was that men had made the war, and it should be women who make—and keep—the peace. The feminist movement took an 'international turn,' both

13

in institutional terms by organizing itself on international and transnational bases, and in ideological terms with its increasing preoccupation with foreign affairs and the status and plight of women in other lands.[4] While at home a pared down feminist movement continued to campaign for franchise reform up until 1928, much of the personnel, spirit, and energy of the suffrage and suffragette movements were already being channelled into international networks and a fresh philosophy and collective identity of feminist internationalism and/or pacifism. But the idealism of the 1920s was to give way under the strain of the ascendency of Nazism. During the 1930s we can observe the crystallization of a feminist anti-fascist mind-set, even if a cohesive and cooperative women's anti-fascist movement never quite materialized.

I propose that we see the phenomenon of feminist anti-fascism as a process rather than a fixed ideological position, and as the outcome of a series of *encounters*. As a conceptual framework, over the course of approximately four decades, from the late 19th century to the end of the 1930s, we can discern three stages that British women passed through as they defined their sphere of interests and interacted with their female counterparts in foreign lands. These stages are the 'colonial encounter,' the interlinked 'International' and 'European encounter,' and, finally, to coin a phrase, the 'Fascist encounter.' Prior to the First World War, post-colonial historians have conceptualized women's perceptual and missionary interaction with imperial subjects as the *colonial encounter*, a power paradigm in which white middle-class women regarded colonized women as the recipients and beneficiaries of their missionary zeal.[5] In their encounter with the colonial 'other,' British women positioned themselves at the apex of a hierarchy of sexual emancipation. With the coming of the First World War and in the immediate decade thereafter, I would propose that the colonial encounter relocated or returned to the European setting, and much of the rhetoric of empire was retuned as a discourse on internationalism. Of course, it is also true that the British feminist gaze was not withdrawn from the imperial stage—there was overlap between the colonial and European encounter. While many of these women were increasingly critical and self-critical about Britain's imperial role, the perseverance of 'feminist orientalism' and 'feminist imperialism' is easily demonstrated by the leadership of the international women's movement by white, middle-class, metropolitans. Bolt avers that the attention of British feminists was directed to three interlinked areas: female emancipation in the various parts of the empire; the activities of the Geneva-centred League of Nations; and, in due course, the relative merits of pacifism and anti-Fascism.[6] For our purposes, the focus will be on the last two of these tendencies.

Public women in the public eye

This chapter plots women's journeys through the political quagmire of the inter-war years. It tracks two consecutive generations of politicized women, the first born in the 1870s and 1880s, thus having come of age during the suffrage movement and reaching their political prime in the aftermath of war, and the generation born in the 1890s and 1900s who came of age in and through the war and who enjoyed political rights on paper as soon as they reached adulthood. It focuses on those women who were active in single-sex organizations, in the newly-reconstituted women's sections of the Liberal and Labour parties, in single-issue campaigns and humanitarian missions, in the administration and advocacy of the League of Nations, and that part of a new generation of women journalists, travel writers, and academics who became 'experts' and authorities on European affairs. Together these women served as the missionaries of internationalism. To be sure, most of the women with whom we will come into contact qualify for inclusion into more than one of these categories. The common denominator of their purpose was to make tangible women's political emancipation by taking advantage of the new spirit and the innovative institutions of post-war internationalism. This is not to suggest the homogeneity of political views, and women devoted to international work, as Rupp has demonstrated, could be nationalist, non-nationalist or antinationalist "but all agreed that women could—and ought to—come together across national borders and work to make the world a better place, and that agreement is what bound them together."[7] The press remarked on the way "conference follows conference in the world of women,"[8] and the energy and ingenuity of an internationalized feminism goes a long way towards contesting an earlier downbeat narrative of post-enfranchisement feminist decline.[9] By their personal examples and through the dissemination of their ideas, these women set the parameters for, and expressed the aspirations of, inter-war British women's citizenship.

What accounts then for this lack of cohesion among politically-engaged women? Predictably, some of the explanations can be found in national, class-based, and party politics, and it is through these prisms that historians have tended to look.[10] But these valuable studies have failed to highlight the international dimension of these divisions, and it is by redirecting the line of enquiry that we gain a deeper appreciation of the impact of international problems and controversies on the women's movement in Britain. Why did freshly enfranchised and politicized women throw themselves into internationalist activism in the post-war years? As educated, enfranchised, often well-travelled, well-heeled and multi-lingual people, how did these women's privileges inform their interpretations of the status of women at home and abroad? How did their mutating relationships with internationalist, pacifist, and socialist politics determine how they positioned themselves during the bitter appeasement debate later in the 1930s? How can we reconcile the imaginative power and courage of feminist anti-fascism with the relative failure of the feminist movement in the same timeframe? Confronting these questions will help us to discern the deeply gendered and contested nature of fundamental concerns in post-war Britain, from the requirements of political engagement in a mass democracy to the nature and responsibilities of citizenship, and to the most pressing dilemma of all by the late 1930s, whether to strive for peace at almost any price or to arm, morally and materially, for an anti-fascist war. An acute feminist internationalist consciousness conditioned the conceptual and psychological outlook of British women as they contemplated a second world war and its alternatives at the end of the 1930s.

Indeed, the scholarship on the inter-war women's movement has taken the same international turn, and in the process recalibrated the political effectiveness and cultural impact between the waves of feminism. Whereas Harrison had argued that "once women had the vote, many feminists moved off into pacifist and internationalist work and partly for this reason domestic feminism went into gradual decline,"[11] the more recent trend has been to reinterpret the international orientation of the women's movement as indicative of its success in adapting to the new world order.[12] There has been some disciplinary cross-fertilization of ideas between theorists of Feminist IR (FIR) emerging in the 1980s, and Gender and IR (GIR),following suit in the 1990s, and practitioners of women's history.[13] The FIR and GIR enterprises are not divorced from contemporary activism, and Peterson has proposed that "by retrieving histories of gender that shaped our international past(s), we improve the quality and likelihood of feminist futures."[14] Much of the historical literature too has been inevitably nostalgic, and many accounts have been written by those with personal histories as activists in the milieu of feminist peace activism.[15] Taylor and Rupp emphasize that "coming together to create the first wave of an international women's movement was no mean feat in a world rent by war, depression, revolution, and the rise of fascism."[16] Bolt has been somewhat more sceptical of their achievements, arguing that Anglo–American "activists defending internationalism failed to advance on the justification for female involvement devised at the end of the 19th century: namely that women's roles as mothers and educators empowered them to protest against militarism."[17] Pugh acknowledges that between the wars "the cause of peace gave women a platform and a degree of authority within what would have conventionally been regarded as male territory."[18] Van Seters has focused instead on the many ways in which engaged women, feminists and non-feminists, sought to penetrate the male world of foreign policy debate in Britain, and concludes that despite the impressive range of their activities during the 1930s, "it was likely the government was influenced by this activism more in the nature of its efforts to present policy to the public (and to women voters in particular) than in the actual policy decisions made."[19] As measured against their pre-suffrage achievements, women's political mobilization was very impressive, but it does not necessarily follow that they made such great strides within malestream political institutions and political cultures. It is to the leading spokeswomen of this vision, women in the public eye, that we must first turn.

The study of women's inter-war internationalism has been especially buoyant for the last 20 years, and the trend has been to examine women's organizations in their own institutional contexts, and sometimes in a vacuum. This has been complemented by biographical studies that have offered many insights into the changing relationship between women and foreign affairs.[20] Building on the rich existing scholarship, here we are concerned with how highly politicized British women related to the international, and a number of brief biographical case studies will inevitably be illuminating. However, in this book I am equally interested to investigate the relationship between the female electorate—the women of the masses as constructed by the media and internalized by many women themselves—and international issues and crises. By taking this multi-dimensional approach, we will see how both the discourses of internationalism and anti-fascism were distinctively gendered and their practices sex-segregated.

Indeed, recognizing the gulf between the sexes in both international and anti-fascist activism is vital to understanding the sense of alienation between the sexes as Britain prepared to fight another world war. Rose has persuasively asserted that during the Second World War itself the People's War mythology of home-front consensus belies the Manichean media constructions of male and female sexual morality, commitment to wartime national service, and citizenship.[21] This was entirely consistent with the real and discursive gender bifurcation in international affairs and foreign policy in the anxious build up to the war, when it was honour, courage, levels of political engagement, and emotional expression that were each gender bipolarized. When war broke out again only 21 years after the end of the last world war (in the same year as women were marking the 21st anniversary of their enfranchisement, and, with even further symbolic charge, as women born in 1918 reached voting age), women and men sensed the defeat of their hopes in different ways and identified war aims along sex lines. There were parallels too in the ambivalent ways in which another 21st birthday was celebrated in the summer of 1939, that of the League of Nations. Emboldened by women's modest but nonetheless path-breaking incursions into international politics, and motivated by feminist critiques of fascism, in some important respects women were fighting their own war against the Axis powers.

There will be more about the construction of 'mass woman' in later chapters, but for now the approach is by necessity a women's history from above. As members of the political, cosmopolitan, educated, and often also the social elite, the women who were civically engaged were not always as finely attuned to the interests and opinions of the mass female electorate as they might have thought. Much of their work was prescriptive and aspirational. Undeniably, there was a significant gap between their extraordinary activism and their opportunities for engagement, supported by a refined political literacy, and the perceived general apathy and political semiliteracy or illiteracy of the population at large. As women eagerly prepared to vote for the first time in December 1918, former suffragette and author Evelyn Sharpe entreated them to cast their minds beyond the private sphere: "I think far too few of us have realised in the past this intimate connection between home politics and foreign politics ... People are turning to women everywhere today, in the hope that they may have some new force to bring to the healing of a tortured humanity."[22] Formulations demonstrating the inextricability of the private sphere from international relations were a leitmotif of inter-war feminism, and New Feminist Independent MP Eleanor Rathbone pointed to "the sphere of effort into which enfranchised women have thrown themselves in the greatest number and with the greatest intensity of interest is the sphere of internationalism."[23] It is, however, difficult to know if this kind of international thinking captured the imagination of many women voters. When Margery Corbett Ashby "spoke of the responsibility of enfranchised women in international affairs, and said that efforts should be made to interest and inform home-keeping women who seldom attended public meetings," she could not have been naïve to the obstacles faced.[24] Vera Brittain actively feared mass women's unreconstructed attitudes to war, believing that they were just as liable as men to be carried away by "wartime emotion and deceived by the shining martial figure of patriotism," and she identified the greatest intellectual handicap in peacetime as "the mass of narrowly pre-occupied housewives who remain completely unmoved by the threat of catastrophe from various parts of the world."[25] It is true of course that most of the 'women on the street' interviewed by Mass-Observation during the Munich Crisis confessed to ignorance of foreign affairs. One M-O interviewee was recorded as saying "I don't believe in foreigners,"[26] and such telling remarks must have come as a hard blow to feminist internationalists. In later chapters we will try to locate the women of the masses in the context of international crises, examining how they were represented by their putative leaders in the women's movement, as well as by politicians, the press, social anthropologists, and pollsters. Nonetheless, we should be wary not to take as final verdicts the opinion-making elite's reductive judgements of the new female electorate, and we will also be listening to otherwise anonymous women who sought direct engagement with the political process on their own terms.

It is true of course that the press and politicians did get into the lazy habit of essentializing and referring to women as a homogenous group, imagining a 'women's vote,' espying a 'women's peace bloc,' segregating 'women's issues,' addressing themselves to women in their roles as wives and mothers, providing woman's pages in newspapers, and often going as far as diagnosing a 'Woman Problem.'[27] Individual women rose to positions of public prominence, and in the aftermath of suffrage there was a media-fuelled fascination with, if not a fetishization of, women as a species. Many political women were accorded public standing and a kind of celebrity status, the male-controlled media eager, for simplicity, to identify and tokenize the leaders of the women's movement, while also quite clearly desperate that women should exercise their political agency as a cohesive whole. As Virginia Woolf noted sardonically, "no age could have ever been as stridently sex-conscious as our own."[28] Similarly, Winifred Holtby observed that "in the second quarter of the 20th century, the very existence of women appears to challenge controversy."[29]

However, the reality was that the women's movement, broadly conceived, only became more heterogeneous and fractious in the course of the interwar years. The definitions of women's political nature have to be deconstructed by developing a more nuanced taxonomy, distinguishing between women on the basis of age, class, region, ethnicity, education, marital status and sexual orientation, political partisanship, profession, and personality, among other factors. When we turn to political women we need to make even finer distinctions according to political pedigree, party affiliation, self-definition *vis a vis* feminism, and access to power and influence.[30] In short, despite the efforts of, for instance, Christabel Pankhurst to launch the Woman's Party in 1918 or Nancy Astor to get different women's groups to work together in the Consultative Committee of Women's Organizations (1922–1928), women were not easily unified on the basis of gender.[31] Further, there is little concrete evidence that women voted on the basis of sex, although more research is required to confirm this.[32]

The women's movement and the international turn

Of course, feminist politics had started to take an unmistakably 'international turn' at the *fin de siècle*. On the one hand, what is remarkable is the depth of politicized women's commitment to international issues given that both some suffragists and the anti-suffragists had assumed that women's political interests would—and should—be confined to the domestic sphere. The pre-war anti-suffragist Mrs Humphrey Ward believed that it would be appropriate for women to be granted a special franchise that gave them rights only in relation to their private sphere, with no authority over imperial and foreign affairs because in these spheres their "ignorance is imposed by nature and irreparable."[33] The mistrust of women to decide matters of diplomatic complexity and of war infused the Parliamentary debates on women's suffrage in the latter part of the war. Sir F. Banbury MP drew on evidence from polities where women had already received the vote to wage his objections, disturbed that in the American states where women had the vote at the last election they had voted against war, and similarly the evidence from Australia indicated that enfranchised women had opposed the vigorous war policy of Mr Hughes. Therefore, Banbury concluded, it was not "desirable to put power into the hands of women who were averse to taking strong action." In the same debate, Mr Burdett-Coutts MP argued that women's suffrage "would not be in the interests of the State from the point of view of its international position," and he was concerned with "what would be the attitude of women if we had to face another great war? The awful experience which they had gone through would probably be more lasting in their memory than in that of men, and if they had the power they might imperil the Empire. So far as war was possible and might be necessary for the safety of the nation woman could never be a complete unit of responsibility in the national life."[34]

On the other hand, these reactionary views of women's domestic short-sightedness lost much of their potency as internationalism became an increasingly important dynamic within European political and intellectual life, and as "leaders of powerful Western states, middle-class women and feminists, anti-colonialists, social scientists, and moral reformers, now organized around the 'international question' as well as the 'nation question.'"[35] The internationalist mind-set permeated high politics as well as social, popular, cultural, economic, and gender discourses, taking on religious proportions.[36] Catherine Marshall hopefully predicted that "women's experience as mothers and heads of households has given them just the outlook on human affairs which is needed in this process of reconstruction."[37] Feminist internationalists stressed that 'politics does not end at home,' and while "most people still think of the women's vote as being concerned only with their home interests and their industrial interests," the truth of the matter is that "women are humanly as much concerned with keeping the world at peace as men are" and "home politics and foreign politics overlap, and what affects the one must to some extent affect the other."[38] The convergence of women's enfranchisement with universal male suffrage and with the broad-based movement to democratize international relations—given institutional form in the highly successful League of Nations Union—created a natural alliance between women and internationalist endeavours.[39]

In structural terms the supra-national perspective was manifested by the placement of the suffrage movement on solid international, transnational, and Anglo–American footings, for instance in the shape of the International Council of Women (1888) and the International Woman's Suffrage Alliance (1904). The international orientation became even sharper during the war, best exemplified by the peace meeting of the International Congress of Women at The Hague in 1915. These networks then provided the framework for feminist pacifist and internationalist ventures during the First World War and after, the most successful products being the multi-national WILPF and, later, the Open Door International. Still excluded from formal diplomacy and peace-making, women organized a women's peace conference in Zurich in 1919, a type of *salon de refusée* where women protested against the punitive terms of the Versailles Treaty, and the WILPF established a permanent base in Geneva at the Maison Internationale soon after.

The first president of the WILPF was the American Jane Addams and another American, Emily Balch, was its first international secretary, while the British Helena Swanwick became one of the two vice-presidents, the other being the German Lida Gustava Heymann as "a healing move."[40]

From the outset of the post-war period and as part of the post-war settlement, women made it clear that they would have a voice in the peace-making and peace-keeping process. Speaking at a Six Point Group (formed in 1921) meeting in London, Viscountess Rhondda explained "[t]he world to-day is becoming more and more a world in which things are done by international action. Today this is the question that faces us: either we must have international feminism or we shall be faced with international anti-feminism."[41] At this juncture Rhondda was campaigning for the Equal Rights Treaty, drawn up by the National Women's Party of the United States, which was soon to be presented to the League of Nations Assembly. Much feminist effort was dedicated to support the campaign for women to be admitted to the diplomatic and consular services. Britain was behind the curve in this respect, as by 1934 Russia, America, Spain and Bulgaria had each allowed women to enter the diplomatic service. Winifred Holtby begged that women should be able to try their hand at the business of diplomacy because "women are not handicapped by a great burden of outworn ritual; they have not learned the elaborations of prestige-hunting; and they care, desperately, earnestly, with an urgency which increases monthly, for peace throughout the world."[42] Further, for women in this milieu, 'abroad' was where the action was, and Vera Brittain told her closest friend Winifred Holtby that "I feel I ought to be in Geneva, in Rome, anywhere but here, marooned in an empty house and an empty London while the League crumbles and the peace edifice we have tried for 15 years to build falls in ruins."[43]

The proliferation of women's international organizations

The range and number of international women's organizations is remarkable, and there was overlap between their memberships, their peace campaigns and tactics, their ambitions and, ultimately, their failures. Rupp has calculated that some 500 international associations were still at work in 1920.[44] As just one example of this proliferation some 16 years later, there were a healthy number of women-oriented organizations that could agree on a *raison d'etre* in 1936:

[w]e are living in time overshadowed by the menace of war, which every day becomes more threatening. The peoples everywhere grow increasingly apprehensive, and in every country the mothers are tortured by dread that their children may be called upon to endure the horrors of another war, made infinitely more terrible than any in the past by the perverted use of scientific knowledge and technical research.

When Lord Cecil (President of the LNU and winner of the 1937 Nobel Peace Prize) and other well-known leaders of the peace movement made their world-wide appeal for an International Peace Campaign "many millions of women were ready to respond, for they knew that the mere desire for peace, mere lip-service to an ideal, is not enough; that there must be incessant striving for its attainment," and the urgent appeal was made "to women in every country, the manual and intellectual workers both in town and country, the housewives, teachers, mothers of families, without distinction of class, religious belief, or political allegiance, to work in co-operation by every means in their power for the success of the World Peace Congress at Geneva early in September, 1936."[45] The signatories of this petition were Margery Corbett Ashby and Germaine Malaterre-Selher, members of the International Executive Committee of the International Peace Campaign; Rose Manus, international secretary; Mary A. Dingham, International Women's Organisations Committee for Peace and Disarmament; Emile Gourd and Gabrielle Duchêne, International Women's Alliance for Civil and Political Suffrage; M.B. Cattaneo, Women's World Committee; Clara Ragaz, International Women's League for Peace and Liberty; M.Y. Prudhommeaux and J. Rugssen, Mothers' and Teachers' League for Peace and Marg. Nobs. Women's World Union for International Understanding.

In addition to the groups that signed the above petition, there was an array of transnational women's organizations with significant British representation. These included the Women's Peace Crusade (formed 1916); the Women's Peace Pilgrimage; the Women's Section of the Labour and Socialist International; the Joint Standing Committee of the Women's International Organisations (formed in 1925 to get women appointed to the League of Nations); and the International Co-operative Women's Guild (founded in 1921 as the international arm of the British Women's Co-operative Guild). Occupation-based international confederations also joined in pressing debates, including the International Federation of University Women (founded in 1919, with a London base in Crosby Hall), and the International Federation of Business and Professional Women (formed in 1930).[46] But it was the Women's World Committee Against War and Fascism (WWCAWAF), founded in 1934 at a meeting in Paris attended by over 1,000 women, and affiliated to the Comintern, that seemed to offer in its very title an opportunity for the convergence of pacifist, internationalist and anti-fascist feminisms.

However, the WWCAWAF never did live up to the potential of its title, and it failed to bring the WIL on side. This was because the WIL was opposed to all wars and all violence, and could not support the latter's pledge "to oppose capitalist war and Fascism and to support all united actions against these menaces."[47] The WIL's resistance to collaboration needs to be seen in context, as its uncompromising pacifism was putting it at odds even with the international WILPF body.[48] Nevertheless, the WIL was not alone in resisting collaboration with the WWCAWAF, whose Communist roots also kept other women away. Nevertheless, it did maintain its presence on both the British and international stages, and in 1938 Charlotte Haldane was approached by the Women's Section of the Comintern to help organize the International Women's Congress Against War and Fascism, which took place in Marseilles.[49] Here the WWCAWAF was renamed as the Women's Committee for Peace and Democracy, and it was under the auspices of this rebranded organization that members made their presence felt with a march to protest against the visit of Hitler's 'perfect woman,' Gertrud Scholtz-Klink, to London as late as March 1939.[50]

The evidence strongly suggests that the influence of these organizations outreached their numerical strength. The coverage of their activities in the mainstream press, and especially by the *Manchester Guardian*—which "preache[d] enlightenment to the enlightened"[51]—offered women's inter-nationalism and anti-fascism generous publicity. In addition, the publicity generated by their own in-house publications and pamphleteering contributed to the impression that feminist endeavours in the sphere of international politics represented a movement. While it is rather difficult to measure the effectiveness of each of these organizations, what is clear is that there was a well-established women's international network that was built on 'peace' work as well as anti-fascist initiatives. What they shared was their rather utopian vision for a peaceful world together with a belief that it was principally in women's interests, as mothers—using "the emotional template of mother love as a universal bond"[52] —to secure that future.

Not all women's internationalism was so directly peace oriented, however. The Open Door International was one of the more ambitious feminist inter-nationalist organizations that had aims supplemental to peace. Formed in 1929 as the international branch of the British Open Door Council (estab-lished in 1926), and likewise dedicated to securing labour and economic equality for women, the ODI held its third annual conference in Prague. The success of internationalist feminism is well exemplified by the attendance at this conference, especially poignant as 1933 was deemed "a black year" for women—one year later the ODI would modify this judgement only insofar as 1934 proved to be even blacker.[53] To the Prague conference delegates from national branches were sent from Belgium, Czechoslovakia, Denmark, Britain, and Sweden; delegates from affiliated societies from Finland, Britain, and Sweden; delegates from associated societies from Australia; fraternal del-egates from Austria, Czechoslovakia, France, and Latvia, as well as the Equal Rights International; other members of the conference hailed from Bulgaria, Czechoslovakia, Norway, Roumania, and Yugoslavia; and government appointed observers from Czechoslovakia, Ecuador, France, Britain, Greece, and Uruguay also took part.[54] The ODI was quick to condemn Nazism, and in July 1933 sent a special resolution to Hitler regarding rumours about the dismissal of German women from their jobs on account of sex.

The short-lived Equal Rights International, like the ODI principally representing equalitarian principles, and fixing its sights on the passage of the Equal Rights Treaty by the League of Nations, provides a good example of the difficulties of uniting women across partisan and national boundaries. It was formed in 1930 at a meeting in Paris chaired by Lady Rhondda and attended by 22 women from five different countries, drawing from the same pool of talent as so many of these other organizations. Flora Drummond wrote to the Chairwoman, Mrs Betty Archdale: "What with the [Women's] Guild [of Empire], Six Point Group, British Women's Hospitality Committee which I have had to rescue and clear up so it can go on with the work of welcoming foreign business women to this country and a few odd other Movements you can see I am kept at it." Old rivalries died hard, and almost 20 years after the suffragette struggle, former suffragette 'General' Flora Drummond admitted that "what made me think we [the ERI] might be getting sedate was my visit to the Liaison Committee here when I saw all the old Constitutionalists haggling away at it. I really wondered if it was necessary for us to be mixed up with them for we were really formed to be more energetic than they are and without red tape." She dreaded the forthcoming Executive Committee meeting "as I feel it is rather a farce that although we are an International Movement there are none but British members sit on the Committee and actually decide what is to be done."[55] It is not hard to see why the ERI folded in 1934, and its failures to find political space suggests the feminist internationalist market was saturated.

Transformative encounters

If by the mid-1930s the unity of feminist internationalism was falling apart, we need to locate the peak period of this *European/international encounter* in the sanguine post-suffrage, post-Versailles 1920s when we see a high level of activism by a wide range of British women working within political parties and in the diplomatic arena, and voicing their attendant concern for the legal status of all European women in the aftermath of total war and women's enfranchisement in some of the democracies. British women were not alone in having been granted the (limited) franchise after the First World War, and they did not rest on their laurels. They worked hard to share the bounty of women's emancipation in countries where women remained disenfranchised, as for example in France or, worse, won and then lost their rights, as for example in Hungary and of course in Germany with the dramatic backlash from Weimar Republic to Third Reich. A sense of desperate alienation was especially marked in the case of Germany, so recently such a modernizing nation in its sexual politics, yet after 1933 under a regime that institutionalized the vilest misogynist excesses, firing women *en masse*, outlawing birth control, subjugating women to male-supremacist militarism, and persecuting the whole sex to the extent that women and Jews were conflated as Hitler's victims (or so these were the ubiquitous themes in feminist anti-Nazi propaganda). Winifred Holtby noted that "because in Germany the Woman's movement appeared to have progressed so far, the retrogression appeared particularly significant,"[56] while Sylvia Pankhurst described the world position of women at present as "terribly bad," because of the "gross and awful reverses" women's movements had suffered in Italy, Germany, and Austria.[57] Ethel Mannin mourned "all that progressive women have worked for for years has been lost,"[58] all the more tragic in Germany than in Italy because "the Roman Catholic hold had kept back the feminist movement, so that Italian women had less to lose by Fascism than had the German women, and the anti-feminism of Italian Fascism is therefore less apparent than with the German brand."[59] The Nazi regime's anti-feminist excesses did much to incense this group of British women, and they felt these setbacks so keenly because many important friendships and collaborations were forged in this transnational context, especially between British, American, German, French and Central and Eastern European women.[60]

The European encounter was given formal institutional shape through the work of the women's delegations to the League of Nations, very frequent political visits to foreign lands by women travelling under the auspices of a political party, women's internationalist peace organizations, and multinational women's groups. European encounters were increasingly possible and numerous for British women, either as research projects whereby women studied women, globe-trotting conference-going, internationalist missionary work, relief work, tourism, or some combination of these. The WILPF nurtured a new contingent of women researchers and experts in international questions. European encounters were pivotal for WILPF activists, and the sharing of grief "was profoundly important as the basis of a shared vision, and the sense of the reality of war was greatly enhanced, especially for the women from the less devastated countries, by their travel through Europe."[61] Under its auspices, for example, Ellen Wilkinson and Helena Swanwick went on fact-finding, bridge-building missions to Ireland in 1920, and Mary Sheepshank to the Ukraine in 1930. In fact, Sheepshank's education was not unusual among women internationalists, and it equipped her well for her many European encounters between 1922 and 1934 when she was Secretary of the WILPF. Born to missionary parents, the family settled in Harrogate, and she went to high school in Liverpool, before being sent to Potsdam, Germany, in 1889, aged 17, to be 'finished,' and she spent all her holidays on the Continent before 1914. She then went on to Newnham College, Cambridge, where she did the Modern and Medieval Languages tripos. Although she regretted not studying history, her true passion, she could not deny that "my thorough knowledge of German proved useful later on, and was an asset in the international organisations for which I worked."[62]

While the WILPF was not geared towards humanitarian work, there were many prominent women who experienced transformative European encounters through relief work with the victims of war. Margery Corbett Ashby visited Germany after the war to advise the War Office on some of the problems caused by occupying troops. Violet Bonham Carter was in the Ruhr in 1923 to ascertain the situation there. Vera Brittain made a tour of the occupied areas of Germany in 1924—the Ruhr, the Rhineland, Cologne, and Valley—and this experience provided the context in which she was later to understand the advent of Hitler. Novelist Phyllis Bottome was involved in war relief work in Belgium in 1914–1915; she lived with her husband in Central Europe from 1930 to 1938, leaving Austria three days before the Anschluss. This first-hand experience of Nazism made her a determined anti-fascist, and it would be the backdrop for her successful novel *The Mortal Storm* (1937), also made into an MGM feature film in 1940 starring James Stewart and Margaret Sullivan.

British women and the European encounter: in search of the real-life Daphne Sandomir

The character Mrs Daphne Sandomir in Rose Macaulay's novel *Non-Combatants and Others* (1916) personifies the mentality, the inexhaustible energy, and the tactics of strident feminist pacifism during the First World War. Sandomir is the type who:

> relieved Belgians, got up Repatriation and Reconstruction societies for them, spoke at meetings of the Union of Democratic Control ... held study circles of working people to educate them in the principles making for permanent peace, went with a motor ambulance to pick up wounded men in France, tried, but failed, like so many others to attend the Women's International Congress at The Hague, travelled round the world examining its disposition towards peace, helped form the SPPP (Society for Promoting Permanent Peace), wrote sensible letters to *The Times*, which sometimes got printed and sometimes did not, articles in various periodicals, pamphlets on peace, education and such things, and chapters in joint books.[63]

In her bid to further the cause of the Society for Promoting Permanent Peace and international understanding among the peoples of Europe:

> [Daphne] usually held them [her meetings] in the village schoolroom. Sometimes she got the vicar's permission to address the children during school hours, sometimes that of the vicar's wife to speak at the Mother's Meetings while it met. But she preferred evening meetings, because of her lantern slides, which showed the photographs she had taken on her

travels of men, women and children in other villages of other countries, thinking, so she said, the same thoughts as these men, women and children in Cambridgeshire, saying, in their queer tongues, the same things, playing very often, with the same toys. (This, of course, was by way of Promoting International Sympathy.)[64]

Part and parcel of women's peace activism was the ever more acute observation of the habits, customs and political cultures of other nations, as the British feminist gaze came to fixate on the European scene.

A number of women could well have been the model for Daphne Sandomir, and it is worthwhile to look at some of these figures and trace their responses and the personal dilemmas they faced through the kaleidoscope of encounters. Kathleen Courtney (1878–1974) was an exemplary feminist pacifist internationalist. After graduating from Oxford where she had read French and German, Courtney emerged as a leader of the NUWSS before the war. She was one of many who made the journey from suffragist to "Peacette"[65] early in the war, and she was one of only three British women who was able to attend the Women's Congress at The Hague in 1915, and she was a founder of the WILPF. During the war she also did relief work among Serbian refugees, for which she was decorated by the Serbian government. After the war she went to Vienna to work with the Friends' Relief Mission, and travelled in the Balkans and in Poland. She regularly attended the assembly of the League in Geneva, and was a member of the executive committee of the League of Nations Union. She served as secretary of the Women's Peace Crusade, was one of the vice-presidents of the Disarmament Committee of the Women's International Organization, worked on behalf of NUSEC and the Family Endowment Society, and she was in great demand as a speaker on international matters at home and abroad. I have looked at her passports among her private papers and they are covered with stamps, with no page blank, and she held an international driving permit.[66] In geographical and conceptual terms, she worked within an international rather than a British framework, becoming an advocate for women who had yet to achieve constitutional emancipation and for the high ideals of feminist internationalism.

For these reasons Courtney was well placed to apprehend the destructive power of totalitarianism over everything she held dear—international understanding, tolerance, freedom and feminism—and her fascist encounters led her to distance herself from pacifism and the British WIL by the late 1930s. The question was unambiguous in her mind "DO YOU WANT HITLER TO WIN OR DO YOU NOT and IF YOU DO NOT WANT HITLER TO WIN, ARE YOU WILLING TO TAKE THE NECESSARY MEASURES TO DEFEAT HIM? [emphasis in original] I have tried to ask this question of some of the leaders of the British WIL and received nothing but evasive and indeed dishonest replies."[67] She embarked on a US lecture tour in 1940 with the aim of breaking down American isolationist resolve, convinced that "we are fighting something which is really evil and is evil most of all in the way that it manages to use the good in human nature for its own sinister purposes."[68] And yet she maintained her faith and commitment to internationalism throughout the Second World War and after she became vice-chairman and joint-President, with Lord Cecil, of the United Nations Association, the successor body to the LNU.

Catherine Marshall (1880–1961) could have been another model for the upstanding idealist Daphne Sandomir. Marshall had been chairman of the Elections Fighting Fund Committee and on the Executive Committee of and Parliamentary Secretary for the NUWSS. She too took the pacifist turn during the First World War, and she was Honorary Secretary of the National Council Against Conscription (which became the National Council for Civil Liberties in 1916), formed to resist the passage of the Military Service (No. 2) Bill through Parliament. She attended the International Women's Congress at The Hague in April 1915, and was another founding member of the WILPF. Internationalist pacifism was her faith, an antithesis to the spirit of war, and it would be the women's movement that would make the greatest contribution.[69] One of a growing class of women experts on external affairs, Marshall was Honorary Secretary of the International Information Bureau which collated and indexed information from the foreign press relating to international questions. She had frequent European encounters after the war, and she was in Germany during the signing of the Versailles Peace Treaty. With so many others in its early days, she regarded the League as a panacea, and was on the Executive of the Council for the Representation of Women in the League of Nations. She was also a member of the Labour party throughout the period. While her connection with the WILPF loosened in the course of the 1920s, she was again working closely with the organization as part of her relief work for refugees from Czechoslovakia. Marshall took an abiding interest in Central European politics, and especially Czechoslovakian affairs. In the late 1930s she was actively involved in relief work on behalf of Czech and some Austrian refugees, many of whom were offered hospitality at her Lake District home, Howse End, in Keswick.[70]

Margery Corbett Ashby: feminist internationalism personified

Indeed, there are many other women who could have been the inspiration for the Daphne Sandomir character, and we could well regard this fictional character as a composite of the above women as well as mother-and-daughter Helen and Betty Archdale, Dr Hilda Clarke, the distinguished lawyer Chrystal Macmillan, Rachel Crowdy, Charlotte Despard, Lady Emmeline Pethick-Lawrence, Sylvia Pankhurst, Maude Royden, Mary Sheepshanks, and Helena Swanwick. However, it was Margery Corbett Ashby (1882–1981) who probably did most to fulfil women's ambitions in the international sphere in this period and lived to the fullest her international encounters. Starting in her youth, Corbett Ashby expressed the excitement she felt when attending her first meeting of the International Council of Women together with her mother in Berlin in 1904: "I can remember the thrill of gazing down on women from many European counties, and especially the brilliant delegates from the USA."[71] Corbett Ashby's reports on the International Alliance of Women's congresses during the 1920s and 1930s, which she served as president from 1923 to 1946, likewise express this fascination with the diverse gender orders in the nations visited, and her narrative voice adopted a top-down perspective as she described in vivid detail the peculiarities of the customs and traditions of different European women.

Her faith was Liberal feminist internationalism, and in 1919 she went on a deputation to the Versailles conference and made successful representations on issues pertaining to sexual equality to the fledgling League of Nations. In 1927 when Corbett Ashby was elected President of the Women's National Liberal Federation, she was already being celebrated for a "most distinguished career in the wider field of international and imperial affairs."[72] As Honorary President of the IAW, Honorary President of the British Commonwealth Union, seven-time Liberal parliamentary candidate (frustratingly never elected), and a leader of the Women's Peace Crusade that claimed to represent two million women in various associations, Corbett Ashby was an exemplar of the woman who stormed the bastion of male-dominated foreign affairs, proved that women were "a new factor in international politics,"[73] and opened the window of the British feminist gaze onto the women of post-war Europe. She was chosen as substitute delegate for the UK to the Disarmament Conference (1931–1935) due to this outstanding curriculum vitae. She had lectured in Canada, the United States, and in every European country, and was one of the leaders of the world peace movement, and "for these and other reasons, including the fact that she is a good linguist, an excellent committee woman, and a sympathetic personality, the women's organisations who had urged the Government to include a woman in the disarmament delegation were delighted when she was selected."[74]

While she had been at the helm of the disarmament campaign as one of the leaders of the Women's Peace Crusade and as a publicist for the Disarmament Committee of the Women's International Organisations, she was deeply disillusioned by the failures of the Geneva Disarmament Conference. At first she had been buoyed by her access to powerful men, excited that cabinet ministers Sir John Simon and Lord Londonderry "listened awfully well," and that the latter even "followed me out and we had a *tête-à-tête* in my room."[75] However, the novelty of her sex wore off and soon became a liability, and in a letter to her husband a year later she confessed that she got very little help from the permanent officials within her delegation who wanted to "freeze [her] out," and this she attributed to "a certain prejudice against women."[76] In a final reckoning, her years as Britain's substitute delegate to the Conference were recalled as "the most miserable of my life."[77] Corbett Ashby experienced many 'totalitarian encounters' during the course of her visits abroad during the 1930s, and as a pro-League internationalist, she did not face as painful a conversion as others when she came to vigorously oppose appeasement and then support Britain's war effort.

The rise of Nazism and the threat of fascism at home were very much on Corbett Ashby's radar, leading her to reason, already in 1934, that "I am sure we should have to contemplate the possibility of the use of war to stop war."[78] It was her feminism, rather than an unmoveable pacifism, that was most offended by the rear-guard acts of totalitarian regimes. The IAW diagnosed the totalitarian state to be "a retrograde man-made organisation where there is no freedom for the work, insight and freedom of women."[79] What she recalled most about the IAW's Copenhagen conference in 1939 was that while there were improvements in women's status to celebrate in many countries, "the threat of war hung heavily over us and totalitarian societies had dissolved or curtailed the activities in six of our affiliates." This IAW conference was also sadly poignant, for while the USA, Sweden and others made offers of permanent hospitality to Czech senator Mme Plaminkova, "she replied 'my country needs me' and she returned to die."[80] In fact, British women were deeply involved in the focused campaign to secure the release of Mme Pleminkova.

As Corbett Ashby later said: "I was rather proud that I was on Hitler's 'black list' and later on that of the Communists,"[81] expressing an organic evolution from the feminist anti-militarism typical of the 1920s to an activist feminist anti-fascism and anti-totalitarianism by the mid-1930s. On their Copenhagen voyage, at a change of trains in Germany, Lady Nancy Astor, her travelling companion and fellow IAW stalwart, danced "up to a group of Nazi youth in their uniform and their contemptuous silence as she told them Hitler could never defeat the United Kingdom."[82] Astor was something of a hit at the IAW congress, "tremendously applauded" and "a great attraction the few days she was there."[83] Indeed, on a metaphoric level, this was a significant transformative encounter for Cliveden Set-anti-heroine Nancy Astor. In contrast, Corbett Ashby was not tainted by association with the appeasers, and she was firmly on the side of the anti-appeasers by October 1938. This was a noteworthy career trajectory for a woman who, despite never having become an MP (not for lack of trying), had probably done most in formal terms, and by gaining the respect of her male counterparts working for the League, to realize the aspiration of feminist internationalism between the wars.

Liberal women, Europe and 'mutually good causes'

Corbett Ashby's internationalist activism and her commitment to the progress of women around the world do not seem at all aberrational when placed in the context of one of the organizations she led. A closer look at the Women's National Liberal Federation gives us insight into the dynamic of the European encounter, and then how internationalist idealism gave way under the expanding range of the totalitarian bombshell. While Liberal women were not alone in experiencing and seeking out these European encounters, and while they were not unique for their interest in a new comparative study of European women, their political standing and the party's ideology and current policies lent themselves particularly well to this perceptual revolution. Why was this?

First, within the Party there was a long tradition of women's philanthropy on behalf of Britain's colonial subjects,[84] women's engagement in anti-slavery campaigns the world over, and dedication to "mutually good causes."[85] Second, in direct correlation to the diminishing electoral fortunes of the Liberal Party after 1918 and thus their dwindling impact on domestic policy-making, Liberal foreign policy and an internationalist frame of reference began to predominate. A reading of the *Liberal Women's News* for the years 1918 up to 1935, when it folded due to loss of interest and lack of funds (it was £200 in debt when it finally ceased its run), demonstrates the gradual but certain drift from domestic to predominantly international concerns, with special attention paid to women's work at the League of Nations, women's involvement in a variety of peace campaigns, the leadership roles played by Liberal women in the international arena, and frequent articles on 'a woman's view' of South Africa, India, Japan, Germany, Northern Europe, Holland, and so on. They took collective pride in the work of Liberal women such as their President Lady Gladstone who had "innumerable committees call upon her services," as she "carried the gospel of internationalism in many directions." Already by 1925 Lady Gladstone had been a delegate on international conferences of League of Nations Societies in Italy, Switzerland, Czechoslovakia, Austria and Poland, and in 1924 she had visited the US and given several addresses on international questions.[86] This interest in women around the world was explained by Corbett Ashby: "We become so absorbed in our own national work, discouraged by our failures or elated by our successes, that it is a good New Year exercise to compare our position with that of women elsewhere."[87] The comparative study of women's emancipation served to buoy the moods of British women Liberals.

Third, Liberal women gave institutional form to their woman-centred internationalism by rarely failing to send one of their representatives to international conferences, by sending numerous resolutions and petitions on foreign affairs to the British Government, and by opening communication with Liberal women in Europe. For instance, in the course of 1924 alone "communication has been opened with groups of women of Liberal opinion in Germany and America," and points "under discussion have been the admission of Germany, Russia, and America to the League of Nations, conditions in the Ruhr, and Equal Franchise."[88] Fourth, members of the

WNLF were well placed, in terms of their political pedigree, class, education (many were multi-lingual—including Corbett Ashby and Enid Lapthorn, the latter's private secretary at Geneva) and family incomes, to embark on frequent trips abroad, which, even if holidays, included a component of politicized tourism for journalistic purposes.[89]

As a function of the deep faith invested in the League of Nations and the 'gospel of internationalism' that dominated Liberal rhetoric and policy, Liberal women had their own difficulties adjusting their political positions when faced with a new world order hijacked by fascist regimes. Indeed, at first their views on Nazi Germany were not nearly as violent or pessimistic as those of Labour women. Throughout the 1920s they expressed real empathy for the Germans. Lady Barlow's few weeks of holiday in Germany in the summer of 1926 convinced her "that nothing can daunt this people,"[90] with special concern for the German woman and her suffering, but within the framework of Anglo–German friendship and in order to facilitate mutual economic benefit, presenting a rather pragmatic and clinical justification for peace. Lady Barlow travelled to Germany again in 1933, after Hitler's seizure of power, writing that "Germany is considered a shell-shocked nation and will have to be treated as the individual in such a case is dealt with—patiently and with understanding. We, the Allies, are largely responsible for her condition."[91] One contributor acknowledged German women's complicity with the Nazis: "although the Nazis are anti-feminist, they had particularly strong support from women electors, the majority of whom are reactionary. From my personal experience of many classes in many parts of Germany, I fear this dictum true."[92] In the early days of the Nazi regime they clung to the hope that the Germans would come to their senses, and they rarely swerved from their originally well-intentioned view that Germany's diplomatic and territorial grievances were entirely justified. This early faith that the Nazi dictatorship was temporary was expressed in the Council of the Women's NLF in May 1933, resolving that it viewed "with deep regret the recent overthrow in Germany of those principles of religious, racial, and political freedom for which Liberalism stands the world over. This Council hereby offers to all Liberal thinkers in Germany the expression of their profound sympathy and hope that the enlightened thought of the great German people may speedily reassert its power."[93] But first-hand experience could be decisive and served to overturn the belief that Nazism was no momentary aberration.

Hilda Buckmaster, the 'lady' Liberal parliamentary candidate for Maldon, experienced a dramatic fascist encounter in the summer of 1933. Having just left Germany, she wrote from Poland to inform readers about the "present loss of freedom in Germany." The danger was great for anyone even slightly connected with any left-wing, international, or liberal movement. She warned that "many people in England, remarking the efficacy of the Italian train-service of today, have shut their eyes to the loss of freedom which Fascism entails." But "now in Germany we have another example of Fascism, nearer our own doors, and among people more akin to us. Let us learn from this sinister object lesson, not to be led away by the specious cure-all of the Locker-Lampsons, Mosleys, and Cripps, but to hold firm to our cherished liberty."[94] In most cases the Fascist encounters proved to be the decisive turning point, after which faith in arbitration alone was abandoned to the realization that fascism could only be stopped by a violent response. Enid Lapthorn, who had served as Corbett Ashby's secretary at Geneva and who was once such a firm believer in the potential of collective security, came to recognize that these ideals were no longer tenable since Hitler had come to power. Joining a party of journalists in 1935 on a tour of Germany meticulously orchestrated by the Nazi Party, Lapthorn informed Liberal women: "It is impossible for those who have not witnessed it first hand to grasp the power of the Fuhrer over the German people,"[95] as the personal Nazi encounter was beginning to tip the scale of Liberal faith in the possibility that the German people would throw off the Nazi yoke. Also in 1935, Lady Rathcreedan, member of the WNLF executive, reported that "she had some opportunities for seeing the dangers and drawbacks of life in the dictatorship countries of Europe ... People in this country had no idea what it was to fear their neighbour informing against their political opinions,"[96] as the true horror of the Nazi regime was beginning to register. Such reports set the stage for the WNLF's acceptance, however reluctant, of rearmament by 1937.

By 1937, under the Presidency of Megan Lloyd George, the WNLF reported the disappointment felt over the past year by supporters of the League, but that the party "still believe that the League function is to secure recognition of the rule of law among nations, and not merely to become machinery to secure international social welfare." From an organization that had been at the forefront of the disarmament campaign, the Liberals now supported the government policy of rearmament "as an unfortunate necessity in a world in which Conservatives had missed every opportunity to encourage a new outlook in Europe."[97] Many Liberal women soon channelled their efforts into Popular Front politics. Liberal women were also involved with Spanish relief, raised money for Spanish refugees, and vehemently objected to the Italian and German intervention in the Spanish Civil War.[98] They also organized relief for Austria, and called for a boycott of Japanese goods.[99]

Overall, the drift of Liberal women to a Eurocentrism was very pronounced. There are some parallels to be observed in this regard with Labour women, as well as significant differences from Conservative women whose attention remained fixed on the national and imperial spheres. It must also be stressed that we need to consider Liberal, Labour, and Conservative women on their own because of the sex segregated structure of all three parliamentary parties. In the shift to the post-war political order in which men had achieved universal suffrage and women had been 'gifted' the limited franchise, all three parties established women's sections that were at once a recognition of women's integration into the political process, but on the other hand placed women in subordinate positions with little access to the levers of power within the parties.[100]

Labour women and the fascist challenge

The parallels to be observed in the changing priorities of Liberal and Labour women does not mean that they were natural collaborators on foreign policy. On the contrary. The records of the Women's Section of the Labour Party do also show how central disarmament, foreign policy, Spain, and later rearmament were for the women of the Party, leaving little doubt that international affairs punctuated Labour women's priorities and anxieties. For example, during the inter-war years the Standing Joint Committee of Industrial Women's Organisations lent its members support to the Women's Socialist International, the No More War Movement, the National Council for the Prevention of War, the Peacemakers' Pilgrimage, the League of Nations Union, the British–American Women's Crusade, the Women's Peace Crusade, and the Women's International League, and in October 1936 set up a "Women's Committee in Aid of Spanish Workers" (in association with the International Solidarity Fund and the Medical Aid Committee). The international conferences which Labour women attended became increasingly focused on women's position in fascist regimes, even if they did not dissent from the orthodox Marxist interpretation of fascism as the last gasp of capitalism, and thus stunted a feminist critique of fascism. For example, when the International Committee of the LSI met in Brussels in 1936, the whole study week took place "under the sign of the necessity to fight to the last breath and on all fronts the rising tide of Fascism,"[101] with the acknowledgement that women were the first to suffer. In the case of Labour women, fascist encounters were counterbalanced by communist encounters, direct or by proxy, as for instance when Labour women in Manchester were addressed by Miss Barnes recounting her recent visit to Russia where she was impressed by advances in education,[102] and Mrs Anderson who gave an interesting account of conditions in Vienna which was then under Socialist administration.[103] Nonetheless, the ambivalence towards the CPGB and hostility to calls for any joint efforts in the fight against fascism was especially evident in Labour's women's section.

The main controversy among Labour women, mirroring that of the party as a whole, was over the United Front and then Popular Front model of anti-fascist militancy. Ellen Wilkinson was confronted by "ironical cheers" when she put forward the case for a United Front with the Communists against the fascist danger at the Labour Party conference in October 1933, and Labour women tended to follow the party line very closely in this respect.[104] In 1937 heated discussions arose at the National Conference of Labour women at Norwich over the question of the United Front, with strong views for and against affiliation with the Communist party. Those in favour tended to be younger women, like Miss Alexander of East Glasgow representing the Shop Assistants' Union, who "said that if they did not have a united front now Fascism would come in and smash them as it had smashed the workers in other countries," and it was feared that Labour's intransigence on this issue was sending young women running into the arms of the CPGB. Overall, there was much division of opinion on international policy, many delegates condemning the Government's rearmament programme, others advocating the policy of collective security, and others like Mrs Hargreaves of Burnley criticizing "Mr George Lansbury for having visited Herr Hitler when the workers of Germany had been tortured and put to death."[105]

Indeed, it was the Labour Women's conference in May 1938 that spearheaded the party's anti-Popular Front campaign, the "highlight" of which "was the overwhelming vote, after a fine debate, for a straightforward resolution affirming belief in Socialism as the only way to peace and security and rejecting proposals for a 'Popular Front'." They continued to regard both the Communists and the Liberals as their political opponents, and even more so would not countenance coming to the assistance of the Duchess of Atholl as she fought her by-election in December 1938 on a Popular Front platform. Labour women were warned against making common cause with this anti-fascist renegade, reminded not to forget that she was a Tory first and foremost, and that she had been a great opponent of trade unionism. However, it was indicative of the marginalization of Labour women that there was an "almost complete boycott in the Popular Front press of our Conference decision." On the day after the conference, the Liberal *News Chronicle* and the Communist *Daily Worker* were silent on the debate and the vote, and *Reynolds's News* did not carry a line about the conference, while the *Tribune* "sneered at the intelligence of the delegates—the usual reaction of the 'intelligentsia' to working women who have minds of their own and not overmuch reverence for those who like to pose as their intellectual betters."[106]

An examination of the records of the Manchester Women's Labour Council illustrate well how heated and personal were these debates over the Popular Front. Up to December 1938 the minutes suggest that the meetings were overwhelmingly consensual and properly officious. But then an unpleasant scene took place when the Council was considering a minority pro-Popular Front resolution to "cement all progressive forces ... at this crucial moment in History." Only one of their number, Mrs Ireland, spoke in favour of the resolution, while nine voted to instruct delegates to vote against, five refrained from voting, and one supported the resolution. "At this juncture Mrs Ireland violently left the meeting slamming the door with the remark: 'I have finished with the whole miserable lot of you.' Members considered her action an insult to themselves and the chairman and secretary was instructed to ask Mrs Ireland for an apology before she attends another meeting of the Council."[107] The altercation with Mrs Ireland continued over the following weeks, the Council demanding her apology and she demanding theirs, nerves were frayed, but a fragile peace within the organization was finally restored. In February, 1939, the delegates of the Manchester Women's Advisory Council "wholeheartedly endorse the action of the NEC in expelling Sir Stafford Cripps from membership of the Labour Party and reject the Popular Front memorandum," and their resolution was sent to the press.[108] Indeed, the Women's Sections remained a stronghold of anti-Popular Front sentiment: in 1939 only 23 out of 1,625 Women's Sections sent resolutions to head office in support of the Popular Front or against the expulsion of Cripps from Labour for organizing a public campaign in opposition to its principles and programme.[109] In the case of Labour women, it seems clear that local issues, grass-roots considerations, and party-wide controversies determined their collective position on international questions.

Conclusion: international solutions to domestic problems

We have been examining a range of women's organizations and different levels of commitment to feminist or women-only politics, but there are nevertheless distinct patterns to be observed. If the 19th-century *Pax Britannia* was underwritten by policies that found imperial solutions to domestic problems—women's emigration to ease demographic imbalance, imperial preference as a solution to trade wars, a consumer revolution of imported luxury goods to enliven the drab English diet and interiors—in the years after the First World War the paradigm shifted to the search for international solutions to domestic problems. Those addressing the new female electorate stressed the cardinal place of international thinking in all spheres associated with women and mothers. Politicians tried to flatter women voters by portraying them, en masse, as the peacemakers and peace-lovers. Typical instances were when David Lloyd George told Liberal women that "Woman is the maker of peace (Applause),"[110] while Labour's Philip Snowden, Chancellor of the Exchequer, speaking at a NUSEC luncheon, said he believed the statement that it was within the power of women to put an end to war: "If ever another war comes—which Heaven forbid—the responsibility for it will be largely the responsibility of women. You can exercise immense influence on politicians. I don't know whether you will believe me or not, but I want to assure you that politicians are amenable to the pressure of outside opinion."[111] The point that the local (family life and women's sphere) and the international (male-identified and traditionally the preserve of the elite) were inseparable was driven home in respect to a whole host of 'domestic' issues, from the price of consumable goods purchased by wives and mothers; to the education of children—and especially boys; to the management, arrangement and decoration of the home; to the worthwhile occupations for 'surplus' women as healers, humanitarians and rescuers; and to the overarching interdependence between grassroots political action and foreign affairs. These themes were also vividly illustrated in a comic-strip titled "For your family's sake" that adorned the back of the National Peace Council's pamphlet in aid of the Charter for "Peace and Social Justice." Here Mrs Smith is made to understand from her husband that much of the money she needs for household expenses and nutritional food for her son is needed to pay taxes which the government uses to build armaments. Mrs Smith spreads the word among her fellow housewives–consumers before coming to her entreaty: "If all women got together and every women's organisation demanded a policy which would bring PEACE, we should get it. Will you help us?"[112]

In her pre-Peace Pledge Union days and before her disillusionment with the League of Nations, Vera Brittain was one of the great purveyors of feminist internationalism. At the height of the Depression, she explained to diners at the Halifax Luncheon Club that we "are made more conscious than ever before of being members of a worldwide community. We are able to see—and indeed are constantly being made to see—our own little affairs are not an isolated phenomenon, but part of great world reactions." Disarmament was vital as "without it there will be even less money to spend on health, on our children's education, upon the reserve for the Mothering Service of mothers who die unnecessarily in child birth."[113] Brittain worked hard to convince female audiences that the domestic and the international were entwined: "How Foreign Affairs affect us as women ... 'Can't bother about Foreign Affairs—must look after home, children and shopping.' But Foreign Affairs specially affects a. home b. shopping."[114] But Hitler's ascension to power in Germany changed all this. Against the backdrop of accelerating international crises, and as they were confronted and affronted by fascist encounters, women were forced to reconsider and reconfigure their national, their internationalist, and their European identities. A minority which Brittain belonged to pursued an absolute pacifist agenda, but the majority of politically engaged women were moved by their fascist encounters to arm themselves for a 'women's war on fascism.'

2
Women's War on Fascism

In the political sphere women had spent much of the 1920s and early 1930s making war on war. The cause of peace and the internationalist orientation gave form and substance to women's politics, and also politicized a wide swath of the female population that might otherwise have been preoccupied with local and domestic concerns. One need only look at the Women's Peace Pilgrimage of 1926 when 10,000 women from all over the country marched, culminating in a great demonstration against war and for disarmament in Hyde Park; the consistent work of the Women's Peace Crusade; how Labour, Communist, and Liberal women came together to organize 'peace weeks;' and the millions of women's signatures amassed for anti-militarist petitions. In particular, by the mid-1920s and into the early 1930s disarmament became a rallying point for women's activism. As Ethel Mannin recalled, "pacifism was all the rage. It really did seem like that—a craze."[1] However, this powerful narrative of the unity of women with peace was critiqued and gradually rewritten under the pressure of international crises in the course of the 'Devil's Decade.' "The whole European situation had been altered by the change-over in this one country [Germany] from a Liberal democracy to a dictatorship,"[2] Storm Jameson admitted in 1934, as the shock of the advent of Hitler came as a terrible epiphany for those who had invested so much in post-war reconstruction and pinned their hopes for peace on internationalism and the new diplomacy. The ideational shift was from war on war to, as the *News Chronicle* put it, "Women's War on Fascism."[3] By no means was this a smooth transition, nor was it made by all women—a significant minority remained pacifist for the duration. For instance, even as a position of pacifist anti-fascism became increasingly contradictory and untenable by the later 1930s, there are many famous examples of those whose pacifism trumped their anti-fascism, including Vera Brittain, Maude Royden, Katherine Londsdale, Sybil Morrison, Sybil Thorndike, Helena Swanwick, and Ethel Mannin, and as late as January 1940 women organized a mass 'Stop the War' meeting at the Kingsway Hall, London.

But what is quite clear is that the tensions and confusion in the women's movement in the 1930s were largely the result of the collision and contradictions of these two militant impulses, both framed in the language of women's special interests and their instinctive self-defence. This tension permeated national as well as international women's and feminist organizations and friendship networks. On the personal level, it caused much soul-searching, anxiety, and depression, and, in the most serious and tragic cases, led to morbid thoughts and suicidal deeds. The weaponry of this new war was ideological and philosophical, as women developed a forceful and largely coherent feminist case against fascism. With this new women's militancy too, words were backed up by deeds, and feminist anti-fascism was also a set of practices and rituals. The inventiveness and energy of women's resistance should not be undervalued, even if in the end we do struggle to identify a unified anti-fascist movement among women, and thus query the overall success of their efforts. The threat of fascism both at home and abroad brought the majority back to contemplating military responses to the terrorism of dictatorships, and to arm themselves emotionally and intellectually for a war on fascism.

In a dialectical process, the hopefulness fed by constructive European encounters, and by the sense that women could make good the responsibilities conferred upon them as a function of enfranchisement, was shattered by *Fascist encounters*. These transformative experiences forced these same women to reassess fundamental principles, and question the efficacy of the women's movement to counter existential threats to feminism specifically and to democracy more generally. These fascist encounters occurred at home in the midst of Mosley's Blackshirts, but just as powerfully in Italy, Germany, Abyssinia, and Spain, foreign and exotic locales where women were already once removed from their domestic comfort zones. "The British intelligentsia brought the experience of Europe to bear on what they wrote and worked with a frame of reference that was anything but parochial, if it could sometimes be misinformed or myopic,"[4] and Overy has further stressed the European-ness of British science, arts, and politics. This sense of European solidarity and shared fate was evident throughout the women's movement as well. The rapid post-war normalization of women's engagement with internationalist, missionary, relief, and diplomatic work meant that many women were already frequent visitors to the Continent and avid pupils of European studies before 1933. Due to the prevalent class (middle and upper middle-class), generational (middle-aged), educational profile (many university educated and multi-lingual), and marital status (either unmarried or married and childless) of the most prolific of these travellers, they could be independent and often travelled alone or with female companions. They were thus firmly embedded in European affairs and familiar with the Continental terrain by the time they confronted or were affronted by fascism.

There can be no exact science to pinpoint the precise moment when women lost the hope they had invested so heavily in well-intentioned internationalism. In the previous chapter we started to look at examples of Nazi encounters that served to tip the scale in favour of support for rearmament and eventually war, and additional cases will be illuminating here. It is true that some did try to fix on a date, and Mary Agnes Hamilton, former Labour MP, cited 1935 as the watershed year, when Italian aggression in Abyssinia acted as the trigger for so many conversions from pacifism to a militant anti-fascism. In 1935 "a profound searching of hearts took place precisely within those groups and sections which had fought hardest for collective security and all-round disarmament. They saw that it was not enough to talk peace; they must be ready to fight for it with the old weapons."[5] Across gender and class lines, the Spanish Civil War was probably the most overruling transformative fascist encounter of the 1930s, with so many experiencing their 'conversions' under the dark shadows, literal and figurative, of pro-Franco bombers over Spanish cities. Indeed, the first British volunteer to be killed in Spain in August 1936 was an artist from a privileged background who had contributed her illustrations to *Left Review*, Felicia Browne.[6] Novelist Rosamond Lehmann foregrounded her maternal role to explain the side she had taken in the terrible conflict:

> As a mother, I am convinced that upon the outcome of the struggle in Spain depends the future, the very life of my children. Up till now a pacifist in the fullest sense, I have come to feel that non-resistance can be—in this case, is—a negative, a sterile, even a destructive theory.[7]

For others, the moment of conversion came later still, Rose Macaulay and Kathleen Courtney by 1938, and Maude Royden not until the end of the Phoney War period in the summer of 1940.[8] The loss of confidence in pacifist internationalism was a highly individuated pattern, and this chapter carries on from the previous one by focusing on how politicized women—most of whom were happy to call themselves feminists—framed their anti-fascism and gave form to their resistance.

The Six Point group: the feminist anti-fascist front

For a moment as the Nazi party was coming to power in Germany one British women's group in particular could well have provided the nucleus for a feminist, progressive, anti-fascist, and still politically ecumenical movement. This was the Six Point Group (formed in 1921), and in 1931–1932 its vice-presidents included the entrepreneurial feminist intellectual, SPG founder, and *Time and Tide* proprietor Viscountess Rhondda; the Tory and feminist Nancy Astor MP; the outspoken and independent Liberal Lady Violet Bonham Carter; the feminist social reformer (Dorothy) Lady Balfour of Burleigh; the composer and suffragist Ethel Smyth; and the brilliant Winifred Holtby who, before her untimely death in 1935, probably articulated the principles of feminist anti-fascism first and most coherently. Also on the SPG executive in 1931–32 sat patriotic anti-socialist feminist Flora Drummond, the pacifist feminist Vera Brittain, and the energetic feminist anti-fascist campaigner Monica Whately.

Feminist anti-Nazism had the power to transcend party loyalties, and the SPG called a meeting on the position of women under Hitlerism in May 1933 at which the right-wing Flora Drummond and Labour's Ellen Wilkinson, who had first-hand knowledge of what was going on in Germany from her many visits there, happily shared a platform.[9] Drummond reinvigorated the militant spirit of suffragette days—she had been known as 'General' Drummond in the WPSU—and warned: "If there are any menfolk in our country who think they will try on the Hitler touch, they may know beforehand that they will have the women to reckon with." The meeting then passed a resolution to send to the German Ministry protesting against "the definite attack that is being made by the National Socialist Government of Germany on the woman's right to earn her living and her right to serve the community on public bodies." In addition, the meeting protested against the ill-treatment of individual women for their political opinions, and "urged Herr Hitler and his Government to realize that none of the urgent problems facing Germany to-day could be solved without the co-operation of women on equal terms with men."[10]

This is not the first or last occasion we come across these women, but it is one of the few when we find them working together in relative harmony. While in the course of the decade the SPG became only more important as a storm-centre for feminist anti-fascist thought and campaigns, and by the end of the decade described itself as the "clearing house of the most tragic cases of the women victims of dictatorship,"[11] it became less able to unite women from all these points on the political spectrum.[12] That is partly because women processed their fascist encounters in different ways. As we are seeing, there was by no means one response to the shock of fascism, and profound fissures erupted in nearly all women's associations due to passionate differences regarding peace and diplomatic strategies, pacifism or pacificism,[13] political partisanship, and personal, spiritual, and national loyalties. Vera Brittain, whose absolute pacifism would come to alienate her from so many of those with whom she had collaborated as a feminist internationalist in the SPG as well as in the LNU, reflected on the crisis of the Left in the immediate aftermath of the Munich Agreement. The effect of appeasement was "the splitting of 'progressive persons' into mutually hostile categories of opinion, which sub-divided further according to strength of their attachment to their particular ideology." Her imagistic summing up of these conflicts was that a "once uniform pattern of cooperative 'leftism' has smashed, with the shattering completeness of a delicate vase dropped on a stone floor, into sharp-edged fragments of incompatible opinion."[14] She could well have been referring to the women's movement in particular.

The shock of the fascist encounter: being in the wrong place at the right time

Already in the summer of 1933, as an eye-witness to Nazi terror and as a representative of the Relief Committee for the Victims of German Fascism, Ellen Wilkinson experienced her transformative encounter, coming back "to this country shocked to the depths of her being at what she had seen, and with a desire to do anything she could to help the victims." Indeed, the reason the above committee had come into being was due to "the fact that she happened to be in Berlin during the worst day of the March terror."[15] Feminist internationalism was also most often intrinsically allied to a feminist-informed pacifism, and fascist encounters set in motion profound soul-searching and eventually 'conversion' to a more active form of anti-fascism and, in due course, support for the war. Wilkinson herself provides a vivid example of the dilemmas faced through these circuitous passages. 'Red' Ellen attended the 1919 Zurich women's congress, and during the 1920s she was an active member of the WILPF, as well as a short-time member of the Communist Party. Throughout the 1930s she would be pulled in many directions as a socialist; as a leading academic expert in the study of fascism and even more specifically as one who carved out the sub-field of women and fascism (she herself was a history graduate); as one of the original sponsors of the World Congress of Women against Fascism and War (meeting first in Paris in August 1934); as a rescuer of the victims of Nazism; as an anti-fascist missionary; as a pacifist but only so far; as one of the minority of Labourites who were willing to join forces to mount the Popular Front; and finally as one of the most trenchant critics of appeasement in Parliament. Wilkinson was already affiliated to the Reverend Dick Sheppard's Peace Pledge Union in the summer of 1936 when the movement's appeal was being extended to women,[16] but she resigned from the '100% peace movement' in March 1938 because she felt that its ideas, "admirable though they were, did not fit in with the facts of the international situation. For us to stand defenceless before the aggressor nations would not ensure peace and freedom to the world."[17]

One of Wilkinson's recent biographers has offered a reassessment of her political trajectory by prioritizing the significance of her transnational practices, and changing the periodization of her career in order to identify 'a second radicalization' between 1932 and 1936 as a consequence of her transformational experiences in Germany and Spain. Perry identifies these as her conference attendance, her journalism and developing roles as foreign correspondent, her acting as a political hostess to Leftist émigrés and exiles, the missions of investigation she made to many countries, and her overwhelming sense of solidarity with fellow Socialists and victims of imperialism and fascism. He argues that "transnationalism became less a compartment of her political work than a permanent orientation, a state of mind intertwined with some of her most mundane activities."[18] Further, we can measure the impact of her interventions in international politics by the fact that the security services were monitoring her 'political tourism,' especially to India and to Spain. They were keeping a personal file on her, which was later destroyed in 1946 when she was appointed Minister of Education.

The direction of Wilkinson's thinking and the redirection of her energies from feminist internationalism to militant anti-fascism mirrored that of the most influential feminist weekly of the period, *Time and Tide*. Indeed, Wilkinson was a frequent contributor and she was able to secure a special issue on Spain. Within the pages of *Time and Tide* we can easily discern the deviation in priorities from equalitarian feminist internationalist aspirations to pressing anti-fascist initiatives among women fortunate enough to live in democracies. In October 1937 Monica Whately wrote a letter to the journal expressing her disappointment that it failed to provide even the briefest report of the proceedings of the 18th Assembly of the League of Nations with regards to the 'Status of Women.' Whately wrote with a sense of achievement how "all the most important women's organizations, representing some 40 million women, had sent their representatives to Geneva, these same societies had sent in their reports of the various aspects of differentiation in the laws as between men and women, which were printed by the League and circulated." In addition, "26 Governments had complied with the League request for information as to the position of women under national laws; the delegates of 23 nations spoke on the subject when it came before the First Commission, some of them more than once." Whately's reproach was followed by a revealing response from the Editor, at once apologizing for not having reported on this heartening news but also implying that in the current climate of crisis there were things more urgent, namely Mussolini's visit to Munich: "In the present state of the world tension it was—in Europe—the most momentous event of the week that took place." The editor then went on to distinguish between the two prevalent dispositions within the feminist movement, the first being the demand for universal legal equality for women on paper, the second:

> maintaining that better results can at the present time be obtained if as many women as possible use the powers which they have acquired, and which in most democratic countries are very considerable, and indeed amount on paper (though not at all in actual fact) to something which in a number of directions approach equality, since by using them they are not only enabled to do good work in the world but also familiarise the general public with the idea that men and women working side by side regardless of sex and on equal terms is for the general good.[19]

It is the latter view that prevailed as the editorial policy of Lady Rhondda's journal, and that was shared by others who took the journey from a 'Me Too'/Old/Equalitarian Feminism that was compatible with a more hopeful age of reform to a *real politic* feminism that was less about women's rights and more about the preservation of democracy as the first necessity.

While we have been focusing here on sex-segregated organizations, it is of course true that women were also channelling their resistance into a wide array of non-sex specific parties, pressure groups, and campaigns. However, within these they did struggle to put forward their concerns as women. There are many examples of what we would have no difficulty in calling sexism within the broader anti-fascist movement, as well as competing agendas among women themselves. One vivid example will suffice for the moment. When Virginia Woolf was approached to take part in an anti-Nazi exhibition initiated by the Cambridge Anti-War Council, she objected to the absence of a woman's perspective. In a 'teasing' reply Elizabeth Bibesco assured her that there would be a section dealing with women under the Nazi regime, but it had not occurred to her "that in matters of ultimate importance even feminists could wish to segregate and label the sexes. It would seem to me a pity that sex alone should be able to bring them together."[20] Woolf was sorely irritated and confided to her diary: "So we go on, sparring and biting. I shouldn't mind giving that woman a toss in the air."[21] The literary world owes a debt to Bibesco's gender blindness, as it was just this attitude that incensed Woolf and inspired the classic of the feminist anti-fascist genre, *Three Guineas*. There is a story to tell about women's roles in the broader but no less coherent anti-fascist movement, but in this chapter I am differentiating between women engaged in anti-fascist activity, and women engaged in feminist and female-centred anti-fascist resistance.[22]

"In great demand as a speaker against these tyrannous dictatorships:"[23] Monica Whately and feminist anti-fascism in action

The editorial scuffle between Whately and Lady Rhondda gives an unfair characterization of Monica Whately's political priorities. In fact, she was an outstanding feminist anti-fascist, and a driving force behind campaigns on behalf of individual women hostages and prisoners in Nazi Germany, each of whom personified the fascist hatred of liberated women.[24] Exemplifying the similarity of their feminist-informed anti-fascism, Whately entreated Virginia Woolf to join a deputation by prominent women to the German Ambassador on behalf of these women victims because "if we can make him feel that British women are deeply concerned at what is happening to the women of Germany, he may be willing to use his influence with his Government."[25] The plight of these persecuted women was taken up by the SPG and each case was also well publicized in *Time and Tide*.[26]

Whately (1890–1960) had been a member of the WSPU, and after the war she was involved in famine relief work in Austria, Germany, Poland,

and Russia. Her career followed a familiar trajectory, and she was a member of the Peace Army, the No More War Movement, and an LNU speaker. As a key figure in the SPG which identified "Resistance to Fascist Anti-Feminist Philosophy" as one of its main tenets immediately in 1933, Whately was addressing 'At Homes' such as at the Lyceum Club with Ellen Wilkinson on 'Women Under the Hitler Regime.'[27] She and Dorothy Evans were sent as SPG representatives to the World Conference of Women Against Fascism and War in Paris in the summer of 1934. She actively sought out Nazi encounters, travelling to Germany on missions on behalf of women imprisoned by the regime. The cases of Liselotte Herrmann, Elsie Evrert, and Olga Prestes, and Else Steinfurth, Frau Beimleer, and Mrs Fridel Worch were the ones that most aroused the vehement indignation of British anti-Nazi feminists, and Whately led the charge.[28] She wrote the pamphlet "Women Behind Nazi Bars," revealing "forcibly the degradation of women under Fascist dictatorships" and containing "a moving call to women to band themselves together as a protection against this world-wide menace." Hundreds of thousands of copies were printed and circulated by the Women's Shoppers League, of which she was Chairman, and copies were also sold in the streets of the West End "where for many years no feminist publications had been so offered for sale."[29] Motivated by the urgent need to turf out *Blackshirt* paper sellers on the streets, copies of the pamphlet were also sold in Piccadilly by a girl whose salary was paid by one of Whately's friends, as well as by other volunteers. Although she had made common cause with the CPGB in many campaigns, including consumer boycotts and protests on behalf of women prisoners in Nazi Germany, her Catholicism and championing of religious freedom made her personally unsympathetic to communism.[30]

Herrmann's case was a "very tragic one" for it was the first purely political trial in Germany in which a death sentence had been passed on a woman.[31] Whately had travelled to Germany at the end of 1934, observing in a letter to Nancy Astor that every step was being taken by the German Government to close all avenues to women. "She is being deprived of her right to higher education, of entering into the Trades and Professions—ruthlessly she is to be forced back into the home, the unpaid servant of her husband, but not the legal guardian of her own children."[32] From here she went on to detail individual cases of women being persecuted or held in prison. Astor, however, did not feel that "constant badgering of the Ambassador about individual cases is going to help," and therefore she decided not to join this deputation to the German Embassy. Whately expressed her disappointment, and asked Astor to reconsider. She reassured Astor that the SPG had also intervened in cases of injustice to women in Soviet Russia in 1934. Nevertheless, Astor felt she could not join the deputation because:

I have always felt that I can get our common opinions across more effectively by a private word in season that [sic] as a member of a deputation, and that to join in an organised expression of feeling (which could, however incorrectly, be construed as being actuated by purely political hostility) would merely diminish what little influence I have at the Embassy.

Astor also admitted how "I do feel the weight of protest from left-wing opinion is too one-sided to be fully effective; but I assure you that that has nothing to do with my decision."[33] Although Astor was reluctant to use up her capital with the German ambassador in London to act as advocate for a Communist woman, this did not stand in the way of Whately's campaign. Whately dispatched telegrams to the German Chancellor pleading for the death sentence on Herrmann to be commuted, and she fronted many meetings and fundraisers. There can be little doubt that these attempted rescue operations of individual women victims drew anti-fascist women together by offering the prospect of achievable goals when the overthrow of the whole regime was far more unfathomable. Despite their energetic efforts, however, the death sentence was carried out on Herrmann in June 1938, as she became "the latest of a long line of victims of Nazi dictatorship in Europe."[34]

Elected to the London County Council for the Limehouse Division in 1937, Whately confronted domestic fascism as well, and she was exposed to face-to-face confrontations with Mosley's Blackshirts. She described her election fight in Limehouse as "a very bitter one" for amongst her opponents were "two members of the British Union of Fascists, whose hooligan and brutal methods were reminiscent of the days when uncivilized crowds of young men and women tried to drive off the street women, who were demanding their political emancipation." The Blackshirts were "driving decency and tolerance from our public life."[35] Whately was also instrumental in launching a number of economic anti-Nazi boycotts as a leading figure in the British Non-sectarian Anti-Nazi Council, and as Chairman of the League for the Boycott of Aggressor Nations (1938). She travelled to Spain on several occasions during the Civil War. Her *ODNB* biographer has suggested that "her career might seem to epitomize the dissipation of energy which fragmented the inter-war women's movement. But it was precisely because she channelled her feminism into many diverse campaigns and issues that she showed its relevance to all the key movements of the 20th century."[36] There was nothing passive about her fascist encounters, and they reignited a militancy that had driven her commitment to women's suffrage before the First World War. What she lacked, as exemplified by her correspondence with Astor, was official status and greater influence that came with holding a Parliamentary seat. Like other former suffragettes, this was not from lack of effort, and she had stood as a Labour candidate for parliament in St. Albans in 1929 and again in 1931, and in Clapham in 1935.

Witnesses to the world in crisis: modes of anti-fascist travel

In spite of Whately's position on the LCC, the effect of her anti-Nazi initiatives were hampered by her limited access to formal power. We have already seen how she had to appeal to the reluctant Nancy Astor MP to advance the cases of individual women prisoners, and the impact of extra-parliamentary pressure inevitably had its limits. Arguably, Ellen Wilkinson was more effective because she held a parliamentary seat, as was the Independent MP Eleanor Rathbone who deserves a starring role in any study of feminist anti-fascism. Of those women who did manage to enter the House between the wars, Rathbone was the only one who had been a leader of the women's movement. She had been a suffragist, and then the President of NUSEC, and it could not have been predicted that once an MP she would become so fixated on foreign policy at the expense of feminist and even social issues. Her long campaign for the endowment of motherhood, for example, started to take a back seat during the late 1930s, even if it is its eventual success in the post-war welfare state in the form of family allowances to be paid to the woman that is the achievement for which she is most famous.

Rathbone was anti-Nazi from the first, and she was the only woman to take part in one of the earliest Parliamentary debates about how Britain should respond to the new German regime on 13 April 1933. She staked out her position during this debate: "given Hitler's racial ideas and treatment of the Jews, it would be a crime to accede to German requests for mandates or to purchase its good will by allowing a measure of rearmament."[37] Nor did she swerve very far from this position, and henceforth her political life was dominated by advocacy on behalf of the victims of Nazi Germany and Mussolini's Italy in Germany, in Italy, in Abyssinia,[38] and in Spain, and, as long as it still held out any hope, tenacious support for the League of Nations. Not only was she profoundly offended by fascism, sensitive to its specific assault on women, and outraged by the treatment of the Jews, but as early as 1933 she took to task anyone who was either too naïve or actually mendacious enough to regard Fascist Italy and Nazi Germany as desirable tourist destinations.[39]

By making assumptions from our post-Holocaust vantage point, we can easily forget the continued popularity of Italy and Germany as tourist destinations throughout the 1930s. "The roads of Europe soon carried more American and British than native vehicles, in the summer; the new German and Italian roads, like the clean and punctual trains, did much to reconcile travellers to dictatorship."[40] Nor would Rathbone have had to look beyond her own circle to find examples of those who partook of political tourism to Nazi Germany. We are less surprised to hear about Right-wing women's conspicuous consumption of carefully orchestrated and lavishly conducted tours of the Third Reich, and the uncritical spectatorship of Nazi showpiece projects like the Nuremberg rallies, the 1936 Olympics, or the autobahn. Unity Mitford, her parents the Redesdales, her sister Diana Mosley, 'Commandant' Mary Allen, the author Enid Bagnold, the women's exercise entrepreneur Prunella Stack, and Lady Londonderry were just a few of these eager tourists, and unambiguous fellow travellers of the far Right. However, among others, Vera Brittain, Thelma Cazalet-Keir, Diana Cooper, Mary Agnes Hamilton each travelled to Germany to take in the political spectacles mounted by the Nazi regime to impress Germans and foreigners alike. Fighting windmills perhaps, Rathbone was adamant than no one "should put himself in the position, even for a day, of accepting the protection and authority—as every traveller must—of her present Government," and travel and economic boycotts would show "in every possible way that Germany is regarded as the leper camp of Europe, which healthy people avoid because they cannot separate the sound from the corrupted."[41] She was only too aware of the transformative power of fascist encounters, and justified her uninterrupted protestations against 'unethical tourism' by citing cases known to her personally where visitors to Germany had "come back full of admiration for Nazi-ism."[42] What we see in the 1930s is a battle of travellers, and a battle of the travel narratives that articulated indelible foreign encounters.[43] On the one hand, travel and tourism were facilitated by technological innovation, social mobility, the economic upturn from the mid-1930s, the expansion of the leisure industry, the resources put into state-managed tours for foreign officials, and personal relationships across borders. Simultaneously, travel was becoming highly politicized and Continental tourism was hotly contested terrain, well exemplified by the rise of the figure and the phenomenon of the 'fellow traveller.'[44] Fellow travelling "captured the link between traveling as a physical activity and as a state of mind or radical political orientation," and for the generation of writers and intellectuals who reached maturity between the wars, travel abroad was a compulsive habit.[45]

Rathbone will receive the fuller attention she deserves in the final chapter of this study, when she emerges as one of the most formidable anti-appeasers and women Churchillians. For the time being though it is important to emphasize how politicized women sought out fascist encounters as concerned feminists bearing witness to the victimization of women; as anti-fascists intervening to rescue the persecuted and to protect democratic values; as an extension of the missionary and relief work that had occupied many of them for decades; and in order to conduct informal diplomacy, the only kind that was open to them as they were still barred from the diplomatic service.[46] That this exclusion was a serious handicap is difficult to dispute. For example, Catherine Marshall visited Czechoslovakia and Germany in the spring of 1936, and upon her return she requested a private meeting, rather than an official deputation, with PM Stanley Baldwin in order to convey a message from the WILPF conference about the necessity to intervene between the French and the Germans and draw his attention to problems that "can be solved only by international agreement made in a spirit different from that which inspired the peace treaties."[47] She does not appear to have been given the hearing she requested.

Where women faced fewer obstacles and met less discouragement was in humanitarian and relief efforts. Predictably, women's commitment to anti-fascist work was only redoubled by taking part in organized missions to Germany, Abyssinia, Spain, and Czechoslovakia. Lady Marley, wife of the Labour member of the House of Lords, went to Germany "in connection with the work of relief" and there met German men and women who had suffered, "who had come back from Germany and told of the most appalling tales." She was most revolted by the Nazi attitude towards women, which she "regarded as key to the whole of its actions."[48] Lady Marley shared these experiences with the Manchester Committee for the Relief of Victims of German Fascism, exemplifying both the power of atrocity stories at exposing the regime's misogyny, and the vibrancy of anti-fascism in the North of England.

Sylvia Pankhurst had been a committed anti-fascist from the outset of Mussolini's regime in Italy, but it was with the Abyssinian conflict especially that she and her partner Silvio Corio swung into action. When her usual methods of recording her vehement protest against British foreign policy in the form of petitioning, and sending letters to embassies, the press and politicians did not have dramatic enough effect, she started her own newspaper, *The New Times and Ethiopian News*, first published on 5 May, 1936— by 1938 it was subtitled 'The National Anti-Fascist Weekly.' She conducted very personal relief work on behalf of Emperor Haile Selassie and his family, merging colonial and fascist encounter. Indeed, it was remarkable that it was she, and not the King or the Prime Minister, who waited on the platform for the Emperor and his family when they arrived as exiles at Victoria Station, London, in June 1936.[49]

Rathbone, Whately, Wilkinson, Dame Rachel Crowdy, Edith Pye, and the Duchess of Atholl were each deeply involved in Spanish relief work.[50] Edith Pye worked with the Friends German Emergency Committee, and Edith Summerskill MP with the National Women's Appeal for Food for Spain. Representing all three parliamentary parties, Irene Ward, the Duchess of Atholl, Rathbone, Wilkinson, Megan Lloyd George, and Thelma Cazalet were members of a committee of MPs concerned with the evacuation of women and children in Spain. Nor should we only recognize the efforts of an older generation of women, and Edith Gow, a member of the Labour Party Clerical Staff, went to Spain as part of a Youth Delegation in late 1937 to deliver food and milk and help the refugees, and there are numerous other such examples.[51] Eleanor Rathbone made various trips abroad, including to the Little Entente countries in 1937, and she was much in demand in Czechoslovakia in the lead up to the Munich Agreement as an outspoken friend of Czech democracy. Another cohort of women active on the LNU's

Women's Advisory Council benefitted from its tours and summer schools to various countries in Europe, and these were still being planned for the 1938 season.[52]

Gendered practices of anti-fascism

From the biographical mode we turn to the structural perspective in order to examine the practices of feminist anti-fascism. Some of these practices were overtly political and derived from longstanding rituals of women's political engagement, while others were more innovative and the product of women's enfranchisement. Radical feminist interpretations of fascism were disseminated through conventional democratic means, such as petitioning, drafting resolutions, and organizing deputations to ministers and foreign diplomats. With business-like efficiency, women organized day schools, 'At Homes,' and conferences to hear lectures by activists as well as by a new breed of woman expert and academic in the fields of international politics and women's social studies. Carrying the banners of the peace movement but increasingly chanting anti-fascist slogans, women participated in marches, protests, and direct confrontations with the BUF. Recognizing their micro-economic power, women spearheaded and supported consumer and travel boycotts, organized bazaars, sent 'snowball' letters to urge women to refuse to buy goods coming from Italy at the time of Abyssinia, and opened and patronized charity shops. Cooperative women sold milk tokens on behalf of Spanish children and refugees, and likewise Labour women ran a 'Milk for Spain' campaign.[53] Labour women collected wool and knitted garments for Spanish workers. LNU women organized the No Silk Campaign to protest against Japanese aggression in China. Women were involved in a wide range of charitable work for various anti-fascist causes, and in a more hands-on way they activated their social maternalism in their work with refugees and the victims of dictatorship.[54] Jewish refugee and film star Elizabeth Bergner donated the proceeds from the performance of her latest film "Stolen Life" (1939) to be shared by the Lord Baldwin Fund for Refugees and to the Women's Appeal Committee for German and Austrian Jewish Women and Children. On one night at the Palace Theatre in London, with 2,000 people in attendance including the great and the good as well as a party of five German refugee children accompanied by their British foster parents, Bergner raised £3,370 from the screening.[55] All these methods were harnessed specifically to advertise the position and the extreme vulnerability of women and children under the fascist yoke.

Women played roles on both sides of a 'culture of collection,' as fundraisers and as those making significant donations. The coming quick and fast of crises at home and abroad made shrapnel of women's efforts, and prominent women especially became inundated with requests for contributions of their time and money. For example, after the success of her *Testament of*

Youth, Brittain confided to Holtby that "one of the minor trials of my existence recently has been confident appeals for money from practically every organization with which I have ever been associated and a great many that I haven't."[56] But others did make grandiose financial gestures such as when novelist Ethel Mannin realized her life saving of £1,000 to help the ILP buy a food ship to run the gauntlet of the Spanish blockade to Bilbao.[57] In the most famous example of a prominent self-supporting woman being consistently hit up for donations, Virginia Woolf's literary persona eventually conceded to part with three guineas for three carefully-chosen causes: women's education, a women's professional association, and peace.

In most cases women were employing these gendered methods of anti-fascist protest on home soil, and as part of grass-roots political activism. Therefore it is important to remember that for the majority of women their only direct encounter with fascism was with its indigenous expression. Indeed, ocular encounters with British Blackshirts could have transformative power. Evelyn Sharpe lamented the peace movement's poverty of imagination and the dowdiness of its feminine symbols as compared to the theatricality, ceremony, and visual impact of Mosley's Blackshirts. Sharpe recognized the paradox that to fight the spirit of militarism it was vital to play the same game, to recapture "the glory of pacifism."[58] Holtby was one of the few feminists who took such a sustained interest in covering and monitoring BUF activity, and she sought out fascist encounters close to home. She claimed that the first BUF meeting she attended was in May 1934 at an East Coast watering hole, where she could not help but be impressed by the stage-management and the discipline of youth.[59] Vera Brittain was one of the many curious anti-fascists who attended the BUF's notorious Olympia Rally on 7 June, 1934, and she contributed her eye-witness statement to the Gollancz pamphlet that recorded the range of atrocities committed by the Blackshirts. A recurring theme in this pamphlet was Blackshirt brutality against women, and the fascist desecration of female bodies. Whately too was a regular at fascist meetings, and she had attended the Mosley meeting at the Albert Hall as an observer on behalf of the National Council for Civil Liberties.[60] However, what she refused to do was to give the fascists a platform, and when the BUF proposed a debate on equal pay for equal work with the SPG, there was little doubt that it was "seeking to obtain propaganda by this means," and the offer was refused.[61]

The pen as the sword: feminist anti-fascist writing

Indeed, these anti-fascist initiatives were mirrored by the feminist perspective in studies of fascism. In retrospect, what they accomplished was to carve out of the sub-field of gender studies of fascism. As the more constructive international encounters gave way to destructive fascist encounters, women authors responded by building a library of anti-fascism texts. Women's literary output in the varied forms of journalism, non-fiction and current affairs publications, fiction and hauntingly vivid dystopias, and theatre contributed to the potency of an increasingly hegemonic anti-fascist national discourse. Since the 1990s, literary critics and cultural historians have finally paid critical attention to this impressive body of women's writing in these thematic veins.[62]

Holtby wrote a number of articles pillorying the BUF and recognizing its contradictory appeal to women to embrace antiquated sex roles while dressing them up in black blouses and sending them on marches in the suffragette-style. In her book *Woman and a Changing Civilization* (1934)— which Swanwick admired for "the close packing of so much matter into a little space"[63]—Holtby took Mosley to task for his call for Blackshirt men to be men and women to be women, predicting that British fascism would soon send women back to the three Ks. Holtby would be recognized today as an advanced theorist of gender and citizenship, noting that "whenever women hear political leaders call their sex important, they grow suspicious. In the importance of sex too often has lain the unimportance of the citizen, the worker, and the human being."[64] It was significant too that Holtby was most impressed by the BUF's power to make politics into theatre, because she opted for the stage as a platform for her feminist anti-fascism. Her play *a clef* "Take Back Your Freedom," written in 1934 with the original title "Hope of Thousands," was published and staged posthumously in 1939. Based on her first-hand experience of domestic fascism, the play offers a scenario set in the foreseeable future where Britain is ruled by a latently homosexual dictator whose mother has dominated him too long. The dictator, former academic Clayton, is the leader of the People's Planning Party, and his mother is installed as Honorary Commander of the Women's Legion of his Grey Guards. The climax of the play is reached when a woman character attempts to assassinate the dictator because under his rule she has been deprived of her profession and hence her life has become meaningless. Mosley was obviously the model for Clayton in many respects, and the PPP closely mimics the BUF. Mosley's mother, known in the movement as 'Ma' Mosley, was for a time leader of the BUF's Women's Section. But the similarities end there, and Mosley was a notorious ladies man and philandered—the 'Rudolf Valentino of fascism.' Latent homosexuality was certainly not one of the 'Leader's' prevalent characteristics, and instead Hitler must have been the inspiration for that. More successful as a work of unambiguous propaganda than as great theatre, with the backing of Vera Brittain who held the rights after her best friend's death, the play was nonetheless being considered for production by the nascent BBC television.[65] It was also being considered as the basis for a feature film, and at various points Robert Donat, Lawrence Olivier, Tyrone Guthrie, and Noel Coward were tied to the project. It should not come as a great surprise to anyone who has insider knowledge of the workings of the movie industry that none of these ambitious plans materialized, and it was never filmed, although her *South Riding* was adapted for the cinema and released in 1938.

The woman would-be assassin in "Take Back Your Freedom" is most certainly the alter ego of the playwright herself, and there were a number of other women who expressed their rage at the backlash against women's rights by attempting to assassinate Europe's new breed of dictators. The unbalanced Violet Gibson shot Mussolini in 1926, and even the feminist Tory MP Thelma Cazalet fantasized about shooting Hitler when she was his official guest at the Nuremberg rally early in 1938—she later claimed that she had "such an impression of impending tragedy that the thought passed through my mind that if only I had a gun and the guts to use it ... [ellipses in original]."[66] Further, while Holtby's anti-fascist heroine did not make it to the screen, we do not have to search far for celluloid sirens of resistance. There are well-realized examples in Hitchcock's thriller *The Lady Vanishes* (1938); in the film version of Bottome's *The Mortal Storm* (1940); as the eponymous protagonist in the Oscar-winning *Mrs Miniver* (1942); in the film version of the Lillian Hellman play *Watch on the Rhine* (1943); and we should not fail to mention the most unforgettable of them all, Ingrid Bergman's Ilsa Lund in *Casablanca* (1942), even if she was not herself a political heroine but rather married to the resistance.

The Fifth-Columnist-scare film based on the Graham Greene story, *Went the Day Well* (1942) also represents many anti-Nazi heroines among the resisters at the 'Battle of Bramley End.' The war-time demographic of the chocolate-box village of Bramley is made up of children, women in uniform, mothers, and middle-aged and old men not of fighting age, with only one soldier among them, home on leave to celebrate his wedding. The women protagonists range from the nubile and plucky ATS women who bear arms to take out the invaders; the vicar's spinster daughter who point blank assassinates the turn-coat Oliver, who had doubly betrayed her by posing as a patriot and an honourable suitor; the lady of the manor Mrs Frazer who saves the village children when a grenade is lobbed through the nursery window by grabbing it and taking it with her into the corridor where she is, we must extrapolate, blown to bits; the widowed telephone operator who manages to knock out one of the German invaders before she herself is martyred at the end of the enemy's bayonet; and the simple-minded Post Office assistant who overcomes more Germans to regain control of the telephone exchange. All these heroines, the female stock types of the cross-class People's War, are pitted against a unit of German invaders made up of baby-killers, murderers of the pious (their first victim is the vicar, shot as he tries to ring the church bell to alert the Home Guard), 'Gerry' thugs, and women-beaters. Anti-fascist heroines personified the purity of democratic values. In all these films the women represent the antithesis of the Nazi construction and delimitation of womanhood. They project the quiet courage of anti-fascist resolve. And they act as a reminder of the potential of a persecuted 'minority' to rise up and overthrow their victimizers.

The fact that two of these films were made in Hollywood, catering primarily to the American market, and not so subliminally intended to break down isolationism, should not distract us from the fact that both *The Mortal Storm* and *Mrs Miniver* approached contemporary dilemmas from a British feminised anti-fascist viewpoint. The former film was immediately understood to be "a trumpet call to resistance," "one of the most inflammatory fictions ever placed upon the screen," and it was the first American film to depict Nazism in Germany.[67] Both were scripted by British screenwriter Claudine West who had been a code-breaker for British intelligence in the First World War, and in the Second had five brothers serving in the RAF. Furthermore, Bottome herself was reluctant to relinquish creative control as her novel was transposed to the screen, and insisted on remaining involved in the adaptation. West also wrote the scripts for *Random Harvest* and *The White Cliffs of Dover*, almost single-handedly creating "the noble, heroic image of Britain that dominated American cinema in those years."[68]

It speaks to the confidence of British women writers in this period that they carved out their own sub-field of feminist anti-fascism, the conceptual and theoretical complexity of which was articulated in books like Winifred Holtby's *Woman and a Changing Civilization* (1934), Naomi Mitchson's *The Home and a Changing Civilization* (1934), Hilda Browning's *Women and Fascism and Communism* (1935), Hilary Newitt's *Women Must Choose: The Position of Women in Europe Today* (1937), Ethel Mannin's *Women and the Revolution* (1938), Katherine Thomson's *Women and Nazi Germany* (1943), and, of course, Virginia Woolf's seminal *Three Guineas* (1938). Never completed, Sylvia Pankhurst began writing a monograph-length manuscript in 1940 titled *Fascism As It Is*, and it included a chapter on 'Women under the Nazis.' One can thus talk about a feminist anti-fascist genre, which extended to the fiction of Katherine Burdekin (*Swastika Night*, 1937), Margaret Storm Jameson (*In the Second Year*, 1936), and Phyllis Bottome (*The Mortal Storm*, 1938), and the American Lillian Hellman. However, it should also be noted that the very practice of women writing the history of European women was at an early stage of development, especially when it came to the adoption of methodologies that were political rather than merely social, and broader in their spatial parameters than the confines of the constricted interior of the family. As Winifred Holtby explained: "The historians of women take it for granted that she is primarily concerned, not with geography, but with biology, not with philosophy, but with personal morality and ideal character."[69] Breaking these sexist boundaries, the above texts each entered male-defined spaces of journalistic interest and academic study, and are themselves products of feminist achievement, as well as documents that could only be produced outside the fascist context. What we have, in fact, is an embarrassment of riches. Cumulatively, these works provide incontrovertible evidence of the continued creative vibrancy and theoretical sophistication of British feminism between the wars, catalyzed not so much by women's domestic concerns but much more so by their deep engagement with the foreign, the European, and the international. Furthermore, their writing was an act of self-defence and self-preservation, both as women and as intellectuals. As Storm Jameson, President of PEN, put it: "At this moment unless we writers are eager in defence of human dignity we shall find ourselves at its grave."[70]

Women and the study of international relations

The widely recognized blurring of boundaries between home front and battlefield during the First World War led to the breaking down of gendered barriers in intellectual life too. Among the male-defined roles women came to occupy were political journalist and foreign correspondent (more examples of American than British women in this role), expert in national and regional histories, and theorist and practitioner in the emerging academic discipline of International Relations. It would be wrong to think that the academic sub-disciplines of FIR and GIR as they emerged out of Second Wave Feminism were without precedent, and between the wars a number of women were professionalized in this field as employees at the League of Nations Union headquarters, and in association with the Royal Institute of Foreign Affairs at Chatham House, while Helena Swanwick was editor of *Foreign Affairs*, and commissioned her feminist friends to contribute, such as economist Barbara Wootton and Winifred Holtby.[71] In another example, in May 1938, the International Conference of Women met in Marseilles on the subject of 'Moral Strength in International Relations,' the British patrons being the Duchess of Atholl, Dr Hilda Clarke, Margery Corbett Ashby, Carmel Haden-Guest, K.W. Innes, Eleanor Rathbone, and Ellen Wilkinson. However, one should not overstate the admission of women to the emerging academic institutions of international studies, which were dominated by men.[72] There were numerous reasons why women were attracted to the nascent and liberal-minded field of study, and one inspiration was to step into the breach left by the Missing Generation. Vera Brittain certainly felt the need to devote herself to international affairs because "nowhere has the shortage of first-class minds, due to the sacrifice of the war generation, shown itself so clearly as in the field of politics and international relations."[73] Whether as self-styled substitutes for absent men or as women breaking new ground, a group of women did make some noteworthy incursions into the study of 'chaps and maps' between the wars.[74]

Women were more successful as authors of studies geared to a wider readership. Women were writing books on current affairs and international relations faster than the Nazis could burn them, and their bibliography of European affairs books in these fraught years is breathtakingly long. Most of these women wrote under their own names, and some of the most successful and prolific were Naomi Mitchison, Helena Swanwick, Eleanor Rathbone, Katherine Duchess of Atholl, Ellen Wilkinson, Elizabeth Wiskemann, Shiela Grant Duff, and Dorothy Woodman. Secretary of the WIL and later of the Union of Democratic Control, Woodman was a prolific pamphleteer on internationalist themes, and she had written the first full-length study of German rearmament, *Hitler Rearms*, in 1934. A notable number were published as Left Book Club selections or by Allen Lane as Penguin Specials. In fact, the second ever Penguin Special was a translation into English of French journalist Geneviève Tabouis's *Blackmail or War* (1937) which was published two weeks after its delivery to Penguin and quickly sold 200,000 copies.[75] The Duchess of Atholl (1938), the Polish-born political cartographer Marthe Rajchman (1938), Shiela Grant Duff (1938), Phyllis Bottome (1938 and 1944), Emily Lorimer (1939), Dorothy Frances Buxton (1939), Nora Waln (1942), and Dorothy Woodman (1942) all authored Penguin Specials in the international relations and current affairs genre. Clearly, publishers were confident that the reading public would tolerate female authorship.

Women's expertise in international politics became normalized, and while many women writers did consider international problems from a woman's perspective, just as many were eager to be at ease in the company of men by remaining, at least superficially, gender neutral. Each publishing under her own name, Elizabeth Wiskemann's and Grant Duff's respective books on Czechoslovakia avoided discussion of women's issues. This does not mean, however, that they were immune to sexism, and each author was the victim of the condescension and patronizing attitudes of male university tutors, professional mentors, and colleagues. These experiences as women in homosocial foreign-correspondent and diplomatic circles have been preserved in their respective post-war memoirs. Well-born Oxford PPE graduate and author of *Europe and the Czechs* (1938), Grant Duff (1913–2004) entered the world of foreign journalism with great determination and the inexhaustible energy of youth, persuading the American foreign correspondent Edgar Mowrer to become her mentor, continuing to cultivate her intellectual and personal relationship with Adam von Trott to gain access to the diplomatic top brass, and in the process "getting used, in journalistic circles, to finding myself the only woman."[76] Grant Duff was also well connected through family ties, and as a relation of Clementine Churchill, she used her access to Winston Churchill to good effect, as we will see later.

Born in Britain to a German father, Wiskemann (1899–1971) gained some celebrity in 1936 when she was arrested by the Gestapo for her anti-Nazi articles published in the *New Statesmen* (she also contributed to the *Economist*, the *Daily Herald*, the *Scotsman*, and the *Manchester Guardian*). She was not allowed to return to Nazi Germany from that date, and she would take some pride in the fact that her name too was on the Nazi black list during the war. A tireless traveller who combined tourism with academic and professional pursuits, she spent the next years networking around Austria,

Czechoslovakia, Yugoslavia, Hungary and Roumania, and Poland, and on lecture tours to the USA. Early in 1937 she was approached by Chatham House to study the Czech-German problem, a surprise invitation as her journalism had made plain her anti-Nazism, whereas Chatham House was known to sympathize with German grievances and make excuses for Hitler. Among the obstacles she faced in conducting her research for the book were those thrown up by her sex, and she found that in Prague the "British Legation was on the whole unhelpful, making it clear that its staff, naturally enough, did not care for young women who might get themselves into scrapes."[77] Her *Czechs and Germans* came out on 2 June, 1938, just in time to bear symbolic if not entirely tangible influence on the course of events, as it was her book that Lord Runciman was photographed reading on the Prague-bound train as he was setting off on his famous if ineffective diplomatic mission. Despite her successes and training herself "as an observer abroad," she was sorely frustrated that the Foreign Office declined to employ her during the war, illustrating all too well how women struggled to be recognized as officials and experts in international relations.[78]

Oddly enough, though, while they both published influential and widely-read books on Czechoslovakia that fortuitously coincided with the Czech Crisis itself in the autumn of 1938, and therefore sold very well, neither had very much to say about the other.[79] One obvious explanation for this was professional rivalry, and one should take care not to suggest that the shared condition of a sore head caused by hitting the glass ceiling fostered sisterhood. Still others feared that they would not be taken seriously if it was known that they were female, and this can explain why Emily Lorimer used E.O. Lorimer as her pen name,[80] whereas in the literary genre Katherine Burdekin's powerful dystopia *Swastika Night* was published under the name of Murray Constantine, despite the seal of critical approval it gained as a Left Book Club selection. Women also played some of the leading roles in the campaign to get an unexpurgated translation of Hitler's *Mein Kampf* published, the Duchess of Atholl the most relentless in pursuit of this object, understanding full well that "[s]ometimes the warlike character of the original is concealed by mis-translation."[81]

Conclusion: the fascist war on women and the feminist war on fascism

How did British women come to terms with fascism? But for a minority of women active in Mosley's Blackshirt movement and a few other marginal extreme-Right organizations, the vast majority of politicized women were engaged in some form of resistance to fascism, both in its more irritating domestic variant and even more concertedly in its menacing Continental manifestations.[82] Even in Britain, a 'bystander' nation that never succumbed to fascism, it did not take long for the political classes to demonstrate the specific threats posed to women by modern authoritarian, terroristic, socially rear-guard, racialist, and male-supremacist movements. British women came to realize that Feminism could only function within a democratic framework, and as Storm Jameson put it: "only under Western democracy is it still possible for a feminist movement to exist."[83] Women on the left were attuned early on to the threat posed to them both as a sex and as class warriors. Already in 1932, the National Conference of Labour Women discerned that "what fascism means to women" is "a menace which especially endangers the political emancipation of women ... Fascism exalts all those human qualities which react most strongly against the welfare of women in family, social, industrial and professional life."[84] The Communist Party of Great Britain also gained mileage from the conflation of fascist tyranny and fascist misogyny, understanding Nazism as a form of 'masculine madness,' and carrying blazing headlines declaring "Fascism degrades women,"[85] prefacing statements by disillusioned German women under Hitler's regime. A surprisingly large number of the entries to a poetry competition 'Lines on Lipstick' in the *Manchester Guardian* touched on the theme of "the Nazi ban on lipstick and cosmetics for women supporters of Herr Hitler's rule,"[86] as British women feared a backlash against their hard-won emancipation. The WILPF recognized only too well that "every inch won by Fascism, under whatever guise, is ground lost to women," although the British branch of the movement would struggle to reconcile pacifism with the necessity of military means to destroy fascism.[87] Pondering what women could do to prevent the spread of British Fascism, Oliver Baldwin, the PM's Labour son, was under the impression that women, in their traditional feminine roles, were best placed to deflate its homo-social and aesthetic appeal, because "women can do so much more than men to stop tyranny, as they can do to stop wars." This is what Baldwin proposed:

> Instead of 'How nice you look in your uniform' or 'Blackshirt,' I suggest, 'You look a bigger idiot than ever,' or 'Bring in the cat; he'll have a laugh at any rate' ... A non-cooperation movement of mothers and sweethearts will prevent their sons from finding an early grave and their lovers from being maimed, for such is bound to be the result if doctrines of Nationalism become the order of the day.[88]

In February 1934 the Oxford Union debated the resolution "that Fascism is a menace to world peace," and N. MacDonald, the student who proposed the motion, argued that "Fascism is not only a menace to international peace, but to the peace between the sexes and the peace between the classes."[89] Cooperative and trade union women picked up on a common melding when they noted that "Hitler set out to victimise two sorts of people—the Jews and the women," and they worried too that "what the Germans had done to women was not unpleasing to many people here in England."[90]

Many women writers identified fascism with patriarchy, Naomi Mitchison observing that "in the re-constituted Teutonic home, the patriarch is again supreme. The state has solidified itself out of the Hegelian abstract into the concrete father god, Wotan, the most sworded and hairy-bellied and prolific of them all."[91] Similarly Rebecca West interpreted fascism in psycho-historical and Freudian terms, namely that men supported dictators because "they wish to return to the psychological conditions of an ideal childhood, in which they will be given every provision and protection by an all-powerful father if only they are good and obedient children."[92] Woolf took this interpretation of fascism to its logical feminist conclusion by comparing and contrasting women's historic struggle against patriarchy with men's current fight against fascism—women "were fighting the tyranny of the patriarchal state as you are fighting the tyranny of the Fascist state," she contemptuously informed her putative male reader.[93] In 1936 Ray Strachey prophesized that "if fascism, or some form of military dictatorship, is established, women will probably lose every scrap of freedom they have won."[94] Speaking on behalf of the Women's Freedom League at the point at which another war seemed inevitable, Corbett Ashby spoke from bitter experience when she observed that "wherever this doctrine prevails the women's movement has disappeared."[95] There was an unmistakable consonance in the political chorus of the 1930s that fascism posed the gravest threat to women's personal and democratic achievements, that it denied them their citizenship, and their humanity. Fascist regimes recognized their sex but denied them rights as citizens, workers, and human beings.

There are therefore important reasons to write a *women's* history of British anti-fascism. As all these notes of deep alarm suggest, women *qua* women had both a role to play in and a particular stake in the defeat of fascism. A women's history of anti-fascism gives due recognition to the determined work that women did within sex-specific organizations and campaigns, either in the feminist movement or in the women's organizations of the main political parties. Within these structures they worked self-consciously as woman and most frequently for women and children, feminizing the practices of anti-fascism. In many cases we can easily understand why they opted to work alongside other women—in unisex and usually unquestioned male-dominated campaigns they rarely held leadership positions, were less free to articulate their sex-specific anxieties about dictatorship, and suffered from sex discrimination.

Joint purpose and shared anxieties did not, however, result in easy collaboration, and while the theoretical partnership between feminism and anti-fascism was tenacious, the relationship between feminists and anti-fascist activism was more insecure.[96] That we struggle to identify a sufficiently broad-based feminist anti-fascism movement, or even consensus and effortless collaboration between feminist organizations about how to respond to fascism in the 1930s, illustrates the diversity of opinion, tactical variances, the schisms and parting of ways between friends and colleagues, and the emotional, intellectual and psychological dilemmas these women activists faced as the fascist threat intensified. The schismatic character of feminist anti-fascism mirrors that of British anti-fascism more generally, culminating in the animosities in Popular Front politics in the late 1930s.[97] Further, some of the ideological and spiritual crises of conscience faced by pacifists were common to men and women, while other dilemmas were not, and these important gender differences get lost in the ether in much of the scholarship of Britain's inter-war peace movement.[98]

However, the most important reason we need a gendered history of anti-fascist resistance is because these feminist and feminized warnings about fascism were loud and powerful contributions to national debates about foreign policy and to the British construction of the Nazi 'other.' This feminist anti-fascist discourse permeated well beyond a handful of ginger groups of women political activists, and it was this viewpoint that informed and conditioned women's responses to the looming world war. In fact, in many respects war had begun for women well before September 1939. This was 'Women's War on Fascism.'[99] Running the lines of the feminist anti-fascist script was a dress rehearsal for the ideological and rhetorical articulation of Britain's war aims, as women were pressed to justify—to their families, to their colleagues, and to themselves—going to war again so soon after they seemed to have won the argument that as sisters, wives, mothers, social mothers, and nature's diplomats they were the world's natural peace makers.

3
'Guilty Women:' Conspiracy and Collusion

In the second week of March 1939, and only days before Hitler sounded the death knell of the Munich Agreement by marching into Prague, members of London society and an array of women representing women's social work and civil service organizations played host to yet another in a string of visiting Nazis. This time the visitor was a woman, and, according to Hitler, the 'perfect Nazi woman,' Frau Gertrud Scholtz-Klink (1902–1999), the *Frauenführerin*, leader of 30,000,000 German women. Met at Croydon airport by the German Ambassador's wife, Frau von Dirksen, and hurrying herself into a waiting car as she did not wish to speak to anyone, least of all to the pack of journalists angling for a scoop, Scholtz-Klink was in London ostensibly to study 'social conditions.' Her visit was at the return invitation of Prunella Stack (who had recently become Lady Douglas-Hamilton) of the League of Health and Beauty, and a dinner was held in her honour at Claridge's hosted by the Anglo-German Fellowship.[1] Among those seated at Scholtz-Klink's table at the dinner were Lady Cynthia Colville (President of the Townswomen's Guild and of the Over Thirty Association), Viscountess Halifax (wife of the Foreign Secretary), the Dowager Countess of Airlie, the Dowager Marchioness of Reading (Chairman of the Women's Voluntary Services for Civil Defence), Miss Florence Horsbrugh MP (Conservative), Lord and Lady David Douglas-Hamilton, and Lady Violet Astor (Controller of the County of London Auxiliary Territorial Service). And that was just at her table, as women representatives of over a dozen other women's organizations also attended, including those of the British Red Cross, the Royal Institute of International Affairs, the National Women's Citizens' Association, the National Council of Women of Great Britain, and the National Council for Maternity and Child Welfare.[2] Was this to be women's Munich?

The guest of honour gave a speech in German about women's work in the Reich, and Miss Horsbrugh MP replied with a speech about the work done by leading women's organizations in Britain. Scholtz-Klink then spent the next couple of days visiting various ideologically-compatible women's organizations, such as the Mothercraft training school at Highgate, the League of Health and Beauty, and the Lapswood Training School for girls. Those of a more conspiratorial bent believed the real purpose of this latest example of shuttle diplomacy was much more sinister, however. One of the many reporters there to greet her at the airport, Richard Baxter, author of *Guilty Women*, would allege that she was in England to touch base with German and Austrian girls who had been planted as domestic servants in the homes of the powerful by their spy ringleader, the wife of the former German Ambassador, Frau Anna von Ribbentrop.[3]

Gertrud Scholtz-Klink's visit was noteworthy for several reasons. Not surprisingly, her presence in London was met with some feminist anti-fascist protest. This was one Nazi encounter too many, far too close to home, and conspicuous for its poor timing. Twelve members of the Women's Committee for Peace and Democracy (formerly the WWCAWF) walked in a single line from Tottenham Court Road to the German Embassy in Carlton House Terrace, their posters reading 'Clear Out Scholtz-Klink,' 'Hitler Wants War, We Want Peace,' 'No Nazi Klink for British Women,' and in German 'Freedom for the Women of Hitler's Concentration Camps.'[4] Her presence was an affront to British feminism, and her status as the leader of the reactionary *NS-Frauenschaft* that had risen to displace and then replace the once vibrant German women's movement meant that Lady Nancy Astor—whom we will be meeting at various junctures in this chapter—had no interest in making her acquaintance, judging that her activities "give no recognition to the rights of women in any sphere but the home."[5] Monica Whately, Honorary Secretary of the Six Point Group, wrote an open letter to the Nazis' 'Perfect Woman' when she visited, "pointing out to her the disgust that British women felt about the treatment of women in Germany," and the *Daily Express*, the *Daily Telegraph*, the *Daily Worker*, the *Daily Herald*, the *News Chronicle*, *Time and Tide*, and *Woman To-day* received the story.[6] Many journalists had little good to say about her and noted with irony her personification as the 'perfect Nazi woman,' Baxter, taking exception to her lack of sex appeal, remarking that she had the "biggest pair of feet I had ever seen on a woman," and describing her as "a dour, irritable Hun who could not even sum up sufficient decency to be civil to the authorities at Croydon, much less the representatives of the Press who had come to welcome her."[7] Others regarded the iconic duo of Prunella Stack, 'Britain's Perfect Girl,' and Scholtz-Klink, Hitler's ideal woman, as an opportunity to compare and contrast ideal Anglo-Saxon female types in a duelling atmosphere charged with political, ideological, and racial tension.[8]

What was the significance of her visit at this most strained moment in the lead up to war? Scholtz-Klink's visit punctuated—and with an exclamation mark—the varied roles played by women in Anglo-German relations in the 1930s. Scholtz-Klink was not herself a diplomat *per se*, but her visit was certainly intended to foster mutual understanding between British and

German women. Indeed, it was not only among feminist internationalists that shared gender identity could transcend national antagonisms, and, as we will see, the Munich Agreement was widely perceived to be a great success with *all* the mothers of Europe. Stack was returning the hospitality Scholtz-Klink had shown her when she had taken a League delegation to a Physical Education Congress sponsored by the *Kraft durch Freude* in Hamburg in the summer of 1938. This was shortly before Stack married David Douglas-Hamilton, the youngest son of the 13th Duke of Hamilton, on 15 October, 1938. The coverage of this celebrity-society wedding had coincided, of course, with the Prime Minister's own honeymoon period with the public in the weeks after his return from the Four Power Conference at Munich. (The Hamilton family had a tangled relationship with Nazi Germany, and when Rudolf Hess flew to Scotland on his ill-fated peace mission in May 1941, he claimed he had come to meet the Duke of Hamilton.) Scholtz-Klink's trip to London therefore was one of many attempts at Anglo-German *rapprochement* through travel and cultural exchange. While it would be rash to tar as pro-Nazi all the women who gave the time of day to the *Frauenführerin* on this occasion, this visit was nonetheless one of many efforts by women to avert war and to demonstrate their appeasement credentials. Further, the suspicion that she was a player in an espionage ring placed her in a long line of real and mythical women spies, *femmes fatale* whose only means of entry into the shady and exclusive world of diplomacy was via their sex and sexuality.[9]

The 'appeasettes': gendering Anglo–German Relations

Scholtz-Klink's visit to London was covered rather frivolously in the press, albeit worldwide,[10] suggesting both the gloss over women's issues and the fact that she was regarded in the public perception as a curiosity, if not a figure of fun. Nonetheless, we could be forgiven for asking why these British women who hosted her did not appear, at least outwardly, to have any qualms about offering her hospitality, and at this portentous time. Was it not odd that the leaders of all these women's organizations, many engaged in the enterprise of mobilizing women for wartime national service, should have supped with the probable future enemy? The seeming incongruity of this visit becomes less unfathomable when we approach the history of appeasement and Anglo-German relations in the 1930s from a gender perspective, and retrieve women's experiences of, and trace their reactions to, the coming of war.

This chapter is concerned with locating the women who played more instrumental roles than has traditionally been acknowledged in the high politics of appeasement. The first thing is to identify the 'Guilty Women' who colluded with, assisted, and celebrated, and who played hitherto largely unrecognized supporting roles beside the 'Guilty Men' who brokered the very fleeting phase of 'peace with honour.' However, this is not an exercise in naming and shaming, nor does it set out to corroborate the vivid and fanciful story of intrigue recounted by Richard Baxter in *Guilty Women* (1941), the provocatively-named red-covered booklet in which this sensationalist Allied propagandist uncovered Hitler's alleged grand plot to press German and British women into the service of the Third Reich. Baxter made the case that Hitler had enlisted the women of his inner circle to convince British women that he "was a peacemaker, a man to be trusted" and thereby to "keep the war spirit down in England even though a few bold politicians dared to foster it."[11] According to Baxter, Hitler's efforts in Britain were proving successful, and "in 1938 'appeasement' and 'peace at any price' reached a flood tide. The full weight of the guilty women was being experienced throughout the whole country."[12] Still, there is no smoke without fire, and some of Baxter's allegations can be substantiated. There was a visible minority of misguided women who played their roles in Britain's Fifth Column, which was, from a comparative perspective, nonetheless a rather diminutive number of subversives.[13]

This chapter seeks to demystify rather than perpetuate these myths, discerning that the international emergency also contributed to a crisis in the relationship between men and women writ large. Relentless tensions in international relations in the later 1930s led to the search for scapegoats—by the press, by various political interests, and by politicians, and sometimes even by women themselves—and culminated in the accusation that the women of Britain were accountable for the policy of appeasement and for its blatant failures. It was common to hold women accountable for sapping the spirit for national service among potential army recruits, and there was a "wide popular acceptance, especially among women, of a well-intentioned but ill-reasoned no-more-war creed."[14] Male critics also identified one of the causes for the perceived effeminization of the nation's youth to be the sharp rise in the number of women teachers in boys' schools since the war.

The 'Guilty Men' were easily identifiable individuals in the form of Devil's Decade-Prime Ministers, their Cabinets, and elite figures in the diplomatic corps and in the Tory establishment. According to 'Cato's' seminal work of Churchillian propaganda, *Guilty Men* (1940)—the text to which Baxter's booklet was surely intended to be both a supplement and a rejoinder—the men culpable for the jeopardy in which the bravest sons of Britain were placed on the beaches of Dunkirk in May–June 1940, the men who conducted the empire "to the edge of national annihilation,"[15] were a long succession of hapless politicians. This line started with Ramsay MacDonald, Stanley Baldwin, Sir Thomas Inskip, and Sir Samuel Hoare, before the reins of the National Government were passed to Neville Chamberlain and his band of Sir John Simon, Sir Horace Wilson, and the Rt. Hon. Capt. David Margesson, the Tory Chief Whip. Together they represented the "regime of little men."[16] More concisely, and from his insider's view as a member of the Cabinet, Duff Cooper identified the "Big Four" responsible for the policy of appeasement: Chamberlain, Samuel Hoare, Sir John Simon, and Lord Halifax.[17]

On the other hand, the 'Guilty Women' were a more amorphous lot. Baxter categorized "two distinct types of guilty women, those who were consciously guilty and those who did not realise until almost too late that they were being used as tools of the Nazis." The unconsciously guilty outnumbered the consciously so, and "they were supporters of the policy of appeasement, disarmament, and no more war."[18] The troupe of Guilty Women was made up of famous and notorious figures. Many were to be found among the Tory elite, such as Lady Austen Chamberlain, Lady Nancy Astor, Edith Lady Londonderry, the Rt. Hon. Unity Mitford, and London hostesses who entertained Nazi dignitaries without compunction. Some were members of the European aristocracy (or had married into it), such as the London-based 'Nazi Princess' Stephanie Hohenlohe. The Princess was employed as Press Baron Lord Rothermere's European emissary. She was on intimate terms with Hitler and the lover of the Fuhrer's personal adjunct Fritz Wiedemann—despite the fact, apparently known to the Nazi elite, of her Jewish parentage. She had wormed her way into London society and spread Hitler's message through her networks that included the Cliveden Set, the circle around the Prince of Wales and Wallis Simpson, and the Londonderrys while she was accompanied on her visits to the Nuremberg rallies by Ethel, Lady Snowden, the latter having moved quite a distance from her feminist and Christian Socialist roots to become an admirer of the Nazi regime. The Princess was credited with "straightening the relations" between Britain and Germany, and Wiedemann revealed this in a letter that became public when the sensational case she brought against Rothermere for breach of contract was tried in November, 1939: "It was her groundwork which made the Munich agreement possible."[19] Indeed, she had been instrumental in arranging Sudeten leader Konrad Henlein's informal talks with British MPs in London in May, 1938, and, at Hitler's suggestion, she hosted Lord Runciman in the summer of 1938 at her Austrian palace, Schloss Leopoldskron (confiscated from Max Reinhardt), persuading him of the rectitude of Nazi ambitions in the Sudetenland.[20] It was no wonder then that Baxter identified her at the centre of the conspiracy of the guilty women.

Others came from the opposite political direction but by taking a position of absolute pacifism were among Chamberlain's grateful admirers in 1938, Helena Swanwick and Maude Royden being prominent examples. Important roles were also played by more anonymous cohorts of women who voiced their feelings in private and public forums, from diaries and letters, to enthusiastic participation at spontaneous demonstrations. In locating women in this well-worn narrative of appeasement I am concerned to reveal the ways in which women could exercise their influence in high politics in the years after achieving equal suffrage, and how this influence was received by their male counterparts, fellow politicians, husbands, and family members. Once these have been established, we can begin to speculate how their support also provided the male actors in the piece with justification for carrying out policy and diplomacy as they did.

'The wife of the man who had made the peace': Annie Chamberlain

Elite women have always had access to power through their husbands and kin, and thereby exercised 'power behind the throne,' while they have also had to tread carefully in order to avoid the charges of illegitimate influence.[21] More, specifically, the figure of the 'female intriguer' who dabbled in foreign affairs was a well-established stereotype in the long 19th century, embodied by women like Madame de Stael and Dorothea von Lieven. In this respect that there should be 'guilty women' during the appeasement era is no surprise. However, in the aftermath of equal suffrage, when women represented more than half of the electorate and when a small but a no less painstakingly scrutinized minority were MPs, the nature of women's influence no doubt took on different forms. (There were only 36 women who became MPs between the wars.) There is solid evidence to suggest this was the case with the man who came to personify Britain's appeasement policy, the Prime Minister Neville Chamberlain, who confided his most intimate thoughts about politics to his sisters; who placed great store in the plethora of letters he received from women from around the country and around the world feeding back to him portraits of himself as hero, saviour, great statesman, and man of peace; and whose wife Annie Chamberlain, his junior by 14 years, acted the model Tory wife by playing the devoted helpmate in private and political life. If we begin with Chamberlain's inner circle we encounter among the Prime Minister's closest confidants his wife and his sisters, as well as the wife of his late brother, Lady Austen Chamberlain.

Mrs Annie Chamberlain became a focal point for public attention during the Munich Crisis and she was the recipient of an outpouring of affection from all over the world. The notorious pro-Nazi London hostess Emerald Cunard waxed lyrical at the Premier's efforts, confiding in Mrs Chamberlain:

> I must write to you at once to say that history has ... produced so great a man as your husband—he is far greater than Alexander, Caesar and Napoleon—History has never produced such a hero. I am ill in bed from a bad heart attack and refused to leave London because of my faith in our PM. His courage, cool ability and genius has no equal in history. No honour is too great for him and you are to be envied, to be as you are, the companion of his life.[22]

Thousands of letters in the same vein were sent to Mrs Chamberlain by the famous and more anonymous. She received letters from Lady Londonderry, Florence Horsbrugh MP, Lady Baldwin, and Christabel Pankhurst. In Chapter 7 we will see how women correspondents felt appreciably more at ease sharing their private responses to world events with her, a fellow woman. And the impact of these intimate letters was reciprocal. Annie Chamberlain made a special broadcast to the 'Women of France' on 31 December, 1939, acknowledging the deep impression made on her by the many letters she received from French mothers, wives, and soldiers, expressing admiration for their fortitude and courage.[23]

The Conservative Party regarded Mrs Chamberlain as an asset, and Central Office's Press Department circulated an information sheet that portrayed her as a loyal public servant, commonsensical, with a long history of working for her husband at constituency level and for the party at local and national level. She used her bicycle to get between meetings. Impressively, since 1918 she had only missed one national annual Conservative Women's Conference. Her interests were principally national and domestic, especially housing. Contact with the international sphere was limited to recreational travel, with a special affection for France. Not afraid of hard work and, like her husband, not of aristocratic stock but born in Edinburgh the daughter of a soldier who died in India when she was young, she was one of the people, and as such she was "intensely interested in people—all sorts of people."[24] Her husband was full of praise too, admitting to his sister Hilda that "I should never have been PM if I hadn't had Annie to help me. It isn't only that she charms everyone with her good humour & makes them think that a man can't be so bad who has a wife like that." More to the point "she has softened & soothed my natural impatience ... and saved me from making an impression of harshness that was not intended."[25] He reiterated these sentiments throughout his premiership, suggesting a successful companionate marriage in which they shared fundamental understandings about love, life, and political work. They also shared a love of home life and the comforts of a shared domestic space, and soon after taking up residence at No. 10, Annie transformed the interior design of the house to the acclaim of political friends and journalists.[26]

She was closely observed and her image widely disseminated by the press. When Chamberlain addressed a packed House on 28 September—the speech that took an unexpected turn due to the dramatic finale in the form of the invitation from Hitler to the Four Power Conference—"in a high gallery over the Speaker's chair sat Queen Mary, in tears, the Duchess of Kent at her side. On the other, her eyes never leaving the Prime Minister, was Mrs Chamberlain."[27] She became an even greater object of attention during all the dramatic scenes staged on the balcony of Buckingham Palace,[28] at the sash window of 10 Downing Street, and in St. James Park that made up the now iconic cinematographic moments of so-called 'Peace Night' on

30 September, 1938, and the days of jubilant mass relief that followed. Indeed, she did not meet her husband at the airport upon his return from Munich but in a private room at Buckingham Palace in the company of the King and Queen, and she remembered that "the King sat on the sofa right of the fire and the Queen sat on the arm of a chair and when I said how nice it was of them to ask me to come there to greet Neville, the King said: 'We can't do without our wives.'"[29] By noting this she was not in any way objecting to being deemed complementary, and from her notebooks it is clear that she was not the type to be drawn into intense political debate. In fact, at least once in the same notebook she congratulated herself for being able to steer clear of political subjects altogether at a diplomatic function.

Her sidestepping of political controversy made her universally likeable, and women were drawn to her. Widely represented at prayer in Westminster Abbey during the Crisis, she also personified women's religiosity and devotion. On 1 October, 1938, "arms outstretched to greet the wife of the man who has made the peace," and "women in Downing-street sob their thankfulness" as Mrs Chamberlain left the residence for her daily walk in St. James's Park. "And the Premier's wife, with tears in her eyes, replied, 'Thank you—thank you ever so much.'"[30] Her quiet strength and soothing influence were even more important to her husband, and he confided that "only Annie knows what I went through in those agonising hours when hope seemed almost extinguished and only I know how heroically she maintained her courage and her confidence."[31] It was noted that "when she left No. 10 Downing-street the cheers which greeted her were as loud, if not louder, than the cheers which hailed her husband." But only a couple of months later, she was portrayed with pathos, at least by the anti-appeasement press, as the one woman "carrying a cross heavier to bear than any of you can imagine," as she had to watch "her husband struggling to retrieve the wreck of his hopes. And the wreck of world peace, too."[32]

Certainly Annie Chamberlain remained a visible figure in the aftermath of the Crisis, still contributing that consoling feminine touch to her husband's policy. For example, at a meeting of the Swindon Conservative Women's Association (CWA) she was received with a great standing ovation by over 1,500 people when she opened their bazaar, pleasing the crowd further by saying "'I think the most hopeful feature of the talks which led to the Munich agreement was the way it brought out the universal horror of war among all nations: A great desire for peace was shown.'"[33] Neville recognized her qualities and their sexual division of political labour. In a week where Annie had three speaking engagements to open different events, Neville noted that "women are very different from men (or perhaps I should say from one another). This last job that would have thrown me into a fever never gave Annie any mental anxiety though it did involve a certain amount of concentrated work."[34] She continued to convey messages of reverie, and to the women's branch of her husband's Edgbaston constituency she assured them that he had faith that 1939 would be better than 1938, and that he "has tried to get away from the old idea of the inevitability of war. He has never lost hope. Had he done so, war would have come."[35] The same week Hitler's troops marched into Prague, Neville relied on Annie's support and was grateful that she "is wonderfully good in a crisis ... the blacker the outlook the calmer she grows and where many women would be an additional burden she helps me because she can stand anything I tell her."[36] During the early stages of the war itself she was seen to provide balance in her husband's life, persuading him to take "a breath of fresh country air to disperse the cob webs of office." She "herself, busy though she is, is the picture of health and serenity. Many women in her position would find the responsibility almost overwhelming."[37] If they were all politically consoling partners to their 'Guilty Men' like Annie Chamberlain then there would not be much more of a story to tell, and women would only merit a footnote in the history of appeasement.

However, there were many women far more formidable than the PM's wife, a woman who was nevertheless more of a partner in politics to her husband than her immediate predecessor at No. 10, Lucy Baldwin. Recalling a private lunch with herself, her husband Duff Copper and the Baldwin's in the South of France in 1931, Diana Cooper recalled having chided

> with a total lack of inhibition: 'Come on now, tell us every word Ramsay [MacDonald] said, for Duff tells me nothing.' There was a smiling grunt as an answer ... and Mrs Baldwin, astonished and horrified, said: 'My husband tells me nothing either, but then I would *never* ask him.'[38]

This anecdote provides an interesting juxtaposition of different types and two generations of Tory wives. During the Munich Crisis Lady Baldwin sent a supportive but very brief missive to Mrs Chamberlain, to the effect "My dear what a happy happy [sic] woman you must be, my warmest congratulations and good wishes to you both."[39] Furthermore, after Baldwin resigned the premiership, both he and even more so his wife, retreated from the political spotlight. As a response to *Kristallnacht*, in December 1938 the former Prime Minister launched the Lord Baldwin Fund for Refugees, which raised £522,000 by the summer of 1939,[40] and Lady Baldwin regularly attended their fund raising functions but was otherwise quite removed from public life.

Not mere 'yes-women': Chamberlain's sister-in-law and sisters in awe

In his most immediate circle it was Neville Chamberlain's sisters who exercised more political influence on him. In his in-depth study of the letters between members of the Chamberlain family from the twilight of the

19th century to the Second World War, Marsh demonstrates the crucial influence of women, sisters Ida, Hilda, and Mary on the three illustrious Chamberlain men, 'Papa Joe' and half-brothers Austen and Neville. Ida and Hilda were unmarried and each was involved in numerous political commitments, and all were seasoned world travellers. Neville conducted consistently weekly correspondence with his sisters on matters of national and international politics, regarding them as his most trusted confidants, these handwritten letters amounting to an average of 80,000 words a year, and providing "a poignant, emotionally honest and extraordinary insight into his mind and emotions."[41] He listened to their counsel and considered their opinions the proof of public opinion. His habits of correspondence were noted and derided by fellow politicians, and 'Chips' Channon, the parliamentary private secretary to the under-secretary of state for foreign affairs, confided to his diary: "the PM gets all his mental stimulus and confidence from his two maiden sisters with whom he corresponds constantly."[42] As a lifelong loner and solitary thinker, "nothing pleased Neville Chamberlain more than praise," as he was "peculiarly reliant on the approval of others— and not just his sisters—for his own peace of mind."[43] He tended to look for any indicators of public opinion that reinforced his sense that he was doing the right thing.

Nor was this feminine influence all behind the scenes, and Ivy Chamberlain, his sister-in-law, acted the informal, and to the mind of Anthony Eden, the meddling diplomat in Italy in late 1937 and early 1938.[44] She herself had received the Italian Gold Medal of Merit. In her own mind Ivy was trying to maintain the good Anglo-Italian relations that her recently deceased husband Austen (died March, 1937) had worked tirelessly to cultivate. By so doing she ended up triggering the decisive rift between the Prime Minister and his Foreign Secretary. On her visit to Rome in December 1937 she was invited for a private visit with Mussolini. Entirely convinced by his overtures of friendship to Britain, she duly conveyed this in her letters to the PM. Her interventions were considered significant enough to induce Anthony Eden to ask Neville "to beg [Ivy] to desist from further interviews"[45] with Il Duce. Eden recalled being "much annoyed" when he found out she was visiting Mussolini and Ciano and reading to them letters from the PM. In Eden's opinion this was "no way to conduct diplomacy," and her activities created confusion, placing him in "a most difficult position." In his letter to the PM on 8 February, 1938, Eden saw that "Mussolini has clearly and, as he should, very skilfully, taken every advantage of the opening which Lady Chamberlain afforded him and will no doubt gain the impression from that interview that we are most eager for conversations."[46] Following Eden's resignation over his fundamental disagreement with Chamberlain about whether to enter into closer negotiations with the Dictators—which Eden opposed but which Chamberlain thought instrumental to the success of his appeasement policy—Chamberlain thanked Ivy for "her invaluable help which has certainly contributed materially to create the atmosphere in Rome necessary for the opening of conversations."[47] This is how Eden later presented it, but the degree of their disagreement has been challenged. She was also in Rome on the occasion of Neville Chamberlain's visit in March, 1938, the visit that brought about the provisional withdrawal of foreign volunteers from Spain, for which Labour MP Arthur Barnes accused her of "meddling in British foreign affairs."[48] Her unofficial diplomacy did not stop there, and Chamberlain told his sister in September that "Ivy's doings in Franco Spain are causing me some embarrassment as they have been reported in the press and have been the subject of a good deal of unpleasant comment in unfriendly quarters."[49] The press did indeed like to imagine Chamberlain cowed and under the influence of excessively powerful female personalities. In one such spoof Chamberlain was imagined to be meeting his "Inner Inner Cabinet" in a bomb-proof shelter when he looks anxiously at his watch:

'She instructed me to be here at 4 o'clock,' he muttered, 'and now it's half-past. I hope nothing's wrong. I shall get a fearful telling-off from her if I've made a mistake in the time.' Just then a flunkey flung open the door, and in hastened the Premier's sister-in-law. Herr von Cliveden clicked his heels as he bent to kiss her hand. 'But,' he said, suddenly, seeing her frown, 'it is oop, is it nod? Dot is, somezings is oop?' [sic] 'Yes, something IS up,' retorted Lady Chamberlain. 'Franco refuses to recognise us.' 'Oh dear!' said the Prime Minister. 'Oh dear! And did he say why?' 'Yes,' said Lady Chamberlain. 'He wanted Canada, as well as Gibraltar and Malta. I told him the British Empire wasn't to be dictated to by a little, upstart whipper-snapper like him, and the conversations ended rather suddenly.' 'You must have been crazy' gasped the Premier. 'He'll be ever so annoyed. He may even refuse our money.'[50]

Neville Chamberlain's easy rapport with women in his immediate entourage and beyond would also be made to count against him.

These incidents demonstrate two things. First, notwithstanding women's official exclusion from the diplomatic corps until well after the Second World War, their interventions could be decisive. Further, that these interventions were characterized as undue influence and meddling render in bold relief the male-chauvinist attitudes that were typical of those conducting foreign affairs. Looking ahead, it is quite plausible too that Eden's scepticism about the suitability of women for the diplomatic corps stemmed from this incident. Second, women could still have a tangible impact on international affairs via private and unofficial diplomacy. In fact, this had not been Ivy Chamberlain's first such intervention, and she had been a very effective diplomatic wife, her part in the Locarno negotiations of 1925–1926 recognized in a positive way with the conferment of the Grand Cross of the

Order of the British Empire. However, as a widow acting on her own, her actions were rather differently construed.

Richard Baxter identified Lady Chamberlain as a Lady Macbeth-type of 'Guilty Woman:' "already a woman relative of Mr Chamberlain's had visited Rome to be feted by the Fascists, who possibly at the order of their master in Berlin turned on the poison gas." Baxter posed the rhetorical question: "Did she in any way influence the decision of the Prime Minister to fly to Munich and thus lower the dignity and prestige of Great Britain and the Empire?"[51] Ivy Chamberlain was also acknowledged to be one of the "wittiest of the aristocrats and Tories who gathered at Lady Astor's residence, Cliveden House," and her own London residence at 24 Egerton Terrace was the infamous gathering place of the so-called "appeasement bloc," and as such when Chamberlain was PM it was dubbed "an underground station to 10 Downing Street.".[52]

In the case of Neville Chamberlain then we see the powers behind his throne, not so much in the shadow cast by his wife Annie, but those of his politically ambitious but no less obliging sisters and his brother's widow. During the Munich Crisis itself the Chamberlain sisters acted as sounding boards for their brother, as well as serving as sources for certain types of information, especially for conveying their impressions of public opinion to him, which duly became or helped to reinforce his. He understood the role they played in his political decision-making process, and wrote "My sisters are not mere 'Yes-women,' they have minds & brains of their own and I know that if they approve of what I am doing it is not because it is I who am doing it."[53] Indeed, he relied on them for developing his understanding of Nazism, and it was Ida who convinced him that:

> while I feel fairly confident that Mussolini if we make an agreement with him will keep his word we know from Hitler's own lips that in his opinion agreements are only valid as long as they suit him, & he sees no reason for keeping them as long as he is strong enough to be able to defy the other Power (15 April, 1938).[54]

As the crisis deepened so did the sisters' encouragement of their brother's efforts. As March puts it, "his womenfolk rejoiced."[55] The succour he gained from the counsel of his womenfolk was pitted in diametric opposition to "busybodies of all kinds [who] intrude their advice, and the papers [which] do their best to ruin one's efforts. (11 September, 1938, Neville to Ida)."[56] After his visit to Hitler at Godesberg between 22 and 24 September, the second of his three flying visits, "he agreed with his sisters that what he had done was in line with the family tradition and entirely after their father's 'own heart.'"[57]

After his return from his first meeting with Hitler he preferred to be in the company of his sisters and family rather than among colleagues; and after his return from Munich he was most buoyed by the tearful enthusiasm of his sister Hilda, who wrote:

> Millions bless your name today, & your happy sisters are uplifted beyond words, by the thought of all you have been able to do! ... We lift our hearts in thankfulness for you, for your character, trained & disciplined all through your life so that the great emergency found you armed at all points (Hilda to Neville, 30 September, 1938).[58]

Thus we see the importance of the intimate communication with his siblings in setting the Prime Minister on his course in foreign affairs. We might also speculate that the nature and frequency of this correspondence predisposed him to believe what his correspondents told him, intellectually and emotionally. The story of the women of the Chamberlain family is an important chapter in the appeasement saga, their more hidden and private but nonetheless often pivotal roles having been neglected by historians until only very recently.

Indeed, while the correspondence between Neville Chamberlain and his sisters has been scrutinized by historians and biographers, in 2005 when Robert Self published an edition of Chamberlain's letters and diaries, the way he frames the material is another stark reminder of the androcentrism of the historiography of appeasement. Self only includes Chamberlain's letters *to* Ida and Hilda, and does not include any of their replies—the women's missives are missing. The Chamberlain women have been disappeared from the history of appeasement, and denied agency. By implication, their only historical interest is as they functioned as soundboards for the musings of their Great Man/Guilty Man brother, and as recipients of his revelations. Marsh does much better to validate Ida and Hilda as political actors in their own right, and to demonstrate the influence they had on their PM brother, while from Self's editorial choices we can only guess what views they might have held from their brother's responses.

After the fact there was fiction: Lady Astor and the Cliveden set

And now back to the task of writing women back in to the story. Indeed, certain women quite clearly fit into the 'Guilty Women' category due to their direct influence on the evolving policy of appeasing Germany. Nor did it go unnoticed at the time that "several women of social position have figured in the political news lately."[59] Always angling to expose a conspiracy, journalists were fascinated by the string-pullers, and especially the women among them: "Meeting discreetly at luncheons, the dinner-table and at week-end house parties their influence on the Nation's destiny is great ... Lady Nancy Astor, head of the 'Cliveden Set,' comes first, and that no doubt, will not cause her displeasure," while at "No. 4, St. James Square, a great town house ... other strictly political parties are given."[60] Chamberlain was courted by two circles of power brokers in political and diplomatic affairs, the so-called Cliveden Set and the Londonderry circle, each of which was headed by an audacious woman who managed to merge Tory principles with a distinctive brand of active feminism. Indeed, while Lady Nancy Astor and Lady Londonderry were not far apart in their views, and they were sometimes guests at each other's social occasions, they were rivals for the mantle of supreme Tory hostess. Further, while they were both formidable female figureheads of their respective political salons, they enjoyed their own status among powerful men. Neither was especially trying to widen the circle to include other women who might have been aspiring to achieve commensurate influence.

The demonized Cliveden Set, so-dubbed in 1937 by Claud Cockburn, the Leftist journalist and publisher of the cyclostyled *The Week,* to describe the pro-Nazi members of the Tory establishment who frequently met at the Astor's Cliveden estate in Buckinghamshire, had the 'opinionated' and 'prejudiced' American-born Nancy Astor as one of its central protagonists. Nancy Astor has been a recurring subject of biography and biopic, her life story and career as dynamic, explosive, and controversial as her temperament and idiosyncratic personal style. Her biographers have come to different conclusions and placed different emphases on her engagement in the politics of appeasement, most eventually vindicating her because she was the target of a Communist-led smear campaign, because she had the sense to turn on Chamberlain in 1940 and transfer her support to her long-standing rhetorical sparring partner Winston Churchill, and because she had a 'good war' as an active patriot and a champion of women's rights.[61] Indeed, after Nazi troops marched into Prague she "startled" the House with the question "'Will the Premier lose no time in letting the German Government know the horror this whole country feels about the Czech outrage?',", at which the House broke out in tumultuous cheers, and journalists were sure that her challenge to the PM showed that "the Cliveden group had revolted at last against the dictators."[62] Furthermore, her name did eventually appear on Himmler's Black List of those who were to be arrested immediately in the event of a German invasion of Britain.

However, there is no disputing that she demonstrated friendly feeling to Germany well after the Nazis came to power, and that she entertained Nazis and Nazi-sympathizers.[63] She was a great collector of people, but a less good judge of character. Waldorf Astor was not quite as convinced in the pro-German direction as his wife, and thus she was not merely parroting her husband's viewpoint. Waldorf had been one of the first British politicians to meet Hitler, on which occasion he spoke frankly with the Fuhrer and asserted that Anglo-German relations could be improved only if the Nazis alleviated the plight of the Jews. This did not go down well with Hitler.[64] For her, however, the wellsprings of her pro-Nazism "appear to have been largely visceral—Francophobia (linked to anti-Catholicism), anti-communism, and an element of anti-Semitism."[65]

Lady Astor nonetheless took great exception to the 'Cliveden Set' label.[66] She was deeply disturbed by the many thousands of abusive letters she received weekly on the premise that she was the Set's most publicly visible and familiar representative. One such poison-pen writer, who would only identify himself as "Pro-Eden," sent this:

> Nancy had a fancy
> Boy named Hitler.
> When's the baby arriving?
> You blasted American whore of a chorus-girl.
> Go back to your own country![67]

In response to this onslaught of hostile publicity she persuaded her dear friend George Bernard Shaw to write an article that denied the existence of "any such sinister Whipsnade."[68] On 5 May 1938, she herself wrote a letter to the *Daily Herald* to deny the existence of the Set, claiming that there was "no group which week-ends at Cliveden in the interest of Fascism of anything else."[69] But the name stuck, and the stain was difficult to wash away; the more she tried to deny it, the more her critics took the view, to quote Shakespeare, that 'the lady doth protest too much.'

In Parliamentary debate in November, 1938, as Labour's Stafford Cripps inveighed against what he deemed the wasteful way in which the Government was proceeding with rearmament, Lady Astor felt she was scoring a point by saying that it was the Labour Party that wanted war, to which Stafford Cripps retorted:

'The people do not fancy their country as does Lady Astor and her set.'

Lady ASTOR: What set?

Sir STAFFORD CRIPPS: I apologise and withdraw the word 'set' and substitute for it 'gang.' (Laughter.) People do not fancy the future of this country as does the gang of Lady Astor as being that of a junior partner in a Fascist international, ruling the common people of all countries by methods hitherto reserved by that gang for natives in colonial territories—methods of brutality, exploitation, and denial of freedom. (Opposition cheers.)[70]

The controversy about whether there was such a cadre as the Cliveden Set, and if so, how and precisely by whom it was constituted, has raged since it was first named and shamed. By now there is virtual consensus that the Cliveden Set was more myth serving the purposes of the fledgling Popular

Front than it was an organized or an effective conspiracy. However, the interpretive path hardly travelled is the one in which we come to understand how the sex of the Set's figurehead contributed to the construction of appeasement as a feminine, and an effeminate, policy.

As the first woman to take her seat in the House of Commons as MP for the Sutton Division of Plymouth in 1919, a seat she held until 1945, Astor was also persistently ambitious for women's rights. She expressed this in both serious and more whimsical ways. For example, in 1930 she hosted "a manless dinner as a novel means of celebrating feminine achievements during the past year,"[71] her only oversight being that male waiters had been engaged for this otherwise women-only event. She regularly reminded all who would listen how politicians could not afford to ignore the women of the country, representing as they now did more than half of the electorate, not to mention that as a sex they could not possibly make the same mess of the world as had men. This ambitiousness included agitation for women's entry into the diplomatic service. She was deeply frustrated by the lethargy of the Committee on the Diplomatic and Consular Service in reporting and confessed that it was the "most dreadfully discouraging thing to come up against their diehard attitude. Really I think the Foreign Office is the most benighted spot in England!"[72] In April 1936 during the debate over whether women should continue to be excluded from the Diplomatic Service, Lady Astor was livid but not in the least surprised by the decision of the Foreign Office to maintain the sex bar. She was especially frustrated by their "reactionary" and "illogical" view because

> the old diplomacy has failed, as the chaotic state of the world testifies. The very desperation of civilization's plight should be sufficient for us to insist that those petty barriers of sex be swept away to give place to the larger and far more vital consideration of the best brains for the best job, wherever they may be found.[73]

She thus led by example and by playing hostess to ambassadors, visiting dignitaries, and leading politicians, she more than made up for women's official exclusion from diplomacy.

Historians of appeasement have virtually ignored women actors, and they have overlooked gender as a category of analysis. Even when they have included the 'women worthy' Nancy Astor in their accounts, they have barely considered the link between her feminism and her anti-war and pro-German views. Similarly, feminists and some women's historians have found it difficult to embrace Astor due her chauvinism and racism, her social privilege, and the fact that she was a Conservative (even though she often came to blows with the men—and women—in her own party because she stood fast and firm on women's issues and proved rather annoying to many when she rode her other political hobby horses, temperance and child welfare). In many ways she was far too idiosyncratic to be representative of women MPs, or for that matter of women's place in British high society, in diplomatic circles, or among political power brokers in the 1930s. Indeed, no other hostess would have thought to entertain Joachim von Ribbentrop with a game of musical chairs, and, furthermore, whisperingly instruct all the other guests to let the Germans win the game.[74]

Appeasement with a feminist twist

And yet, I would argue, her pro-appeasement stance developed in tandem with her feminism, while her feminism made it impossible for her to be unthinkingly pro-Nazi. Her anti-war position made perfect sense in the feminist pacifist circles in which she was active, and she frequently made the point that peace was a women's issue. In 1921 she joined with feminist internationalist Millicent Fawcett, Ethel Snowden, Margaret Wintringham, and Maude Royden to initiate the movement to send a God-speed from British women to the Prime Minister as Britain's representative on a mission of peace when he sailed to Washington.[75] In 1928 she was part of the Women's Peace Crusade, asserting that "Peace mainly depends on women, and it is our duty to reach the millions of women who genuinely want peace but who are not thinking about it. It is our duty to make them think, not nationally or internationally but rationally."[76] She was synchronous with feminist anti-fascists too when in May 1933 she carried a unanimous resolution drafted by the NUSEC that was sent to the German ambassador expressing dismay at the Nazi dismissal of women from government services. In a show of feminist solidarity, she declared that "any injury done to women of one nation must be deeply felt by women of all nations."[77] She stood out among Conservative women at their annual conference in 1934 by taking an anti-rearmament and pro-peace position, making a show of not supporting a resolution on the need to "strengthen our defence forces to such a degree as shall be conducive to the future security and peace of the country." She was subjected to noisy opposition and loud jeers when she spoke in favour of an amendment, stating that "'England never stood higher than she does to-day,' and it is because she has been strong in leadership towards the path of peace." Marking herself out from the defencists who dominated her party, she exclaimed "We are not afraid of being fifth air power, because it is quality, not quantity, that counts in the end." (Ironic laughter.) The disapprobation did not deter her and she went on: "'I have won and held a naval constituency for 15 years, but not by beating a big drum and shouting about England ruling the waves.' (Loud hoots)."[78] She was very much in the minority, and the resolution she opposed was carried without her amendment.

When Astor spoke in Parliament on foreign and defence policy her concern in navy debates was for sailors' and dockworkers' welfare rather than strategic arguments. Her fondness for Chamberlain originated with her admiration for his record on social reform, while she had enmity for Churchill due to their deep disagreements on feminist issues. While her rancour for Churchill was reciprocal, her admiration for Chamberlain was less mutual, and the PM understood that she was a loose cannon. After one particular incident in June 1938 he confided in his sister Hilda: "Heaven save me from my friends."[79] At the Fulham Town Hall in support of her son W.W. Astor, MP for East Fulham, she said

> I believe so much in peace that if it meant doing away with the British Navy to achieve it I would say do away with it. I loathe war ... What has happened in the last three days is going to make for peace. I admire Mr Chamberlain for the way he has come out and left no stone unturned to get peace. If it is humanly possible, Mr Chamberlain will strive to get peace. The world knows now that England leads the way in armaments.[80]

Her reputation and reach transcended the national, and also in February 1938 she made an international broadcast from the BBC's Plymouth Studio under the auspices of the International Federation of Business and Professional Women, together with prominent women from Italy, Norway, Switzerland, and Eleanor Roosevelt representing the USA. Again Astor made the point that women's first essential duty in a free democracy was to preserve world peace. She claimed that "if they could bring their womanly understanding into their work they might succeed where politicians failed." She continued, "'[i]t is true we women start thousands of years behind the men, but I believe we start with a better background than they do. We are less cynically minded, statistics show us to be fifteen times better behaved, and that's something.'" Her essentialist reading of women's nature led her to "'believe that women's most important function in every country is to try to bring to their work those spiritual values which alone can make a better world.'" She referred to the progress made by women in Britain and America in the past 20 years as "really the one bright spot in an otherwise gloomy world."[81] As Harrison argues, Astor's "support for appeasement in 1938, far from reflecting fascist values, embodied (however misguidedly) their opposite: a hatred for war, a respect for women, and a down-to-earth preparedness to face realities and seek a middle way."[82] There was thus a clear trajectory in her alignment with feminist pacifism from the earliest phase of her political career to the flashpoint of appeasement. This is what only a womanist interpretation of the Cliveden Set can elucidate.

Astor was especially invested in the work of the International Alliance of Women (IAW), where she was a close associate of Margery Corbett Ashby. It was also in the context of the IAW that the allegations of pro-Germanism can be mitigated. In 1935 she spoke at the IAW's Congress in Istanbul, singling out the European dictatorships for their mistreatment of women. She told the audience that "Hitler's failure to let women help Germany seems to be far more dangerous to the peace of Europe than all his armies and aeroplanes."[83] Astor attended the IAW's Copenhagen Congress of 1939. The Congress was recognized as a success as it provided the opportunity to share news of improvements in the status of women and their presence in cabinets, parliaments, and senates, only to be sadly contrasted with the fact that six of their affiliates in totalitarian countries had either been dissolved or curtailed. Corbett Ashby recalled: "On our journey out at a change in Germany I remember Lady Astor dancing up to a group of Nazi youths in their uniforms and their contemptuous silence as she told them Hitler could never defeat the United Kingdom."[84] Astor emphasized how her feminism acted as a prophylactic against Nazism, and she worked hard to make her case against the Cliveden Set charge with evidence of her feminism. In that respect this interview was revealing:

Q.   Do you mean that your aim in life is not to preserve your position into which you have married?
A.   How can it? I am a feminist. How can a feminist want to preserve the social order. We have already changed it so that you can hardly recognise it. But we are not changing it in the way the Communist and the Fascists and the Nazis want us to.
Q.   What you mean to say is that you are not plotting to keep things as they are, and to prevent progress?
A.   How could I a feminist.
      ... A. In spite of being a Virginian I am an internationalist too. After the War they wanted a body to meet each other. We had them at Cliveden, German, French, Swiss, and that was entertaining with a purpose, and a very good one too.[85]

We will also remember how Astor refused to take part in the festivities to welcome Gertrud Scholtz-Klink to London on the grounds that Hitler's 'Perfect Woman' was a symbol of Nazi anti-feminism. Astor was in penitent mode and attempting an image makeover precisely when Scholtz-Klink was dropping in on other pro-German Londoners. Astor explained:

I am still a Virginian, and still a democrat and an ardent believer in women's rights and social reforms. Well, how on earth could such a combination as that believe in Mussolini, or Hitler, or Stalin, or in any dictator? ... How anyone who is a feminist and has seen the effect of the women's interest upon public affairs could believe in dictators, I can't conceive.[86]

Nancy Astor was a more complex figure than the Cliveden mythology allows: she was a Vice President of the Six Point Group and she was active in the campaigns to free women prisoners held as hostages for their husbands in Nazi Germany, campaigns that were vigorously driven by Monica Whately. In 1939 this resulted in some success as Mrs Prestes was granted a visa owing to the fact that Whately had persuaded Lady Astor and Lady Huntingdon to write to the Foreign Office.[87] However, even as her interventions did lead to some successes, Astor expressed her deep reservations about getting too involved in these cases, she was unsympathetic towards any of these women who were Communists, and she was careful not to alienate her contacts in the German Embassy.[88] Thus there can be no doubt whatsoever that she was as aware as anyone of Nazi atrocities, and that her anti-Nazism was informed by her feminism.

Nancy Astor as token woman appeaser

Furthermore, there is another angle that is illuminated by espying appeasement through the gender prism. Astor had already been the token woman in so many respects since her election in 1919. By 1937 she was seen as a frontwoman of both the Cliveden Set and an exemplar of the women's viewpoint. In an article entitled "A Portrait Gallery of Women in Parliament" which appeared in *Queen* in February, 1937, J. Henderson Stewart MP described her as "quite unique," and it was his view that:

> Lady Astor stands apart ... poles apart from the other Members, male or female. She alone can claim to represent that illusory thing called 'the woman's point of view.' The other women Members are each in their way distinctive, but their contribution to the business of Parliament, whether in style or in matter, is not essentially different from that of the average male Member.[89]

By 1937 she was also seen as representative of the Cliveden Set, its figurehead, and her prominence was one important contributing factor to the feminization of appeasement. As the one Labour MP put it when addressing a mass meeting at Hyde Park on 28 February, 1938, Britain was now in "a position when we must have society ladies determining our foreign policy. The foreign policy of this country is no longer settled by the Cabinet in Downing St. but at the country house of Lady Astor at Cliveden."[90]

David Low's series of cartoons of the "Shiver Sisters" did much to cement Astor's reputation as the bossy foreigner who, however slight of build, was able to get everyone that counted to goose step from her Christian Science hymn sheet. In one of the "Shiver Sisters" series, the text inset reads:

> Play the Game, Cliveden!: Sinister reports appear that at the meeting of Nancy's Inner Cabinet of Shiver sisters held at Cliveden last week-end members played 'THE GAME.' First prize (a signed portrait of Hitler went

to sisters Halifax, Lothian and Nancy and 2nd prize (a bound volume of '27 Ways of Persecuting a Jew') to sisters Chamberlain and Inskip.[91]

Astor was not only pilloried for being a woman in a man's world, but it was her nefarious influence that emasculated all who accepted her command, and in the same cartoon a cross-dressing Chamberlain is struggling to keep hold of an obese cross-dressed Inskip.

The imagery of a foreign-born woman string-puller whose political leanings could be seen to have more in common with pacifist women worldwide as well as with the priorities of American isolationists (among those she entertained were Charles Lindbergh and Joseph Kennedy) than with those who were working to maintain Britain's prestige was powerful.[92] She herself recognized this, and when she addressed the Oxford Union in February 1939 she noted that she was being portrayed by the press as leader of the Cliveden set, a "combination of Cleopatra and Jezebel."[93] It followed that once one woman was to blame, it was not a grand conceptual or a psychological leap to make it out that all women, or the majority of women, were like-minded, likewise guilty, and part of a treacherous sorority.

4
'Guilty Women:' Powers behind Thrones

On 14 February, 1939—St. Valentine's Day, appropriately enough—the Prime Minister announced to Parliament that the French President wished to visit both Houses on his forthcoming State visit. The occasion was to be "open to Members of both Houses," and those who signified their intention to attend were "invited to bring a lady with them." Chamberlain loyalist Miss Horsbrugh was a bit concerned, and asked "whether lady members of the House may bring a man?" to which the PM replied: "naturally there will be reciprocity."[1] Horsbrugh's demand for clarification on this point is a good indication of the symbolically important gains women had made in reforming parliamentary procedure and etiquette, and the strides they had taken to be included in matters of international relations. Further, the PM's response revealed "a mind filled with thoughts of appeasement,"[2] as appeasement had developed into the ways and means of pacifying both dictators and the battle of the sexes.

Women had inscribed themselves at the heart of the politics of appeasement, and Richard Baxter must have had quite a number among the social elite in mind when he levelled his charges against the 'guilty women'. In this chapter we continue to explore how elite and notable women were implicated in the story by dint of marriage and family connection, political conviction and activism, or both. Support for appeasement and pro-Nazism intermingled in the informal political spaces created and ordered by elite women. Lord and Lady Londonderry were renowned for entertaining Joachim von Ribbentrop, Hitler's special envoy and later German Ambassador in London, as were the well-connected but no less politically naïve and unreliable Lady Colefax and Emerald Cunard. It was widely rumoured that Cunard was responsible for infecting the then Prince of Wales and his then mistress Wallis Simpson with pro-Nazism.[3] These hostesses "helped make Nazism fashionable in smart circles," and all of them enthusiastically accepted invitations to the Nuremberg rallies and formal dinners in Berlin, as did Lady Redesdale, Mrs Ronnie Greville, Lady Diana Cooper, and Sir Frank and Lady Newnes.[4] It was no accident that both the

Londonderrys' and Cunard's letters of praise were among the fan mail sent to Chamberlain in the autumn of 1938. And of course there was Edward VIII and Wallis Simpson whose pro-Nazism was well known within their own circles and has become public record since, their visits to Nazi Germany as Duke and Duchess of Windsor giving very public expressions to their sympathies. Just as ominously, Sir Oswald Mosley, leader of the British Union of Fascists, and Lord Halifax, British Foreign Secretary, actually shared a mistress and confidant in these years. This was Alexandra 'Baba' Metcalfe, the wife of 'Fruity' Metcalfe, Edward VIII's equerry, as well as Mosley's sister-in-law (it was alleged that their affair only started after the death of his first wife and her sister in 1934, Cynthia nee Curzon).

Lady Londonderry as arch appeaser

Edith Lady Londonderry (1878–1959) was possibly as or even more influential within the Conservative Party and with Britain's governing elite than Astor, although as a famous and lavishly generous political hostess rather than an elected representative she was not as recognizable as Astor to the general public. While she was not identified with a 'set' *per se*, Lady Londonderry was also more directly and undeniably implicated in the behind-the-scenes advocacy of appeasement. Well born and marrying into one of the wealthiest and grandest aristocratic families, she was an *a priori* High Tory. However, she was also the product of her generation of 'new women,' she supported Millicent Fawcett's women's suffrage campaign before the war, and in the course of her lifetime she was most impressed by women's advances in the spheres of sports and fashion. She practiced what she preached by dressing *à la mode* to facilitate her own sporting pursuits which ranged from riding to flying. Driven by a patrician sense of duty, Lady Londonderry carved out various civic roles for herself, beginning with the Women's Voluntary Reserve (later the Women's Legion) during the First World War; in 1919 she was sworn in as the first woman JP for Durham; she was a chairman of the Red Cross; and she was one of the founding members of the Townswomen's Guilds, a movement started in the late 1920s along the lines of the WIs in rural districts in order to train women to become conscious and effective citizens. She was also active at the local level in the Conservative Party, serving as President of the Conservative Women's Advisory Committee, Northern Counties Area (1930–1946), and at the national level she served as the party's glittering tiara-adorned hostess at Londonderry House in London, throwing an annual eve-of-Parliament reception. Significantly, she did not host such an event in 1936, expressing sour grapes for Lord Londonderry's dismissal from the Cabinet and their subsequent fallout with Stanley Baldwin; and again it was called off in 1938, in the shadow of the Munich Crisis.

While many among her peers recoiled at the sexual liberalization occasioned by the Great War, she celebrated how the war completely altered the status of women. She reconciled feminism with ultra-patriotism, conservative social values, and unapologetic elitism. This 'Conservative Feminism' or 'Patriotic Feminism' was a far more detectable strain of post-suffrage feminism than many women's historians have acknowledged, and it was cultivated by feminists no less prominent than Emmeline and Christabel Pankhurst themselves.[5] Lady Londonderry was a gender democrat, and felt strongly that women must play an equal role in public and municipal life. Even as she sought Anglo-German understanding in the 1930s, she found much to object to in the fascist attitude towards women, and explained how:

> I feel convinced that a country in which public opinion represents the views of its citizens of both sexes is less liable to blunder into errors and tumults than those continental nations today, where women are allowed no say in the government or national affairs but are sternly relegated to the home and kitchen.[6]

It was also appropriate that she supported the view that "women would make excellent diplomatists," although she envisioned this to be more problematic for married women.

Her marriage was not without personal challenges, and Charley, Lord Londonderry's, infidelities were deeply injurious to her, but otherwise married life expanded her potential for influence in the public sphere. She was no mere appendage to her husband, and her biographers have tended to suggest that she was just as politically astute, affable, and able, if not the more intelligent of the two. The Londonderrys' hospitality was legendary, as was 'The Ark,' a political, artistic, and literary dining-club for the rich and famous, patronized by all the inter-war Prime Ministers. She established it in 1915 and it remained in existence throughout her life. In the Ark "[a]mid the harmless amusements, contacts could be made, connections established, relationships built up, gossip exchanged, and minor plots hatched."[7] All the members were given names of mythical creatures. She was called 'Circe the Sorceress,' Lady Astor 'Nancy the Gnat,' Baldwin 'Bruin the Bear,' Neville Chamberlain 'Neville the Devil,' although her most infamous affair, generally believed to be platonic, was with a later initiate into the Ark, the Labour and National Government Prime Minister Ramsay Macdonald, 'Hamish the Hart' in Ark-speak. This odd pairing excited much speculation and gave her considerable access to power.[8]

By the 1930s, how did she facilitate and endorse her husband's notoriously ill-advised attempts at Anglo-German rapprochement? Much of the evidence strongly suggests that she shared her husband's outlook on the Nazis, and if he was the most identifiable arch-appeaser-Nazi-sympathiser then she deserved to share this epithet. Their ostentatious effort to foster Anglo-German friendship was a shared endeavour. De Courcy, who would later go on to write the authorized biography of Diana Mosley, judged that

Lord Londonderry's "intentions were honourable but the course he followed was to blemish his reputation and earn him the description of 'Nazi sympathiser' and, later, 'appeaser.' Edith, always unquestionably loyal, backed him wholeheartedly."[9] According to Lord Londonderry's biographer, Lady Londonderry was "the central prop in Charley's career,"[10] and Kershaw acknowledges her complicity in Lord Londonderry's deepening relationship with the Nazi leadership. This contrasts with Lord Londonderry's other biographer, and Fleming has very little to say about Lady Londonderry during these years—a typically androcentric reading of even the personal politics of appeasement.[11]

When von Ribbentrop was in London in 1934 Lady Londonderry was one of the first to shower him with invitations to her salons. Despite not being able to speak German, she was her husband's enthusiastic companion on several of his trips to Nazi Germany. After their lavish welcome and audience with high-profile Nazis on their trips in 1936, Lord Londonderry was "dazzled by his experiences in Hitler's Germany."[12] There was no doubt that the Nazis had worked their magic on the couple, the German Ambassador, Leopold von Hoesch, telling the Foreign Ministry that "it was unmistakable that Lord and Lady Londonderry were extraordinarily satisfied with their stay in Germany and took the most favourable impressions home with them."[13]

Upon their return to Britain, both husband and wife did what they could to sustain and share their enthusiasm—their Nazi string-pullers could hardly have scripted it better themselves. However, their efforts were curtailed because they were now so obviously situated at the outskirts of power. Lord Londonderry was humiliated to find that few wanted to meet with him, neither Baldwin nor King Edward VIII wished to hear about his German trip, and among those in government only his own son-in-law, Lord Stanley, expressed an interest. He joined the newly reformed Anglo-German Fellowship at Ribbentrop's urging. Women were involved with the AGF, Lady Redesdale and her daughter Unity Mitford would attend its functions in the late 1930s, and Edith contributed to the *Anglo-German Review*.

Edith found more outlets for her pro-Nazism. Her effusive letters of thanks to her hosts "surpassed those of her husband."[14] She carried on a correspondence with both Hitler and Göring, Hitler writing to her how he was particularly "overjoyed" to learn that "you and your husband sympathised with my efforts to bring about a genuine peace,"[15] while to Göring she explained how she was using her influence with many MPs and with the press—which she alleged was "largely hostile and controlled to a great extent by Jews"[16]— to sway public opinion in favour of Anglo-German understanding. She was "more prone that her husband to allowing her new-found enthusiasm for Nazi Germany full expression,"[17] early in May 1936 publishing in the *Sunday Sun* a fulsome portrait of Hitler and a rave review of their winter visit. More surreptitiously, she passed on a letter penned by Göring pleading for

Anglo-German friendship to the most influential people she knew, including to Neville Chamberlain, which he "politely received ... and ignored."[18]

When Ribbentrop became the likely replacement for von Hoesch, who died in his post as Ambassador to London on 10 April, 1936, the Londonderry hospitality kicked into high gear. Ribbentrop and his wife Anneliese, another woman who had the reputation for being the power behind the throne, were invited to the Londonderrys' Mount Steward estate in May, a long-weekend party upon which the press lavished much attention. While both parties tried without much conviction to convey the message that they were meeting because they had struck up such a warm friendship, it has been claimed that Charley found Ribbentrop to be rude and Edith thought him loathsome. The weekend cemented the Londonderrys' reputation as the nucleus of a pro-German lobby.

The replacement of Baldwin by Chamberlain as PM in May 1937 created a possible route back from the political wilderness for the Londonderrys', and they were especially hopeful when Chamberlain asked them to revive the tradition of the eve-of-Parliament grand reception at Londonderry House, London.[19] While Lord Londonderry did in the end agree to host the event, the chip on his shoulder still bore down on him, telling Chamberlain how he had "tried to take a prominent part in connection with improving relations between Germany and this country, I was deliberately cold-shouldered by everyone with very unfortunate results .... Our support and loyalty to Conservatism is the same as ever but my effectiveness has been sadly damaged."[20] Easing their way back into the inner circle of the Conservative Party, Edith also hosted an 'At Home' at Londonderry House to meet the Prime Minister, at which the Astors were among the guests.[21] That they were again deemed political insiders was demonstrated by the fact that Hore-Belisha (of Jewish origin), Secretary of State for War, flew to Northern Ireland as the Londonderrys' guest in January, 1938.[22] In April, the Chamberlains were invited by the Londonderrys for a "pleasant holiday" and a weekend of river fishing. Their personal and ideological proximity to the Prime Minister was illustrated well when Lord Londonderry saw Chamberlain off at Hendon airport on the first of his three meetings with Hitler in September. However, Lord Londonderry did overstep the mark and cause the Prime Minister embarrassment by coming to Munich under his own steam to meet with several German leaders while Chamberlain was negotiating with Hitler at the Four Powers Conference. Further, in the immediate aftermath of the Crisis, suffering from a near nervous breakdown, the book that Chamberlain turned to for lessons from history and for some comfort was *Letters of Benjamin Disraeli to Francis Anne Marchioness of Londonderry*, edited by Edith Londonderry and published that year by Macmillan.

It was due to her intimate friendship with the PM that Edith could write so candidly and full of praise for his actions at the Munich Conference. She felt that at Munich Chamberlain had fulfilled her dreams:

At the certain risk of adding to your post, you must forgive me for sending you a line to say how splendid it was of you to fly to Hitler. It has always been Charley's and my dream—if I ever even hinted as much—I was told I was mad! Now you have done it—I do think more than courageous—as there will be a [lot] of hostile opinion against you here—all bent on facing a war or otherwise making grievous trouble ... May you have all the luck you deserve so well.[23]

Nonetheless, in the shadow of the Crisis the Londonderrys thought it more appropriate not to host the customary eve-of-Parliament reception at Londonderry House that autumn. In practical terms, the aftermath of Munich was also energizing, and the Londonderrys cut short their stay in Scotland to get back to London as the Crisis reached an acute stage, becoming frequent visitors to the Dorchester because they had turned Londonderry House into a recruiting depot for women motor transport drivers.

Edith Londonderry's memoir was published on the cusp of earth-shaking events, shortly after the Munich Agreement and still before the war, and she reflected back on her life as a Tory grandee devoted to public service and the exercise of women's patriotic duty from the vantage point of late 1938. For her the Munich Agreement represented the wisdom of her generation against the superficiality and contradictions of the post-war generation of "pink boys," preoccupied by "pink thoughts," and all "marching along, armed to the teeth in the cause of peace!" Lady Londonderry opined that:

The great danger from which the nation was only averted on the brink of disaster by the singular courage, resolution, and the ingrained habit of being able to take sudden responsibilities, such as Mr Neville Chamberlain recently displayed, may yet prove to be the turning point in the 'laissez-faire,' easy-going, lives of so many people today.[24]

The Munich Agreement was the culmination of her ambitions, and it had been secured by a PM whom she had ably cultivated. That her husband regarded her as an equal and a close collaborator in the role of British advocate of friendship with Germany was further exemplified by the fact that his controversial Penguin Special, *Ourselves and Germany* (April 1938), was dedicated to Edith.

Lest she should come across as the greatest villainess of the appeasement debacle, to her credit she did try to use her influence with the Nazis to do good on at least one occasion. In the spring of 1938 she wrote furiously to both Ribbentrop and Göring, only receiving a reply from the latter, when two Austrian guides she knew and who were trainers for the Londonderry Snow Eagle Race, an international competition, were arrested on suspicion of being anti-Nazi. They were eventually released.[25] While this rescue attempt hardly compared with the valiant efforts to come to the aid of

myriad victims of the Nazi regime by British women from across the political spectrum, as discussed in Chapter 2, it did illustrate how Edith's eyes
were opening. Both she and Charley were disturbed by *Kristallnacht* and
told their Nazi friends how the Nazi anti-Jewish campaign made their own
self-appointed task of Anglo-German rapprochement very difficult. Both
were anti-Semitic and condoned or turned a blind eye to Nazi racism, but
their anti-Semitism was not of the Nazi genocidal variety.[26]

The first part of 1939 brought the Londonderrys even deeper disillusionment with the Nazis, especially after Hitler occupied Prague in mid-March.
Edith also changed gear and immersed herself once again in the work of the
Women's Legion.[27] She was also active on behalf of the Spanish Children
Repatriation Committee, which campaigned for the return of Spanish children to Spain, and she wrote letters to the press explaining that conditions
in Nationalist Spain where much better than those represented by 'Red'
propaganda. However, both Edith and Charley had burnt too many bridges;
they spent much of the war feeling embittered and undervalued.

If Nancy Astor's feminism developed in tandem with her pacifism and
thereby can provide one convincing explanation for her support for appeasement, how should we understand Edith Londonderry's commitment to the
same policy? As we have seen, Edith Londonderry was highly suspicious of
the peace movement, nor did she make that common conceptual conflation
between women's nature and peace. On the contrary, she was a 'defencist,'
with an almost fetishistic fascination with modern modes of transport and
weaponry. Between the wars she had no formal links with the feminist
movement either, interested more in how women could use their rights
to fulfil their patriotic duties rather than with the furtherance of women's
rights themselves. The Women's Legion was a quintessentially nationalist,
'Me Too' feminist organization—thus attracting the ire of the newly created
Men's Defence League—and it was in sync with other such independent
militarized women's formations like the voluntary women police and Flora
Drummond's Women's Guild of Empire.[28] She did genuinely wish to prevent another world war, and from her elevated social position she had the
contacts and the means to exert influence on those in power, occupying a
role that had already been open to women in high politics and in the realm
of diplomacy well before women's suffrage. Among the elite the advent of
suffrage did little to diminish, nor did it significantly enhance, their leading
roles in the cloak-and-dagger of high politics.

When appeasement sundered the marriage of minds

So far we have seen how support for appeasement reflected the meeting
of minds between husband and wife. While each coupling had its own
particular power dynamic, there was a sense of shared endeavour on this
count in the Londonderry, the Astor, the Redesdale, the Windsor, and the

Chamberlain marriages. However, the appeasement question could also be discordant within families and between husbands and wives, and there were some quasi-guilty women who were partnered with the anti-appeasement men. Duff Cooper remembered that:

> among my own acquaintance, twelve happily married couples ... were divided on the issue of Munich, and in every case it was the husband who supported and the wife who opposed Chamberlain. Many would have expected that women would have been more ready than men to accept the spurious peace at its face value. But it was not so.[29]

This was something of a strange recollection, and perhaps this was one of the things that this old man misremembered. Not only have I found very few instances where the wife was anti and the husband for Chamberlain, but in the Cooper marriage itself it was the other way around. Similarly, Anthony Eden said nothing about his own wife's feelings about appeasement (they would be divorced by the time he wrote his memoirs); and Leo Amery's wife disagreed fundamentally with her husband, although she never made this public.

Duff Cooper's wife Diana (nee Manners), the famous actress, was swept up in the public mood of relief and gratitude to Chamberlain. In fact, she was in Geneva, where the Assembly of the League of Nations was taking place, when the Crisis first broke in mid-September, enjoying it as the place to be for "a lady who needs her confidence and her desirability bolstering up ... I haven't seen one woman under 60 and the intellectual boys are just spoiling for diversion."[30] When the news broke that Chamberlain proposed to visit Hitler at Berchtesgaden, Diana was seated at a British Empire dinner next to Eamon de Valera, PM of the Republic of Ireland, who responded to this news by saying "this is the greatest thing that has ever been done."[31] She appeared to share the sentiment.

Diana could hardly be described as an anti-appeaser, and her reaction to the crisis was physical more than it was morally or politically-charged. She recalled:

> My own condition was deteriorating fast. Fear did more harm to my physique than to my morale. Sleep was murdered for ever. My heart quaked, yet I must appear valiant. My hands shook, so work must be found to steady them. Always a pessimist, I could imagine nothing worse than what must happen perhaps tomorrow—war, death, London utterly demolished, frantic crowds stampeding, famine and disease .... I had found occupation at the WVS, a body some years old, of voluntary women who gave their services to a wide number of causes. Lady Reading, its begetter, had organised her helpers to assemble gas-masks for civilians, so Venetia Montagu and I sat in the Tothill Street workrooms

clamping snouts and schnozzles on to rubber masks, parcelling them, and distributing them to queues of men and women.[32]

Duff Cooper decided to resign from the Government soon after Chamberlain's first visit to Hitler, but only actually took the decisive step on 30th September after the terms of the Munich agreement were published. Significantly, he spent the evening of 29 September at "a dinner-party of men only," among the guests MPs, newspaper proprietors, and prominent journalists, and this 'old gang' listened intently to the news as it was broadcast in instalments.[33] Diana had mixed feelings about her husband's stand, and "in the evening the thunder of cheering, that I longed to be part of, filled our ears from Whitehall."[34] All her instincts, her maternal worry, her fears about a repeat of the last war, and her first-hand experience with the Women's Voluntary Service in preparing for a gas attack made her an instinctive appeaser. While in her own account she never seemed to try to dissuade her husband from resigning, it is clear that she would have been just as suitable as the wife of a pro-appeasement MP. She was related to the anti-appeasers only by marriage.

Diana Cooper's fear of the coming war only mounted, and the rift between husband and wife was especially palpable on 3 September, 1939, when Duff was horrified to discover that his wife found the German 16 points to Poland, as reported on the wireless in the morning of that fateful day, not unreasonable, and he realized that "the reactions of millions of people might well be the same as those of Diana." He confided in his diary how "I think we are all in pretty good spirits except Diana, who, poor darling, cannot face the war at all."[35] While Duff noted, perhaps with some envy, that Clementine Churchill was "more violent in her denunciation of the Prime Minister even than Winston,"[36] he was faced with a wife who was in "a state of almost suicidal depression," and he was "terrified lest she should indeed commit suicide, which she thinks she might do if I were obliged to leave."[37] While Diana appears to have tolerated Duff's serial infidelities and even remained on good terms as friends with many of his romantic conquests, such sophisticated understanding in the battle of the sexes was not extended to tangible battlefields. They could not agree on the necessity for war.

Diana's mother, the Duchess of Rutland, was also puzzled by her son-in-law's resignation, and while she admitted that she disliked "the Germans because they are an unattractive race and I hate their methods," she felt that "[o]ne can't exterminate them like they try to exterminate the Jews. One has got to deal with them reasonably and without prejudice for the sake of peace." She was wholeheartedly for Chamberlain: "Oh Duffie why can't you believe in the policy and the man I so sincerely admire. He has shown courage, imagination and patience and not for the first time." She realized that her opinion probably did not count for much. "I have no inside knowledge like you. I can only judge by results. I cannot think of anyone who would be a better PM ... What does it matter what I think—only I am *very* distressed and puzzled at your resignation."[38] [underscored in the original] It was just this kind of feeling, more frequently expressed by women, that Chamberlain came to rely on to see him through the Crisis. Within the Cooper marriage this fundamental difference of opinion probably had little impact on his political strategizing. While Duff made it abundantly clear how immensely he enjoyed women's company, he was a sex segregationist when it came to politics. His position was quite remarkable two decades after women had achieved the vote and the right to sit in the House of Commons, and he explained that although he "always had a great respect for the political judgement of women," he "never thought that the House of Commons was the right arena in which they should display it."[39] It was even more striking that he should publish these sentiments in 1953, 35 years after women had secured these rights. In his view the House of Commons was a man's house with "no place in it for women, and women cannot excel there any more than they can on the football field."[40] Further, I would argue that Duff Cooper's representation of the Munich Crisis contributed a great deal to its reputation as a feminine policy not worthy of men of courage and virility. He mocked Chamberlain for admitting in the Cabinet meeting on 17 September, 1938, that he had been flattered by Hitler who "had said to someone that he felt that he—Chamberlain—was 'a man.'"[41] Quoted in both Duff's and Diana's memoirs, Josiah Wedgwood wrote to congratulate Duff upon his resignation, concluding that "I do dislike belonging to a race of clucking old hens and damned cowards."[42] Duff Cooper played an instrumental role in gendering the crisis, depicting the masculine response as resistance to Chamberlain, the feminine response as the Munich Agreement itself and all the desperate gratitude paid to it.

This dynamic was mirrored in the private life of another leading Tory anti-appeaser, Leo Amery. Amery was the MP for Sparkbrook (South Birmingham), his wife Florence was President of the Sparkbrook division Unionist Association, Christ Church Women's Branch. She was the type of political wife who followed her husband's star, an even more acquiescent type than Annie Chamberlain. She, or at least images of her in pieta-like configurations with their two sons, had been trotted out for her husband's election material since the early 1920s in appeals for women to vote along Conservative lines. As the Crisis was brewing, she was at the Matterhorn in the Alps and away from her husband. Her diary entry for August, 1938, gives us some insight into her sense of self and the value she placed on diary writing: "I think I ought not to keep a diary. I usually write in it when I am tired or not very well or a bit dense. It is so silly." She admitted that:

the meaning of my life is my love for Leo and the boys. I would like to be all a wife could be to Leo. He deserves the best in every way and I would like his sons to be worthy of him. Those are all the things I really care for.[43]

Husband and wife found themselves on opposing sides of the appeasement debate, which is all the more striking considering how she had expressed her selfless devotion to her husband only a couple of weeks earlier.

Her diary entry for September–October reveals how her views diverged from Leo's. "Leo unhappy and uneasy about Europe .... The Neville going to Germany. To me it seemed an answer to prayer. He's repeated attempts and when we really thought war was upon us Munich and Peace. I think this country and Europe owes him an unpayable debt of gratitude." She let loose her political prejudices, noting to herself that Chamberlain's:

> enemies who want war were those who but a very short time ago were shouting drastic reduction of arms—This incredible to me. They seem to be playing the Bolshevists' game for them and would embroil Europe in all the horror of war, to prove their theories right, and to save a fictitious country .... The soft babbling of Bob Cecil, V. Lytton, the Socialists and Jews, and last but not least Leo's secretary, fill me with gloom.

Florence admired Chamberlain in particular: "I think Neville's persistent determination to secure peace the most glorious thing England has done since Dizzy—and his critics are like the mean unholy things that come out in the dark but do not face the light." Her sentiments resonated with a wide swath of public opinion but contrasted with her husband's. As she noted: "Leo's attitude is a mixture of idealism and a curious sentimentality which I own I do not understand. If National Service, which he espouses comes out of it, it will be good for us all. I do not follow his reasoning except for this."[44] Her reaction gives further substance to the view that Munich was a women's peace.

Like Diana Cooper, Florence Amery's health was also to suffer as a direct result of the Crisis, possibly exacerbated too by the related marital discord. She experienced high blood pressure and heart strain but found an effective cure in a reduced work schedule and three days in bed in Switzerland.[45] Her diary ends on 1 September, 1939, by which stage she is no more reconciled to the necessity of war, feeling "rather numb, no doubt everyone does and I am conscious only of longing to be at home, for there I should feel nearer the boys and Leo's work and might be able to help someone."[46] Indeed, Duff Cooper's anecdote of the dozen faceless anti-Chamberlain wives and pro-appeasement husbands seems to be based on little substantial evidence. If there is a pattern to be discerned, it is the opposite one. This corroborates with the persuasive evidence that demonstrates how Chamberlain had a special rapport with women in his inner circle and with women in the Conservative party. As we will see, this perceived special affinity extended even further to women of the nation and of the world. This was not lost on some of these very protagonists, and among Amery's notes for his autobiography we find this: "Sybil Colefax told me (April 1949) that in July 1938

Neville Chamberlain had said to her that there was no possibility of war because the women of Germany would not allow it."[47] But, as it happens, Amery never incorporated this telling conversation into his autobiography, in which we also do not find any mention whatsoever of women in the chapter on Munich.[48] While Leo Amery distanced himself from the 'Guilty Men' by defending the betrayed Czechs and stepping up the campaign for a system of national registration, he was nonetheless one of the many who was blameworthy for writing women out of the history of appeasement.

Women on the peripheries of Anglo-German diplomacy

In high politics few women were given the political latitude to influence policy or even to persuade their husbands who made policy. Lady Dorothy Onslow, wife of Lord Halifax, Chamberlain's Foreign Minister, is a case in point. While Lady Dorothy was invaluable in advancing his career, and she was regarded as "a paragon amongst women," "she never had, nor sought, any influence over policy."[49] If his memoir is any guide, the proper and bone-dry Halifax displayed passion for only two things, English Catholicism and foxhunting, and he was careful not to betray much emotion in public life.[50] Similarly, while women were able to navigate the peripheries of diplomacy and play their parts in various intrigues, their formal exclusion from the diplomatic corps meant that their activities were regarded as interference. We have seen how Lady Austen Chamberlain made her presence felt in Anglo-Italian relations, but the same opportunities for women to involve themselves in Anglo-German affairs were curtailed. The British Ambassador to Berlin, appointed near the end of Baldwin's term in January 1937, was the unmarried Nevile Henderson. He was widely acknowledged to be the foremost representative of Neville Chamberlain's foreign policy, and even a mini-Chamberlain in look and attitude. Martha Dodd was the anti-isolationist and anti-appeasement daughter of the American Ambassador to Germany who was in Berlin to witness the handover from Sir Eric Phipps to Henderson. Her memoir of 1939 served as much as a witness statement as it did a warning, and she asserted that Henderson had been appointed to prepare "the way for Chamberlain's vicious and cowardly sellout [sic] of the Western world."[51] Henderson's marital status probably did him no harm when it came to trying to establish a good rapport with Hitler, the famously abstemious bachelor who regarded female company and female bodies as merely ornamental. Indeed, when Chamberlain first went to meet Hitler at Berchtesgaden on 16 September, one of the things that struck him most about the dictator's lair were all the paintings of nudes on the walls.[52]

Nonetheless, Henderson did recognize the importance of getting women on side in order to preserve the fragile peace. One of his first speaking engagements upon his arrival in Berlin was at a dinner hosted by the German English Society, which was the German equivalent of the

Anglo-German Fellowship. Henderson recalled: "Towards the end of it, with a view to enlisting the support of German women for the peace for which I pleaded, I quoted a verse of a song which, if I remember rightly, had been popular in America during the anti-war Wilson election there in 1916." The song ran as follows:

> I did not raise my son to be a soldier,
> I brought him up to be my pride and joy;
> Who dares to put a musket on his shoulder
> To kill some other mother's darling boy?

"I was told afterwards that it had been purposely omitted lest German mothers should really think that their sons were not solely born to die for Hitler and for Germany."[53] Unknown to them, the 'mothers of Europe' were players at the highest levels of Anglo-German relations.

While Henderson was unmarried and thus navigated the mainly homosocial diplomatic circuits with ease, he did credit the wife of the Italian Ambassador to Berlin with influence well beyond her official capacity. Bernardo Attolico was as anti-war as Henderson, but how they differed was that Attolico was "ably seconded by his wife, who spoke German fluently, which the Ambassador did not."[54] The Pact of Steel was cemented with some feminine solder. At the same time as Henderson and Attolico were together travelling down by train to Munich for the Four Power Conference, "Madame Attolico, unknown to her husband, was herself travelling to her favourite shrine in Italy to pray for that peace which he had worked so hard to ensure."[55] Similar scenes of women at prayer were taking place in Britain. Most famously Westminster Abbey was packed to the holy rafters on the same day, photos of the scenes suggesting that women represented the majority of worshippers.[56] It was prayer too that carried Annie Chamberlain through the hours of high suspense when her husband was in Munich, "her own religious faith and the conviction that the prayers of so many millions could not be in vain upheld her most."[57] Again, we see women's influence bearing on the process in more subtle ways.

Guilty women and fellow travelling

There were of course, plenty of British guilty women using what influence they had to manipulate events, and now is a good opportunity to discuss the mainly aristocratic women who were courted by the Nazi propaganda army's top brass.

Lady Londonderry was one of many women 'fellow travellers,' her social status making her one of the Grand prizes in the Nazi game to win over the British aristocracy, a classier, more mature version of Unity Mitford. The phenomenon has been well documented in the ground-breaking work of

Richard Griffiths in the early 1980s, and his supplement to *Fellow Travellers' of the Right, Patriotism Perverted* deals very specifically with a small but potentially dangerous pro-Nazi and subversive element that functioned at the level of the British establishment downwards to disaffected émigrés and middle-class eccentrics. In both works Griffiths has given the women protagonists their due.[58] In addition, fascination with the notorious Mitford sisters and Mitford-Nazi relations has spawned its own cottage industry, and since Diana Mosley's (nee Mitford) death in 2003 even more has come out about her behind-the-scenes activities and the fact that MI5 regarded her as more of a threat to national security than her husband, Britain's fascist leader.[59] There has also been some illuminating research on the high rate and cultural impact of actual tourism and the movement of politically-engaged travellers between Britain and Germany in this period.[60] In fact, there was nothing unusual about Britons from across the social spectrum choosing Nazi Germany as a tourist destination; sadly, what was more unusual were those objecting to such conspicuous tourism on ethical grounds, Eleanor Rathbone MP being one of the few to mount such a protest. Nor was politically motivated travel on an official or semi-official basis at all unusual, and most of the figures covered in this chapter embarked on one of many such excursions at the invitation of the Nazi elite.

While there is no need to substantially repeat this material by providing detailed itineraries of women's Nazi encounters, it is important to remember that many British women were willing and eager publicists for the Nazi regime. They made incendiary statements and gave public voice to their admiration for the regime and its leaders precisely when the appeasement debate was raging. They ranged from the travel writer and adventurer Rosita Forbes who had been a guest of the Fuehrer on several occasions and considered him an intimate friend;[61] to eccentric Policewoman and later British Union member Mary Allen;[62] to the author of *National Velvet* Enid Bagnold who embarked on a motoring tour of Germany in November, 1938;[63] and, to return where we started, to women's fitness guru Prunella Stack.[64] And coming from further on the extreme Right, Nesta Webster remerged and contributed to the debate by publishing her pamphlet "Germany and England" in October, 1938. The head-writer of the Judeo-Masonic-Communist world conspiracy, Webster's view of the Munich Agreement was predictable enough, appreciating that Hitler represented 90% of the German population, seeing him as "a plain man of the people, an ardent social reformer, too Socialistic for us but clearly sincere, a leader who whilst restoring the confidence and self-respect of the German people has quelled in them the spirit of hatred towards our country." She was also moved to see "the youth of Germany cheering Mr Chamberlain as the messenger of peace through the streets of Munich. And this is the moment when we are told that a world war is inevitable in order to crush the 'German menace.'"[65] We have already seen in Chapter 1 how very important travel and personal, tangible, emotional and ocular encounters were for refining political intentions and inspiring action.

British feminists and support for appeasement

Even among British feminists there was a cohort who, in 1937–1938, felt passionately that Hitler had to be given the benefit of the doubt, and who accepted Chamberlain as the nation's saviour. Together this cohort of feminist appeasers were the ones that Richard Baxter obliquely referred to as the unconsciously guilty, "the 'peace at any price' clique."[66] The former suffragette leader, who had moved with her mother Emmeline decisively to the Right during the Great War and by this point had distanced herself from politics in favour of Christian Adventism, Christabel Pankhurst, felt much relief and was brimming over with gratitude. She wrote to Annie Chamberlain:

> May I tell you how grateful I am in the Prime Minister for his effort to preserve world peace. Though I have long ceased to take any part in politics, I am moved by the clamour of his misguided critics to send, through you, this assurance of loyalty and thanks to the PM.

Pankhurst believed she spoke for the voiceless: "The vast silent majority of the people are certainly of the same way of thinking. The PM's action affords the only human hope of preventing a world war and the prayers of all good and intelligent citizens should uphold him."[67]

Sharing a spiritual motivation with Christabel but otherwise coming from another point on the political compass, feminist internationalist pacifist preacher Maude Royden also wrote to Chamberlain:

> Dear Sir, I fear that it may perhaps be wrong to add even one to your colossal mail, and yet the fact that a few—I am convinced that they are not more than a few—people are trying to make capital out of the present situation and, in doing so, to detract from your marvellous achievement as a peacemaker, impels me to add one word of passionate and lasting gratitude to all those which must have been rained upon you. Some friends of mine, who were giving out leaflets in Whitehall two or three days ago, told me that before people accept them they frequently and anxiously asked 'is it anything against Chamberlain?' And only when assured that it was not, received them eagerly. Many of us believe that in your magnificent break with old traditions, which no longer fit the new world, a new world will be ushered in. [68]

Chamberlain was evidently moved by her "long and passionately enthusiastic letter."[69] Royden was so overwhelmed by the promise of peace that she lost sight of many of the promises she was breaking. It would not be until later in 1940 that she came to support the war, and not before getting herself mixed up with the anti-war, pro-Nazi and rabidly anti-Semitic British People's Party (founded in April 1939) and the British Council for Christian Settlement in Europe in 1939–1940. H. St. John Philby stood as BPP candidate in the Hythe by-election of July, 1939, and Royden was among those who spoke in support of his campaign. She "can hardly have been unaware of the company she was keeping."[70]

Former suffragist Cicely Hamilton, who had spent the inter-war years coming more and more in sympathy with the dictatorships as revealed in her travel books, was in equal measure impressed by Chamberlain and irritated by the Leftist intelligentsia's critique of the Munich Agreement. She shared her observations of working women's response to the dénouement of the Crisis, contesting Malcolm Muggeridge's statement that it was the rich and businessmen who were most relieved that war had been averted. Within a feminist frame she observed that:

> the crowd that stretched along the Cromwell Road for Mr Chamberlain's return, and through which his car had to thrust at walking pace was not composed of wealthy stockbrokers; my immediate neighbours were two wage-earning women who told me they had hardly slept for a week and who brought their small families to wave their gratitude for peace.[71]

Ethel Smyth also went against the editorial tide of *Time and Tide* by confessing how "it seems impossible adequately to express one's admiration for Mr Chamberlain."[72] The Munich Agreement was 'peace with honour,' and Smyth was overwhelmed by his achievement.

Of this cohort Helena Swanwick was the most uncompromising appeaser. Her route to becoming one of Hitler's most outspoken apologists in Britain was via the peace, civil liberties, and feminist movements. She is portrayed in distinctly different ways by scholars drawn to her for various reasons, either as a prime example of feminist pacifist resistance to the technology of modern warfare,[73] as a pioneer in the discipline of feminist IR,[74] or as an exemplar of international and transnational feminist networking during and in the interwar.[75] From the vantage point of the late 1930s, however, she comes across as rather less sympathetic and possibly misguided. As revealed in her correspondence with Winifred Holtby, Swanwick's willingness to give the Germans the benefit of the doubt was well rehearsed, based on her reading of the Treaty of Versailles as a "Carthaginian Peace, smeared over with American flap doodle, French rhetoric and English religiosity." At the time of the Reichstag Fire trial she revealed her sympathy for the Germans and railed at the "intemperate and sanctimonious attitude of the English Press" for making it difficult for the German judge to act fairly, and she expressed her disquiet that *Time and Tide* was going down the road of anti-Nazism.[76] She became an increasingly isolated figure,[77] and with the publication of

Collective Insecurity (1937) and *The Roots of the Peace* (1938) she lost much credibility by equating Hitler's foreign policy ambitions with other imperialisms, and relativizing, rationalizing, and normalizing his domestic policies. Ellen Wilkinson deemed the former book "the perfect expression of the 'nursery-governess' case against mankind which will persist in being naughty. It is difficult to argue against Mrs Swanwick's conviction that if all men behaved as she would like them to do, violence would cease. But what if they won't?" and she described Swanwick as "a wise Nannie."[78] Even as Nancy Astor considered feminism and fascism mutually exclusive, she was persuaded by Swanwick's line of argument in *Collective Insecurity* "concerning the folly of the treatment of Germany, after Versailles," and defended Swanwick by emphasizing that "this exposition of our and (mainly) French short-sightedness does not make the author a Nazi, nor does it cause us to approve of Nazi methods in foreign policy or in dealing with political, religious, or racial minorities."[79]

Munich was an answer to Swanwick's prayers too, and while she knew full well that she was far outside the editorial lines of *Time and Tide*, it was there that she declared her position on the Munich Agreement. "I will say that I, who have so tediously often been called unpatriotic because I disagree with my Government, am now most happy to feel myself in agreement with Parliament in its support of a Prime Minister whom I respect for his courage, his political imagination and his modesty." She was especially grateful to the PM on a personal level:

> Neville Chamberlain appears to be the only man who has any chance of averting the Nemesis due on account of Lloyd George's infatuated policy of vindictive penalties, insincere pledges and illusory security. For the first time since 1919 it is possible to look forward, and not only, with shame, back.[80]

As an absolute pacifist[81] Swanwick embraced Chamberlain, comparing him favourably with Richard Cobden, and opined that "our treatment of Germany was such as to convince her Government that nothing could be obtained from us save by force; that Germany had 'nothing to lose but her chains.'" Then came Chamberlain 'the peacemaker' who:

> has tried to change this disastrous state of mind, and if Herr Hitler can be persuaded to prefer peaceful negotiations that will seem to me good pacifism as well as good business. Whether this policy succeeds or not, it is infinitely worth pursuing, and much more interesting than mere opposition to war.[82]

Swanwick's faint hope was soon extinguished, and in her despair at the outbreak of war she took her own life on 16 November, 1939.

Conclusion

In the first systematic study of British women and foreign affairs debates in the period, Van Seters notes that "the potential roles for women in the behind-the-scenes setting which are often so crucial to policy formation would appear to warrant further research."[83] That is precisely the research gap these two chapters have sought to fill. Again and again women have either been absentmindedly left out or explicitly written out of the story of appeasement. As we have seen, there were women who wielded their influence behind the scenes, and some even more publicly, both in Britain and in Germany. There were also women among the Fifth Columnists, often trying to use their sex and sexuality to achieve their ends. While Baxter wished to expose these women and make sure they would not be forgotten to history, his over-the-top portrayal of them as cartoon-like anti-heroines and schemers probably did much to forestall a serious exploration of their influence and their legacies.

Nonetheless, even as there can be little dispute that it is important to rescue the memory of the 'Guilty Women,' it cannot be denied that foreign policy was formed and performed in male-defined spaces and mainly within the confines of male-only associational life. Women were formally excluded from the diplomatic corps; no woman sat in the Cabinet at this crucial time; there were very few women political journalists and there was no female daily newspaper editor or proprietor (that is after the death of Lady Houston in 1935).[84] At the highest levels of high politics where women who were so inclined found their opportunities was in the interlocking social and private spheres, as political hostesses, as wives, as sisters of great men. (We will see how women activists and women MPs need to be written into the story as well.)

Indeed, in the search for women's agency and for gendered representations much too is revealed about the cultural constructions of masculinity, and social expectations of manliness and gentlemanliness that underpinned the politics of appeasement. Those leading figures who made self-portraits, both the appeasers and the anti-appeasers, were anxious to defend their claims to heroism, honour, valour, and manliness. This was well exemplified by the way Chamberlain took special gratification from Hitler's regard for him as a 'man,' as well as the way Duff Cooper and others took some glee in diagnosing in the PM's gullibility on this count his sexual insecurity. These sexual insecurities were projected onto the national level too as appeasement was understood to mark the nation's emasculation and the triumph of the sensibility of old women.

There are many new insights to glean from a gendered (re)vision of the Guilty Men/Guilty Women narrative. From the point of view of diplomatic history, a womanist reading of the evidence can uncover far more about the cultural and the psychological frameworks in which foreign affairs were conducted. These power dynamics had new meaning in the aftermath of suffrage, and when male political actors could not cross women out of the equation, no matter how much sexism and male-supremacist attitudes persisted. We have also seen how the power struggles between the sexes intertwined with those contests between entrenched positions in foreign policy debates. From the point of view of women's history, this approach provides an important acknowledgement of women's presence, participation, and emotional and intellectual investments in the sphere of international relations, a relationship that came to a head in the autumn of 1938. Part and parcel of the neglect of the women's history of appeasement has been the neglect of gender studies of the Conservative Party, and in the next chapter we will see how the success of appeasement hinged not only on grass roots support, but even more specifically on Chamberlain's popularity with the women of his own party.

5
'To Speak a Few Words of Comfort to Them:' Conservative Women's Support for Chamberlain and Appeasement

Any account of the 'women worthies' variety of the 'Guilty Women' is inevitably haphazard.[1] High politics, and especially diplomacy, were still very much male domains in the late 1930s. Women's influence, their impact on crises in international relations, and their culpability and agency too, manifested itself in more subtle ways. Taking account of the women in and around the Cliveden Set and those who were in intimate contact with the 'Men of Munich' can therefore only reveal so much. To provide a more nuanced women's history of the political and international crises of the late 1930s we need to consider how women in the Conservative Party provided emotional subsidy, intellectual justification and the indelible impression of firm public support for appeasement and for the appeasers. Arguably, it was their support at the party level that gave their mainly male political leaders in the National Government the confidence to proceed as they did.

Our understanding of the politics of appeasement has become more textured and multi-layered with attention paid, for instance, by Nick Crowson to the relationship between grass-roots Conservative politics and foreign policy questions, and Daniel Hucker's study of the construction of public opinion in appeasement debates in Britain and France.[2] However, in neither case has gender been a category of analysis, notwithstanding the fact that women represented more than half of Conservative Party membership. There were one million women members by 1928, 940,000 in 1934,[3] and their strength was back to one million subscribing members by April 1939. The Women's Unionist Organisation (WUO) or the Conservative Women's Association (CWA) "was the largest, most active political organization in interwar Britain, and Conservative politicians were aware of its benefits to their party."[4] The CWA certainly did not see itself as a feminist organization; its strategies were locally-based; and it was not concerned with promoting women or sponsoring female candidates. Historians of Conservative women have rightly discerned that during the earlier years of the inter-war period Tory women's political interests were social issues, bread-and-butter economics, defence of empire, and anti-Bolshevism, while it is also clear that the social and leisure aspect of participation in Tory politics was often the spur for political commitment.[5] The purpose of the Women's Conservative Organization was to carry out the work of mass politics and to create women Conservative voters, making efforts at all times to avoid sex antagonism. But the Conservative conceptualization of women was not static, and Hendley has observed a shift in the construction of female voters from "embryonic citizen in 1918 to consumer in 1945."[6] Furthermore, while sex segregation determined the structure of the Party, women were not entirely excluded from leadership roles. When Lady Falmouth resigned from the vice-chairmanship of the Conservative Party in 1939, she had already been the second woman to hold this post, having been preceded by Lady Hester Bourne.

There is less written on women in the Conservative Party than one would expect, and "political historians have dismissed right-wing women as political ciphers."[7] Perhaps this is because "political partisans who tend to support the existing social and political system are not likely to attract progressive-minded feminists,"[8] and Campbell's trailblazing *The Iron Ladies: Why Do Women Vote Tory?* (1987) was written as an anti-Thatcher polemic. Further, it is striking that the preponderance of studies focus on the 1920s and early 1930s, and the role of women in the party after the 1935 General Election is a blind spot in the historiography. Nor are there any studies of British women's support for causes deemed nationalist and patriotic and their mobilization in favour of rearmament and defence in the 1930s, whereas such a study exists for the American context.[9] The result is that historians of appeasement have taken almost no interest in women, let alone in Conservative women. Historians of Conservative women have glossed over the later 1930s and in so doing hardly interrogated Conservative women's relationships to appeasement politics. Further, diplomatic historians have disregarded wider responses in the British population to the actions of 'Great' and 'Guilty' men.

We also find that while women's historians have started to probe the very strong interconnection between feminism, pacifism, and international politics, Conservative women are again regarded as extraneous. With a few exceptions, Conservative women were much more ambivalent than women in the Liberal and Labour parties and in women's movements about the League of Nations, and mostly unconvinced that collective security represented a panacea. However, as we will see, Conservative women voiced their opinions about foreign policy matters in the 1930s, even if these were often an echo of the party leadership. Therefore as we resituate women in the narrative of appeasement, we must pay due regard to women in the Conservative Party.

Conservative women MPs' engagement with foreign affairs

During the first years after the war Tory women were primarily absorbed by their local context, home affairs and the shoring up of Empire, but their concerns did change with the times. Indeed, imperial affairs should not be conflated with foreign affairs. Conservative women were tasked with oversight of imperial issues, given roles to play as the champions of empire and defenders of an imperial consciousness, organizing Empire Day events, etc., and these were distinct from 'international relations' and European affairs. Considering the high ratio of women to men in the party, the number of women Conservatives to hold Parliamentary seats was disappointingly low, although it did not follow that these few Conservative women MPs were not colourful figures. We will be making the acquaintance of the Conservative women MPs who sat in Parliament between 1935 and the outbreak of the war. These were Lady Astor, Lady Davidson, Thelma Cazalet-Keir, Florence Horsbrugh, Mavis Tate, and Irene Ward. The story of the Tory rebel the 'Red' Duchess of Atholl belongs to the chapters to come.

These Conservative women MPs did not confine themselves to domestic issues or remain close to their constituencies in a physical sense. They engaged with foreign policy; many had an international profile and paid official foreign visits; and at the height of appeasement most proved themselves to be great backers of the Prime Minister. Women MPs were consistently seen to stand for the 'woman's point of view,' be in the service of women nationwide, and represent the broad spectrum of women voters rather than their party interests alone. The press was fond of publishing pen portraits of the women MPs, grouping them together as "the nine women MPs are good champions of their sex,"[10] or the "dozen daughters of Parliament."[11] As they took their public stands on foreign policy issues and had themselves counted among Chamberlain's most loyal supporters, Conservative women MPs unwittingly set in motion the process of the feminization of appeasement politics.

Miss Margery Graves, the granddaughter of an MP, entered Parliament in 1931 by defeating Herbert Morrison in South Hackney, but she lost her seat in 1935, and was therefore not in Parliament during the Munich Crisis. Nonetheless, we start with her because she provides a good example of a woman Conservative politician whose interests transcended the domestic sphere. During the war she had been attached to the Foreign Office, and she had gone to the Paris Peace Conference in an official capacity. She then went on to become secretary to the Intelligence Department of the Home Office. She was a seasoned traveller in America, Canada, and on the Continent, and a writer of books on French history.[12] In July 1932 she gave her maiden speech on the Lausanne conference, defending the agreement reached there on war debts. In itself this was exceptional, as of the 35 maiden speeches made by women MPs between the wars 21 were on welfare issues, nine on taxation or tariffs, and only three on foreign or defence policy, thus seemingly justifying the neglect of the study of women's engagement with foreign affairs at the level of parliamentary politics.[13] While she rarely spoke in the House, she was acknowledged to be one of the women MPs who "have gained considerably in knowledge of foreign affairs since they were elected."[14] She supported collective security through the League, and was active in the LNU, but she was also ready to make concessions to Hitler—and visited Germany in 1935—and to Mussolini in Abyssinia. She was chosen to be the token woman on the British delegation to the League assembly in the summer of 1936, because "it happens that she knows more about foreign affairs than most women in the public service."[15] She remained active in the party after losing her seat and had a presence in the West Country where she became prospective candidate for Barnstaple, lecturing at Conservative political schools on 'The Present Situation in Foreign Affairs.'[16] She was a headliner at a three-day political school organized by the Women's Advisory Council (Western Area), speaking on 'The Treaty of Versailles as it affected the map of Europe.'[17] Addressing the West Dorset CWA on the foreign situation in 1937, she spoke of the importance of maintaining the balance of power and explained that "It is our duty as an old nation to extend not only toleration, but understanding, to the new powers of Germany and Italy."[18] She was also high up in the structure of the party, becoming the first women to serve as chairman of the metropolitan area of the National Union of Conservative and Unionist Associations (1936–1937).[19] She was again in Central Europe in the spring of 1938. Graves was one of the few Conservative women so focused on foreign affairs, and one of the few women experts in the party on international issues, speaking with authority on the principles that undergirded the policy of appeasement.

Irene Ward, who had won her seat at Wallsend in 1931 by defeating Britain's first female Cabinet Minister, Labour's Margaret Bondfield, hardly devoted herself to domestic issues to the exclusion of international affairs. In 1936, Ward was in New York City representing the Government's rearmament programme coupled with an appeasing attitude towards the Nazi regime.[20] She took a keen interest in anti-fascist relief work, and in 1937 and 1938 she was a member of the committee of MPs involved in the evacuation of women and children during the Spanish Civil War. As MP for a shipbuilding constituency, she also engaged with defence matters, asking questions in the House about naval construction, anxious that Tyneside should get its fair share of contracts. She made her "debut in international affairs" as a substitute delegate to the General Assembly of the League of Nations in 1937, specializing in the League's work regarding white slavery and child welfare.[21]

At the height of Chamberlain's popularity Ward was regularly at hand to support pro-appeasement by-election candidates. Ward addressed a women's meeting in support of Henry Hunloke in May 1938, together with the National Conservative candidate's wife and his mother-in-law, the Duchess of Devonshire. She remained committed to appeasement, headlining a meeting in Bude in support of the National Conservative candidate Mr Whitehouse in the North Cornwall by-election in July 1939.

The central issue of this by-election was seen to be 'peace or war,' with the Conservatives targeting women voters, and "pressing home at women's meetings all over the division the debt of gratitude women of the country owe to Mr Chamberlain for saving their homes and families by his Munich intervention." Ward "appealed to [women] to show the dictators that Britain was solid behind the Prime Minister by returning Mr Whitehouse."[22] These were also good examples of how local party organizations targeted women voters by fusing their interests as women with the Prime Minister's foreign policy.

The backbencher Mrs Mavis Tate, MP for Frome since 1935 (she had won the West Willisden seat in 1931), likewise did not quite play to type. She engaged with 'unfeminine' concerns in the realm of defence policy, and she also took a strident feminist position on women's issues.[23] While interested in questions of health and agriculture, she was an avid airwoman, gaining a reputation as "the only woman in Parliament who is a champion of increased air defences, backed with experience and technical knowledge of aviation." She had considerable flying experience, and had "studied the engineering principles of aviation as few men Members have done. Not one of her Parliamentary sisters has ever been up in a ' plane, so far as most Westminster authorities know."[24] She was regarded:

> as one who knows what she is talking about. Yet she is not a terrifying person. Like Miss Megan Lloyd George and Miss Thelma Cazalet, she brings a pleasant femininity to the debates of the House—and, unlike one or two of her sisters, she can sit quite still for an hour at a time.[25]

Her 'defencist' agenda placed her on the Right of the party and in company with the Rothermere circle, which explains why in June 1938 she was at a "Right-wing meeting at Lord Bute's house, with Archibald Ramsay in the chair."[26] Ramsay, leader of the Right Club, would end up interned under Defence Regulation 18B during the war.

Indeed, it is worth pausing for a moment to consider the important relationship between women and flight, both in real terms as a significant number of women on the Right embraced modern aviation as both sporting pastime and political cause, and on the metaphoric level. Lady Londonderry established the Women's Legion Flying section in the early 1930s, enabling women interested in aviation to put their skilled service to the country's disposal in the time of emergency. The British Union of Fascists also established a Women's Flying Club. In the mid-1920s former suffragette and wartime founder of the Women's Police Service and later the Women's Reserve[27] Mary Allen learned to fly at Stag Lane aerodrome, Hendon, and Lady Bailey and Lady Heath were fellow pupils, and she also overlapped there with Amy Johnson who was completing her licence.[28] Like Lady Londonderry, Allen's feminism from the Right was premised on women performing their patriotic duties unmolested by antedated sexism, and she suggested that "we women drop, for good and all, the tiresome reiteration of 'Women's Rights,' and substitute for it 'Women's Responsibilities.'"[29] The eccentric and wealthy Lady Lucy Houston DBE (died 29 December, 1936), who had been a generous donor and active speaker for the WSPU in suffragette days, was by the 1930s Baldwin's pro-fascist scourge, relentlessly attacking the National Government in her newspaper the *Saturday Review*. Lady Houston's great cause was defence and particularly air armaments.[30] The Nazi woman aviator Hanna Reitsch also became an international icon. These women 'speed freaks' tended to identify with the Right or even the extreme Right in British politics, placing Tate's interest in aeronautics in context.[31]

Tate's record as one who had urged air rearmament since 1934 might explain why she was a bit 'flighty,' at least privately, during the Munich Crisis. She wrote to Duff Cooper upon his resignation: "I myself am miserable and undecided, but it should be a help to all of us to hear your views. In any case I deeply admire your courage and disinterestedness."[32] This did not stop her from publicly identifying with the appeasers, and along with 70 Unionist MPs, including Lady Astor and Miss Horsbrugh, she joined an appeal to the electors of the division of East Perthshire to vote against the Duchess of Atholl and for the National Conservative candidate Mr Snadden.[33] In the end, however, she was among the group of Ministerialists organized by Clement Davies KC and Robert Boothby, with Leo Amery as chairman, who voted against the Government on 8 May, 1940, drawing up the three-point policy that called for Chamberlain's resignation. Mavis Tate was a late addition as a 'glamour girl,' joining the group of rebels who ousted the PM, together with Duff Cooper, Hore-Belisha, Earl Winterton, Richard Law, Harold Macmillan, Henderson Stewart, Ronald Tree, Harold Nicolson, Sir Derrick Gunston, and S.H.M. Russell.[34]

Lady Davidson played more to type, and she was focused on constituency issues as well as the internal politics of the Conservative Party. She had been a member of the council of the National Union of Conservative and Unionist Associations since 1925, and she was chairman of the Young Britons, in 1938 remarking on the relative lack of progress of the Tory's youth movement in comparison with those in the totalitarian states. An intimate friend and regular correspondent of Stanley Baldwin, she entered Parliament by winning the Hemel Hempstead by-election in June 1937, after her husband's (Tory party chairman J.C.C. Davidson) elevation to the House of Lords, taking advantage here of the so-called 'halo effect.' Essential to the Party's appeal to women was to equate them with peace and the politics of peacetime only, and court the notional 'women's vote' by representing itself as the party of safety and security. They did this by portraying their opponents as the warmongers, and themselves as not entirely unsympathetic to internationalism but eager to remain out of foreign quarrels. The League of Nations card was most usually played by their Liberal and Labour challengers.

The Hemel Hempstead by-election of 22 June, 1937, was typical of the Party's rhetoric and the framing of the peace debate, but less typical for being contested by two women. Lady Davidson was running against Margery Corbett Ashby, the distinguished Liberal feminist internationalist for whom this was a seventh attempt to enter the House of Commons. Corbett Ashby stood for a progressive attitude to peace and social justice which cut across all party distinctions, and as such demonstrated how women candidates at by-elections could fight on those big, male-identified foreign policy issues. For her part Davidson asked electors to affirm their faith in the National Government, pointing to successes in trade recovery, the economy, the expansion of social services and housing and "Fourthly— the National Government has maintained peace and has prevented Britain and the Empire from being involved in a European War." She asserted that "I am convinced that the constant criticism indulged in by the Socialist and Liberal oppositions and their desire to interfere in the affairs of other countries if carried into effect would have led to a conflagration in Europe."[35] Her non-interventionist stance was clear during this second summer of the Spanish Civil War.

While Lady Davidson's achievements in her own right should not be dismissed, when it came to foreign policy she was clearly marching to her husband's drum beat. Her husband's endorsement appeared on the back of her election address. When he was guest speaker on the topic of Britain's defensive position at the annual meeting at Ashridge College in June, 1938, she accompanied him, saying a few brief words about the vital importance at present of education in citizenship.[36] She also remained loyal to Chamberlain. While on 8 May, 1940, Astor and Tate withdrew from Chamberlain the votes they had cast for him on 6 October, 1938, Davidson, Horsbrugh, and Cazalet-Keir, did not join the revolt.[37] During the war Davidson did take some interest in women's potential roles in international affairs, joining a deputation of 32 representative women, led by Thelma Cazalet-Keir, at the Foreign Office in September 1941 that asked Anthony Eden to consider their case for admitting women to the Diplomatic Service.[38] Overall, Davidson did not distinguish herself in foreign affairs but instead represented that type of aristocratic Tory political worker who prided herself on loyalty to party and to leader at all costs.

The daughters of parliament and the father of peace

The MP for Dundee, Miss Florence Horsbrugh had a deeper interest in foreign affairs, and was delegate to the League of Nations in 1933, 1934, and 1935. Most of her time was devoted, however, to 'domestic' issues, culminating in her appointment as Parliamentary Secretary to the Ministry of Health in July, 1939, thereby becoming the second Conservative woman MP to be a member of the Government of the day. On this occasion she told a reporter that the subjects "she will have to deal with—housing, health, and child welfare—have been among her chief interests since she entered the House of Commons."[39] Just three years earlier, in November 1936, she had scored symbolic 'firsts,' making constitutional history as the first woman to move the reply to the King's speech in the House of Commons, and by being the first Empire politician to be televised from the Alexandra Palace.

Horsbrugh did engage in the national debate about defence and rearmament, in March 1936 explaining "that the only way to reply to international bullies who had been spending millions on armaments was to face up to them. If Britain was going to have defence forces at all they must be adequate."[40] She also engaged the LNU in debate, not hostile to, but not uncritical either of the League of Nations. Addressing the East of Scotland District Council of the LNU and speaking on "The League of Nations: The Ideal and the Machine," she believed that as it stood collective security could not be tried out, and recommended a major overhaul of the League structure and a scheme of federation.[41] She was also a staunch anti-interventionist in the Spanish Civil War.

Arguably, of all these women Conservatives sitting in the House at the time of the Munich Crisis, Horsbrugh was possibly the most forthright Chamberlain loyalist. She was very protective of him, in March 1938 moving a resolution at the annual Conservative conference castigating the BBC for broadcasting criticism of the Premier. She felt a great affection for and intimacy with Neville and Annie Chamberlain, reaching out to the latter on 28 September: "this afternoon I had the chance of saying 'thank you' to the PM and I feel I want to say the same to you. I hope you will realize that those two words carry thoughts of gratitude I cannot fully express." Horsbrugh also empathized with her as a woman, appreciating that "your wait must have been almost unbearable—the woman's—to wait—is almost more of a strain than activity however terrible the responsibility."[42] She supported the Munich Agreement without reservation, "proud of what the Government had done and convinced that we had taken the first step in the right direction."[43] When she contributed to the debate in the House after the Munich Agreement, she stood proxy for 'the Women's View,' speaking:

> not with humiliation, but with pride, because the people of the world had looked at war and found it hateful and they had a greater determination than ever before that quarrels must be settled not by bombs from the sky and misery but by human beings getting together, with consultation and negotiation, each trying to see the other's point of view. Messages received by women members made it clear that the women of the world were thanking God that the means of averting the disaster was found and that men and women of good will had been given once again the chance of working for peace. When the British mothers put labels and warm coats on their children preparatory to sending them away, possibly never to see

them again, it was not only of themselves that they thought of but the mothers and children in Germany and Czechoslovakia. (Hear, hear.) They realized that war was not worth the price. She believed that the Prime Minister took the spirit of the League out of the ritual and machinery into which it had got, and took it to the dictator countries. (Hear, hear.)

Her interlocutor on this occasion was Ellen Wilkinson, who replied:

> that no one would disagree with the passion for peace throughout the speech of Miss Horsbrugh, but what they objected to was the personal policy of the Prime Minister, which had landed the country in a position where only some dramatic improvisation in the last five minutes, and the throwing away of practically everything this country cared for, could rescue us. But the Prime Minister should not have to bear the burden alone. A number of influential people had been saying to Herr Hitler, and to Herr von Ribbentrop, that in no circumstances would the people of this country fight for Czechoslovakia or Austria.[44]

Horsbrugh expressed her belief in Chamberlain's foreign policy by pitting herself very publicly against his foremost woman critic and her fellow Scottish Conservative MP, the Duchess of Atholl. Horsbrugh campaigned in Dundee on behalf of Atholl's National Conservative challenger in the by-election of December, 1938, believing it "a tragedy that your Member was not in London or in the House of Commons on September 28 when Mr Chamberlain received the vital summons to Munich or she would not be doing what she is doing now."[45] Had Atholl been there in person and not in America, Horsbrugh was convinced she would have been swept up by the mass sense of relief.

Horsbrugh remained a voice for a policy of peace and reconciliation, expressed in Christian terms, and on Sunday, 12 March, 1939, she told a meeting of the Dundee Brotherhood: "We should be able, even now, to send out a message throughout the world that we are willing to be brothers and to meet as one family, each willing to learn about the other everything that is true, and good, and noble."[46] This was four days before the Wehrmacht moved into Czechoslovakia and Hitler proclaimed Bohemia and Moravia a German Protectorate. Even that summer, in July 1939, she was campaigning on behalf of the National Government candidate at the North Cornwall by-election, when she and the candidate's wife addressed two enthusiastic women's meetings in the area appealing "to all women in the division to remember Munich, when Mr Chamberlain saved their homes and their families by preventing a war with Germany."[47] Horsbrugh's loyalty paid off, with a government appointment that same summer, while her gratitude for being promoted to the government is also the plausible explanation for her remaining loyal to Chamberlain up to May 1940.

No women's party: women MPs in schism

The women MPs, so often portrayed by the press as a group despite significant ideological differences and divergent party affiliations, were understood to be in schism by the summer of 1938. The Independent Eleanor Rathbone, Labour's Ellen Wilkinson and the Conservative's own Duchess of Atholl were regarded as the "most embarrassing to the Government," while "at the other end of the scale—unswerving support for all aspects of Government foreign policy"[48] stood Horsbrugh and Miss Thelma Cazalet, a junior Minister.[49] Thelma Cazalet was in step with her female Conservative colleagues when it came to foreign affairs, and she voted for the Government in the motion of confidence in mid-October, 1938, despite the fact that her brother, Captain Victor Cazalet (MP for Chippenham) voted against the Government on this occasion. She was nonetheless at the progressive end of the party.

Thelma Cazalet was first elected for the LCC in East Islington in 1925, holding the seat until 1931 when she became an alderman, and elected Conservative MP for East Islington in 1931. In 1935 she was one of 16 MPs who was a supporter and signatory of the Next Five Years Plan, a scheme that combined the retention of private enterprise with public control in the private interest. In 1937 she was made Parliamentary Private Secretary to Kenneth Lindsay at the Board of Education, a first for a woman. She was best friends since school days with the Liberal MP Megan Lloyd George, the twosome frequently referred to as 'The Inseparables' or the 'Dolly Twins,' and they appeared to "agree on everything under the sun except politics."[50] Her credentials as a progressive and a feminist were further strengthened when she married David Keir, the *News Chronicle* parliamentary correspondent, in August 1939, a wedding that was newsworthy for many reasons, and again presented an opportunity to score a number of 'firsts' for women. It was the first engagement and then first wedding of a sitting woman Member of Parliament; she was the first woman MP to be married in the House of Commons' Crypt Chapel; the bride kept her maiden name; and the transcendence of the affection of friendship over partisanship was demonstrated by her choice of Megan Lloyd George as her maid of honour. While the wedding was marked by a liberal spirit in all these things, the timing of their honeymoon in August meant that Irene Ward was chosen as a Government delegate to the League of Nations instead of Cazalet-Keir, who would otherwise have been the first choice for the posting. Having missed the opportunity to make a mark in international relations that summer, she was the first woman MP to be sent to France during wartime in December 1939, and it certainly helped that, of French extraction, she was fluent in the language. The causes she espoused and the committees she headed up during the war demonstrated her commitment to expanding the role of women in international affairs and diplomacy.

Considering Cazalet-Keir's pro-Chamberlain position, it is clear that in later life she was anxious not to be classed with the Guilty Men. In the post-war years she was anxious to provide her political alibi, using her memoirs to demonstrate "the completeness of my detestation of Hitlerism," and pressing the point that "I can also prove that I never advocated that we should strip ourselves of adequate means of defence."[51] She had the ear of many of the leading players in international affairs, including Lloyd George, Baldwin, and Chamberlain. From the vantage point of the 1960s, she sought to defend Baldwin against two charges, first that he was unduly friendly towards Ribbentrop, and second that his foreign policy was naïve. She reasoned that Baldwin, "like most of us," was "inclined to believe what he wanted to believe, and part of such wishful thinking was that it would be possible to organise the same sort of fraternity between nations as he had tried so hard to create among classes in Britain." She provided the reminder that "Appeasement was not then a dirty word; it was by no means apparent that its parent was ignorance and its child disaster."[52] True, Cazalet-Keir's main interest as an MP was in educational matters, and she admitted having "no particular prescience" when the Nazis came to power in 1933, recognizing too that in the early 1930s Winston Churchill was "no repository of wisdom or even of sense." However, in her memoirs she emphasized those episodes that made it appear that she took a firm stand against Hitler once she was directly confronted by the 'truth' of the Nazi regime. "It was my visit in 1938 to the famous Nazi rally in Nuremberg that really completed the sweeping of the scales from my eyes." She was among those visitors Ribbentrop had been recruiting in Britain, yet she felt his efforts revealed "the depth of his psychological folly," not realizing "how uncongenial it would be to people like myself." She had accepted the invitation "for the very obvious reason that it was the duty of an MP to see at first hand what was going on in Germany. I had been to Russia in 1937, without being dubbed a communist; and was planning to go to Washington in 1939."[53] Of the crisis itself, she stated:

> I wish I could claim that my eyes were not wholly gummed up with sleep. Indeed, by the end of 1937 I was fully disillusioned, and at the height of the Munich crisis, on 28 September of the following year, I actually sent President Roosevelt a personal telegram asking him to fly himself to Europe and try to maintain peace. This was not as brash as it may seem because I had met Mrs Roosevelt when on a visit to the US in 1933 and had a long interview with her in the White House ... My telegram was not taken amiss. When Mrs Roosevelt came to London in 1940 it was I, as a member of the Anglo-American Committee, who helped to show her round both Houses of Parliament.[54]

As we can see, Cazalet-Keir was making every effort to relocate herself in, even impose herself on, the history of Anglo-American resolve and anti-appeasement inclination. Her rather small efforts were given inflated significance by this retrospective approach, and she tried to show, with some feminine modesty, that she was a determined anti-Nazi. But perhaps her point that her "specialities were in fields more modest than foreign policy," and that she was thus justified to focus on local and social issues, such as schools and housing, rather than to "bridle or cower at Hitler's antics,"[55] underlines women MPs disabilities as women to partake in a meaningful way in staunchly male-dominated foreign policy-making. The reality of this was only reinforced during the war itself when Cazalet-Keir, a self-avowed feminist whose mother had been a confidant of the Pankhursts' before the First World War (and she had the honour to deliver the obituary broadcast on Mrs Pankhurst), had an interview with Anthony Eden, Foreign Secretary, "to induce him to allow women to enter the Diplomatic Service and thus to become ambassadors. Nobody could have been more charming or more non-committal. His last word was: 'Tell me, Thelma, what exactly would happen to the husbands?'"[56]

However, try as she might to exonerate herself post-war, Violet Bonham Carter was not ready to forget Cazalet-Keir's alignments in those over-wrought days before the war. Bonham Carter wrote to Churchill in the run-up to the 1945 General Election:

> Well—there we are—on opposite sides of the line, we who have felt and fought and thought together—in fair weather and foul—but especially foul. And ranged behind you I see—Thelma Cazalet! (poor, dull, industri-ous goose! Who junketed at Nuremberg) and all the old appeasers, and that Vermiform Appendix, the National Liberals—which I do not grudge you.[57]

In the eyes of one of the most distinguished anti-appeasers, Cazalet-Keir would not be let off the hook for her collusion with the guilty men.

Given their unswerving endorsement of Chamberlain, why do figures like Horsbrugh and Cazalet-Keir not emerge in accounts of appeasement? First, it is because they were *woman* MPs and as such of little consequence despite, or maybe because of, their achievement of so many 'firsts,' Second, their dis-tinguished wartime service might well have functioned to provide each with a clean bill of political health. Third, although we find them staking their positions on the international crisis at constituency level, representing the pro-Chamberlain position across the country, and even paying him tribute in Parliament on behalf of the women of the nation, their positions exem-plified those of the Party as a whole. These women were too representative of mainstream opinion to stand out, and at the centre of party consensus.

In this discussion of Conservative women MPs and their engagement in foreign policy debate it would seem logical to include Lady Nancy Astor. However, these aforementioned Conservative women MPs played for the second team of guilty women, whereas Astor was, of course, on the first team in her role as hostess of the Cliveden Set. Her case was treated in finer detail and in a different frame in the previous chapters. For now what needs to be explored is the extent to which Conservative women MPs represented Conservative women's attitudes towards foreign affairs and their mentality more broadly. How did Conservative women respond to and participate in the controversies in foreign policy and the ensuing crisis?

'Keep smiling faces': conservative women's education in international affairs

As international crises came quick and fast, Conservative women could be found busily playing catch-up, and seeking to educate themselves in matters of foreign affairs. Throughout the 1920s and well into the 1930s Labour and Liberal women left no stone unturned to achieve disarmament and collective security. In contrast, Conservative women were more sceptical. At their annual conference in April 1934, attended by Anthony Eden, Conservative women showed that they did not quite speak with one voice on defence policy, the majority supporting a resolution "to strengthen our defence forces to such a degree as shall be conducive to the future security and peace of the country,"[58] while Lady Astor adopted an anti-militarist stance. Astor was subjected to noisy abuse when she spoke in support of the amendment, and because she was much more in tune with her sisters in the Liberal Party when it came to disarmament and defence matters than with the women, and men, in her own party. Astor demonstrated both the influence of feminist pacifism on her politics and a spirit of independence on defence questions, and she was an aberrational figure in the party for it.

The political curriculum for Conservative women developed with the exigencies of the times, and there was a shift from a focus on topics that were deemed most interesting to women, such as the servant crisis or housing conditions, to world affairs. At a political school for Conservative women in Christchurch in 1934 (attended by 130 women) the keenest interest was taken in speeches upon disarmament and agriculture. At the morning session Major J.D. Mills MP spoke on disarmament, paying lip service to the ideal of disarmament but noting that "if we continue to stand still while other nations increase their arms we shall—one day—find ourselves in a position of great danger."[59] At their Political School in Ashridge in 1935, Conservative women were given a syllabus that included lectures by historian Arthur Bryant on 'The National Tradition,' and Sir Edward Grigg speaking on 'Germany and Italy.'[60] However, Berthezène has shown that women's influence was conspicuously weak among the Tory 'Fabians' of Ashridge College.[61] A series of lectures on 'National Defence and Collective Security' were held at the Ladies Carlton Club in the autumn of 1935, addressed by Sir Charles Petrie, Miss Marjorie Graves MP, Leo Amery MP, and Sir Arnold Wilson MP.[62] In 1936 between 300 and 400 women attended a political school arranged by the Manchester Women's Conservative and Unionist Association, and again the most popular session was Captain Malcolm Bullock MP on 'Foreign affairs.'[63] In 1937 "it was decided to hold a Political School at Falmouth. The syllabus was to be on 'Foreign Affairs.' It was the unanimous wish that Miss Marjorie Graves be asked to give two lectures."[64] In the Home Counties South-East Area (35 constituencies), the Annual Political School for women Conservatives was held in Cliftonville in February 1939, attended by 120 resident students, and the subject studied was foreign affairs.[65]

The pressure was on from party level to provide education on current events via political schools, and women were especially targeted. However, some MPs were dubious of the value of committing so many of the party's resources to women. When Cuthbert Headlam gave a lecture on 'Problems at Home and Abroad' at such a political school organized by the Central Division, Newcastle, and attended by 50–60 people—"mainly middle-aged and ageing women"—he wondered if more good would come from directing efforts to "more active propaganda," as "none of the people to whom these lectures are given is likely to take any really active part in politics either canvassing or on the platform."[66] Only two days later he was similarly discouraged at a meeting at Dumfries, attended by 70 women, as "it is boring to have to address a small meeting of women who never utter a sound of approbation or disapprobation from the first moment to the last—and are all waiting for their tea!"[67] He remained cynical about the value of 'political education' after attending another "dull as usual" meeting of the Education Committee, but he was resigned to the fact that "we shall have to waste money on it so long as Lady Falmouth and Dame Regina Evans so wish!"[68] Even if in private Conservative MPs expressed their scepticism about ploughing their energies into educating and mobilizing Conservative women, it was the order of the day as delivered by the party's wire-pullers.

Mobilizing consensus at CWA annual conferences

With the foundations of their education in foreign affairs set at the local level of the party, it was not terribly surprising that when Baldwin addressed a meeting of 7,000 women at the 16th annual conference of the CWA in May 1936,[69] his whole speech should have dealt with international affairs, striking a decidedly cautious and protective paternalistic tone. Baldwin said:

> 'Speaking to a British audience, can I be blamed if I put as my first object the safety of our own land and of the Empire!' He hastily corrected the phrase saying, 'our own land—that would have been true up to a few years ago, but when you think of war and of preserving our people from it, it is not only our own land, it is our people, our men, women and children.'[70]

The rhetorical mould had been set by the time Chamberlain addressed the same conference two years later.

Chamberlain was even more popular with the women in the party than his predecessor, his recipe of gestures of goodwill in Europe blended with gradually increasing defensive strength calculated to be the comfort food for women in the party and in the electorate at large. He was clear about how profoundly he had been influenced by women's concerns, knowing from their letters that:

> the fear of war has been hanging over countless homes from many months past and filling the hearts of mothers and wives with the gnawing anxiety unless their menfolk may have to take part in it. If there are any of them here to-day, I should like to speak a few words of comfort to them.

The policy of appeasement was hardly a hard sell to women Conservatives, and he explained that:

> [t]he main object of this Government's foreign policy is the establishment and maintenance of peace so that, instead of building up armaments against one another, we may settle our differences and then devote ourselves to make the world a better place to live in. If anyone was to attack us, we should have to defend ourselves. That is the purpose of our armaments.[71]

On several occasions Chamberlain confessed to how profoundly he was influenced by female public opinion—or at least his reading of it—and the letters sent to him from appeasement-minded women anxious to evade another war reinforced his own isolationism.

Indeed, he took this Albert Hall speech to the Women's Unionist Association very much in earnest. After the fact he considered the speech to have been "very successful," and was gratified to find out that:

> they had been 'torn out of the place' for tickets and much to my surprise I saw no vacant places. I had taken a good deal of trouble over the speech—in fact I didn't get more than 5½ hours sleep any night last week—but it was worth it.

He clearly basked in his celebrity status with Conservative women, noting that: "[w]hen I got up to reply to the vote of thanks I had a tremendous ovation, people rising & waving their handkerchiefs for what seemed a long time." He was even more gratified to hear that the wife of Conservative MP Herbert Williams told her husband: "That it was the best Leader's speech she had ever heard."[72]

Campbell has discerned how "loyalty prevailed again when Conservative women endorsed the government's appeasement of Hitler in Munich in 1938."[73] At the same conference and attended by 3,000 delegates in May 1939, Chamberlain was still celebrated by a resolution thanking him for his untiring efforts for world peace, but by this stage in the game a few dissenting voices were raised. Mrs Jenkins (North Kensington) said that she had the greatest admiration for the courage displayed by Mr Chamberlain during the September crisis, "'but while London was rejoicing, Czechoslovakia was in mourning.' 'There are black words on England's record,' she exclaimed. They could not feel that England was in the position she used to occupy." Several delegates retorted "Yes, we are," and one voice interrupted her protesting "we ought not to criticize." Jenkins did not leave it at that and replied:

'I don't think that interruption is in accordance with the traditions of England, where we have free speech.' ... 'It sounds to me to savour a little bit of dictatorship.' She added that while she believed most firmly in the National Government, 'we are a little bit tired of seeing the British lion wag its tail so slowly.'

It was Mrs Chamberlain who tried hard to forge consensus, insisting that "in the past year they had been faced with great troubles and difficulties, and she thought that they had perhaps emerged rather different people. It was impossible to exaggerate the importance of unity." Indeed, the widely disseminated images of Neville and Mrs Chamberlain arriving at this conference show how enthusiastically they were fêted by Conservative women. Further, the Premier's wife confirmed the importance to her husband of women's support. Speaking in dulcet tones about peace and her husband's achievements at this late hour of the antebellum, Mrs Chamberlain underscored that "One of the most moving things, and one that has touched my husband deeply, has been the message of confidence which have been sent to him from the women of the country."[74]

As with his speech to the same conference a year earlier, it was clear that Neville Chamberlain took Conservative women seriously and felt particularly comfortable in their company, regarding them as the backbone of the party, if not as representative of popular opinion across the board. While the speech gave him "an unusual amount of trouble and worry for in these days every word I say is examined under a microscope & weighed & measured," he was encouraged that several people who heard it told him it was the best he had ever made.[75] That he would make such a critical and policy-setting speech to the CWA strongly indicates the PM's ease with his women constituents, which was clearly mutual, and probably too that he felt he could count on an audience of women Conservatives to give him a reasonably quiet if not fawning hearing.

Conservative women's organization in comparative perspective

Conservative women did increasingly take an interest in international affairs. However, from a comparative perspective they were still very noticeably behind their female counterparts in the Liberal and Labour parties, whose sex-segregated party organizations, the Women's Liberal Federation and the Labour Party's Women Sections, were ever more dominated by concerns with international issues. There are a number of reasons for these dissimilarities. At the ideological level a tradition of anti-Bolshevism meant that Conservative women approached fascism from a very different starting point than others for whom—as feminists, as Liberals or as Leftists—anti-fascism was instinctive and visceral. In this vein Lady Maureen Stanley, wife of Oliver Stanley, the Minister of Labour, explained why she adhered to Conservatism, which she regarded as a faith: "'We do not experiment in theory on the great masses of people in this country,' she said. 'We are much more inclined to sit down and watch experiments in foreign countries, which to my mind is a very good idea.'" She added "that it was essentially a broad-minded party, and in it could be found those who might be described as Socialists, Liberals, Fascists, Communists, and almost anything."[76] Lady Stanley regarded Conservatism as a broad church that could even accommodate those of fascist faith, entirely consistent with her positive Nazi encounters as a guest of the regime.[77]

At the structural level the relative narrowness of the international perspective among Conservative women was due to the absence of international networks and organizations in the realm of Conservative politics. Since the later decades of the 19th century feminists and suffragists, Socialists and Liberal women had already been well integrated into transnational networks, with their attendant ideologies of internationalism. The very basis of socialism was the international unity of the working classes, and Labour women were active in the International Women's Committee of the Labour and Socialist International (LSI), the International Federation of Trade Unions, and many Labour women also subscribed to the Open Door International (founded in 1929 in Berlin) that sought to work for the economic emancipation of women. Even more so were Liberal women preoccupied with world affairs, to the extent that as the national fortunes of the party declined, the Liberals' investment in foreign affairs increased dramatically. Liberal women were actively involved in the WILPF, the International Alliance of Women, the International Council of Women, they dominated the League of Nations Union, and many Liberal women were also representatives at the League of Nations assemblies. As a consequence, Liberal and Labour women were much more able, immeasurably better educated, and self-sufficient in international politics. In addition, while Conservative women were most often addressed by male speakers regarding foreign affairs, this was much less frequently the case at Liberal and Labour women's own meetings. A few Conservative women did participate in some of these non-party internationally-based organizations—for example Nancy Astor who was active in the International Women's Alliance—but they were the exception rather than the rule. Conservative women were only tenuously linked to this institutionalized feminist internationalism and feminist pacifism.

Conservative women's interpretation of fascism

If we want to determine how Conservative women reacted to appeasement, we need to understand how they interpreted fascism. How did Tory women relate to the home-grown variety in the form of the British Union of Fascists (BUF)?[78] In the middle of the decade there was a feeling that the Party was in direct competition for certain types of members. They came to understand that just because they shared an enemy in Socialism that did not make Tories and Blackshirts natural allies, and Mrs Montague, a Conservative Central Office speaker addressing the CWA in Exmouth, warned that "We Conservatives must watch these Blackshirts, for it is our vote they are most likely to catch."[79] The Conservative Mrs Bell Cairns was concerned that her Bristol East Branch might have to close down if it could not secure more funding from the Party's central administration, especially as the Fascist Movement was attracting the young men of her district and they only had to pay 12 shillings in annual subscriptions to the BUF.[80] Indeed, shortly after the BUF's Olympia rally in June, 1934, the party leader, Stanley Baldwin himself was alert to the Blackshirt threat, issuing this warning to his followers:

> The policy of Fascism is what you may call an ultramontane Conservatism. It takes many of the tenets of our Party and pushes them to a conclusion which, if given affect to, would, I believe, be disastrous to our country. But it has taken from the Continent one thing that is completely alien to the Englishman, and that is a desire, ultimately, common to the Communists, to suppress opposition and to be able to proceed by dictatorial methods.[81]

While not in such numbers as would ever be a cause for serious concern, the allure for some of British Fascism as a more militant conservatism which could appeal to youth did tempt them away. The Labour Party Questionnaire of 1934 found that the Labour party was not too likely to lose many of its members to the new Blackshirt movement, while at the grass roots the BUF was arousing the attention and support of local Conservatives, many of them women.[82]

Nonetheless, an examination of the administrative records of the Conservative Central Women's Advisory Committee and local women's organizations tends to suggest the relative absence of interest in fascism, both national and international variants. The exception to this was in the North West where the Women's Advisory Committee for Lancashire, Cheshire, and the Westmorland Provincial Area, felt compelled to pass the following, still rather anaemic, resolution in 1934: "That in the opinion of this Conference, neither Fascism nor any form of Dictatorship is a suitable method of Government in this Country."[83] They were very much in tune here with the party leadership. Stanley Baldwin stressed the similarity of Fascism and Communism, describing them as "those two alien plants."[84] A year later the same branch resolved that it "is of the opinion that the Fascist Movement is not in accordance with the democratic principles of Government as established in this country."[85] The same branch recorded an interesting discussion that took place after their 9 July meeting on 'The Progress of Fascism in the North-Western Area,' and at their subsequent annual conference in October, 1934, the first subject for discussion was 'The Dangers of Fascism to our Party and to our Country.' Arguably, local circumstances rather than a heightened awareness of international politics accounts for the greater concern about fascism among Conservative women in the North West. The BUF had a conspicuous presence in the region. Its Northern regional headquarters were opened in 1934 (although they closed in 1937); much of the BUF's focus of recruitment shifted to the North-West after failures in the South and in the hope of making political capital out of the unemployment crisis in the textile industry; with Mosley even contemplating moving the national headquarters to Manchester.

Otherwise, among the records of other branches of the CWAs the term 'fascism' was rarely used; the term 'dictatorship' did appear from time to time, but as a blanket expression meant to refer to extremes of both Left and Right, appearing with greater regularity as war loomed. The consistent enemy was the 'Socialists,' the whole spectrum of left-wing politics from the Labour Party to the Communist Party of Great Britain and its alleged publicity machine the Left Book Club. Instead, Tory women encouraged their members to join the competing Right Book Club, founded in early 1937 by Christina Foyle of bookshop fame, the thread of whose publications was "defence of 'traditional values,' anti-Communism and pro-appeasement."[86] Conservative women's anti-communism continued almost unabated through the war itself, illustrated by some resistance on their part to make any significant contribution to Mrs Clementine Churchill's Aid to Russia Fund, believing that while what was once a non-party organization was now being taken over by the Left, and Conservative women "finding themselves outnumbered, outvoted and literally swamped by the unscrupulous activities of those who put Party first and country afterwards."[87] Throughout the period anti-Communism was a more significant strain in Conservative thinking than anti-Fascism, and this no doubt accounts for the ease with which women in the party accepted Chamberlain's vision of Hitler as a figure who could be trusted. Their ability to give Hitler the benefit of the doubt was also facilitated by the reports and accounts given by women among their number who visited Germany, studied there, and enjoyed the hospitality of the Nazi public relations machine on carefully orchestrated tours and events.

Conservative women, the LNU, and the politics of peace

Where did Conservative women position themselves on the thorny issue of peace and peace politics? They belonged to a movement that is not usually associated with pacifism, and there is plenty of evidence to suggest that Conservative women were hostile to the pacifist movement as such, and ambivalent about the League of Nations Union. Still, all political parties represented themselves as a pro-peace party, and in its appeal to women the Conservatives made clear that it:

> is a party of peace: While it has consistently striven—and will continue to strive—to secure reductions of armaments by international agreement, the Conservative Party recognises that the country must be made strong in its defence if its safety is to be ensured and its voice is to be treated with respect throughout the world. A policy of rearmament must, however, be accompanied by positive endeavours to remove by negotiation and conciliation the suspicions, injustices and fears that are the underlying causes of war.[88]

Until late into the 1930s 'pacificism' represented the mainstream position in the population at large, and even many leftist anti-fascists argued against rearmament until the late 1930s, and the electorate had consistently supported party programmes dominated by the peace message. Yet Conservatism jarred with absolutist pacifism that tended to be associated with leftist cowardice and shirking, or internationalism that was associated with Judaeo-Communist conspiracies and malevolent anti-national tendencies. Finishing her memoir in October, 1938, Lady Londonderry waxed lyrical about "the engrained habit of being able to take sudden responsibilities, such as Mr Chamberlain recently displayed,"[89] and she made a very clear distinction between Conservative appeasement and leftist peace activism.

How did Conservative women feel about the League of Nations Union, the most popular and successful non-party organization to emerge from the Great War, and invested with the hope that the elitist secret diplomacy that led to war could be replaced by a democratized international system? If the mantra of the 1930s was 'collective security,' Conservative women were not doing a very good job at reciting it. Pugh has noted that in the mid-1920s right-wing Conservative women treated the League of Nations with suspicion, seeing it as a threat to the Empire and Britain's imperial authority.[90] While the Conservative Central Women's Advisory Committee did send a representative to the League of Nations Union, Mrs Wilson-Fox, its attitude to the LNU was usually non-committal. For example, the Committee's response to appeals on behalf of Spanish victims or Czech refugees was lukewarm at best, if not dismissive of the suffering of foreigners. In fact, it does appear to be the case that Conservative women sought representation in the LNU in order to monitor the organization, rather than to collaborate with it. Conservative Women Organizers saw the importance of sending representatives to meetings of the LNU and the Peace Council, and stressed that these women must be of "strong conservative principles and prejudice, as otherwise if weaker representatives are sent to such meetings, they sometimes get impressed with the views of the other side."[91]

Even more worrying than the possible penetration of fascist ideas was that of pacifist ones. At the local level, this tenuous connection with the LNU was seen by some to be an issue, and Conservative women in the North-West passed a resolution in November 1937 stating that their conference "recognises the vital importance of creating sound opinion on peace problems and feels there is need for more individual Conservative support in the branches of the LNU."[92] At the national level, however, when questions were raised concerning the International Peace Campaign and the organization of Peace Weeks, "Lady Falmouth stated that the question of participation in Peace demonstrations needed careful consideration, but that on the whole the Central Office thought it was advisable to take part, where possible, in order to try to keep the movement on the right lines."[93] While Marjorie Graves was very involved with the Peace Week organized in Barnstaple where she was the Conservative prospective parliamentary candidate, and these Peace Weeks were held in 111 places, the LNU recognized that they were not universally popular with all their affiliate organizations, and in High Wycombe, for instance, "Conservatives and British Legion refused to take part."[94] But even taking part mainly in order to keep the LNU on the straight and narrow became problematic a year later. This was because "lately the LNU has organised Peace Weeks in conjunction with the National Peace Campaign and PPU, and that both of these organisations are Communistic in outlook, Party Headquarters now advise constituencies not to take part in Peace Weeks."[95] As late as June 1939 the Women's Advisory Committee agreed "they did not wish to take any further part in the birthday celebrations of the LNU, either by sale of stamps or attendance at the mass meeting in December."[96] It is thus little surprise that the Committee discontinued their representation on the LNU in October 1944, deeming the organization of little account.[97] Overall, Conservative women were diffident about the international system and women's potential to affect change within it, and mercurial on the whole question of peace. Their wariness of the League of Nations is quite understandable, especially given their party perspective. During these years it was at Geneva that pacifist feminists found a voice, demonstrating for disarmament, leading on peace missions, and opposing imperialism, hardly the central concerns of Conservative policy.

'Guilty women' at the grass roots of the conservative party

How did Conservative women respond to the policy of appeasement and react to the rapidly changing circumstances of the deepening crisis? The appeasement debate was highly gendered, and we see again this rather too neat bifurcation between feminine pacifism—and the equation of women with their essentialist biological identities (mother, wife, and sister) with support for peace at all costs—against masculine belligerence and hotheadedness that risked international conflict. Of course, this gendered configuration was not confined to the Right, and it had been expressed by feminist pacifist movements since before the First World War and in the years that followed. For example, in 1915 Catherine Marshall told the ILP in Bradford that "the sense of common motherhood of women which the Women's Movement is awakening will, when fully realised, make it impossible for one nation to shoot down the sons of another."[98]

If the records of the Conservative women's associations are a guide, Conservative women had little influence on policy-making nor did they seek to challenge paternalism, all the more striking given the party's great success in mobilising and organizing women. Conservative women represented themselves as loyal supporters of the party leadership, with aspirations neither to question the male leadership nor to raise their own status in the party hierarchy. The sentiment was one of deferential gratitude, as exemplified by this 'Crisis Letter' addressed to the Prime Minister's wife by members of the Ladies Grant Council of the Primrose League, expressing:

> to you the deep and heartfelt admiration which we all feel for your husband for the way he has handled an international situation almost without parallel in the World's History. We, together with millions of women of all nationalities, owe him a debt of gratitude impossible to compute in mere terms of words.[99]

Indeed, it seems that, at the local level, support for Baldwin and then for Chamberlain was much stronger and more defensive than support for the wartime Prime Minister, Winston Churchill. What is certain is that there is little evidence that there were many women Churchillians within the party before 1940, although in Chapter 9 we will be making the acquaintance of an eclectic, growing, and distinguished group of women who followed Churchill's star from outside it.

One of the more outspoken and proactive branches, the North-Western Provincial Area, energetically endorsed appeasement, resolving that they "heartily appreciate the services to this country and to the cause of peace rendered by Mr Neville Chamberlain," but with the proviso of "an extended re-armament programme and of comprehensive defensive measures" to maintain peace and security. "They earnestly hope that a scheme will be introduced at an early date to organise, in time of peace, the work of national service of every able-bodied citizen so as to achieve the maximum of national effort in time of war."[100] In fact, it was two women from this branch who respectively moved and seconded the resolution thanking the Prime Minister for his untiring efforts on behalf of world peace, assuring the Government of their whole-hearted support of their foreign policy at the CWA conference in May, 1939. Miss E Evelyn Pilkington "said that Mr Chamberlain no more wanted to crush the German nation than we wanted them to crush us. He was a man of peace to the depth of his soul." Similarly, Mrs Worrall "declared that when history came to be written the honesty and statesmanship of the Prime Minister would shine out against the perfidy and treachery of Hitler."[101]

Chamberlain's popularity with conservative women

Indeed, Chamberlain's rapport with Conservative women is unimpeachable. Chamberlain had been popular with the women of the nation from the 1920s with the success of the Housing Act (1923) which had led to the construction of 150,000 homes. As Minister of Health in the late 1920s Chamberlain continued to play to women. For example, when he addressed a mass meeting of 2,000 women at Kingsway Hall, London, to introduce the Government's far-reaching measures for reform of the Poor Law, he was "assured of a rousing reception, for no minister has played a bigger part in securing those social reforms in which women have an outstanding and direct interest," such as the Widows,' Orphans,' and Old-age Contributory Pensions Act, the record erection of houses, and the vast improvement of the public health service.[102] It was presumed that Chamberlain had benefitted from a surplus of women voters in his wealthy residential constituency of Edgbaston where "there are 7,000 more women voters than men" and which returned the Premier at the 1935 General Election with a majority of 21,000 votes.[103] By the late 1930s, lacking the glamour, the youthful vigour, or the Romantic heroic potential of the younger and defiant men in his own party, Chamberlain was instead a trusted father figure, a protector, a soothsayer who empathized and was in turn himself comforted by the nation's women. As the Palestinian Ragheb Nashashibi told Chamberlain: "Your excellency [sic] has everywhere acquired the title The Father of peace."[104]

Starting at the level of his constituency of Edgbaston, in early October, 1938, an adoption meeting "was really devoted to an attempt on our part to express our thanks and our gratitude to you [Mr Chamberlain] for all you have done during these last weeks." The:

> feeling of the meeting went far beyond anything the wording of the message can convey ... Nearly half the people there spoke and the women in

particular ... sent their most affectionate good wishes to Mr Chamberlain and their thanks for the great part he has played. I think the general sentiment of the Meeting can best be summed up in the words of one elderly lady who just stood up and said 'It is impossible to tell him how much we thank him.'[105]

Throughout the autumn and winter of 1938 and 1939, across the country the meetings of Conservative women celebrated their Prime Minister.

In the absence of systematic files for the CWA in the Conservative Party papers, reporting in local newspapers opens a window on the mood and content of these self-selecting but still public meetings. Messages to and from the PM, generously covered by the pro-appeasement national and provisional press, emphasized the intimate connection between Chamberlain and women in the party. So, for instance, when Mrs O. Boonham, chairman of the Tamworth CWA, sent a letter to Chamberlain expressing her appreciation for his success in averting war, she was only too delighted to receive a reply from him as follows: "Please accept my very warm thanks for your kind message. During these difficult and anxious times through which we have been passing, the expressions of sympathy and goodwill which I have received from all quarters have been a source of great strength to me."[106] The relationships cultivated were not so much chivalric romances but considering Chamberlain's age and his self-styling as a respectable figure from a pre-flapper by-gone age, the more apt analogy might be with the Electra complex. Nor was this tale going to end with happily ever after, and in due course the fairy story of wishful thinking was unmasked for what it was. This is not just me getting carried away on the white horse of extended metaphor, because fairy tales were very much in the public consciousness at this time, and especially at the cinemas with the blockbuster success of Disney's *Snow White* (released December 1937 in the USA and the highest grossing film to date). We will explore this very public love affair further in the chapters to follow, seeing how women's opinion and their putative electoral choices when given the opportunity of expression in by-elections suggest that the tryst between Chamberlain and the women of Britain was more than just salacious rumour and extended beyond the Conservative family.

Up and down the country women Conservatives showed their consistent and unquestioning support for appeasement, their meetings becoming thanksgiving celebrations for the Prime Minister. At the Hull Women's Conservative Club it was a woman expert on Czechoslovakia who had lived in and studied the conditions in the country, Miss Caytor, who gave a vivid presentation on its history and geography, leading to loud applause for Chamberlain by concluding that "If war had come we could not have saved Czechoslovakia."[107] At Twyning Mrs Atherton, who had visited Germany, had a favourable impression of the Nazi regime and recognized that "the people of [Czechoslovakia] had made enormous sacrifices to preserve peace and save lives. We in England, she said, must also prepare to make sacrifices in the same way." This was followed by the passage of a resolution conveying:

> hearty appreciation of the strenuous efforts of the Prime Minister for peace, and that it approves of any measures that he and the National Government may take to strengthen our Army, Navy and Air Force, and to organise the civil population so that a strong nation will help to ensure the future peace of the world.[108]

At the Cullompton Women's Section of the Conservative Association, enthusiastic endorsement of appeasement was brought together with light entertainment when a New Year's Eve party consisted of speeches congratulating Chamberlain for saving the peace with a performance by the Cullompton Women's Institutes Nigger Minstrels.[109] During the crisis it was clear that Conservative women worked hard to legitimize, rationalize, and promote Chamberlain's foreign policy, getting their heads around a policy that sought to balance appeasement with preventative rearmament.

'Women unionists are absolutely for Mr Chamberlain and his peace policy'

Conservative women showed their unquestioning support even after the Munich Agreement was proved to be an abject failure in March 1939. The Bristol North Unionist Women's Association sent a letter of confidence and trust to the Prime Minister, and Mrs Robinson White remarked that "Mr Chamberlain has said that he will work unceasingly to bring peace to this country, and we, in our turn, must do all we can to support him. He is our leader, and we give him our full trust" she said.[110] Similarly, Mrs J.H. Dent Brocklehurst told women Conservatives in Cirencester that "We must put our faith in Mr Chamberlain and his Government in the present crisis."[111] In Dover the CWA enrolled 454 new members over the year just past, and Lady Violet Astor "felt very strongly that the less they talked or listened to rumour, and the more they backed up their Prime Minister, Mr Neville Chamberlain, the marvellous national leader that England was so fortune in having, the better. They could help by showing that they were united."[112] There was little dissension within the ranks in the CWA, with women expected to be the fixers in this kind of consensus politics.

Conservative women's loyalty was demonstrated further by their distancing themselves from the Tory rebels. Upon Eden's resignation in February 1938, for example, Mrs Trench of the Women's Branch in Poulton gave "a full account of the events that had led up to the recent crisis and spoke sympathetically of the difficulties confronting Mr Chamberlain, asking for the loyal co-operation of all those present in his support,"[113] while Lady Nancy Astor expressed her sympathy but not her support for Eden's resignation, which she regarded as an "unwise decision" and put down to "his being overwrought."[114] Viscount Cranborne, who had been Undersecretary for Foreign Affairs under Eden and who had resigned with his chief in February, also emerged as a critic of the Munich agreement in and outside Parliament, in the process threatening "a split in the Conservative Party in South Dorset." He was eager to answer his critics at a meeting in Weymouth on 12 October, delivered to Conservative women who were waiting to start a whist drive. While he offered Chamberlain some faint praise, he objected to the phrase 'peace with honour' for "it means that it is a peace which has added lustre to our country and enhanced its position," which it had not. "Rearm, rearm, and rearm," was his alternative. "Mrs D.F. Daw and other women leaders tried to persuade him to remain silent but he said, 'I am determined to speak.' His speech was heard in silence. At the end there was a vote of thanks, but the chief applause was given for Mr Chamberlain."[115]

Similarly, the Carlisle CWA cancelled a meeting where Leo Amery was to speak in protest at his abstention from voting in the House on the motion of confidence in the Government in the Munich agreement. The Chairman in Carlisle claimed that while they had no personal objection to Amery "we women Unionists are absolutely for Mr Chamberlain and his peace policy, and are nervous about Mr Duff Cooper, Mr Churchill, and Mr Eden, because we fear their policy may lead to war.'"[116] We have already seen how Amery's own wife Florence was ranked with the appeasers, and how she did not "follow his reasoning."[117]

While selflessly devoted to her husband and keeping her opinions to herself in this matter, her point of view is further evidence of the feminine reaction to appeasement and women's gratitude to Chamberlain. Conservative women felt an intimate connection with Chamberlain and with appeasement, and felt especially nervous in the company of anti-appeasers.

What patterns can be discerned in the relationship between Conservative women and foreign policy? First, it was more often the custom for men to address Conservative women on matters of foreign affairs, and usually with at least a touch of condescension. Second, Conservative women's political education was very much top down, and their deference was expected, towing the party line on foreign policy as obedient daughters and grateful wives rather than as independent free-thinking citizens. Third, Chamberlain enjoyed a love affair with women in the party, and this was projected onto women in the electorate. The relationship between Neville and Annie Chamberlain and the women's sphere of the party was especially strong from the start. In 1920 Annie Chamberlain was already addressing the mass meeting of women at the National Unionist Association, and when in the 1920s many Conservative Party clubs clung to male exclusivity, women took their own initiatives in single-sex 'clubability,' and among the women's clubs formed was one by Annie Chamberlain in Birmingham. At conference Mrs Chamberlain told Conservative women: "I have always been a worker in politics like you. I have not spent the whole of my married life, as some have suggested, in darning my husband's socks," and she came across as a diligent party worker.[118] In a similar vein, Neville Chamberlain was aware of the overwhelming success of the WUO which was revealed in his 1931 investigation of the party's organization.

The appeasement policy appeared to have only increased female recruitment for the party, and there was a rise of 4,000 subscribing members for 1938; at the end of 1938 there were 135 constituencies employing Women Organizers, as compared with 117 in 1937; women speakers were sent by headquarters to address 3,698 meetings, in addition to the thousands of meetings held in Women's Branches and Sections; and for 1938 the circulation of *Home and Empire* was nearly 223,000, an increase of nearly 9,000 over 1937.[119] These increases might be explained away by suggesting the logic of an upsurge in women's politicization with the coming of war, but it is just as convincing to argue that is was indicative of Chamberlain's popularity among women.

While some examples have been provided of Conservative women taking the initiative in foreign affairs, overall the impression one gets is that Conservative women cultivated a position of isolationist parochialism when facing the challenges of the international crisis. This is not to ignore the attention paid to foreign affairs in their political education, but in relative terms it was far less than that conferred on this sphere in women's education in the other parties. Their spirit of insularity was further exemplified by their apparent lack of involvement in philanthropic efforts on behalf of the victims of fascism.[120] Conservative women were truly Chamberlain's handmaidens, and thus great defenders of the policy of appeasement, the 'guilty women' *en masse* committed to a traditionally subservient and overly trusting marriage with the 'guilty men.'

The guiltiest of all: British fascist women and appeasement

However, at the fringes of the Conservative Party and where certain elements of the party blended with Britain's fascist movement, we do encounter women who were less acquiescent and readier to take risks in the name of their deep conviction that Britain should not go to war with Nazi Germany. Women in the British Union (BU) spearheaded the movement's peace campaign, launched with the 'National Campaign for Britain, Peace and People' in September 1938. Awaiting Neville Chamberlain's return from the Munich conference, BU mothers demonstrated with a poster parade in Whitehall; their pickets read "Our Children Were Young in 1914 – Have We Brought Them Up for War?"[121] At least one Fascist woman joined countless other Britons in the outpouring of personal gratitude immediately after Chamberlain's return, Daisy di Mobilant penning a 'Crisis Letter' to this effect:

> The Premier's photo that I owe to your kindness has been on my table all through these weeks of ordeal: and I wish to let you know that we fascist women look up to this real english [sic] statesman, above and outside parliamentary strife, and know he is holding vigil where the spirit is needed and senses are taut.[122]

But this appreciation for government policy was short-lived.

BU women were openly contemptuous of the Government for calling on women to volunteer and organize for an imminent national emergency, increasingly setting themselves apart as dissidents and revolutionaries. They were particularly derisive of the WVS, ARP, and the alleged frivolity towards these exemplified by "fashionable gas parties" in Mayfair that provided "novelty for jaded debutants."[123] Fascist women differed from their Conservative counterparts by wholeheartedly supporting Mosley's Peace Plan, which necessitated a commitment to a campaign that was incrementally subversive and anti-government. However, they mirrored Conservative women in their unquestioning devotion to their leader, even if they exercised some independence in organizational terms.

Women's contributions to the BU press during the Munich Crisis hardly exuded enthusiasm or approval for Chamberlain. Florence Hayes highlighted the estimated cost of the crisis week as £40,000,000, and lamented "what could we have done with a grant of that nature?—houses for workers, homes for the aged, schools, sanatoria." Revealingly, this was not mere parochial isolationism, and it thinly veiled the real point, which was the undesirability of provoking the fascist powers whom she admired. Hayes continued: "how very unnecessary it seems to spend it on precautionary measures against a nation that only desires our friendship."[124] BU women felt more than ever alienated from women politicians representing other parties, although their ire was directed more at the Independent Eleanor Rathbone, and Labour's Ellen Wilkinson, than at the Conservative Miss Horsbrugh, who, at a meeting of the Women's International League, was credited with having expressed "most nearly the sentiments of British womanhood."[125]

A more organized form of government opposition was inaugurated when BU women launched their Women's Peace Campaign at a public meeting at Holborn Hall on 28 February 1940, the BU's first large-scale indoor meeting to be organized, addressed, and stewarded entirely by women. This meeting was followed by week-end rallies on the afternoons of 3, 10, and 17 March, throughout parts of London. At a women's peace meeting at Friends' House on 13 April 1940, Mary Allen, ex-suffragette and Commandant of the Women's Auxiliary Service who had openly joined the BU in December 1939, gave an address. By May 1940, with the passage of Defence Regulation

18B 1 (a) many of these women were interned as their work for 'peace' was deemed a threat to national security.[126]

While rank-and-file BU women were beyond the pale, there was more overlap at the elite level between women Tories and the pro-German pressure groups, in which women could play active roles in this kind of auxiliary diplomacy. According to Richard Baxter, members of the pro-Nazi Anglo-German Fellowship "came back to England impressed by all they had been shown in Hunland, thoroughly blinded and bluffed, and the women amongst them worked harder than before to advance the cause which the Nazis were so anxious to see prospering in this country."[127] The overwhelming majority of members of the Anglo-German Fellowship and The Link were Tories, some of them even members of the Prime Minister's own family. Neville Chamberlain's cousins, Alderman and Mrs Byng Kenrick of the Birmingham branch of The Link lent their garden at the Grove, Harborne, for a meeting of the branch in July 1938.[128] Griffiths claims that the Birmingham branch, where Miss Margaret Bothamley (also a member of the Nordic League) was its secretary, was one of the most violently pro-Nazi and anti-Semitic branches of The Link. The membership list of the treacherous and noxiously anti-Jewish Right Club consisted of 100 'ladies' and 134 men.[129]

The imminence of war drew some Conservatives much closer to British Fascists, illustrated well by the guest list at a dinner party hosted by Diana and Oswald Mosley on 26 July, 1939, which included MPs sympathetic to the BU, pro-Nazi journalists, and prominent pro-Nazi and anti-Semitic personalities connected with the Anglo-German Fellowship, the BU, The Link, and the Nordic League. As reported in the *Evening Standard*: "Lady Mosley emerged last night as a new political hostess. She and Sir Oswald gave a dinner party at their house at 129 Grosvenor Rd."[130] However, the pattern to be discerned is of the odd Tory joining in ill-advised partnerships with British fascists, while there is very little evidence of British fascists infiltrating the Conservative Party.

Conclusion

The sociable and non-confrontational forums in which Conservative women met and oiled the party electoral machinery did not lend themselves to the politics of dissent or to polarizing debates. The CWA was the essence of appeasement, as the form of political engagement complemented the content of political ideas and policy. Considering the influence and political success of the Conservative Party, much of which comes down to its masterful if not entirely intentional mobilization of women in the post-1918 period, the limited range of the scholarship on Conservative women is surprising. Of this historiography, most of it is focused on the 1920s and early 1930s and therefore preoccupied with the Tory construction of women's citizenship after the two extensions of suffrage to women in 1918 and 1928. Especially during the first decade or so after the First World War, Conservative women were relatively speaking uninterested in European affairs, other than a sometimes paranoid fascination with the new Soviet Union and the alleged intrigues of its agents and would-be-emulators closer to home. But there has been very little research on Tory women in the late 1930s and their 'special relationship,' both with the architect and the dissemination of the policy of appeasement. How can we explain this gender gap? Perhaps it is because all the focus shifts to the Guilty Men and to the Conservative party and foreign policy, where it has hitherto been more difficult—or the will was just not really there—to identify the women protagonists in the narrative. And we are back to that same problem in that the area most neglected in the study of appeasement, public opinion (other than in its formal expression through the organs of the press) has received, until very recently, only passing interest. The Tory anti-appeaser Robert Boothby called the Munich Agreement "the most cowardly and sordid act of betrayal ever perpetrated by a British or French Government. The fact remains that it had the full support of the British and French people,"[131] and for too long commentators have got away with such blanket condemnations.

   Women, women's organizations, and the women's associations of national organizations are regarded as minorities and in their cumulative form constitute public opinion—i.e., they have an ethereal presence and everyone in power thinks they know what they are thinking, but they have no power themselves, nor is there systematic or scientific collection and analysis of their views. The next three chapters are concerned with women's public opinion, the way it was constructed, the claims that were made in its name, how it was disseminated, politicians' exploitation and responses to it, and the emerging recognition of its value.

Figure 1   Peace delegates on their way to the International Congress of Women at The Hague in 1915 to campaign for a resolution to the international conflict
Source: Image from Historic Collection/Alamy.

Figure 2   Women MPs elected in 1931: (back row, left to right) Lady Astor, Mrs Helen Shaw, Mrs Tate, Miss Cazalet, Mrs W.J. Ward, Miss Ida Copeland, and Miss Horsbrugh. (front row, left to right) Mrs Runge, Lady Iveagh, the Duchess of Atholl, Miss Irene Ward, and the Hon. Mary Pickford
Source: Courtesy of the Nancy Astor Papers, University of Reading Library.

Figure 3 Targeting the 'Woman Voter': 1935 National Conservative General Election poster emphasizing what were presumed to be women's priorities of peace and security. Oxford, Bodleian Library, Conservative Party Archive: Shelfmark Poster 1935–14.

Figure 4 Feminist pacifist and internationalist Vera Brittain became a leading member of the PPU and was committed to an anti-war position throughout World War II
Source: Image from Mary Evans Picture Library/Alamy.

Figure 5 'Red' Ellen Wilkinson, Labour MP, Popular Front supporter, feminist anti-fascist, whom Richard Baxter regarded as one of the very few women who was not guilty
Source: Image from World History Archive/Alamy.

Figure 6 Lady Nancy Astor, first woman MP to take her seat in the House of Commons in 1919, and by 1937 hostess of the so-called Cliveden Set
Source: Image from Bert Morgan Archive/Alamy.

Figure 7 Cliveden House, seat of the Astor family and centre of the activities of the so-called Cliveden Set
Source: Courtesy of the Nancy Astor Papers, Special Collections, University of Reading Library.

135

Figure 8 David Low, "Where Our Foreign Policy Comes From," *Evening Standard*, 23 March, 1938
Source: Courtesy of the Nancy Astor Papers, University of Reading Library.

Figure 9 Virginia Woolf, whose feminist pacifist *Three Guineas* had been published in June, experienced the Munich Crisis as an emotional cycle, concluding that 30 September, 1938, was "a very fine day"
Source: Image from Heritage Image Partnership Ltd/Alamy.

Figure 10 Eleanor Rathbone, feminist, anti-fascist, and anti-appeasement 'Glamour Girl'
Source: Courtesy of the Eleanor Rathbone Papers, Special Collections, University of Liverpool Library.

Figure 11 The Munich Agreement was described as 'poisonous as Snow White's apple,' referencing the block-buster Disney film *Snow White and the Seven Dwarfs* (1937) that was still playing at cinemas during the Munich Crisis
Source: Image from Pictorial Press Ltd/Alamy.

Figure 12 David Low, "The Dashing Young Man and the Flying Trapeze," *Evening Standard*, 2 March, 1938
Source: British Cartoon Archive, University of Kent.

Figure 13 Poster-father of Peace: "The Man of To-day" poster with Neville Chamberlain on the steps of an aeroplane prior to his departure for his second meeting with Hitler, 22 September, 1938
Source: Cadbury Research Library: Special Collections, University of Birmingham.

139

Figure 14 David Low, "Mein Kampf," *Evening Standard*, 24 September, 1938
Source: British Cartoon Archive, University of Kent.

Figure 15 Neville Chamberlain declaring "peace in our time" upon his return from the Four Powers Conference in Munich
Source: Image from INTERFOTO/Alamy.

Figure 16 The Adulation of the Women of Britain: Anne Chamberlain in front of 10 Downing Street after the signing of the Munich Agreement, 30 September, 1938
Source: Cadbury Research Library: Special Collections, University of Birmingham.

THANK YOU MR CHAMBERLAIN

Figure 17 The world's gratitude: postcard of Neville Chamberlain [September, 1938]
Source: Cadbury Research Library: Special Collections, University of Birmingham.

Figure 18 Public Support for the Munich Agreement: Car procession and cheering crowds in London, 30 September, 1938
Source: Cadbury Research Library: Special Collections, University of Birmingham.

Figure 19 The Roaring Crowd: Neville Chamberlain arriving back at 10 Downing Street in the evening after seeing the King at Buckingham Palace, greeted by large crowds
Source: Cadbury Research Library: Special Collections, University of Birmingham.

Figure 20 The *Vox Populi* on Appeasement: Anne Chamberlain greeted by large crowds on Downing Street before her walk in St. James's Park after the signing of the Munich Agreement, 30 September, 1938
Source: Cadbury Research Library: Special Collections, University of Birmingham.

Figure 21 Neville Chamberlain helping Anne Chamberlain out of car on his return to Downing Street (Central Press Photos Ltd)
Source: Cadbury Research Library: Special Collections, University of Birmingham.

Figure 22 For the Mothers and the Children: Before leaving for Chequers, Neville and Anne Chamberlain talking to a girl outside 10 Downing Street, 1 October, 1938
Source: Cadbury Research Library: Special Collections, University of Birmingham.

146

Figure 23 Neville and Anne Chamberlain, Lord Halifax, Edouard Daladier and others on an official visit to France, November, 1938
Source: Cadbury Research Library: Special Collections, University of Birmingham.

Figure 24 Ever popular with the French people, Anne Chamberlain presented with flowers on a visit to France in November, 1938
Source: Cadbury Research Library: Special Collections, University of Birmingham.

Figure 25 Mother and child wearing gas masks (1939). Populations were preparing themselves for, as Viscount Halifax put it when he addressed the House of Lords on 2 October, 1938, a European war in which "men, women and children would have to take part in the dance of death"
Source: Image from INTERFOTO/Alamy.

148

Figure 26 Neville and Anne Chamberlain outside 10 Downing Street buying a flag from Lady Malcolm on Trafalgar Day, 21 October, 1938
Source: Cadbury Research Library: Special Collections, University of Birmingham.

Figure 27   David Low, "Low's Christmas Dream," *Evening Standard*, 24 December, 1938
Source: British Cartoon Archive, University of Kent.

ALL BEHIND YOU, WINSTON

Figure 28 David Low, "All Behind You," *Evening Standard*, 14 May, 1940
Source: British Cartoon Archive, University of Kent.

Figure 29 Poster for *Mrs Miniver* (1942), the film based on Jan Struther's columns in
The Times
Source: Image from Photos 12/Alamy.

6

'Women Are the Best Friends of Mr Chamberlain's Policy:' Gendered Representations of Public Opinion

Michael Barsely's little ditty, "Mess Observation," brilliantly captures the sense of disarray within a middle-class British family in the fallout of the Munich Crisis:

> Ever since the Crisis came,
> Nothing's really been the same.
> Blight has settled on 'The Limes,'
> Father cannot trust *The Times*
> Mother, fresh from the *Express*,
> *Still* believes we're in a mess.
> Tom's been drinking with his lunches,
> Dick's developed awful hunches,
> Harry, if the truth be told,
> Looks preposterously old.
> Aunt Matilda says we must
> Stick to Chamberlain or bust,
> Captain Trumpet blames the Yids,
> Mildred says she won't have kids,
> George just goes on saying 'Spain,'
> Like an animal in pain.
> No one bothers to repair
> Household fittings anywhere,
> Precious ramblers go unpruned,
> Grand pianos go untuned.
> And it's eerie, after dark,
> By the trenches in the park.
> Advertisers all implore
> Everyone to purchase more,
> But the shade of Ribbentrop
> Wanders into every shop.
> In this year of 'peace and plenty'

No one's happy over twenty,
Joan's been fitted for a tunic,
On my heart is written 'Munich'—
Nothing's really been the same,
Ever since the Crisis came.[1]

Gently parodying Mass-Observation, this poem reveals as much through gallows humour as any contemporary poll about the divergences in public opinion along gender, class, generational, and ideological lines. Indeed, at the height of the Crisis the majority of British women were represented as Chamberlain's champions, and many among them were understood to support peace at any price. In the previous chapters we examined the intriguing intertwining biographical and institutional story of women's support for appeasement, identifying those individual women and groups of women whose presence has too often been obscured in accounts of the international crises that precipitated the Second World War. Even if we see Richard Baxter's *Guilty Women* (1941) as the rather crude piece of wartime propaganda that it is, a female version of the 'Guilty Men' narrative does provide an important corrective, and restores women to the plot of domestic and international politics in the late 1930s. But that is only one aspect of a gendered history of appeasement, and the next chapters resituate women within the cultural memory of the Crisis by examining the representations and self-representations of public opinion on appeasement. By so doing we gain some further insight into what 'Mother,' 'Aunt Matilda,' 'Mildred,' and 'Joan' thought and felt; how they and their like sought to convey their views and emotions to politicians and the press; and, in turn, how the agents of civil society portrayed them and then made efforts to satisfy them *en masse*.[2] It will become clear how dramatically gender affected the way that appeasement was discussed and the ways in which the Crisis was experienced.

The discussion of the gendered nature of public opinion and the Munich Crisis will be divided into three sections, according to source genre. This chapter focuses on representational sources, elite readings of public opinion as disclosed in textual and visual sources from newspapers, opinion polls, and the contrasting visions of public opinion in the imaginaries of those most closely involved in foreign policy debates. These are 'impressive' sources where an interpretation of response has been imposed upon women by others. Looking at elite opinion of public opinion is not the same as trying to drill down to the bedrock of popular sentiments, however, and the chapter to follow is based on expressive sources. These are more intimate means by which women from across the social spectrum were able to document spontaneous emotion and record immediate intellectual responses. Women's experiences of the Crisis and the coming of the war is preserved in two rich sources bases, Mass-Observation material, and in the Crisis Letters written to Neville and Annie Chamberlain. Third, we will look at how the appeasement debate was gendered in the series of by-elections in 1938–1939 that were together seen as a referendum on the Prime Minister's foreign policy. From these gauges of public opinion distinct and powerful constructs emerge, namely that British women as a group considered themselves to be the world's natural pacifists; that across class lines women showed disproportionate and gushing support for Prime Minister Chamberlain during the Munich crisis; and that, as a consequence, women also provided the most solid grass-roots support for the policy of appeasement.

Public opinion in the historiography of appeasement

Very little attention has been paid to both the real and the perceived gender differentials in public opinion at the time of the Munich Crisis, but then again, public opinion is one of the least studied aspects in the vast historiography of appeasement.[3] Why has the study of public opinion been the poor child in appeasement scholarship?[4] Dilks has explained how "the historian of the 20th century, who has more normally to bewail the abundance than the paucity of records, is forced to acknowledge that the sources for the study of public opinion between 1915 and 1940 are too patchy to allow of firm conclusions." More barriers come up when historians are faced with the task of defining public opinion and "it is an area in which the historian is peculiarly tempted into generalisation, or into judgements which can be made to fit his own inclinations, and a celebrated political scientist has detected more than 50 interpretations of the term."[5] Boyce suggests that in the period after the Great War "public opinion was equated with the masses, the crowd, its non-rational, emotional aspects were emphasised, and the competence of public opinion was questioned."[6] Pronay has delved deeper into politicians' anxieties about satisfying and educating the public about rearmament, but he too focuses on "the role of perceived public opinion."[7] Scholars have conducted case studies of particular projects or discrete moments to capture public opinion, such as the 'Peace Ballot,'[8] the Abdication crisis,[9] and the Munich by-elections,[10] but until recently there was no systematic survey.

Hucker's study is the first monograph to take public opinion and appeasement as its focus, although he confines himself to sources that reveal how public opinion was perceived by the political elite. His helpful taxonomy differentiates between 'reactive' representations of opinion, i.e., immediate responses to the public as represented to political elites by newspapers, police reports, election results, and printed material; and 'residual' representations, i.e., retrospective sources and mainly printed. He is not interested in public opinion *per se* but "seeks to recreate the constituencies of opinion that informed and influenced policymakers."[11] It follows then from this top-down approach that Hucker underplays gender, asserting that women had "no impact on the foreign policy-making process," that "their influence was marginal," and that "representations of opinion that informed elite perceptions were dominated by a largely male and, moreover, a largely upper-middle-class establishment."[12] However, his conclusions are determined by his selection of sources, and while Hucker's work represents a breath of fresh air in terms of taking public opinion seriously, its assumptions about women are more stale. In the British case it is clear how invested women were in the appeasement debates, and how they exercised considerable influence on the Men of Munich. It would appear that the same was true in the French case. For example, when French PM Edouard Daladier travelled to Munich he had in mind a widely circulated anti-war petition disseminated by the largely feminized teaching corps, and in the months that followed many feminists were outspoken critics of peace at any price.[13]

The historiography of interwar British politics and especially the nature of citizenship after universal male and partial female (1918) and finally equal enfranchisement (1928) has increasingly been revised and rethought through the lenses (and often bi-focally) of gender and cultural history.[14] As a general trend, "in pointing to this role of gender in the signification and articulation of relationships of power, gender history has opened new paths of inquiry in political history."[15] In line with this approach, this chapter offers a gender and cultural history of domestic responses to Britain's entanglements in international politics. In addition, historians of women have contributed a great deal both to the narration and the demystification of the People's War. However, they have had far less to say about the years of intense ideological, intellectual, and emotional instability in the prelude to the war. Therefore this study should also be seen as providing a preface to the powerful narrative of the People's War, tracing the nation's journey from this 'People's Crisis' to the People's War.

Furthermore, by caring about what is being said about women and what women are saying about themselves, the approach here also proposes a paradigm shift in appeasement scholarship. The handful of historians who have studied the Crisis from the vantage point of public opinion have added a vital third dimension to what has very much been a two-dimensional tableau of elite appeasers versus anti-appeasers (and their respective progeny). When we add gender to the picture, a four-dimensional perspective on the Crisis emerges, and we can start to see appeasement in the round.

The *vox populi* and the democratization of foreign policy

Why have historians of appeasement been reluctant to study public opinion? One can suggest various explanations. From its outset, politicians and the educated public judged social scientific investigation of public opinion unreliable. While polling was an almost immediate popular success, the method encountered scepticism and even hostility from government officials.[16] Public-opinion polling began in Britain in 1937 with the launch of the British Institute of Public Opinion (BIPO) on 1 January by its director Henry Durant, only two years after Gallup, the first opinion-poll organization, was founded in the USA in 1935. Gallup polls were used and the method was shown to be predictive of the results of the 1936 American presidential election. Mass-Observation was also launched in 1937. Soon a rivalry developed between the latter two due to their very different methodologies.

For the British, suspicion about polling based on its novelty was compounded by its American origins. "Polls of public opinion taken by newspapers or organisations are not much favoured here, but in the United States such efforts to diagnose public opinion are taken quite seriously." This observation prefaced the reporting of one of the early Gallup polls conducted in Britain in March 1938 following Anthony Eden's resignation as Foreign Secretary. Significantly, the poll in question found that "women are the best friends of Mr Chamberlain's policy ... In favour of Mr Chamberlain's policy: men 21%; women 27%."[17] The BIPO qualified its findings by emphasizing that "the measure of public opinion is still in its infancy," and confined its claim to being able to show "a photograph of opinion *taken at a particular point in time* [italics in original]."[18] In point of fact, the results of their polls demonstrated the shifts within a short span of time in attitudes to fascism and communism respectively, in feelings about Chamberlain, and in morale during the early phase of the war. However, and for our purposes disappointingly, the BIPO did not offer a breakdown of opinion along gender lines on any but one question, and that was about attitudes to voluntarism. When in November 1937 they asked men "If there is another war, would you volunteer?" and women "Would you urge your husband to volunteer," 38% of men and only 22% women replied 'Yes,' against 62% of men and 78% of women replying 'No.'[19] Clearly the majority of women were not going to mobilize willingly for war.

At the time and since, public opinion is acknowledged to be fickle and measures of public opinion are regarded as not always reliable. That aside, it is important to note the extra weight this force of public opinion was gaining precisely at this time and because of the political crises. Whatever the shortcomings of techniques to measure public opinion, there was perhaps never as much curiosity about it, as many experiments to measure it, as frequent evocation of it being on the side of the speaker of the moment, and as much reliance on its guidance and notional good judgement than during the long months of Crisis.

There was a "time-lag between the advent of polling and its integration into political life," and anti-appeasers were especially keen to use public opinion polling data to substantiate their case, the Liberal *News Chronicle* leading the charge in October 1938 with the BIPO surveys. While "most of the journalistic establishment lined up behind Chamberlain's foreign policy, the polls were one of the few organs of public opinion that opposition MPs could point to as illustrating a strong anti-Hitler bias within the British public."[20] Complementing the development of devices for opinion measurement by Mass-Observation and BIPO, the *Illustrated London News* produced a 'Fever' Chart covering the 19 days between Hitler's Nuremberg speech on Monday, 12 September, and the Four Power Agreement signed at 12.30 a.m. on Friday 30 September, showing the percentile shift in probability for war and for peace.[21] The press certainly narrated the events of September, 1938, as a war of nerves.

Simultaneously, public interest in foreign affairs was understood to be at an all-time high, the culmination of the process of the democratization of foreign policy since the Great War. The institutional expression of "the internationalisation of British civil society"[22] was the popularly successful and non-party League of Nations Union, which by the late 1930s veered to the Left and vigorously opposed appeasement, while the launch of Air Raid Precautions (ARP) in the autumn of 1935 demonstrated government commitment to mobilize civic engagement for civil defence. According to Harold Nicolson, public opinion now made a difference to the conduct of foreign affairs as it had not done in the past because "the rapid expansion of aerial warfare, and especially the dreaded implications of bombardment, have convinced the British people that any future war will not be an affair of professional fighters but an affair by which every citizen will be directly menaced." This spurred demand for popular accountability in foreign policy—which continued to gain momentum with the 'Peace Ballot,' and popular mobilization around the Hoare-Laval episode and the bombing of Guernica—and:

> the British public today claims to exercise direct, and not merely indirect, sovereign powers in regard to foreign policy. Our external relations have thus been brought down from the cabinet room to the arena of party controversy; and the press as well as the propagandists have joined in the fray.[23]

Foreign policy debate was conducted across the country and across the social spectrum. For example, "three or four years ago a prominent member of the Government in private conversation in a Manchester political club said that at no time in his experience had the mass of the people taken so much interest in foreign affairs as they do in these days."[24] This was facilitated, of course, by radio, and Mass-Observation volunteer Miss French confided in her directive response on 24/25 September, 1938: "My knowledge of the crisis comes from the wireless, for I never miss any news bulletins that I can possibly have."[25] It was Conservative politician Cuthbert Headlam's experience too that "foreign affairs nowadays is the only thing which seems to exercise the minds of people."[26] Others felt that government was under its yoke, especially with regard to the languor of rearmament, and

The Times special correspondent, A.L. Kennedy, thought "real statesmanship, in the old sense of the term, resides rather in the dictators than in the democracies" because the former could "formulate long-distance policies & carry them through, & can up to a point defy ignorant public opinion."[27] In direct contrast, from the Left, it was emphasized that under the present constitution "policy is tempered by public opinion," however "Tory control of the greater part of the Press and other means of propaganda enable public opinion to be swayed to suit Tory policy,"[28] with the disastrous result that 'appeasement' was "the outcome of a policy akin to betrayal."[29] With both interest in public opinion and foreign affairs at all-time highs, it would seem natural to investigate more closely the intersection between the two.

Public opinion on foreign affairs issues was represented in starkly gendered terms. To start off with, despite the fact that ballot papers are inconveniently not gender differentiated, since women first got the vote there was much speculation about voting habits according to sex. Further, it was widely held that women's patterns of media consumption differed from that of their men-folk, and that women were considerably less interested in foreign affairs than their male counterparts. "Readership surveys found foreign politics to be one of the least-liked categories of news, especially among women."[30] While men took an interest in current affairs and sports, most newspapers provided women's sections, pages or columns full of fashion, domestic tips, and celebrity news. Indeed, advertisers sought to capitalize on the regrettable distraction the crisis had provided, expressing the view that "there can hardly be a woman who did not feel that she left something of the smoothness and ease of her looks behind at the time of the crisis. That is why beauty-gifts, gratefully received by any woman at any time, are particularly good this Christmas."[31]

The same was true of broadcasting. Indeed, feeding the public interest in international affairs, among both men and women, was not facilitated by the BBC which made the effort to avoid courting political controversy. Its reporting of the Munich Crisis was carefully censored. More generally, much of broadcasting was directed to a female listenership and these programmes barely touched upon current affairs and politics.[32] The situation was even worse in the USA as *Manchester Guardian* correspondent Mildred Tonge Brown found when she was tuning in to heavily commercialized American radio for news of the European crisis, and it was "in a frenzy that we twirled the dial to find any other station that was breaking into the morning's fashion hints and cooking recipes to bring last-minute news."[33] The European news was drowned out by swing music, the Lambeth Walk, baseball scores, and the only crises mentioned were the personal ones experienced by soap opera characters. It followed that in the context of 1938–1939, in an array of sources we find the polarization between men's and women's attitudes to war, to readings of the character and achievements of the Prime Minister, to the nature of support for Britain's foreign policy, and to the quality and pitch of political engagement at times of acute world crises. These representations were embedded in the perceived feminine predilections for peace, isolationism, and disengagement, while the masculine was epitomised as war-willing, oppositional, and confrontational. This dichotomy was reinforced by representations of the ordinary British woman as preoccupied by domestic issues, possessing an inferior political education, and being wilfully ignorant of the outside world. Indeed, it is vital to differentiate between sex and gender, and the attribution of feminine characteristics to men or masculine temperaments to women only reinforced the continued adherence to gender structures that unquestioningly overlapped with political hierarchies. This gender bifurcation both shaped the whole appeasement debate at home, and meant that, in a figurative sense, one of the first battles of the Second World War, of the 'People's War,' was, in fact, a battle of the sexes.

This was especially well exemplified in the popular press, and Bingham has offered an illuminating gendered reading of the coverage of the Sudetenland Crisis in the *Daily Mirror*, comparing the columns of 'Cassandra' (the pen name of William Neil Connor) with women's feature-writer Eileen Ascroft. Ascroft was a reporter-participant of the women's story of the Crisis, joining scores of other women who went to Westminster Abbey to kneel in front of the tomb of the Unknown Warrior. As Chamberlain and Hitler were meeting, her prayer (which, incidentally, the *Mirror* published again when war loomed in August, 1939) was as follows:

> O Lord ... we, the women of England, are on our knees to You today ... The storm clouds gather all around us and men talk and argue about peace and war. And we are afraid for our husbands and our sons and our dear ones. We are prepared to see them fight for justice—but we long for peace ... Hear the united prayer of the women of Europe. We are the mothers, Lord, who have cherished and loved our children ... We are wives ... we are sweethearts ... we are friends.[34]

During the 1930s editors were happy to draw attention to what was packaged as the 'woman's point of view,' and this made perfect sense when 957,000 women constituted 70% of the *Mirror's* readership (while men represented 70% of the readership of *The Times*). However, this kind of woman-focused coverage, steeped in the language of domesticity and maternal love, carried little discussion of actual events or the hard news of the unfolding Crisis. In contrast, 'Cassandra,' who had been the anti-appeasement voice of the *Mirror* since the Spanish Civil War, wrote 'like a man,' with access to insider diplomatic knowledge and recent experiences in both Berlin and Prague, articulating "a cynical, pragmatic masculinity, sceptical of grand rhetoric, traditional heroism, and the blandishments of the establishment, but also proudly patriotic and determined not to see grave international injustices go unpunished."[35] Surely it was encouraging that women were on the ascendency in the journalistic profession in this period, but it is also clear that those writing for the popular press did tend to reinforce rather than destabilize gender stereotypes. It would be left to a smaller cohort of women journalists and scholars, those who were practitioners of democratized and more equalitarian international relations, to cover the hard news of the crises and thereby contest these stereotypes.

The construction of the female public and women's public opinion

Nevertheless, what the agents of civil society meant when they used the terms 'public opinion,' 'popular opinion,' and 'popular feeling' lacked precision. More often than not they used the terms as shorthand for an amalgam of press reports, anecdotal evidence, subjective impressions, and wishful thinking. During the Abdication Crisis less than two years before Munich, Duff Cooper remarked how his peers went about gauging public opinion. He found it curious "how everybody who had sought the views of taxi-drivers, hairdressers, hospital nurses, clerks and servants had heard exactly what they wanted to hear, that is to say their own opinion."[36] Most politicians turned to newspapers as the main source to ascertain public opinion, employing clipping services to survey the national and regional press, and developing mutually beneficial personal relationships with editors and journalists.[37] Indeed, Cockett has made an irrefutable case for collusion between the appeasers and the press, although he does not differ from other historians in ignoring women's part in the story. Arguing that there was a conspiracy of silence between Chamberlainites, with Samuel Hoare taking the lead, and the newspaper proprietors and editors—the roles of arch conspirators played by Lord Beaverbrook owner of the *Daily Express*, and Geoffrey Dawson of the *Times*—about the whole Sudeten business meant that the press generously underwrote the Conservative Party's foreign policy. What was called 'public opinion' was almost entirely fabricated, and during the Munich Crisis large sections of the press "had clearly abandoned their role of articulating public opinion in favour of a religiously partisan support for Chamberlain." In so doing the press was "quite consciously spurning its popular mantle of 'watchdog of government' ... and was instead seduced by the glittering prize of political power."[38]

It was as a response to this collusion and due to the evident limitations and undemocratic implications of reading public opinion from these top-down sources that systematic public opinion polling and various social scientific experiments were launched at this precise historical juncture.[39] These were BIPO and Mass-Observation, the former offering less scientific but more qualitative and textured evidence of popular opinion. While newspaper editors, politicians, and pollsters invariably regarded the public as 'them,' Mass-Observation's impetus was to write 'the anthropology of ourselves.' However, it is also important to note that the protagonists in the appeasement story hardly ever referred to Mass-Observation or to opinion polls; their glimpses of public opinion relied on the time-honoured unscientific methods of information-gathering as detailed above.

But *who* was the public imagined to be? Which segments of the population did the umbrella term shroud? As I will argue here, the 'public' was now understood to include the female population, and in some cases it was even understood to be disproportionately constitutive of women, or it was feminized, and sometimes both.

In the context of the Munich Crisis, the press and politicians understood that 'public opinion' represented the views, the fears, the anxieties, and the homebound and domestic concerns of the nation, of the non-combatants. Grayzel has made the case that with the advance of aerial warfare, civilians—whom contemporaries usually signified as women and children—became targets of war rather than a group shielded from its impact. This process of signification, she argues, was something new during the First World War, when the rise of the expression 'home front' was gendered feminine, 'war front' where soldiers were to be found gendered as masculine.[40] Thus when Chamberlain was on his way to Munich for the "last supper" to "placate the greatest of all tyrants," he was going on behalf and in defence of "our mothers, our sweethearts, and our children [who] must cower and hide in holes in the earth from an appalling terror."[41]

If civilians were figured as women and children, and the home front was women's domain, where did things stand discursively by 1938 as the nation looked down the barrel of the anti-aircraft gun at another world war? The domestication of warfare became a clear leitmotif, as "the development of the bomber has brought the front line of war to the very doors of a nation which for centuries had been safe from invasion." The object of the bomber was "not to defeat the rival air force but to terrify into submission populations whose women and children and homes are attacked and destroyed by fire, explosives and gas."[42] Modern warfare represented the ultimate violation and the unsustainability of women's private sphere. It failed to differentiate between civilian and combatant, and likewise made no distinction between male and female. As the war clouds again hung over Europe, mothers who had been young during the First World War and who had daughters now in their twenties could hardly fathom what lay ahead for them, other than the tragic realization that death "will threaten their girls as swiftly as their boys."[43] A sort of sexual equality had been achieved through the spectre of shared suffering. It was taken as read that those being represented by this still relatively modern term—and 'public opinion' had so much added resonance when the relative freedom of its expression within mass democracies was inevitably contrasted with its violent suppression under dictatorships—were the women of the nation and the 'man on the street.' In David Low's political cartoons 'public opinion' was personified either by a man attired in aspirational lower-middle-class costume of overcoat and fedora hat, or by a sister (nurse).[44]

Both working-class men and women had been the beneficiaries of post-war franchise extension, and both cohorts had made fewer advances towards emancipation in its aftermath than their respective leaders had hoped. Disappointment with women was widespread. The ILP's Winifred Davies, for example, accepted that women had fought like Trojans for the vote, and so great things were expected of them for "if they can fight like cats and dogs before they have the vote, what will they not accomplish when they have won it? They have, actually, accomplished very little." On the Left there was understandable frustration that women either failed to vote or that large numbers voted Tory. "But the most pressing problem which is daily threatening the future of women is war ... And women look on with indifference ... An International League of Women, properly organised, could achieve more for the cause of Peace than the League of Nations."[45] The backlash against feminism was palpable, and as Helen Fletcher was told by one of the fathers at a children's party: "Liberty! It's not liberty we need but discipline ... And feminism, I didn't know anyone remembered the word. It belongs to bicycles and Battersea Park."[46] Outside election time, women turned to different and even innovative methods to communicate with their parliamentary representatives. Letter writing to politicians and diary-keeping on behalf of Mass-Observation were two energetic gendered exercises of power, and, paradoxically, at the same time compelling evidence of women's powerlessness. But there was a parting of ways between these two main constituencies of 'the public,' with the women of the people widely regarded to have sided with the appeasers, while the restive male working class was raring for a fight.

For example, this conflation of women and the public took both literal and figurative form in this report of the frantic scenes that greeted Chamberlain upon his return from Munich. The reporter:

> clung to the railing of No. 10, with perspiring men and women crushed against me on three sides. 'Pneumonia Corner' was now trying to make amends by providing us Pressmen with a Turkish bath. 'You are lunch,' said a colleague to a typical Cockney woman just behind me. 'This place is really reserved for the Press.' 'S'all right, guv'nor,' she replied. 'I'm in the press now.'[47]

This Cockney woman—this 'Jane Public,' this 'woman on the street'—stood proxy for the women of the nation. She became the public. Similarly, Virginia Woolf confided in her diary: "The obvious feeling everywhere We dont [sic] want this war. No glorification, as Mrs Dean [the smith's wife] remarked: the mouthpiece of the nation, as much as Chamberlain."[48] The growing recognition of women as the majority voice within public opinion makes sense in the first decades after women's suffrage. This was when women joined 'the public' as citizens, and when politicians needed to pay heed to what the new majority of the electorate thought. In 1918, 8,800,000 women were enfranchised, with a 3,000,000 male majority, but with the equal franchise in 1928 there were 2,000,000 more women than men among eligible voters. At the time it was felt, as the *New York Times* put it:

> that Britannia, not content with ruling the waves, has stepped ashore and intimated John Bull, politely but firmly, that the Englishman's house is no longer his castle, but hers. The United Kingdom, already bereft of the Irish Free State, has become—if not in actuality at least in prospect—a kingdom of women.[49]

These anxieties were not eased in the decade to follow, and Britain's female citizenry came in for harsh criticism and frequent condescension.

Despite the tireless efforts of women activists, the slow progress of women to be elected to political office was found to be attributable to "the indifference of women themselves" the world over.[50] This was the conclusion reached in a survey conducted by the International Federation of Business and Professional Women through its branches in 25 countries early in 1938. In the wake of the Crisis, S.C. Leslie's survey of "How the Public Thinks," in the anti-appeasement *Spectator*, suggested how "extremely difficult" it was for the minority of "politically active and interested to realise just how indifferent, and how passive, how many people are nearly all the time," and he honed in on the "politically backward status of the mass of women," those most bereft of "political consciousness." In his interpretation this "large class of ignorant or depressed persons is obviously a menace to a democracy, and a potential asset to dictators."[51] Leslie was profoundly worried about the influence of apathetic working-class women, identified them as a threat to an enlightened democratic consciousness, and by implication too as those responsible for a foreign policy that embraced the saviour of peace while condoning the aggression of dictators.

The sexual politics of the crisis

On the one hand, we see women's increasing visibility among those who constituted the public, and the accompanying ambivalence about it. On the other hand, we can also identify a process whereby this public was feminized and sexualized. Public opinion had to be led, it had to be seduced. It had to be made to submit. From the point of view of the pro-Chamberlain press, public opinion could even be creatively fabricated Pygmalion-like to serve policy. Upon his arrival in Munich, Chamberlain was "received a rapturous greeting from the German people."[52] In symbolic terms in Nazi Germany the massed crowd at great displays like the Nuremberg rallies was a woman, the leader her seducer or even her rapist, bringing the crowd to climax with his oration.[53] The British press evoked this rhetoric of sexual violence again during the Anschluss which was described as "the rape of Austria,"[54] and in March 1939 when the Nazis marched into Prague one headline read "the Rape and after."[55]

In the context of Britain's mass democracy we discern fewer overtones of sexual violence and domination, but nonetheless we see a feminized (and infantilized) public that requires patriarchal guidance, and in turn expresses its affection in romantic terms. Public opinion, in its formlessness, its naïvety, its whimsy, and its need to be courted and flattered was discursively linked to culturally constructed traits of femininity. By pandering to this feminized public opinion, by seeking arbitration rather than confronting Hitler, and by failing to come to the aid of Czechoslovakia or later even Poland, the appeasers too were feminized and exposed as less than men. From his privileged position inside the Cabinet, Duff Cooper detected that "Hitler has cast a spell over Neville."[56] From there on it did not take long for the ranked opponents of appeasement to feminize the whole policy, to feel that the nation had been emasculated at Munich, and to blame the women of the world for the whole diplomatic debacle. Richard Law, a leading parliamentary opponent of appeasement, alleged that it was the influence of women that had been the obstacle to a strong foreign and defence policy, and that they had "brought nothing but degradation and dishonour to politics."[57]

Chamberlain was consistently cast as the enemy of the young and of the working man, but as the best friend of the women. Liberal public intellectual Gilbert Murray alleged that "millions of young men" were filled with "savage mistrust of the PM's motives,"[58] but with only a few exceptions the women supported him. We will recall that women electors strongly backed the National Government, which in 1935 held 132 of the 134 constituencies where women voters composed more than 55% of the electorate. We also saw how Chamberlain relied on his personal popularity with women, earned since the 1920s for his progressive social policies.

It was entirely consistent then that Gallup poll data should show that support for Chamberlain was higher among women in March 1938. "Women, according to this survey, are the best friends of Mr Chamberlain's policy ... In favour of Mr Chamberlain's policy: men 21%; women 27%. Opposed: men, 60%; women 51%. Undecided: men, 19%; women, 22%."[59] The Gallup poll of October 1938 revealed "that PM Chamberlain is much more popular with Britain's women voters—who, incidentally, outnumber the men—than with men voters."[60] Pro-government Conservative candidates relied on this female franchise factor during the Munich by-elections. This gender pattern persisted as the Phoney War came to an end, and in the summer of 1940 on the vital questions on war and peace, BIPO found "the young were less militant than the old, and the women, of course, less so than the men."[61]

Crisis mothers and the mother of all crises

While the Conservative-dominated National Government failed to placate working-class popular opinion (and the dynamics here were both class conflict and that between youth and age, inside and outside Parliament), the appeasers took some solace from the belief that their actions satisfied women's public opinion, and that they were in harmonious union with all the world's mothers. In this vein Dino Grandi, Italian Ambassador in London, wrote a personal note to Chamberlain on 16 September, 1938, in admiration for what he was doing to "save our world from a catastrophe which only two days ago seemed to be inevitable, just because the situation was getting out of control of statesmanship." Grandi continued that "difficulties ahead are still so great, but you have broken the evil spell and millions of mothers in Europe and in the world over are blessing you to-day."[62] Similarly Nevile Henderson wrote from the British Embassy in Berlin:

> It was quite impossible for me to say in words this morning what I really felt. I was thanking Heaven that at this critical hour we had got a Man as Prime Minister. Providence has long been kind to England, but never more so than during this last month. Millions of women will tonight throughout the world be blessing you your courage and energy.[63]

His own ministers understood the Premier to embody civilized manhood, and in turn Chamberlain understood his nearest colleagues to represent archetypal males. Chamberlain regarded his Foreign Secretary Halifax as "an ideal companion for the occasion [of their visit to Rome in January, 1939] & made a great impression as the type of English Christian gentleman."[64] As the British press's paeans narrated the days of celebration after Chamberlain's return from Munich, it was the *Sunday Dispatch* that reiterated the diplomats' impressions, with the added corporeal imagery of feminine gushing, remarking that "the greatest gratitude of millions of mothers, wives, sweethearts pours out to feed a flood which will sweep Mr Chamberlain to a high pinnacle of history."[65] This evocation of mothers marked out a political space between the intimate and the public.

Women speaking for women in conservative organizations echoed these messages. The Ladies Grand Council of the Primrose League noted that due to Chamberlain's handling of the international situation "we, together with millions of women of all nationalities owe him a debt of gratitude impossible to compute in mere terms of words."[66] The Women's Institutes, with their motto 'For Home and Country,' warmly welcomed Chamberlain's efforts as a fulfilment of what was a women's desire for tranquillity and an end to anxiety: "The dark cloud of war hung over them, and they, as women, felt the terrible anxiety of wondering whether they would be called upon during the next few weeks to lose their nearest and dearest." The

WI's Lady Inglefield felt sure that it had been "the earnest prayers of the Empire and the work of the Prime Minister that brought about the peace."[67] Similarly, Sir Edward Benthall, prospective National Conservative candidate for the North-West Devon Division, told a Conservative women's luncheon meeting:

> I believe tremendously in the power of thought ... and I cannot help thinking that during those anxious days it was largely the unanimity of thought, particularly the thought of women throughout the various countries, and also the prayers of millions, which in the end probably unconsciously influenced Hitler to change his mind.

Benthall also remarked on the very different mood as compared to 1914, the absence of hysteria or jingoism, mainly because "everyone realised, and women in particular, that in the next war everybody would be involved. Women would not have only a passive role."[68] Women in the LNU were encouraged that a sense of sisterhood transcended national antagonisms and one contributor noted that:

> judging from letters from German friends of my own, the main reactions of German women during the week of crisis were deep gratitude for expressions of friendliness and sympathy for this side, a passionate longing for peace, and a very real appreciation of, and immense thankfulness for, Mr Chamberlain's efforts at conciliation.[69]

It was reported that at Godesberg the Premier had had "a hearty 'Heil' from mothers and elderly civilians, but from the vast crowd of youth and maidens in uniform, the reception was severely official."[70] Awaiting Chamberlain's return from Munich, women members of Mosley's British Union marched in a poster parade outside Whitehall, their posters reading 'Our Children Were Young in 1914: Have We Brought Them Up for War?' Upon his return from a visit to Germany as "sleuth," T.P. Conwell-Evans estimated that German opinion was still definitely favourable to Chamberlain, and growing less favourable to Hitler: "Esp: the mothers—they find their children are taken right away from them & made over to the State, probably to be used as cannon-fodder."[71] These accounts suggest that mothers had been those most moved by the Crisis, and those most relieved by the promise of 'peace in our time.'

The media certainly represented Chamberlain as the hero of mothers everywhere. The Prime Minister became an international celebrity with whom other world-class celebrities wished to be associated. Mistinguett, French chorus-line leader and "personification of Parisian gaiety, the star with £200,000 legs, friend of Kings and Princes," flew to London in mid-October to propose the health of Mr Chamberlain at the monthly literary luncheon at Grosvenor House.[72] Chamberlain was more than happy to fan the flames of French ardour, and he explained that the reason he had decided on a trip to Paris in November with Halifax and their wives was "to give French people an opportunity of pouring out their pent up feelings of gratitude and affection."[73] Indeed, among the waiting crowds outside the Gare du Nord where the Chamberlains and Halifaxes arrived were a number of delegations, "including several women's organisations" such as the French League for Women's Rights, "who were anxious personally to testify to their gratitude to Mr Chamberlain for his part in preserving the peace."[74] According to Nancy Astor, Lubska Kolessa, the world-class pianist who hailed from the Ukrainian part of Czechoslovakia, "adores the PM," and Astor was trying to arrange a soiree as Kolessa was "very anxious to play for him."[75] In these ways notable women gave their celebrity endorsements to appeasement.

In institutional terms, of course, the Crisis mobilized mothers specifically as facilitators of the various civil defence projects. Mothers were responsible for collecting gas masks for all members of the family, and instructing their offspring in their use. Mothers prepared themselves for voluntary service in ARP, in the WVS, and in the newly-formed ATS, among other organizations. And mothers were faced with a new quandary due to the nature of modern warfare: the evacuation of children. Local authorities realized that the evacuation of children would be a hard sell, and, in Preston for example, councillors were aware that "mothers would want to be with their children in an emergency."[76] Thus government propaganda and newspapers, such as the *Daily Mirror* extolled mothers to act "Now, Before it is Too Late," because it is "every mother's duty" to send her children to safety.[77]

Further, from our contemporary vantage point, we can also see the Munich Crisis as 'the mother,' as the rhetorical womb, of all post-1938 crises. From Suez in 1956 to Syria in 2013, to the Ukraine in 2014, Chamberlain has cast a long shadow; the 'Munich moment' is relived; public debate is framed by the bitter divisions of 1938 and by the shaming of men (and women) who, for whatever complex reasons, do not stand up to dictators; and in each subsequent crisis protagonists identify with those same moral and psychological dilemmas faced by politicians and the public confronting another war.[78] This would be the legacy of Munich, but in the short-term the world's mothers were seen to rejoice.

The gift (and giftware) of appeasement: commodifying crisis

After concluding the Munich Agreement Chamberlain was showered with gifts from around the world, and in one of her speeches Nancy Astor made much of the fact that "Portugal wants to put up a statue from 'Grateful Mothers.'"[79] The women of Brittany sent the Chamberlains a 'Livre D'Or' bearing 903 signatures of mothers, wives, and sisters of war veterans and young French soldiers as "a token of fervent admiration and deep gratitude for their noble and successful work in favour of the maintenance of peace."[80] German mothers and the PM's admirers in Munich sent him two huge volumes labelled 'Deutschland.'[81] Chamberlain was also profoundly uplifted by this story, as related to him by Bill Astor, son of Nancy:

> Just before he left Greece he [Bill Astor] met an old peasant woman who asked whether he would be seeing Mr Chamberlain. On being told that this was possible she showed him a cross which like most Greek peasants she was wearing round her neck. In the cross was a tiny hole for the reception of a relic of the true cross, (of which there is apparently an unlimited supply to be obtained). You see, she said, I haven't filled up my hole. Now when you go to London I want you to get for me a little bit of Mr Chamberlain's umbrella to put in my cross.[82]

He savoured his iconic status as saviour, and he was guided in his policy-making by these sentimental, spiritual, and material signs of approval.

Closer to home, Chamberlain was flattered that the *Daily Sketch* offered its readers an 'Art Plate' of a photo of he and Annie at Downing Street after Munich.[83] Readers had to fill in a coupon and forward it with 3d in stamps, and by mid-October already 90,000 applications had been made.[84] W.W. Hadley, editor of the *Sunday Times* of which the *Daily Sketch* was the daily sister newspaper, told Chamberlain that "they had never seen anything like it."[85] We can safely assume that it was women who were targeted by the *Sketch's* promotion, and that they outnumbered men among those who sent away for this celebration in ceramic. Similarly, ornately decorated loving cups were manufactured, adorned with the portrait of the PM and a banner reading 'Chamberlain the Peace Maker,'[86] while Paragon china produced a perpetual souvenir commemorative plate with the PM's portrait, the rim decorated again with the words 'Chamberlain the Peacemaker,' and a plaque quoting his remark 'I am myself a man of peace to the depths of my soul.'[87] The popularity of the "remarkable photograph" of Mr and Mrs Chamberlain, which was bought in the thousands by the PM's admirers, represented the renaissance of the type of hero-worship that Victorian Premiers had enjoyed, but had been absent since the war. This at least was the opinion of novelist and essayist Edward Shanks, who assigned the decline of political idolatry to the fact that "politics and the politicians involved in them bulk much less largely in our lives than formerly,"[88] and the entertainment value of political meetings by now could not compete with games, cinemas, radio, and gramophones. Photographs of the King and Queen with Mr Chamberlain and his wife on the balcony of Buckingham Palace were sold as Christmas cards, bearing the motto 'Peace on earth and goodwill to men,' and were available from *The Times'* shop in Queen Victorian Street, London. This angered critics of appeasement, estimated to be "fully half of the people of this country [who] do not agree that Munich brought 'Peace and Goodwill to men.' ... the Czechs couldn't either."[89] Nor was the tragic irony highlighted by the Anglo-German comparison lost on *Times* roving reporter, the American Virginia Cowles.

> On that same day people in England were opening Christmas cards from Mr Chamberlain, showing the picture of an aeroplane with the simple inscription: 'Munich.' People in Germany were stopping in the streets to look at the New Year's posters showing the picture of a soldier in a steel helmet with a fixed bayonet. These, too, bore a simple inscription: '1939.'[90]

For the antis, this way of packaging appeasement was the merchandising of mendacity.

The negative reaction to this commercialization of appeasement notwith-standing, the market for these cards would have been women who were the conspicuous consumers of appeasement and its merchandise. Words were not always enough to convey spontaneous and powerful feeling, and what we can identify through these artefacts and by examining the material culture of the Crisis is the importance of a ritual of gift-giving. Gift-giving was one effective and also affective form of political expression and engagement. With almost child-like glee, Chamberlain referred to the bounty of gifts received at No. 10 Downing Street, regarding each token as a confirmation of his policy.[91]

What Chamberlain possessed in those autumn months of 1938 was nothing less than star power, and messianic star power at that. A feature film entitled *Chamberlain, the Man of the Hour* covering his activities from his early days to the Munich conference was released in cinemas all over the country in the second week of October, 1938.[92] An avid collector has recently brought to light the vast number of medals and commemorative coins depicting Chamberlain the man of peace and his co-signatories at Munich.[93] Hagiographic portrayals of Chamberlain may not always have been tasteful but some could actually be tasted. The celebrated Maitre Chef at the grill-room at the Dorchester Hotel, Park Lane, invented a new dish called 'Coeur de Filet Neville Chamberlain,' consisting of a fillet of English beef in port wine sauce, garnished with marrow on toast, and surrounded by croquettes of potatoes and almonds, asparagus points fried in the Italian way, and croustade of cherries done in the German fashion. "Created by a French chef, and named after the British Premier, the dish is fully represent-ative of the new 'concert of Europe.'"[94] To wash down this new dish, a new cocktail named for Chamberlain was launched for the House of Commons Cocktail party, 'the umbrella.'[95]

The easing of mass anxiety and the setting in of mass relief was also signalled by a return to joyous expression on the dance floor. In Paris the Umbrella Dance or the 'Chamberlaine' was the latest craze, involving hook-ing your chosen partner with an umbrella.[96] Virginia Cowles was in earnest conversation with Duff Cooper at the Ritz two weeks after his resignation.

While Cowles was impressed by Duff Cooper's rationale for resigning, she observed how "the girl in the scarlet taffeta dress wasn't bothering herself about honour or dishonour and neither were the other couples on the dance floor, from the look of them." What was important to people in general was "Peace," and "once more the music was playing and Mr Chamberlain was the hero of the day." Cowles went on to remark on the way "business firms advertised their gratitude in the newspapers; shops displayed Chamberlain dolls and sugar umbrellas; and in Scandinavia there was a movement to present the British leader with a trout stream."[97] In addition to Chamberlain dolls, mask jug heads of the PM were also produced.[98] It is striking how material things, how consumable objects designed with the symbols of the 'Man of Peace,' made people feel secure. Overy has summed up these anxious months by observing that "anxiety was democratic, certainty totalitarian." [99] To extend this formula, capitalism sold relief.

Chamberlain's matinee-idol status was confirmed by the exhibition of his waxwork bust at Madame Tussaud's in December, 1938. In fact, Chamberlain had done a good deal to cultivate his star power, and a David Low cartoon a year earlier had satirized the Conservative Party Film Association for taking advice from film moguls Alexander Korda and Michael Balcon on how to sell the PM's image.[100] Under the banner "A Star is Born" Korda holds the PM's face in his hand and contemplates whether to make him up as a Robert Taylor type, a Jack Hulbert sort of fellow, or "something glamorous and exotic like Merle Oberon."[101] It might seem odd to speak glamour and Chamberlain in the same breath, but that is just what a jury of Americans did when it declared Chamberlain the 'glamour leader' of 1938, "chosen because he made America conscious of preparedness whether for rain, with his ever present umbrella, or the war, with his unshakable British calm."[102] Whereas since the Great War a critical mass of the public had been intent on democratizing foreign policy, foreign affairs were domesticated, and the appeasers were glamourized.

It was therefore natural that Chamberlain and his umbrella should impact the world of couture that season. A well-known Paris couturier revealed that two famous people had influenced Paris fashion more than anyone else in the 1939 season, Queen Mary and Chamberlain. Chamberlain influenced the details of design, such as "neat little day frocks will have pockets shaped like umbrellas. There are Chamberlain hats, too, to say nothing of actual umbrellas." In jewellery as well "they reproduce the famous umbrella. There are tiny gold umbrellas to pin to the lapel of your coat. There are also medals of Chamberlain made up into brooches and Chamberlain medals dangling from key-holders, fobs and all kinds of ornaments to women's dress."[103] It was mainly the ever fashion-conscious French women who adorned themselves with these accessories of appeasement.

Women also filled their domestic spaces with the spirit of appeasement and the images of the appeasers at that 'Munich moment.' Inadequately provided for with worldly power, women exercised 'flower power.' For LNU women the Crisis "brought home to some the realisation that we women have a very vital part to play in the establishment of peace." The same writer mused:

> What is the psychological connection between flowers and peace, or the ending of tension? Many of you, I'm sure, were among those who, in relief at the sudden ending of the crisis, hastened to fill their homes with flowers. My own first impulse on that Friday morning, when the garden looked lovelier than ever, was to pick every single bloom ... and rush out and given them to someone, anyone, quickly.[104]

In another vivid example, a photo shows a woman placing a portrait in oil of the PM framed with flowers and banners reading 'We are Proud of You' and 'God Bless You' in front of a florist in Ludgate Circus, London, in October, 1938.[105] Further, many expressed their gratitude by sending bouquets of flowers to Mrs Chamberlain at 10 Downing Street.

An affective history of the crisis mind

Only that summer Selfridges & Co. had defined Britain as a "non-hysterical old country," and its men and women "sane" and not easily hustled by newspaper campaigns or film and stage propaganda that sought to sway public opinion.[106] However, the electric pace, the terrifying suspense, and what one paper called 'a vague but ubiquitous peril' made the Crisis a deeply visceral experience for all involved. The Munich Crisis is ripe for an interpretation from the perspective of the history of emotion, and the contemporary representations of Crisis Week and the months after were of a nation submitting to feminine emotionality, only to generate male apprehension about its unchecked expression. Overy has shown that the Crisis "prompted the public to brace itself for a war they had been told for years would be a cataclysm of terrible violence," thus unleashing a barrage of private and public emotion, from spontaneous crying, to anxiety attacks, and suicidal thoughts.[107] The cultural historian Susan Grayzel has provided an emotional history of the Crisis with regard to ARP mobilization and the material distribution and the potent symbolism of gas masks.[108] Grayzel has found that the on 25 September, the day that became known as 'Gas Mask Sunday,' press coverage "was nearly unanimous in its emphasis on the calm that prevailed as families lined up for gas masks," with women in particular being praised for being calm and collected and ready to do their patriotic duty as air raid wardens.[109] However, these kinds of newspaper reports have to be taken with a pinch of salt in view of the appeasers' success at getting the press to urge peace and downplay public anxieties in the cause of the 'national interest.'[110] Further, such positive portrayals of women's collective behaviour were not sustained in the weeks to come.

In fact, the popular response to Crisis week, the widely documented scenes of mass celebration and hysteria, the feverish atmosphere, was seen by many commentators to fly in the face of the national character, and to be undignified and unmanly. A population of hysterics amplified the narrative of a once 'Top nation' being divested of its manly eminence by its unstable leaders, its stiff upper lip trembling with fears of war.[111] The very use of term 'hysterical' is significant, its etymological meaning being a form of illness originating in the uterus, and throughout the 19th century it was a form of neurosis diagnosed mainly in women. At the dawn of the 20th century the misogynist proto-Nazi Jewish philosopher Otto Weininger "defined hysteria as 'the organic mendacity of women.'"[112] The great versifier of the English national character, J.B. Priestley pronounced the phenomenon of the 'crisis mind,' "the sort of person who is shaken out of his or her ordinary life by a crisis, but does not arrive anywhere else." Priestley was struck by how the audiences stayed away from the theatres that week, as they had done during the Abdication Crisis, and he was concerned that "[i]t encourages an uneasy feeling that an hysterical strain is rapidly developing in us, and that we are in danger of losing at least one very characteristic English virtue."[113] These diagnoses of mass pathologies illustrated well the mainstreaming of Freudian and psychoanalytical concepts in Britain, and even the most academic practitioners of International Relations were willing to entertain the psycho-historical theory that war was an 'erotic outburst' from the sex repression of civilization.[114]

We can discern the diffusion of the psychoanalytical and popular psychology discourses in the many descriptions of the atmosphere of those weeks. Admiring Duff Cooper's decision to resign, one of his intimate friends Betty, Lady Cranborne, wife of Lord Cranborne who had been Under-Secretary to Eden at the Foreign Office and who had resigned together with him earlier in 1938, told him how she felt at "this particular moment too, when most people are suffering from hysteria, and the PM is on the top of the wave—I think it is wonderful."[115] The overwrought behaviour of Parliamentarians added more shame to the humiliation of the Munich Agreement. Delia Macdonald was one of many who turned to Winston Churchill for "courageous leadership," because as "the hopelessness of many can find no expression, and it becomes despair when the hysterical behaviour in Parliament last week is the lead given to the nation by those to whom we look for serious consideration of such a grave step."[116] Along the same lines Marjorie Stephenson prognosticated how the "mass hysteria cannot last, but meanwhile it obscures the shameful betrayal of democracy and the surrender to brute force."[117] 'Cato' would describe the public and parliamentary reaction on 28 September, 1938, as analogous to "the dance mania" that spread all over Europe several hundred years before in which "women gashed themselves with knives as they capered. Men dashed their heads against the walls." 'Cato' regarded as unseemly and un-English that "sixteen men and two women as they walked out of the Chamber were sobbing and crying with emotion."[118] In short, both Parliamentarians and the general public were acting like histrionic women.[119]

Blaming the women: 'while men had been resolute women had only been afraid'

Whereas in January 1937 Harold Nicolson had cautiously welcomed the democratization of foreign policy, even then he had been concerned about how uncharacteristic of the national character it was to exhibit a "nervous temperament." He felt strongly that the people should take their place in foreign affairs but he fretted that due to their inexperience in this sphere they might fail to approach these matters with characteristically English judiciousness, moderation, and sense of humour. Feeling hopeful, he predicted "in a few years we shall recapture our former equanimity and the peculiar British virtues which derive from it." At that time he could "have little doubt that in a very short time the British public will realize that emotionalism can lead only to confusion of foreign policy, and will return to the doctrine of enlightened self-interest and realistic humanitarianism."[120] However, the Crisis was the realization of his worst fears in this regard, and women especially dashed his hopes.

Drawing the battle lines of a sex war, the Crisis created an atmosphere of deep suspicion about women's political power and influence. Addressing the annual conference of the feminist National Council of Women in early November, 1938, Nicolson castigated the women of England for their alleged lack of courage during the recent Crisis and for their instinctive pacifism and insularity. Nicolson's impression would have carried some weight as a former diplomat, the husband of respected author Vita Sackville-West, National Labour MP, and anti-appeasement Edenite. He portrayed women as the guilty party, more culpable than any of the men who actually played the real leading roles in bringing about the national dishonour that was the Munich Agreement. He claimed that during the recent Crisis:

English women showed fear, not courage; that women had still to show whether they were brave or not. In no previous time of international difficulty had they felt themselves and their homes to be endangered, it was suggested, and on this first occasion of realising the proximity of danger, while men had been resolute women had only been afraid .... One can feel a new fear that the cause of pacifism may even have been engendered by general insistence that fear of war is women's prerogative and that naturally to them the fate of peoples is of less importance than the immediate preservation of family skins. It has been assumed that though men can be afraid and active, women must always be paralysed by fear—the old 'women must weep' idea. A great body of women rendered nationally immobile by fear without resolution must be regarded as a dead-weight, a restrictive influence on national policy. With a majority population clamouring for peace at any price, what, we may wonder, can any Government do but clinch a bad bargain and snatch a peace that is momentarily presentable but as poisonous behind its exterior as Snow White's apple?

Nicolson argued that the Crisis had tested women's courage and they had been found wanting. Nor was he heartened by how easily women recovered from their fear and returned to business as usual once the agreement had been struck and war had been, for a time, averted.

Should one rejoice that women can so quickly recover their balance and, having become blind to the shadows outside their present circle of light, devote themselves again to the trivialities of domestic and social life? Or is it perhaps not reprehensible to decide that if women with at least leisure to enable them to lessen their ignorance of international issues can be content to know no more than that business and pleasure can be continued as usual for the time being, we shall only be taking our due place if we are degraded in the hierarchy of nations? If the real but selfish fear of more than half the population is succeeded only by a lapse into a former state of uninterest in public affairs, is any but a defeatist policy possible?[121]

Nicolson established a very stark binary between the sexes in their reactions to the imminence of war. His real object, it seems, was to jolt women into a sense of duty and service and kick start their volunteerism, but his approach was to shame women by drawing on the worst stereotypes of female domestic myopia and maternalist navel gazing.

It was only odd that he should have addressed this speech to an audience made up of women. Indeed, Nicolson's speech left its audience dumfounded and insulted, one member of the NCW explaining how he:

inveighed against the cowardice of the women of this country. The withers of these jades were unwrung [sic], and they listened and gazed in mild surprise while four or five times he repeated the accusation with all the assumed passion of an actor's art. Finally, as a last resource, he was driven to the somewhat gross expedient of stating baldly that while he had every confidence in the spirit of those of his own sex, it was the lack of courage he observed in the women that was causing him so much anxiety—and this time he produced the desired effect. The audience protested. And Mr Nicolson bowed and smiled and thanked them for so kindly reassuring him on the point. Unfortunately he had failed to interpret the protest aright. The women present had no desire whatever to vindicate their courage in the opinion of the speaker. They were expressing their own opinion of the frivolity of his approach to the deeply serious problems confronting us.[122]

Nicolson was not the first nor would he be the last to misread and misrepresent women's responses to the Crisis, yet it would be his allegations that received the widest press coverage and set the tone of alienation between the sexes. (Surprisingly, nor would this ill-judged speech dim his star status on the circuit of women's political meetings.)[123] 'Women' were scapegoated for their suspected collective cowardice and small-minded isolationism, which was seen to be holding men back from doing the honourable thing of facing up to the Dictators. Britain's female population came to serve as the 'whipping women' for the strategically and ethically precarious policy of appeasement. As implied by Nicolson's address to the NCW, women had to be awoken from their apathetic slumber and made to acknowledge the gravity of international affairs. What is clear is that the Crisis presented a new battle ground in the war of the sexes, at least in discourse and political debate if not in the actual home and in front of the hearth.

Miss Dartle and Mrs Miniver: the everywoman in the press

How was the experience of women at home and in front of the hearth imagined by opinion makers? We can compare two fictional characters who made regular appearances, Miss Dartle in the anti-appeasement *Time and Tide*, and Mrs Miniver in the pro-appeasement *Times*. Both principals were meant to epitomize the women of their respective social class, and they also give us some insight into how the contributors to these contrasting newspapers construed women's public opinion. Both are well-observed gentle caricatures; neither figure is overtly politically engaged; and the episodic nature of the diary or story column allows their creators to convey seemingly impromptu reaction and emotional response to the coming of war. While as fictional characters they are imaginative representations, we can nonetheless locate authentic emotion through the depictions of their intimate lives and the access we are given to their interior monologues.

Time and Tide, with its origins as a journal representing enlightened feminist opinion, provided an outlet for women's frustration at the political ignorance of their own sex.[124] P.Y. Betts spoofed the suburban housewife who was so overwhelmed that "something dreadful is happening somewhere," that she relied on her husband Henry to explain the news to her, and, in the final reckoning, she reverted to political complacency.[125] *Time and Tide* ran a series of mock letters to the editor written by a Miss Rose Dartle of Old Brick House, Highgate, a suburban, politically naïve everywoman who voiced what the journal presumed to be the opinion of mass womanhood. These satirical letters highlighted her passivity and her growing confusion when confronted with all the dangers of the world. The writer always identified herself as 'only an ignorant woman,' but this self-deprecating moniker tended to preface a perceptive point made with irony. For example, her friend Miss Elizabeth Prig had heard Dame Christabel Pankhurst lecture and was impressed how the former suffragette leader had "developed a remarkable gift of prophecy. This lady addressing a crowded meeting in Miss Prig's part of the world ... announced that she had always foreseen General Franco's triumph and that this event would shortly be followed by Our Lord's Second Coming."[126] After a regular run of letters, Miss Dartle wrote to the editor:

> it had been suggested to me that I should, from time to time, resume my pen in order to enquire into matters which puzzle me in public affairs. But I am only an ignorant woman and, in this present state of the world, I find it impossible to formulate my constant perplexities.[127]

This ordinary woman was so flustered by events that she could no longer formulate her thoughts. However, Miss Dartle was to chime in again to offer a comic subversion of Chamberlain's public claims to the deep impression the Crisis letters had made on him. She enquired:

> I am only an ignorant woman and shall therefore be grateful if you or one of your clever readers can explain how, since he has not yet had time to read any of the thousands of letters sent to him since his return from Munich, our brave Prime Minister can be so sure that all of them are full of praise. I only ask for information.[128]

Miss Dartle was a vehicle for the journal's deep scepticism not only about the policy of appeasement, but also about the claims the appeasers were making about the public's approval.

The feel of Jan Struther's Mrs Miniver is quite different and more in keeping with the tone of the newspaper in which the column began appearing precisely one year before the Munich Crisis. In addition, we know more about Mrs Miniver and her creator, Jan Struther. Struther was approached by *The Times* editor Peter Fleming to contribute to the Court Page. He wanted her to write about a woman. Struther asked what kind of woman, and Fleming replied "'Oh, I don't know—just an ordinary sort of woman, who leads an ordinary sort of life. Rather like yourself.'"[129] While Struther would continue to emphasize that her creation was not autobiographical, there are many parallels between author and creation. Mrs Miniver is the mother of three, married to a domestic architect called Clem, living in Kent, well-educated and able to quote John Donne and carry on a conversation in French, and freed from drudgery by domestic help and a nanny. The first few columns are taken up with middle-brow quotidian matters, but gradually the political tensions of the day intrude. On a Sunday in March, 1938, the Minivers' take a family day out at Hampstead Heath where they come upon rival political meetings of extreme Right and extreme Left. "It was hard to take in the sense of what the speakers were saying so confusing was the double clamour. But one thing was certain, that the fabric of both speeches was shot through with the steely tinsel of war."[130] The family hear a shrill third voice and they are only too pleased to discover it is coming from a Punch and Judy show. They take immediate refuge in the children's entertainment.

Mrs Miniver is able to sidestep serious issues for another few months, but the gravity of the situation engulfs her by the end of September when she has to take her children to collect their gas masks. Waiting in the queue she reflects on the meaning of war, if it comes, and how different it is this time than it was in 1914. She takes some consolation in believing that this time at least they know what they are fighting for—against an idea and not against a people.[131] In the aftermath of the Munich Crisis she comes to appreciate the little things in life: "Another thing people had gained was an appreciation of the value of dullness. As a rule, one tended to long for more drama, to feel that the level stretches of life between its high peaks were a waste of time. Well, there had been enough drama lately." With so many others she shares a feeling of exhaustion.

> They had lived through seven years in as many days; and Mrs Miniver, at any rate, felt as though she had been wrung out and put through the mangle. She was tired to the marrow of her mind and heart, let alone her bones and ear-drums; and nothing in the world seemed more desirable than a long wet afternoon at a country vicarage with a rather boring aunt.

She is struck by how much has changed since the previous autumn. "Just a year ago, she remembered, she had stood at that same window putting the summer away and preparing to enjoy the autumn. And here she was again: only this time it wasn't chrysanthemums she was rearranging, but values."[132] Her reflections take us through the emotional cycle of the Crisis.

The next violent intrusion from the outside wider world is Kristallnacht. In a daze:

> she put on a mackintosh and struggled up the square to the pillar-box. Outside the little newsagent's the evening paper placards were flapping under their wire girds like netted geese. The lower half of one of them had been folded upwards by the wind, hiding everything except the word 'JEWS.'

Her emotions may be mixed but they induced a physical reaction, as:

> Mrs Miniver was conscious of an almost instantaneous mental wincing, and an almost instantaneous remorse for it. However long the horror

continued, one must not get to the stage of refusing to think about it. To shrink from direct pain was bad enough, but to shrink from vicarious pain was the ultimate cowardice. And whereas to conceal direct pain was a virtue, to conceal vicarious pain was a sin.

She is moved to charitable work on behalf of the Jewish refugees, because "only by feeling it to the utmost, and by expressing it, could the rest of the world help the injury which had been caused. Money, food, clothing, shelter—people could give all these and still it would not be enough."[133] In fact, the fictional Mrs Miniver launched a real appeal on behalf of Jewish refugees in *The Times* and linked to the Lord Baldwin Appeal Fund. By December thousands of donations of parcels with clothes, books, and toys were received.[134]

Visiting France in the summer of 1939, Mrs Miniver gives voice to the author's internationalism, and her advocacy of a Federal Union premised on cultural exchange for the sake of international understanding as the only chance to save the world from war. Nevertheless, by the end of the summer, Mrs Miniver is ready for the war, even appreciating:

one great compensation for the fantastic way in which the events of our time are forcing us to live. The structure of our life—based as it is on the ever-present contingency of war—is lamentably wrong; but its texture, oddly enough, is pleasant. There is freshness about it, a kind of rejuvenation: and this is largely because almost everybody you meet is busy learning something.[135]

Mrs Miniver personified the famous poster slogan 'Keep Calm and Carry On.' The 1942 film *Mrs Miniver*, based on Jan Struther's *Times* columns, was a huge popular success and won the Oscar for Best Picture that year. It was also a propaganda coup, and had a "significant impact in generating American sympathy for Britain."[136] The figure of Mrs Miniver was one of the imaginative cornerstones of the People's War mythology.[137] That this fictional woman should have become one of the most recognized emblematic figures of the People's War was facilitated, I would argue, by the ever closer identification of women with the public, and *as* the public in the first 20 years after suffrage. From the pre-war vantage point too Mrs Miniver is a revealing representation of middle-class and middle-English womanhood, displaying a spirit of sacrifice and adaptability to crisis that was altogether missing from Harold Nicolson's hostile analysis of his countrywomen.

Drawing old dames to damn defence policy

Finally, we need to consider how the appeasers and their foreign policy were feminized. Susan Kingsley Kent, Joanna Bourke, Nicoletta Gullace, and

Adrian Bingham, among others, have remarked on the destabilization of the gender order following the First World War, and the shifts in representation of masculinity from images of imperial strength, heroism, and physical superiority to those of dismemberment and Modernist fragmentation.[138] Collins has located the last stand of the quintessential English gentleman in the 1930s, the gentleman who was the product of four concentric circles of exclusive homosocial power: the public school, the empire, the gentleman's club and that 'most exclusive club in the world,' the Conservative Party. By the 1930s, the English gentleman asserted himself in the face of British decline and the rise of totalitarianism, but he proved himself ill-equipped to arrest decline or check the power of the dictators.[139] Munich was seen as 'a gentleman's peace;' Chamberlain beautifully personified the top-hatted, umbrella-ready English gentleman; and Baldwin was still celebrating the English gentleman's virtues in 1940 while also on the defensive against charges that appeasement had been the expression of effetism.[140] The CPGB view as articulated by Simon Haxey—pseudonym for Arthur and Margaret Wynn—was that the Conservative Government was "emasculating the British constitution,"[141] and appeasement had opened the way in Britain for what had been happening on the Continent where "parliaments in many countries have been destroyed or emasculated."[142]

It became common to see the men who made war in 1914 as the 'old men' or 'old women' who sent their young to slaughter in the trenches and were ultimately accountable for the 'Missing Generation.' Again in the late 1930s, it was the old men, Prime Ministers Baldwin (born 1867) and Chamberlain (born 1869), who were cast as responsible for British cowardice and dishonour. In 1938 Emmeline Pethick Lawrence, a leading veteran suffragette, wrote that she had lived through an age "when 'the old maid' was the butt of ridicule, when the term of opprobrium directed on a man who was a fool was 'old woman'!"[143] In the press, in political cartoons, and in popular literature, Britain's ruling elite were seen as 'pigmies,' and as decadent and effeminate. Beverly Nichols greyed and emasculated the nation, encapsulating the 20 post-war years as follows: "England won the war. England has nothing left to fight for. And as a result, England, to many foreign observers, is like a rich old woman whose sole ideal is to keep what she has got."[144] In Nazi propaganda too Britain was increasingly feminized.[145] It was felt that Herr von Ribbentrop's great miscalculation was to make "the traditional and rather silly mistake of believing that Britain is effete and tired," and his "dislike for this country was accentuated by the merciless leg-pulling he received while he was Ambassador in London."[146] Indeed, on many occasions the characteristic English sense of humour was acknowledged to be the strongest prophylactic against political extremism, and it was humour and especially the ability to laugh at oneself that the Nazis lacked.

In British Communist propaganda, such as in cartoons published in the *Daily Worker*, the appeasers were represented as frail housemaids, as rotund old women, and as gossipy old maids. In British Fascist propaganda Britain's leaders were described as 'Mrs Baldwin' and 'Mrs Chamberlain,' and unfavourably juxtaposed with the virile assertions and determination of Mussolini and Hitler.[147] In the cartoons of George Strube in the *Daily Express*, both Baldwin and Chamberlain were feminized, such as the depiction of "Mrs Stanley" the corpulent retiring housekeeper who instructs her successor as cook, "Miss Neville" "give'em good plain, 'olesome, old-fashioned English cookin', non o'them foreign fal-lals and above all, keep 'em guessin'."[148] Here Chamberlain was doubly emasculated, first by being represented as a maiden and then by being portrayed as nothing but Baldwin's inferior, and both equally woeful at moving beyond the domestic sphere and into an international frame.[149]

Even in publications with a feminist ethos Chamberlain's authority was undermined by dressing him in Victorian women's costume. Accompanying Ellen Wilkinson's review of 1937 in Parliament, in which she described the new Premier to be "so mild as to be almost old-maidish," is a cartoon of Chamberlain as a Victorian old maid in pearl necklace and knitting.[150] Using the same iconography another *Time and Tide* cartoon represents Chamberlain as a nanny dressed in Victorian garb handing over a crying and sickly baby (representing appeasement) to nursemaids Hoare and Simon.[151] In *New Times and Ethiopian News*, edited by former suffragette leader Sylvia Pankhurst, Chamberlain is depicted as a nursemaid flirting clumsily with an obese banker-type, the caption reading "If that naughty boy does not want to kiss you, I'll do it myself," while a naughty-boy Eden stomps off in the background.[152] A cartoon in May again depicts Chamberlain as a supplicant Victorian housemaid representing "Chamberlain's Fascist Aid Society" to two other stock types, a well-healed grandmother representing "Great Britain Aristocracy," partnered with her monocled and handlebar-moustachioed spouse representing "Great' Britain Business."[153]

So too in the cartoons of David Low in the *Evening Standard*, Chamberlain's satiric personae were of an easily-led member of the Shiver sisters (a.k.a the Cliveden Set); a gnarled and depleted old man; and a dainty old woman unable to resist the flattery of the puffed-shirted dictators. The Shiver Sisters appeared in David Low's cartoons in 1937 and 1938. Chamberlain was depicted as a circus acrobat in décolleté leotard balancing ever so precariously on a tightrope. He holds a balance beam which at one end supports the Shiver Sisters carrying a placard reading "Any Sort of Peace at Any Sort of Price," while at the other end and starting to weigh him down are the "Blimp Brothers" holding the sign declaring "No Concessions."[154] In "The Dashing Young Men and the Flying Trapeze," the Shiver Sisters appear again as the audience at yet another circus performance, with Chamberlain front row centre among them.[155] Chamberlain was not in the frame of "Shiver Sisters Celebrate," but all those presumed to be driving Britain's foreign policy were portrayed wearing skirts, ladies hats and furs, and goose stepping to the only martial looking figure in the picture, Nancy Astor in Nazi uniform. In the generous caption they were identified as "Ladies Lothian and Grigg," "Old Mother Shaw," and "Frau Garvin ('Observer') and Frau Dawson ('Times')."[156] "Play the Game, Cliveden!" imagined the scenes at the Cliveden weekend where 'sisters' Chamberlain, Halifax, and Lothian were all guests, showing a cross-dressed Chamberlain struggling to keep hold of an obese cross-dressed Thomas Inskip.[157] The 'Shiver Sisters' also attained star billing in *Babes in the Wood—the Panto with a Political Point*, a pantomime produced by the Communist-run Unity Theatre, which played to full houses in the winter of 1938–1939.[158] That same season women cabaret dancers staged a sketch donning the now signature Chamberlain apparel: top hat, moustache, and black umbrella.

The other piece of this iconographic puzzle is to be found in the consistent representations of peace, of the League of Nations, and of Europe all as female figures. This gendered duality has been an established part of the Western symbolic lexicon for millennia, and in the Greco-Roman pantheon Pax is the goddess of peace and Mars the god of war. From its foundation the League of Nations was symbolized by Pax and her female decedents. In the course of the 1920s and 1930s in cartoons of all political hues, this archetypal League woman exhibited the signs of serious and eventually of terminal illness, her once confident stature defeated by world events, and her body ravaged by the violence perpetrated against her by various national governments. The female figure who began as a symbol of hope in the early 1920s, uniting as she did the classical tradition, women's post-suffrage aspirations, and a gentler, more feminine system of international relations, ended up by the late 1930s as the symbol of the barrenness of hope and of death. Virginia Cowles captured the moment as she, "peace was dying." In Paris in August 1938, Cowles looked on as the people:

> kept a vigil in the death-chamber, clasping the patient's cold hands and refusing to admit, even to themselves, the growing pallor of her face. The agony of the long illness was terrible to watch. It lasted over a year, but the anguish of Europe was never again so acute as during those summer months when every type of medicine hope, treachery, idealism and compromise were feverishly injected in her veins in a desperate attempt to keep her alive. Her recovery at Munich was an artificial one. After that she went into a coma and a year later died.[159]

As she—peace, Europe, the League—lay dying, it follows that all who were associated with her and her plight should likewise be feminized.

During the Munich Crisis Chamberlain was also costumed as a hapless 'Sno-Use and the seven dwarfs.'[160] This was particularly salient due to the release in 1937 of Disney's first full-length feature production *Snow White and the Seven Dwarfs*. It was interesting how the Disneyfied Grimm fairy tale was increasingly evoked as an allegory for the high tensions in foreign affairs, and Chamberlain was competing for audiences in search of escapism with the Walt Disney hit. The eponymous heroine represented the unwitting democracies; her allies all dwarfs; pitted against the evil step-mother proxy for the dictators whose hunger for power is absolute but also illegitimate; and the poison apple stood for the Munich Agreement. Further, the eating of the apple also references Eve's plucking the forbidden fruit from the Tree of Knowledge in the Garden of Eden, serving to reinforce the case for women's guilt. We will recall that Nicolson had drawn the same analogy suggesting that "with a majority population clamouring for peace at any price" what "can any Government do but clinch a bad bargain and snatch a peace that is momentarily presentable but as poisonous behind its exterior as Snow White's apple?" In Paris, the revue Vive la France, authored and starring Dorin, included a skit on *Snow White*, with Hitler, Benes, Mussolini, Daladier, Bonnet, Goebbels, and Chamberlain as the Seven Dwarfs. Chamberlain was represented by a marionette wielding the now iconic umbrella, which was judged to have eclipsed Baldwin's pipe as an expression of all that was most British.[161]

Of course feminizing and cross-dressing the subjects of ridicule was nothing new to political parodies and cartooning in the 1930s. However, it is significant that Hitler, Mussolini, and Stalin were not feminized in British political cartoons but, on the contrary, imbued with exaggerated characteristics of machismo and unbridled pomposity. Similarly, Winston Churchill would never be sent up for failing to fulfil masculine stereotypes, and part of his success as wartime leader was to recast English manhood and reacquaint gentlemanliness with virility. Churchill himself would write about Duff Cooper's heroism and dignity in resigning as First Lord of the Admiralty in language pervaded with sexual innuendo and phallic forcefulness: "At the moment of Mr Chamberlain's overwhelming mastery of public opinion he [Duff Cooper] thrust his way through the exulting throng to declare his total disagreement with its leader."[162] Duff Cooper had risen to the occasion. Whereas Chamberlain played to the feminine and feminized crowd and developed a language to suit, Churchill's master term was honour, and his rhetoric of masculine virtues provided continuity with the high diction of imperial and military heroism.[163] Therefore, by 1940 the failed masculinity and decrepitude of the Chamberlain government was contrasted with the hyper-virility and bull-dog masculinity of the Churchill government that replaced it. Edward Hulton, editor of the *Picture Post*, wrote:

> above all the leaders must be *men* [emphasis in original]. For the last 20 years they have been a lot of old women. The Old Woman Democracy of Neville Chamberlain, John Simon and Samuel Hoare has got to give way to the Leader of Democracy of such men as Churchill, Duff Cooper, Bevin, Morrison and Amery.[164]

The Crisis spawned the poetics of national shame. A Swiftian satirical poem ironically titled "Peace with Honour" was sent by its author to Leopold Amery, and concluded on this note:

> O shades of Haig, Hood, Malborough, Nelson, Drake!
> Who with your swords made every tyrant quake—
> Hurled back the ranks of Spaniards, French and Huns—
> And when disaster loomed, stuck to your guns!—
> Thank God you're dead! Shrink back into your tombs.
> We've learned new methods when disaster looms:
> Now when Peace with Honour statesmen speak
> They turn the other fellow's other cheek![165]

These lyrics subverted the heroic diction of patriotic poetry, and as such sabotaged the constructions of masculinity that went with it hand in hand.

It can be argued that Baldwin and Chamberlain's leadership of the National Government came to be seen as the fitting and final inglorious chapter of Britain's inter-war gender disorder and the nation's decline from a manly imperial nation to an inward-looking, gentle, ineffectual, and feminine little England.[166] In the ever more clamorous narrative of decline, sexual anarchy and national emasculation were seen as catalyzing the process.

Conclusion

In the autumn of 1938, at the height of the Munich Crisis, women and mothers—women as mothers—especially were figured as the satisfied party. They were widely represented as 'the best friends of Mr Chamberlain's policy.' The promise of appeasement was one that was made to them and for the sake of their offspring. Arguably, this was the crescendo of the process that Alison Light has described as the 'privatization of national life' in these 'in-between' years of the First and Second World War.[167] However, this affirmative feminization was soon inverted, and increasingly women were represented as subversive, anti-national, un-patriotic, and as acting irresponsibly with their still quite recently acquired citizenship rights. This is the narrative that emerges from an examination of representational sources by the politicians who basked in the adulation of women's public-facing enthusiasm; by the journalists who created composite female figures that they presumed mirrored their female readership or that were intended to mould this readership to their ideals of women's political performance; by the anti-appeasers in search of scapegoats; by the newspapers that merchandised the Prime Minister to satisfy women's putative desire to consume and establish an intimate relationship with the messianic 'Man of Peace;' and by satirists who stoked public anxiety to the unfitness for leadership of Britain's parliamentary leaders. But did women also imagine themselves to be the satisfied party? Did they take up the gauntlet thrown down by their mostly male critics to fight a sex war? In their introspective self-representations, in diaries, letters, and as expressed in more intimate relationships, we can see many women struggling with the negotiations and reconstructions of their sexual and political identities. It is to women's own emotional and intellectual responses to the Crisis that we turn in the chapter that follows.

7
'Anyway Let's Have Peace:' Women's Expressions of Opinion on Appeasement

From across the political spectrum the agents of civil society were keen to speak for British womanhood, some with good intentions to voice their sex-based concerns, others to mock women's alleged collective pusillanimity as part of a satirical subversion of the National Government's foreign policy. Were these caricatures fair representations of British women's opinion and their reactions to the Munich Crisis? How can we hope to access women's intimate feelings as they faced another war? The thoughts and deeds of the more prominent 'Guilty' or 'Innocent' women are accessible to historians through their published material, in media coverage, and in carefully archived private papers. Those of the British 'woman on the street' are less readily apparent. However, we are fortunate that two rich archives, Mass-Observation (M-O) and the so-called Crisis Letters which form part of the Neville Chamberlain papers contain women's confessional sources, and individualized qualitative material that complements but also fine tunes the quantitative finding of the social researchers.[1]

Women's life-writing for Mass-Observation has offered a treasure trove for social, cultural, ethnic, and gender historians, especially those who have taken the 'subjective turn' and celebrated rather than berated the archive's idiosyncrasies and "emotional richness."[2] Mass-Observation was an experiment in social research launched in 1937 by anthropologist Tom Harrisson, poet Charles Madge, and filmmaker Humphrey Jennings. The aim of M-O was to foster a genuinely democratic public sphere "capable of resisting the twin evils of top-down political manipulation and popular political apathy."[3] M-O's Leftist inspiration assured it the condescension of the conservative press, the *Sunday Times* describing it as 'Mass Eavesdropping,' and the *Spectator* characterizing volunteers as 'Busybodies of the Left.'[4] It was organized on a voluntary basis, its volunteers drawn from a wider swathe of political opinion and social backgrounds (although in reality the vast majority were lower-middle or middle-class and on the Left). What they shared was the motivation to be active citizens, and idealism about contributing to the great social good. Mass-Observers were sent regular 'directives,' a series of questions about their own attitudes, personal histories or current behaviour in relation to particular topics, and they would send these in on a monthly or bi-monthly basis. Mass-Observers were out in force as interviewers and as respondents to 'directives' during the Crisis.

Although it was not a consciously feminist-inspired enterprise, Mass-Observation attracted many prominent women intellectuals as volunteers, including H.D. (poet Hilda Doolittle), Bryher (poet Winnifred Ellerman), writer and PEN Club president Storm Jameson, poet and scholar Kathleen Raine (who married Charles Madge), and writer Naomi Mitchison. With women making up one third of volunteers (1,894 men and 953 women responded to directives and wrote diaries for Mass-Observation between 1937 and 1945), "gender themes, and especially women's history, have been the veins in the M-O archive most tapped by theorists and empirical researchers."[5] Hinton has argued that particularly in the case of women volunteers, life-writing for M-O acted as a catalyst for "individual struggles for personal autonomy."[6] While Mass-Observation material has been the basis for many studies, including studies of women, not much use has been made of women's directive replies *before* the outbreak of war. Nor can this gap be attributed to a paucity of sources. Rather, we see the same pattern identified as elsewhere in this study: there is a concentration of scholarly interest in the construction of women's citizenship and radical socio-sexual change in the first decade or so after the Great War; this gives way to relative neglect of the 'messier' late 1930s; and then scholarly interest peaks with near blanket coverage of the war years, especially in the form of 'forgotten histories' of women who defended the domestic front and who need to be credited with their part in winning the 'People's War.'[7]

The second source-base is equally revealing, but for different reasons. In the Chamberlain archive we find the 'Crisis Letters,' thick files full of letters mostly from otherwise anonymous correspondents from around the world expressing gratitude to Neville Chamberlain for his achievements in world affairs. A large proportion of these letters are from women, and each missive represents an act of self-expression, both spontaneous and visceral, and an attempt to reach out and achieve some intimacy with otherwise remote public figures. A textual analysis of the content of women's letters is as interesting as consideration of the significance of this method of political communication. On the one hand, the act of letter writing should be seen as an exercise of women's political power and engagement. That they should write to the Chamberlains about their most private feelings and anxieties also suggests a personal bond with the Prime Minister, as these almost exclusively pro-Chamberlain writers related to him as an accessible and sympathetic father-figure and the prophet of peace.

On the other hand, however, these letters can also be regarded as evidence of women's sense of disenfranchisement. Many writers felt they had not been able to make their voices heard through democratic channels, and former suffragette leader Christabel Pankhurst's Crisis Letter to Annie Chamberlain drives home this point. That these letters were overwhelmingly outpourings of praise and not protest explains why they were so caringly catalogued and preserved by their recipients. While Mass-Observation was not on Neville Chamberlain's radar, the Crisis Letters buoyed him throughout the winter of 1938–1939.[8] The efforts of women letter-writers were not in vain, and they would have a much more tangible and immediate impact on Chamberlain than any other type of public opinion. What both source bases together reiterate is that there was a significant gender gap in how the Crisis was experienced. These sources further confirm that growing sense that, as crisis followed crisis, men and women were working at cross-purposes, with conflicting aspirations for the nation's future.

'This is a woman's attitude:' Mass-Observation surveys

Certainly, Mass-Observation's study of the Crisis indicated significant differences within public opinion along gender lines to the international situation, to the popularity of the Prime Minister, and to the prospect of war. Madge and Harrisson provided their own narration of the British public's response to the Crisis of September 1938 in *Britain by Mass-Observation*, published in January 1939. This study sought to record and recover public opinion as it was, rather than as it was claimed to be by manipulative politicians or by journalists speaking for the 'Man—and Woman—on the Street,' but actually too lackadaisical to collect the data to substantiate their claims.

While Mass-Observation noted the surprising pattern of popular decrease of interest in and weariness with international affairs with each successive crisis, the Sudeten crisis tended to arouse war-ready feelings in the majority of British men surveyed. In contrast, women tended to support Chamberlain and herald him as the returning hero upon his homecoming from his visits to Hitler. "This is a woman's attitude, and there is a marked tendency for the women to stick to it over the following days, when their men are once more saying that Chamberlain was weak and we should have stood up to Hitler." Women want peace and "they hate having to give up the wonderful sense of relief which Chamberlain has given them."[9] As a general assessment Mass-Observation recorded that: "At every stage in the crisis the women have proven the conservative, peace-at-any-price and pro-Chamberlain element." But the time of day the surveys were conducted led to different findings, and "in each one of our snap surveys the results obtained during the day by interviewing women are significantly different from such research when continued during the evening after the men have come home from work."[10] A Labour MP told one observer: "'I was surprised to hear when I got up to Lancs. that the men are for stopping Hitler, they know what it means later. It's the women who are frightened of the chance of a war now.'"[11] Taking Mass-Observation's picture of public opinion at face value, British women, as a group, provided the widest and most resolute support for the politics of appeasement. Indeed, these observations of the masses placed in social scientific context the same pathological suspicion of women that obsessed men like journalist Richard Baxter, and that explain the publication of his little red book *Guilty Women*. Harrisson and Madge were likewise suggesting that women's influence was less legitimate than men's, and they were evidently frustrated by women's higher levels of political apathy and ignorance about foreign affairs. Their frustration at these findings makes sense given that the very inspiration for Mass-Observation was Popular Front activism and an energized anti-fascism.[12]

However, this starkly gender bifurcated construction of British public opinion has to be nuanced, and this can be done with the help of other sources produced as part of the Mass-Observation enterprise. What was quite unique about Mass-Observation was that women were also observing themselves, acting and not just acted upon. Indeed, "no similar enterprise, bringing so much women's writing together and ensuring its survival exists in any other part of the world or for any other era."[13] Mass-Observers did more than experiment with taking surveys or rely upon what they might hear on the bus or in the cinema as an indication of public sentiments. They contributed their own experiences in diary form. Their life-writing bridged the private and the public sphere as it does the intimate and the public document. Volunteers were clearly writing for an audience, even if they were promised anonymity. Mass-Observation volunteers felt they were part of an intellectual community. "The M-O diarist commonly had the feeling that, by portraying their everyday selves, they were producing raw data both for current generalizations about social experience and for posterity's knowledge about the Britain in which they were living."[14] When war broke out, Mass-Observation hit on the idea of asking for diaries as a continuous record of everyday life, anticipating that the disruptions of wartime would make it more challenging to collect the directive replies on a regular basis.

Women's Mass-Observation directive replies for the period of the Munich Crisis and the prelude to war shared a number of themes. Religious faith was often expressed and thanksgiving for appeasement as a means of avoiding war was identified as the true Christian way. Women's language especially was saturated with religious imagery. The flipside of this is that some women betrayed their prejudices, especially anti-Semitism.[15] Unsurprisingly, there was ample praise for Chamberlain and his good works at Munich, but this support was less unanimous or overwhelming than that expressed in the Prime Minister's 'Crisis Letters,' as we will see later. Nonetheless, their gratitude and admiration was far more discernible than criticism of either Chamberlain's foreign policy or his character. These Mass-Observation women and the women whom they overheard in quotidian conversation were little concerned with the nation's reputation or national honour, and only a few despaired at the sacrifice of Czechoslovakia or the persecution of minorities in Nazi Germany. Their main sense of relief came from the fact that war had been averted, a war that they understood mainly in terms of its impact on the home front, on their lives, duties, on the safety of their families, and on their separation from loved ones. Only a few of the women were committed or absolute pacifists, although most could be described as 'antimilitarist' at this moment in time. Some were admittedly excited by the prospect of war and felt exhilarated by the suspense and pace of the crisis itself, and there were strains of war fever in the air in September 1938 that affected some of these women in ways other than fear for their loved ones.

While these subjective reports were being written at the height of the appeasement policy, the term 'appeasement' was never used. This would suggest that the term was not in common usage at the time, but applied retrospectively and more often than not as a pejorative. Further, the understanding of 'fascism' as a political concept and its menace was rather limited, and fear about the consequences of fascism paled in significance to misgivings about wartime deprivations. While many were fairly well-educated and middle-class, understanding of foreign policy issues was variable, with some women rather well-informed, and others quite ignorant. Still, it is obvious that Mass-Observation women were generally better informed and more animated than women sampled in Mass-Observation surveys of the population of Fulham West at the time of the by-election there in March 1938, for example.

There was a preponderance of pacifist sentiment expressed by diarists, and this allows us to see how at the grass roots of the peace movement pacifist belief informed personal choices. Mass-Observation's Muriel Barker was 18 years of age in 1938, and she, her sister, a shorthand typist of 22 years old, and her brother, a clerk of 25 years old, were all pacifists and "intended doing nothing that would in any way further the war." Barker described her sister as "an active worker for pacifism (I won't say peace, because 'peace' workers have been demanding war with Hitler)," illustrating well the suspicion between those working for 'peace,' and the rather loose bandying around of the term to mean one of many possible things. While Barker's siblings were all in agreement about the war and had various ideas about how to resist, they did not come from a family of pacifists, and the father "announced he was going to join up. But he's 56, and has a 'heart,' so we weren't worrying about that."[16] A generational gap existed in the Barker family with regard to attitudes to war, which was not unusual.

Even less unusual were variances of opinion between women and men in the same family, and between husband and wife. For example, Mrs Dawson was filled with gratitude to Chamberlain, while her husband was more dubious:

I felt so relieved and glad for all the world—God bless the PM. Seeing the paper pictures of PM and wife quite brought a lump in my throat. He has done well, and he is a tired old man with not too grand a constitution left him by his naughty old father.

Her husband took a more pugnacious position:

> The hubby thinks he could have stood firm ages ago for Hitler is all bluff—But I tell hubby that he's a rebel, always against authority. But in my heart of hearts I wonder. Anyway C.Slavatika [sic] is only a mixed lot of states and Germans, Poles, etc., therein, must wish to be in their own country. Yet I know old Hitler and Mussolini are pleased and are getting their own way. Anyway let's have peace.[17]

Dawson's point of view illustrates well the concessions women were ready to make to maintain the peace. While the husband asserted the rectitude of war against the aggressor, the wife expressed warm and protective feelings towards the old and ailing PM and rejoiced at any sign of war being avoided. This response was the one most often identified as the female and the feminine response to the Crisis.

While Mass-Observation surveys noted the unreliability of wives' opinions because they would often be different in the evenings when their husbands were at home, the confessional mode provides invaluable glimpses into family and marital dynamics, and suggests how these personal relationships conditioned political opinions. Mrs W. Thompson, for instance, expressed a range of emotional reactions to the Crisis. She discussed these issues with both her father and her husband, before coming to her own independent conclusions. While she believed that Hitler was a madman and she was "sorry that Hitler has made so well out of all this," she felt true sympathy for the Czechs who have been "fed to the wolves" and believed that England and France should "grant them a gift of about £30,000,000" to help them in the distress they were sure to experience in the coming winter, she was nonetheless relieved that "the nightmare is now over" and "we can buy our Christmas cards, and presents, and perhaps plan our next summer's holiday. Life is worth living again. I hope this is a lasting peace."[18] Thompson's appreciation of the moral complexity and the shortcomings of appeasement were not persuasive enough to override her sense of relief, and while her sentiments did not lack generosity towards the victims of Nazi expansionism, they were not powerful enough to transform her from dove to hawk.

Indeed, the advent of Christmas represented an epiphanic bookend to the dragging narrative of the Crisis. The *Manchester Guardian* attempted to replicate the success of *The Times's* Mrs Miniver with its own personification of parochial womanhood in the form of Aunt Maria. For the fictional Aunt Maria, as for Mass-Observations's Mrs Thompson, it was remarkable how attention shifted from international crisis to preparation for the festive period: "It is surprising how rapidly one time of stress succeeded another in Aunt Maria's little Cheshire manor-house. When the national crisis was over and a month has been spent, pleasantly rather than profitably, in discussing it her thoughts turned to the problem of Christmas cards."[19]

Deadlock: women's dilemmas with pacifism and anti-fascism

In an example with some parallels with the two above Mass-Observation respondents, the novelist and pacifist Naomi Mitchison was not persuaded that it was worth fighting a war against fascism, while her men-folk were less convinced pacifists even if likewise unenthusiastic about the war.[20] She seemed willing to help the war effort only in the form of relief work and sheltering evacuated children in her home outside Glasgow.

> I did not purpose to do anything active about the war if there was one, as I am very doubtful of a war even 'against Fascism' under Chamberlain, and equally doubtful whether the country as a whole would upset a conservative Government during a war. I would not encourage any young men to go.

She described the indecision of her husband (48), a Labour MP who "proposed to support a war in alliance with France and the USSR, but not very enthusiastically." Her son too had not yet made up his mind as to the correct course: "My son (19) at Cambridge, was rather torn; he said he supposed that CUSC (the Cambridge Socialist Club) would demand war, but individually were unlikely to want to fight; he himself was not a pacifist, but was very unenthusiastic about this war, on the same lines as myself." She also noted that women's feelings about the prospect of war contrasted with those of men: "I met no woman who was keen on the men fighting."[21]

Mitchison's famously unwavering pacifism aside, a more frequently perceptible pattern by the autumn of 1938 was the mutability of pacifism and the instability of pacifist commitment. In Glasgow Miss French visited the Peace Pavilion at the Empire Exhibition on 10 September, noting that while it was crammed with visitors there was also a book provided for those "who wish to sign their names as associating themselves with the Peace Movement and glancing through it I found only half a dozen people a day signing."[22] In discussion with a close woman friend on 7 September, Mass-Observation volunteer Dorothy Brand gave some insight into the immediate influence of Woolf's controversial feminist anti-fascist text, *The Three Guineas*. Dorothy and her friend were both reflecting on Woolf's incitement to the pacifist woman that, in the event of war, she:

> should refuse even to knit sox [sic] I put this to my friend and asked her what her attitude was. She was quite definite that she was a pacifist but could not go to such lengths. Once we were at war and if she felt it was a legitimate cause she would help.

(Incidentally, Woolf herself claimed to be unconcerned by the reviews of *The Three Guineas*, she was not seeking public approval, and in the bigger picture she felt that "my book may be like a moth dancing in the bonfire—consumed in less than one second."[23]) Brand also noted that people tended to avoid talking about the Crisis and their "knowledge is often very scanty and though they will talk about Hitler and Germany's aims they are generally very vague about Czecho-Slovakia—her history, geography and industries and have little knowledge of the Sudeten-Germans, where they live in Czecho-Slovakia and their grievances."[24] Similarly, Muriel Bennett noted the change of heart experienced by a pacifist, aged approximately 50:

> I don't like this peace. It does not look as though it will last. Of course it is all very well to criticise Chamberlain afterwards, but I don't think when we're so glad to hear about the peace we realised quite how much he had given in to the demands of Hitler.[25]

Like many others, Nazi Germany's naked aggression would motivate a rethinking about the efficacy of pacifism, a process of conversion that was more likely to occur in people who were well informed about international affairs.

The Crisis only made a bigger dilemma of an already existing one of how to be simultaneously against war and fascism. This was a personal and psychological as well as intellectual conundrum experienced by Mass-Observation diarist Margot Jones, a peace activist:

> Wednesday, September 14. No news yet—everything just the same or perhaps a shade worse. Had lunch with my father and said the same old things once again: nobody wants a war, but Hitler seemed mad, and it all depended on him. There was really nothing new to say or think. I made a speech to this effect: It seems there's nothing worse than war. But if we don't resist, if we and the world give in to Fascism, if Oswald Mosley becomes our king under Hitler, wouldn't that have been worth fighting to prevent? But surely nothing can be worse than war? Deadlock.[26]

Arriving at this psychological impasse and ideological cul-de-sac was a trajectory shared by another woman anti-fascist pacifist, Phyllis Perlow: "N.B. Own policy as always—Pacifist, non-Party but definitely anti-fascist. I think with tonight's majority ... Own feeling: that no Peace Conference dealing with minorities can possibly consider it has given moral justice if the Jewish Question is not thrashed out. A lamentable omission." After she attended a meeting on 1 October 1938 Perlow's "General impressions: 'Peace' is what we wanted—we have got it ... for how long?" Her feeling was one of irresolution and cliff hanger: "Relief at peace—but what now? Can anything be done before Germany takes possession of Czechoslovakia .... Chamberlain has pawned democracy rather than risk Communism—The result seems to be Czech-mate—and Germany wins."[27] The wheels were now turning for Perlow as her pacifism became increasingly untenable alongside her anti-fascism. Certainly many experienced mixed feelings, the 80 year-old Mrs Arnold, of Ilford, Essex, recording on 1 October:

> I'm thankful, truly, deeply thankful that the cloud of horror has lifted. Not so much for myself—my race is run—but for the millions who have suffered such agonies to no good purpose. Further my poor old heart can feel the 'Tramp, Tramp, Tramp of soldiers' into Czechoslovakia, and though thankful, I cannot rejoice.

These were "thoughts I may only express in a Mass-Observation report."[28] Mrs Arnold's sympathy for the Czechs, the sacrificial lambs of the Crisis, dampened her sense of relief. Her diary writing for Mass-Observation also provided her with an outlet for these mixed feelings, the type of fitful emotions that could never be expressed in an official or a public source like a newspaper or a public speech.

The political is emotional: confessional histories of the crisis

In general, life-writing comes more easily to women, and women may be better at describing and representing the psychological and emotional dimensions of the Crisis, due in part to socio-cultural expectations about women's nature and the presumed transcendence of intuition over reason.[29] It also goes without saying that women turn to such modes of expression more readily because they have fewer outlets for political expression in the public sphere. Thus I. Blackwell described her reaction to the Crisis in these terms: "I am one of these people who always follow the international news. I have been very worried over it and have been expecting war for a long time." Soon the intellectual is displaced by the emotional response:

> Last week I felt ill with worry and not much better when Chamberlain came to his agreement with Hitler, for I felt if Hitler was allowed to get strong enough to dominate Europe we should have a war sooner or later and I would rather have it now, before he is too strong.

When she had come to terms with the necessity of waging war against Hitler she was overtaken by even more intense emotion:

> Once war seemed a certainty, I lost my worry and began to feel quite an exhilaration in all the bustle and hurry, the anti-aircraft guns, search-lights, trenches, gas masks, queues ... The atmosphere was exciting and chilling, so when the news came through about the Four Power Conference which seemed to cut off the war I felt almost flat.[30]

In the private form of a diary entry she was able to own up to what few would have admitted in print, namely that the achievement of peace terms came almost as a disappointment.

In Ramsgate, diarist M.E. Grant similarly took the reader along on the emotional rollercoaster that was that weekend at the end of September. Her entries also leave little doubt about overwhelming public support for Chamberlain, even if private sentiments are more ambivalent. Grant wrote:

Friday: Early morning. Peace declared, what a relief for everyone, and what a triumph for Mr Chamberlain and Herr Hitler. I most sincerely hope that England and Germany will remain great friends, my husband always says, you can trust a German anywhere, but only trust a Frenchman as far as you can see him ... Friday night: The arrival of Mr Chamberlain was broadcast on the radio and there were great cheers at his home coming, everyone I know seemed to be listening for the news whenever it could be obtained on the radio. Church services had been going on continually during the week, with prayers for peace, it seems that their prayers have been answered. Saturday: people all seem back to their normal again, but everyone is still talking of the news of the last few days, while many seem quite satisfied with the change of events, several men only, not women, seem to think that we had not heard the last of it.[31]

Similarly, on 1 October Mrs Last compared her own feelings of general relief with that of her male neighbour: "Feel bewildered when my next-door neighbour shakes his head over joyful news—he talks about 'betrayal and weakness.'"[32] However, Mrs Last also felt frustrated by the reaction of her sex: "Wish I knew a clever man who would tell me his views. Clever women would be no use. Women's views limited to welfare of loved men—whether grown or tiny."[33] The identification of these gender differentials in feelings of relief that war was averted tallies with many other representative indicators of public opinion.

Another Mass-Observer noted the explicit split of opinion along sex lines:

MEN. Consider Hitler's demands exorbitant and suggest he should have been stopped in the spring. Generally speaking they think they would be conscripted and would stick to jobs as long as possible ... They all joke but in both cases the jokes are a covering for a deep seated dread of war.

In contrast:

WOMEN: An atmosphere of expectancy prevails as most of them expect war sooner or later. They do not joke like the men, most of them dread the calling up of men-folk either at home or fiancés. They tend to count

Britain's defences more than the men. In event of war they would stick to teaching or be prepared to relieve men at boys' schools.[34]

Men's and women's different responses to the Crisis and to the changing nature of war were thus evident in the context of the family, marriage, social life, as well as the workplace.

Many Mass-Observation diarists performed two functions, recording their own personal sentiments and their unmediated reactions to world events, while still fulfilling the hypothetically scientific-observer role by taking literary snap-shots of public reaction. These windows into the anonymous and reified public's reaction were more subtle than the various surveys, while still not entirely reliable and, obviously, very random in their coverage. Margot Edgelow gave "some general impressions," noting "No hatred of Germany, feeling is only Hitler and the Nazis who wish war. Tremendous willingness to help on part of everyone. No grumbling. Great admiration for Chamberlain—is a nation's hero. Have noticed spontaneous clapping in cinemas whenever he is shown in news reel." She had not "found great sympathy for Czechs, or attitude of 'back them up at all costs.'" This was set beside her "personal opinion," namely "that the Treaty of Versailles was very unjust, a wrong that needs righting."[35] Sympathy for Germany persisted well into the Crisis although there was mounting evidence that this willingness to reach an understanding was also gradually being displaced by compassion for the Czech victims of Nazi aggression.

The diarists give us invaluable insight into the rapidity of change in public opinion and in the national mood. As Overy has also speculated, the shift in popular opinion towards support for military confrontation cannot be neatly identified at the juncture when Hitler violated the Munich Agreement in mid-March, 1939, with the occupation of Prague. The "process was both less coherent and less chronologically precise than this."[36] Mass-Observation's Edith Oakley noted that:

> during the last ten days or so I have witnessed some extraordinary changing of opinion ... As the drama has unrolled itself the stronger and stronger has grown my conviction that it will end in a satisfactory denouement ... Peace depended upon finding a way out that would not press Hitler's pride, and I had great confidence in Mr Chamberlain's abilities.[37]

Still in early October this momentum was on the Prime Minister's side, but many a diarist predicted that it would not last long. For example, Collin Brooks, Lord Rothermere's fascist-sympathizing right-hand-man, confided in his diary how "never has the world seen a better example of 'Hosanna today: crucify him tomorrow' than in the treatment of Neville Chamberlain. When he returned and war fear passed he was adulated. Now he is reviled. We deserve bombing."[38]

The people's crisis as prelude to the people's war: correspondence of the crisis

Mass-Observation diarists were not the only ones engaged in these quazi-confidential discursive practices as a record of private reactions to momentous world events. The Mass-Observation enterprise was motivated by a didactic drive; it sought to encourage self-empowerment, greater psychological understanding, and self-awareness; and it strived to counter political apathy and superstition. Harrisson estimated that of an adult population of 40 million, three quarters had left school before age 15, and a quarter did not vote in elections. Writing in 1940, he also found that one in a hundred had written to an MP or newspaper during the past five years.[39] To Harrisson that only 1% was politically engaged and in direct communication with politicians was a woefully meagre statistic. However, it seems clear this 1% was not made up only of members of the upper and educated classes, as exemplified by the Crisis Letters sent to Neville and Annie Chamberlain.

These letters, to which we now turn, represented the widest swathe of the population, correspondents ranging from persons of distinction to fairly ordinary members of the general public. While by no means only from women, a significantly large proportion were sent by women—more than half, and women of all ages, all political affiliations, and all regions, as well as from other countries. Letter writers addressed the Prime Minister and his wife with great affection, expressing their thanks to him for preserving the peace of Europe. Almost without exception these letters were congratulatory and brimming over with gratitude, most demonstrating very little awareness of the complexity of foreign affairs. Peace-making was understood to be a female and a feminine speciality, and it followed that these women were seen as, and saw themselves as, the most beholden for peace and the efforts of peacemakers.

At the time of Anthony Eden's resignation as Foreign Secretary in February, 1938, sources suggested that women disproportionately supported his decision and were correspondingly opposed to Chamberlain.[40] Eden received some 6,000 letters of support.[41] While we do not know how many of these were from his female admirers, we do know that Eden's popularity with women was one of the reasons he was appointed minister with special responsibility for disarmament in 1934, an issue that had been the focus for so much cross-party women's activism.[42] Women politicians of all hues came out in support of his resignation, for instance, the Liberal Margery Corbett Ashby, who had worked alongside Eden at the Disarmament Conference, and Labour's Ellen Wilkinson. It was reported that "two hundred shouting demonstrators, mostly women, were ejected by a large force of police from the central lobby of the House of Commons last night, chanting 'Chamberlain must go. Long live Eden.'" Nor was this an isolated expression of women's support as "the demonstration typified the day-long, spontaneous campaign which women voters all over Britain waged for the ex-Foreign Secretary."

Apparently, "MPs were overwhelmed with telegrams, telephone calls, letters from their women constituents urging them to stand by Mr Eden, warning that this departure might mean the wrecking of the National Government."[43] This report continued with a detailed account of the impact on Eden himself and on his family of his resignation, a personal and domestic dimension not accorded to just any politician. To some extent it was certainly the case that women's support for Eden can be explained by his debonair good looks. There is no doubt that sex appeal enhanced his political success.[44] Eden's personal popularity notwithstanding, it was not long before the weight of women's favourable opinion was again impressed upon the appeasers.

Neville Chamberlain was popular with women voters, and even more the firm favourite of Conservative women. In the previous chapters we saw how since the 1920s Chamberlain had satisfied women's political demands. He deliberately courted the women's vote and paid tribute to his women supporters, an increasingly familiar practice in the post-enfranchisement years (and since). For example, at a meeting in Birmingham immediately after the 1935 General Election he said: "In these days women are not only the predominating factor in an election in numbers but we have found by experience that they do more work and show more enthusiasm than the men. (Cheers)."[45] Still, Chamberlain's popularity with the women in his party and the female electorate fluctuated. In the winter of 1938 Eden's personal popularity with women made Chamberlain the less popular if not the villain of the piece. But when the excitement over Eden's resignation died down and international affairs were again reaching a crescendo, Chamberlain ably conducted women to sing from his hymn sheet, and he certainly made attempts to appeal to what many agreed was his natural constituency. He was persuaded that he had this special affinity with the female electorate by the enthusiastic responses to his addresses to the annual meetings of the Women's Conservative Associations in 1938 and 1939, and by the special rapport he had with his sisters. Francis has argued that Chamberlain was even less excitable than his predecessor Baldwin, "possessing a celebrated aloofness rooted in deep loathing of displays of public emotion or sentimentality."[46] This characterization of his emotional control does not, however, ring true during the Crisis when Chamberlain's communications with the female electorate show a politician much at ease in and ready to confess how moved he was by women's company.

However, what convinced him most of women's support for him personally and for appeasement more generally were the thousands of gifts and 'fan mail' he received from women worldwide. In the days after Munich, Chamberlain received more than 20,000 letters and telegrams.[47] Women had already been corresponding with Chamberlain to some considerable extent, and he told the CWA annual meeting in May, 1938, that "I know from many letters I receive that the fear of war has been hanging over countless homes for many months past and filling the hearts of mothers and wives with the gnawing anxiety unless their menfolk may have to take part in it."[48] In fact, it was his sympathetic response to the sentiments expressed in women's letters that inspired him to conduct face-to-face negotiations with Hitler in September, 1938. It is striking that this has never been taken into consideration in the vast historiography of appeasement.

It is telling that the passages most often excerpted from Chamberlain's infamous radio broadcast of 27 September are those that expose him as a wishful pacifist, naïve about European affairs, and only too ready to sacrifice 'a far-away country' of which 'we know nothing' in the interests of Britain's Empire. But what prefaced his dismissal of Czechoslovakia was his sympathetic response to the letters sent to him and Mrs Chamberlain in the preceding weeks. These letters told of people's "gratitude for my efforts" and assured "us of their prayers for my success." Significantly, "most of the letters have come from women—mothers and sisters of our own countrymen." In addition to these letters from British women were countless ones from France, Belgium, and Italy, as well as from Germany, "and it has been heartbreaking to read the growing anxiety they reveal and their intense relief when they thought, too soon, that the danger of war was past." Therefore Chamberlain was not offering his own assessment of the threat of war but rather echoing these letters when he then went on to say: "If I felt my responsibility heavy before, to read such letters has made it seem almost overwhelming. How horrible, fantastic, incredible it is that we should be digging trenches and trying on gas-masks here because of a quarrel in a far-away country between people of whom we know nothing."[49] Guided by the letters, Chamberlain was voicing what he understood to be the women's reaction qua women to the international crisis.

Indeed, this passage was misinterpreted from the beginning, as pointed out by Miss D.M. Ketelbey, Assistant Professor of Modern History at St. Andrews. In her rhetorical analysis, if the sentence 'a quarrel is a far-away country between people of whom we know nothing' is read in its context:

> it is obvious the Prime Minister was addressing a very special group of people—'mothers and sisters of our countrymen' who has written to him, 'those who are digging trenches and trying on gas masks.' With an imaginative effort to get under other people's skins, which is one of the Prime Minister's most striking and valuable qualities, he was trying to assess the value of the purely local issues of the Czecho-Slovakian question as they must appear to people not on the whole politically-minded or politically well informed.[50]

The selective presentation of this broadcast in so much of the historiography is yet another reminder of how the fixation on building the case against the 'guilty men' has rendered women invisible to the story of appeasement.

And yet it is very clear that Chamberlain was consistent in the due he paid to women's letters. At the CWA conference a year later, Annie Chamberlain reassured women that their heartfelt missives had been heard: "One of the most moving things, and one that has touched my husband deeply, has been the message of confidence which has been sent to him from the women of the country."[51] That Chamberlain himself considered such expressions of support instructive is borne out by his own observation of his disproportionate popularity with women, particularly once public opinion was turning against him. On 11 May, 1939, Chamberlain told the CWA assembly:

> I seem in these days to be the target for a lot of rotten eggs, but I can assure you that does not keep me awake, because I believe that I have the support of the women of the country and that they have a clearer vision than some of those whose sight is obscured by party and personal prejudice. More and more women are making their influence felt in politics, and there is no subject on which they have a greater right to be heard than on foreign affairs, which in these days, as never before, may profoundly affect their chances of happiness in the future and the security of their children. For that reason, you have, as I know from my correspondence, followed the events of the last 12 months with the closest attention. You have watched the old umbrella going around, you have, I believe, approved our efforts, strenuous, and up to now successful to keep Europe out of the war.[52]

His public statements were confirmed by his admissions in private in his letters to sisters Hilda and Ida during the Munich Crisis. Here he fixated on the letters, the gifts, and the enthusiastic crowds that greeted him, using this kind of affective and expressive evidence as a counterbalance to his insecurity and feelings of increasing isolation within political circles.

The letters and gifts had started to pour in from mid-September, 1938, and he told Ida that "You cannot imagine the wonderful letters we have had from all sorts and conditions. Our rooms are a bower of flowers & gifts rain in."[53] Depressed by the continued tensions in Anglo-Italian relations as well as the "stream of vituperation being poured upon me" he "took an antidote to the poison gas by reading a few of the countless letters and telegrams which continued to pour in expressing in most moving accents the writers heartfelt relief and gratitude."[54] He was embarrassed by the profusion of gifts of 'every sort & description' showered upon him, including gold watches, fishing rods, innumerable flies, clocks, umbrellas, and planting bulbs and flowers. The letters were still flowing forth in November, and Annie was receiving at least 70 per day and as a consequence had to enlist more help in addition to her four paid secretaries.

Even a single letter could be enough to convince him of the effectiveness of his speech, broadcast by the BBC, to the Foreign Press Association on 13 December. He related to Ida that "One woman wrote to Annie enclosing a letter from her young son who said 'Wasn't C marvellous? Tears of admiration rolled down my cheeks!' That seems to prove the value of the broadcast."[55] With the proximity of Christmas, festive cards and presents kept arriving, "often accompanied by such touching letters that one doesn't like to leave them unanswered."[56] The process of exchanging letters, and the importance the Chamberlains placed on responding where possible, firmly established another category of political relationship, and one in which women could even be at an advantage.

Chamberlain also basked in the affection of the crowd, a feminized mass. On his visit to Italy in early January the Italians took to the street to express their gratitude and appreciation, "many saying 'You don't know how much we *love* you,'" [italics in the original] while in Turin "some 200 girls in uniform clapped & shouted themselves hoarse."[57] Chamberlain was aware how modern media technologies encouraged a new relaxation of formality in the relationship between 'millions of auditors' and the Prime Minister, and he appeared to be very much in his element. He told Hilda how "quite a number began their letters Dear Mr Chamberlain and then apologise for their familiarity but explain that since they heard my voice they feel I am a friend."[58] It was a combination of his selfbelief that "'I know I can save this country and I do not believe that anyone else can,'"[59] with his conviction that the people were behind him that armed Chamberlain against the mandarins well into the spring and summer of 1939.

While feeling "very dispirited & lonely" in the House of Commons, in mid-April Chamberlain still believed that the country was with him due to the letters he was receiving.[60] There can be no doubt that Chamberlain was concerned about public opinion and desperately wished to win it over. Eschewing public opinion polling and even paying only passing attention to what by-election results revealed about popular feeling, Chamberlain no doubt paid special attention to those expressions of public opinion that corroborated his entrenched position in foreign affairs. Virginia Cowles was given a long interview with Chamberlain and what struck her most was his naïvety about the pro-peace popular feeling in Germany. "Deeply impressed by the German people's desire for peace," and taken in by the cheers even of the SS men, he "didn't seem to grasp the fact that in the totalitarian state public opinion is manufactured and fashioned overnight to suit the purpose of the moment. His remark about Hitler's declining power indicated to me a dangerous lack of understanding."[61] However, this reading of the PM's personality flaws does not cancel out the evidence of popular enthusiasm. Nor does it diminish the significance of women's sense of comfortable familiarity with and support for Chamberlain's appeasement politics.

The Munich mums: maternal gratitude for war averted

What kind of messages were women conveying to the Chamberlains in their letters? One of the predominant sentiments expressed was thanksgiving and gratitude on the part of mothers' and wives' who felt their husbands and sons had been spared. As part of a longer discursive tradition of women's engagement with war, women correspondents tended to highlight their maternal credentials to explain their aversion to war and their growing fear of losing their men-folk in another bloody conflict.[62] The immediate impulse on the part of so many mothers was that they had been saved untold grief. An anonymous correspondent who simply identified herself as "a mother of an only son (just 18 years)," said: "I do wish the 'Women of England' and the 'mothers of sons' could do something for you, to show our heartfelt gratitude to Mr Chamberlain."[63] Julie Aves wrote to say "I feel you have given back to me all what I have in this world, my only son."[64] Mrs Helen Alison felt it her "duty as a mother to show my appreciation to you for what you have accomplished in averting what was certain disaster to our country."[65] E.A. Russell spoke for herself and other mothers: "I, as a great many more mothers lived in an agony of suspense—having a son living in London—just on the threshold of his career. I pray you will have the health and endurance to accomplish your Christian work—so that our children can live in security, may God bless your efforts."[66] Foreshadowing the phenomenon of the so-called 'Security Moms' after another earth-shaking event with global ramifications—the cohort of American women who were not necessarily consistent Republican voters but who nonetheless allegedly contributed to the re-election of George W. Bush in 2004 in the aftermath of 9/11—a similar type emerged from the Sudeten Crisis, a type we might dub the 'Munich Mums,'

Many of the letters showed how deeply moved women were by the apparent triumph of the Munich agreement, and these messages can also be quite moving, written in a style and providing the same kind of impassioned responses that were characteristic of Mass-Observation women's life-writing. Women of all classes and all levels of literacy wanted to write to the PM to let him know how they experienced the crisis and how their lives were transformed by his "epoch-making statesmanship."[67] Women of the upper classes were just as likely to feel gratitude because, as mothers, they believed they had been saved untold grief, and Lady Templemore wrote to thank Chamberlain: "I feel with God's help that you have given me back my boys, at one moment it seemed as though we must loose [sic] all three of them, and it seems so wonderful to feel that there will be Peace after all."[68] From lower down the social ladder, Gladys Turner addressed the Prime Minister without any hint of formality so as not to mitigate the strength of her emotional response.

Now I am going to explain why I am writing. I should not have done so only I feel I have a special privelage [sic]. I am a mother, aged 25, and on September 29th 1938 I gave birth to my third child. It was indeed a Crisis Day for me, on September 28th. I listened to your speech on the radio and there seemed to be little chance of escape from war, things did indeed seem black ... I felt I was shouldering too big a responsibility, another baby to care for and perhaps my husband gone and who knows maybe a widow and the children fatherless, anyway my Baby Boy was born on Thursday the 29th and wasn't I pleased when Friday morning the newspaper came and the storm was over for me and for everyone too.[69]

Even less articulate but just as heartfelt was Mrs Llowelin's letter where she described herself as "only a poor woman" who "may not put all I feel correctly into writing" but who nonetheless "would like you to know how much your efforts to gain Peace for us all, means to me and thousands of Mothers like me, listening to your speech from Grosvenor House last night makes one realise how difficult your task is."[70] Indeed, she had lost her husband in the last war and had been left to raise seven children on her own, one of whom was now in the Navy. Mrs Driver, whose husband had served four years in the last war and whose son had just turned 21, thanked the Prime Minister "in the name of all working-class mothers. Blessed are the peacemakers. You will be blest, even if the other side wont [sic] let it be peace. One in high places gets so much blame, and so little thanks."[71] Another heart-wrenching letter came from Hilda Kent, a bed-ridden invalid who had lost her own son but who could nevertheless "understand what mother's [sic] must have gone through during that great crisis and it is to you, and you alone they owe so much."[72] Another woman begged him to force the surrender of the Czechs; "make the Czechs give Hitler what he wants on Saturday," she pleaded, because, as she predicted, Hitler "will take it any way." She entreated him to "think of England. Already we mothers are in tears and those awful air raids."[73] Presumably she felt somewhat unsure about demanding this sacrifice of the Czechs, signing her letter 'anonymous.'

'It is impossible to tell him how much we thank him'

Complementing the many examples collected by Mass-Observation, the Crisis Letters also conveyed the wider public reaction and reportage, not just intimate sentiments. Mrs Collett's letter included a useful snapshot of the reaction at a Women's Unionist Association meeting, where so many of the members were either widows or spinsters who had lost loved ones in the last war. "Here in Broadway," while Mr Chamberlain was negotiating at Munich:

we were gathered together in our monthly ward meeting and we asked God that in his graciousness he would guide and protect Mr Chamberlain from all harm and bring him back to his own country, to you [his wife] and his people, with 'peace' to proclaim to the whole world. Our prayer was answered.[74]

Nor were these outpourings confined to meetings of women Conservatives. After communicating the meeting's resolution to the Prime Minister, Cyril Yates describing the mood at the Edgbaston Ward adoption meeting:

> Actually the feeling of the Meeting went far beyond anything the wording of the message can convey and I can perhaps express it best by telling you that I have never been to a Ward Meeting which anything like approached it in enthusiasm or sincerity. Nearly half the people there spoke and the women in particular, who as usual were in the majority though not so strongly as in previous years, sent their most affectionate good wishes to Mrs Chamberlain and their thanks for the great part she has played. I think the general sentiment of the Meeting can best be summed up in the words of one elderly lady who just stood up and said 'It is impossible to tell him how much we thank him.[75]

Marion Phillmore had her own observations to share with Mrs Chamberlain, as a means of framing her animosity towards the Prime Minister's detractors. She noted that "everyone I have spoken to, workingmen—people in the train—all sorts—is of the mind that peace is what we want," and she railed against all those who opposed appeasement, "the noisy ones who don't agree," and thanked "our stars that your husband is where he is, and that we are not left to the mercies of Mr Eden or Winston Churchill and the International Peace warmongers."[76]

The Munich Crisis was one of a handful of these poignant moments of national catharsis and emotional reckoning in 20th century British history. As a proximate precedent, the Abdication Crisis of December, 1936, had elicited a similar response from the wider public in the form of 3,500 unsolicited letters sent to King Edward VIII, a lesser number but nonetheless a fair few addressed to the wife of the PM, Lucy Baldwin, and another sizeable batch sent to Winston Churchill, the self-styled leader of the 'King's Party.' While in 1938 the Chamberlains' popularity was greater, if we are to measure this by the sheer volume of unsolicited letters received, Mort has used the Abdication crisis letters to demonstrate the "psychologically expansive and emotionally expressive nature of contemporary opinion formation." The Abdication Crisis put the nation on "emotional display" as women letter-writers, who formed the majority of these correspondents, entered into imagined and intimate relationships with the sovereign. No matter how far removed in terms of social and cultural status, they identified with the King and with his wrenching romantic quandary, regarding him as they might any matinee idol. On the other hand, those correspondents who sided with the Government, and opted to write to Lucy Baldwin, were also mainly women, and they identified strongly with her role as a political wife, "endorsing an energetic version of conservative femininity which countered the claims made by the King's allies for a more tolerant code of personal morality."[77] And of course a later parallel to the mass emotional displays that punctuated both the Abdication and the Munich crises was the seemingly unprecedented extreme public displays of grief, emotion, and the abundance of floral tributes in the wake of Princess Diana's death in 1997.

The great and the good among the crisis correspondents

The Munich Agreement hit the highest notes on the emotional register, and the feeling of relief was nearly universal. Nonetheless, the nature, tone, and impact of the letters were different when they were sent by public figures and/or intimate friends. While thus far we have been concentrating on letters from rather anonymous individuals, Chamberlain was also flattered and reassured in his chosen course by the letters he received from persons of note. Letter writing was also the most readily available political tool for those who felt themselves disenfranchised and outsiders in politics. Therefore Osbert Sitwell—with his credentials and reputation as an author and Bright Young Thing hardly a person one would expect to regard himself as so distant from politics—wrote to Mrs Chamberlain to celebrate the Prime Minister's "boundless moral courage and ability to go straight to the point, and his determination not to be bound by precedents." Sitwell felt it incumbent upon himself to address her:

> because at the moment all the ... self-seeking are stitching attitudes in the opposition forces; and it must be difficult for those who are placed, like yourself, in the centre of things to realize the intense feelings of gratitude and affection that the PM has aroused in thousands of people who are voiceless.[78]

Children's author Enid Blyton expressed her gratitude and pride in his actions in verse, concluding that "The moment came—and with it rose the Man."[79] As we have seen, both Christabel Pankhurst and society hostess Emerald Cunard wrote to Annie Chamberlain to express fulsome support and gratitude. Again, this direct access to the Prime Minister and his wife suggests an alternative, extra-parliamentary form of political communication that should interest the political and not merely the woman's historian. Like the responses to Mass-Observation directives we have just been sampling, letter writing served a similar function and provided an expressive outlet for the writers.

While the Londonderrys had fallen out with the Conservative Party since Lord Londonderry's differences of opinion with Baldwin and his exclusion from the Cabinet, both 'Charley,' Lord Londonderry, and Edith, Lady Londonderry, wrote to Chamberlain to congratulate him on his endeavours. It was an effortless endorsement because, as Lord Londonderry put it: "I feel intensely happy of course because I have been at this for four years but could make no impression on your predecessor and his Foreign Affairs advisor."[80] Lady Londonderry was likewise enthused, telling the Prime Minister "how splendid it was of you to fly to Hitler. It has always been Charley's and my dream—if I even ever hinted as much—I was told I was mad! Now you have done it—I do think it more than courageous."[81] The Londonderrys felt for a moment vindicated. From the same social circle Lady Ethel Desborough wrote to the PM over-brimming with joyous affection for Chamberlain: "One can only gradually believe in the reprieve. We went to London for the speech, at that breathless moment." What she saw there led her to believe that "I don't think there ever can have been such a universal emotion against war, throughout the whole world, every best and worst human quality enlisted against it—but I don't believe that anyone but you could have saved Peace with Honour."[82] She concluded by evoking the memory and legacy of his father, and how proud he would have been.

Indeed, many more of these letters were written by women with Conservative affiliations, and there is no question that Chamberlain was fêted by both moderate and extreme elements of the Right in the autumn of 1938. Thus from the far Right, new formations which were conducting their own anti-war campaigns, Lord Lymington, as president of the following organization sent this telegram: "Crowded Meeting of British Council Against European Commitments at Caxton Hall Last Night Sends You Hearty Good Wishes and God Speed in Your Mission for Peace with Germany—Lymington President."[83] Letters of appreciation came from fascist women too, Daisy di Mobilant writing that she had taken comfort in the past weeks in the photo of the Premier on her table, and she wished "to let you know that we fascist women look up to this real english [sic] statesman, above and outside parliamentary strife, and know he is holding vigil where the spirit is needed and senses are taught."[84] Chamberlain was the object of a leadership cult and a fan club. He had achieved celebrity status with a female population already well versed in the fan culture of the cinema.

Dear Mrs Chamberlain

It is interesting that nearly as many letters were addressed to Mrs Chamberlain, an even larger proportion of these sent by women. Mrs Annie Chamberlain (nee Vere—they married in 1911) was a complementary political wife and provided little competition for her husband for the limelight. One can thus see why many women identified with Annie and reached out to her. She was seen as an extension of her husband and a solid supporter of his policy, a loyal wife who was not much more interested in or capable of understanding the complexities of international politics than they were. Certainly she enjoyed her husband's reflected glory in those dramatic days in late September, 1938. She sat in the Ladies Gallery of the Commons between Queen Mary and the

Duchess of Kent when Neville announced to the House that he was going to attend the Four Powers meeting in Munich, from which vantage point she saw tears pouring down regal faces. Then on the evening of 30 September:

> Crowds of women made Mrs Chamberlain the centre of an affectionate demonstration. She had been at St. Michael's Church, Chester Square, London, where the Archbishop of Canterbury had addressed a crowded broadcast midweek service. When Mrs Chamberlain appeared at one of the doors after the service a crowd of several thousand cheered her continuously for several minutes. As she stepped into the car they surged round. Women grasped her hand and congratulated her, and Mrs Chamberlain was obviously deeply affected. Cheering women clambered on the running-boards of the car, and as it drove away Mrs Chamberlain waved and smiled.[85]

While there were many similarities between the letters sent to her and to her husband, one can also discern some subtle differences, with writers feeling freer to convey sentiment, psychological impact, and anxiety, as if a woman would be more receptive to these inflections. Further, writers took more liberties when they wrote to her as they entered the intimate space of her family life, expressing both respect and sympathy for her in her fulfilment of her wifely and maternal duties. Thus one Richard Wilson wrote directly to her to say that he "felt, like many others, that you must have been the greatest help to him. The photographs of your receiving him back each time from Germany gave us all a sense of security and a homely touch during a very grim period."[86] Beatrice Johnson, a member of the Westcotes Ward of the National Conservative Women's Association, Leicester, asked her to:

> please pardon the intrusion on your privacy at this anxious time, but as one woman to another, I feel I must write to tell you of the great admiration women in all walks of life feel for you, in the help and inspiration you give to your husband, in this time of great effort to obtain peace for the whole world, straining as he is, every nerve, to avoid the unbelievable horrors of war, upon the nations of the earth.[87]

The fact that both writer and recipient were women meant that Beatrice Johnson felt at ease and perfectly justified in making a direct approach, expressed in emotionally effervescent prose, to this prominent national figure.

Although she had already conveyed her appreciation to the PM through conventional political channels, Florence Horsbrugh MP wanted to say 'thank you' to his wife, hoping Annie Chamberlain would realize "that those two words carry thoughts of gratitude I cannot fully express. Your wait must have been almost unbearable—the woman's—to wait—is almost more of a strain than activity however terrible the responsibility."[88] Horsbrugh was so overcome by emotion that she felt empathetically that she could only really express herself to another woman.

Gendered constructions of the PM in the crisis letters

Women wanted Annie to know how proud they were of her husband, and thus how proud she should be of him, and in this vein Eileen Anderson of the Ladies Carlton Club wrote to tell her that we should be grateful to him:

> for the proof to the whole world that personal goodness and strength of character, showing itself in undaunted courage and self-control is proved after all, to be the one thing of all others of priceless value, and the only thing (because God is behind it) which is powerful enough to defeat the power of evil which rules so much of our unhappy world in these days.[89]

Chamberlain was seen to personify the national character and British ideals, while his wife in her quiet fortitude standing by her man was also seen to embody the most prized wifely virtues.

Women, whether from the public at large or from the circle of the Chamberlains' acquaintance, tended to feel more at ease addressing their letters to Mrs Chamberlain. In this outpouring of joy, relief, and admiration, Chamberlain was almost universally acknowledged to be a great 'peace-maker,' a 'prince of peace,' if not a heroic figure and the great man of his age. 'A few Nurses' from Manchester also wrote to say "how proud you must feel of your husband, we are, and think his visit to Herr Hitler the gesture of an 'English gentleman.'"[90] Women shared their appreciation for his more subtle manly qualities, and his understated Englishness as compared to the cunning "mad dog" character of his German adversary.[91]

Unlike more charismatic figures or politicians with sex appeal, the 'good' Chamberlain was made to fit the mould of Victorian respectable masculinity, possessing qualities of integrity, courage, patriarchal reserve, calm, and something approaching spiritual force. This was even evidenced by the *Punch* cartoon of 1 September, 1938, titled "Still Hope" in which he was represented with the wings of an angel. Kathleen M. from Newcastle wanted Mrs Chamberlain to know that "we all trust him as a Father, and we the young wives of England know that even now if it is humanly possible that he will save us from the horror coming so close to our babies in this industrial town."[92] Indeed, the use of language infused with religiosity and Christian imagery was rife in the letters. A more unusual letter because it was from 'a father and husband' thanked Mrs Chamberlain from the bottom of his heart for "being the means of preserving for men, the lives of my wife and daughter, who otherwise might have been killed. I regard yesterday [28 September] as Resurrection Day."[93] One woman had just been reading the story of David and Goliath and was "struck by its similarity to recent events and only pray the result will be the same. I am sure if Mr Chamberlain had lived in Bible times he would have gone down in those chapters as a great prophet."[94] That a granddaughter was born to the Chamberlains during the Crisis in early September, the second child of their daughter Mrs Stephen Lloyd—on 19 November she was christened Anne Mary after her grandmother—and that Chamberlain would celebrate his 70th birthday on 18 March, 1939, certainly reinforced his fatherly and grand-fatherly persona.

To sum up, there are leitmotifs among women's Crisis Letters. As the number of letters to Mrs Annie Chamberlain suggest, women felt more comfortable sharing their personal circumstances with another woman, and a related trope was praise for the forbearance and quite courage of the wife of a hero. To put the epistolary mode into context, in this period "letters remained the most important medium for expressing personal and emotional thoughts and feelings," and heart-felt letters "composed in a direct and natural manner were privileged as part of an open style of popular writing that was championed by women."[95] This can also help us to understand Virginia Woolf's adoption of the epistolary form—even if it was merely a stylistic conceit—in the feminist anti-fascist and pacifist *Three Guineas* (June, 1938). Well-schooled in and at their ease writing letters, the epistolary form became a natural mode for women's political expression between the wars, whether in the form of public letters to newspaper editors, private letters to public figures, or putatively private letters made public (and canonical) by leading feminist modernist intellectuals.

Certainly women's crisis letters tended to adopt a different writing style and adhere to certain conventions of correspondence, often prefacing their letters with an apology for writing in the first place, whether this was a sign of real humility or merely a polite affectation. Yet, more significantly, this spoke for the reality of women's unequal citizenship and comparative political passivity. Women letter-writers felt that they must excuse themselves for troubling men, for interrupting them in their important work. It follows that war would affect them as wives and mothers, and it is mainly on this basis that they had a right to be heard. Consequently, another common thread throughout the letters was a lack of engagement with matters of international politics or any kind of thorough political analysis. There is scarce intelligent or informed commentary on political matters, and not many more had something to say about the cause of the Crisis, while even fewer offered a solution to the Sudeten problem. There is noticeably less understanding of Nazism or sympathy for its victims than in the writings of Mass-Observation women. In the Crisis Letters women's innate and instinctual pacifism is what is most in evidence, as they adhered to their biologically-determined roles and underplayed their status as informed citizens or as politically engaged electors. On this basis we could argue that that on the eve of the Second World War women's citizenship remained a weak construct.

Could we regard letter writing to political leaders as genteel acts by the dispossessed? The large quantity of women's letters among the Crisis Letters must be accounted for. It can be argued that women were more likely to turn to extra-parliamentary methods of representation, and they resorted to non-violent, non-aggressive means of political communication that were deemed acceptably feminine. Letter writing therefore fits into the same category as petitioning, resolutions, peaceful marches, and processions. But these Crisis Letters were not acts of protest, and what was most conspicuously absent from them was any criticism of the policy of appeasement. With only very few exceptions, folio after folio contains letters of support for the Prime Minister.[96] One can only speculate whether this is symptomatic of selective preservation—hostile correspondence was not saved—or whether those who opposed the Prime Minister did not write to him to express their dissent in this more intimate format. By point of contrast, the papers of each Churchill, Duff Cooper, and Amery do preserve some of the hostile correspondence they received in the fallout of the Crisis.

Further, there was an important international dimension too. On the one hand some of the British correspondence yearned for an international movement of women to stop war, and T.M. Rannie asked "Cannot the Women of Great Britain and of Germany unite to avert War, its inevitable destruction of their homes, their husbands and their sons? Can the 'International Council of Women' do nothing? ... Let thoughtful, wise, courageous women of all nations stand together now and act."[97] Others too invested these hopes into women, and Mr Beverley Baxter MP was trying to inspire women to take on the "great campaign of peace yet to be won," and he wished "to see the women of British establish contact with the women of Germany and Italy." He admitted it would need organizing, but it would come naturally to women because it is they "who create life," and "they have a common sisterhood in combining against those who destroy life." Baxter proposed that instead of the usual Cenotaph memorial on 11 November, 100 of each German, British, and French mothers who had been bereaved in the last war might come together to start a movement which would "engirdle the world."[98] Certainly the events to mark Armistice Day in 1938 had added resonances for women and mothers a few short weeks after the Crisis. On the other hand, Chamberlain would have been convinced that appeasement satisfied all women from the many letters and gifts he received from women from across the globe. These letters show us both the universality of the figurative construction of peace-making as a female and a feminine speciality, and the tangibility of women as the most grateful for peace and the efforts of peacemakers.[99]

There can be no doubt that women's support for Chamberlain decreased after that public relations honeymoon period of the Crisis, but many women continued to admire him. There is also a folio of 'Letters of Support' from 1939, which, while much thinner than those from the autumn of 1938, contains some interesting insight into popular opinion. Mary Angel wrote to the PM on the day that war was declared to reassure him that he was:

> a splendid person deserving of all our thanks ... As you said yourself, this had to come, and now it has come we all face it with the courage you wished us to have ... But my heart is full to-day: it is sore, for thinking of the hurt which must come to us all and especially mothers, and wives, through the horror of war, but it is also full of gratitude to you, and admiration for you. I can't resist trying to tell you how much I think of you, and how I love you for your efforts on our behalf.[100]

Public opinion in his favour and the particularly warm relationship between Chamberlain and elements of the female electorate were longer-lived than one might expect, or than the hegemonic mythology of the 'Guilty Men' thesis would allow for. British Institute of Public Opinion polls similarly suggested little variation in terms of satisfaction with the Prime Minister in the 12 month period between October 1938 and October 1939, although we can only speculate to what extent these results were buoyed by the loyalty of women as the statistics do not differentiate by sex.[101]

Conclusion

British women found an outlet for spontaneous political expression in both Mass-Observation life-writing and the Crisis Letters. Paradoxically, their voices did not fall on deaf ears at the time as the Prime Minister himself was especially receptive to their fears and their praise, while these same voices are hardly audible in historical representations of the appeasement. Women found the possibility of integrating themselves into the political process and engaging in active citizenship outside election time by opening up lines of communication between their domestic and psychological interiors and those of the nation's leaders. The insight these sources give into women's feelings about the international crisis and the impact it had on their private lives, their gender identities, and their self-definitions is compelling in and of itself. In the Mass-Observation life-writing, for instance, many women were clearly torn between their socially and culturally constructed roles as mother, wife, chronicler of every-day life, citizen, and patriot, and activist or pacifist. With these sources we are able to reconstruct a women's history of the Crisis, an inclusive panorama of women cutting across class, generational, ideological, and national lines.

But a gendered reading need not only arouse the interest of a feminist or sectionalist readership. The results of the approach taken here should do more than merely right a wrong committed by those who have contributed to a phallo-centric narrative of Britain's place in world affairs and the nation's agency in world crisis, whether by being one of the 'Guilty Men' or by being one of the propagators of the myth that only *men* were guilty or otherwise. Certain types of domestic sources have not been taken seriously, or they have not been seen to count for much when set beside traditional state and diplomatic papers or formalized press reporting, almost all of which was produced by men and for a notional male audience. But when we allow for female viewpoints and make the concomitant methodological shift and valuing of female produced and female-identified source, an alternative narrative of the Crisis emerges.

Indeed, especially in the case of the Crisis Letters, we have seen how they created the emotional and psychological framework for the Prime Minister's experience of the Crisis. What the historians of appeasement have missed by failing to consider gender and by taking little interest in the reception of appeasement 'at home' is the vital domestic aspect of British foreign policy. We are reminded that politicians operate in a domestic political context, and thus have to consider public opinion. Politicians operate both in an intimate domestic context, as we have seen by paying greater heed to Chamberlain's 'sexual politics' and relationships with women in his inner circle, and in the sphere of domestic politics even when they are most preoccupied with foreign policy.

This is by no means an immutable set of circumstances. In fact, we can identify a unique set of factors in this period, and the culmination of three intertwining processes unleashed in the aftermath of the First World War: the political space being carved out by and the accompanying ambivalence about the new female electorate; the democratization of international affairs; and the socio-scientific and ethnographic methods under development during precisely these years that set out to diagnose and empower public opinion. In the chapter to come we will see how these processes conspired in the context of the Munich by-elections, where women were again represented as the best friends of Chamberlain's policy and as exercising an undue and dangerous influence over the nation.

8
'Don't Believe in Foreigners:' The Female Franchise Factor and the Munich By-elections

Quick on the heels of the Munich Agreement there was speculation that a general election would be called to capitalize on Chamberlain's vast popularity with women voters. It was believed that Chamberlain was "being pressed by some of his advisers and some of his newspapers to have a snatch election, in which he is to be paraded before the electorate, particularly the women voters, as the man who saved us from war."[1] In the absence of a general election, the post-Munich by-elections were the most reliable gauges of the Prime Minister's wavering popularity with the electorate as a whole and with women in particular, and the public unease about the power of women as an electoral force.

By mid-October 1938 seven by-elections were due to be contested, and the media soon referred to them as a referendum on appeasement and as a general election in miniature. The by-elections took place in the constituencies of Oxford City (27 October), Dartford (7 November), Walsall (16 November), Doncaster (17 November), Bridgwater (17 November), West Lewisham (24 November), and the Fylde Division of Lancashire (31 November). The eighth by-election at Kinross and West Perthshire on 21 December in which the Duchess of Atholl stood as an Independent against a National Conservative candidate also belongs to this group. Not only was this most revealing in a study of women and appeasement politics but, Ball argues, it is the most significant of all the by-elections as it was the only one to involve a prominent parliamentary critic of appeasement, it arose directly from controversies over European affairs, and it was a test of public attitudes to foreign policy.[2]

An earlier version of this chapter appeared as Julie V. Gottlieb, "'We Were Done the Moment We Gave Women the Vote': The Female Franchise Factor and the Munich By-elections, 1938–1939," in Julie V. Gottlieb and Richard Toye (eds.), *The Aftermath of Suffrage: Women, Gender, and Politics in Britain, 1918–1945* (Basingstoke: Palgrave, 2013), pp. 159–180.

The conclusions that can be drawn from both representational and expressive sources can only reveal so much, and it is a truism that in a democracy the most carefully examined evidence of public opinion is the election. By-elections in particular serve a number of functions. They offer opportunities to try out new party tactics; they have been used to test innovations in publicity; and they present opportunities to field new organization; but most crucially they are thought to reveal the state of public opinion in relation to both specific issues and the likely outcome of subsequent general elections.[3] However, while these Munich by-elections have been subjected to some psephological scrutiny, the instrumental role of gender in the choice of candidates, in voter choice, and in the tone of party appeals has been overlooked. On the eve of by-elections in Fulham and Litchfield earlier in 1938 the anti-appeasement *Daily Mirror* was in little doubt that electoral success hinged upon appealing to women voters, with headlines such as "Women can Make Premier Change his Policy."[4] The conservative press was just as sure that it would be the pro-Chamberlain women's vote that would decide these post-Munich by-elections, while Mass-Observation, which made close studies of these Munich by-elections, noted with growing frustration that the mass of women electors were pro-Chamberlain, instinctively pacifist, and ignorant about the wider world. As early as 1940 political scientists made a forensic study of these by-elections and concluded that they were geographically and demographically so random that they could neither prove the public endorsement nor the rejection of Chamberlain's policy. Rather, the low voter turnout and the continued stress on local issues in the majority of these cases demonstrated a heightened level of political apathy.[5] With more hindsight, Eatwell has shown how the government did badly in the seven by-elections in October and November 1938, even as the Munich Agreement "was believed to have been received with great rejoicing by the majority of the people of Britain." However, while Eatwell's analysis is entirely convincing, especially his assertion that "foreign policy in the two months after Munich attracted greater public attention than at any time since the clash between Gladstone and Disraeli over the Bulgarian massacres," at no point does he remark upon the polarization of opinion along gender lines.[6] In regard to the Oxford and Bridgwater by-elections, MacLean does, in contrast, recognize the importance of the perception of women's identification with the appeasers, but presumes that there is a lack of social scientific evidence to substantiate such a hypothesis.[7]

Allowing for the shortcomings of available data, gender did play an important part in these by-elections. There were many women among the by-election candidates; at all points of the political spectrum there was much concern and debate about the impact the female electorate would have on the results; and the whole appeasement debate and support for Chamberlain had already been gendered by the political parties and the press. The addition of 4,750,000 women voters to the British electorate with the Equal Franchise Act (July 1928) amplified the homogenization of women voters as a bloc. The study of the representations of women's engagement in the political process in these post-Munich by-elections speaks for more than the sum of its parts, as the most acute crises of the late 1930s—of democracy, of international relations, sexual, personal, and psychological—converged to feminize the policy of appeasement.

'Bewildered in our foreign policy:' gender and the West Fulham by-election

The West Fulham by-election of March 1938 is part of this story even though it took place before the Munich Crisis. The by-election in the neighbouring constituency of East Fulham in late October 1933 "became notorious as a political symbol of the locust years,"[8] and likewise due to what it revealed about public opinion on foreign affairs. Labour snapped up the seat with one of the most remarkable swings ever recorded, 29.2%. As the result strongly suggested wide public support for complete disarmament, it was among the early motivations for the organization of the LNU's (League of Nations Union) Peace Ballot.[9] (However, it returned to the Conservatives in 1935 when William Astor, son of Nancy Astor, won the seat.)

The West Fulham by-election was similarly noteworthy and newsworthy. It came at a critical time, shortly after Eden's resignation as Foreign Secretary over his opposition to the appeasement of Fascist Italy, after Chamberlain's assumption of control over foreign relations, after the Anschluss, and shortly after the Government's sacrifice of Spain to its friendship with Mussolini.[10] The candidacy of Labour's Dr Edith Summerskill was significant in itself, and her sex was both a point of strength and a liability. On the positive side, she had the ear of women voters and played on her distinguished medical career and her specialization in welfare issues. On the down side, it was noted that women voters had little to no interest in the European situation, and it was to this burning issue that Summerskill would really have wished to direct voters' attention. In the early stages of the campaign she represented herself as standing for the removal of all the disabilities of women whether legal, economic, or social, and it was duly noted that she had "lectured frequently on equal pay and opportunity and the problems of the professional woman and the status of women under democracy and under dictatorship." She had gained this deeper understanding of the worrying variations in women's status across diverse political systems on her visits to Italy, Germany, and Russia, making her "an advocate of peaceful methods of settlement of disputes between nations, of full and free use of democratic machinery nationally and internationally, and of the official Labour programme."[11] In short, she was both a feminist and anti-fascist, as well as a feminist anti-fascist, her European and fascist encounters sharpening her political conviction.

Against such a formidable woman politician as Summerskill, it was good practice for the Conservatives to send Nancy Astor to Fulham to campaign for their candidate Charles Busby, "a good-looking coal merchant."[12] Astor addressed a meeting of 175–200 women, mainly middle-aged, where she supported the Prime Minister and highlighted the failure of the League.[13]

Even though Summerskill had the support of Lloyd George's Council of Action, the LNU, and the Liberals, with figures such as Wilfrid Roberts and Megan Lloyd George appearing in the constituency to speak on her behalf, and at the beginning of her campaign at least one third of her speeches were devoted to foreign policy, she increasingly redirected her speeches to social questions. In contrast, Busby kept foreign matters and defence policy in the forefront.[14] In Fulham Mass-Observation observed that women voters "remain, as they have always been in lower middle-class constituencies ... concerned chiefly with such things as rent, rates, employment, and the price of food."[15] Once it seemed clear that women voters were repelled by discussion of foreign affairs, Summerskill changed track and profited from her expertise on issues most closely allied to women's sphere. As Mass-Observation's tallies show, in the speech at her opening meeting 52 minutes were devoted to foreign affairs, five minutes to personal, and nil to non-foreign, whereas at her third meeting the figures were 57, seven, and 53 minutes respectively.[16] Summerskill tailored her appeal to the domestic front, to such an extent that the *Observer* surmised that she was "hardly happy when talking of foreign affairs, and her replies, when questioned on Socialist policy in the present tangled skein of international matters obviously failed to carry conviction."[17] It would seem that Summerskill was bowing to public pressure, and Mass-Observation conducted a straw-poll survey on the eve of the by-election which revealed a number of interesting tendencies.

M-O asked 'Which is more important, home or foreign affairs?' There were apparent gender differentials, with the predictable penchant of women taking less interest in foreign affairs. However, these polls also offered some more indefinite revelations, and men also expressed ignorant, xenophobic, and isolationist opinions. Women's views on the relative importance of foreign affairs ranged from "Woman, 60: 'Both equally interested. One depends on the other. We must not interfere in Europe. Believes in the League," to "Woman, 35: 'No interest in either. My own home is all I live for,'" to "Woman, 60: 'Don't believe in foreigners.'"[18] Overall, of a sample of 250 people interviewed over a 24 hour period, the total that favoured foreign policy was a meagre 18%, home policy 66%, and both together/equally 16%, and less women than men thought that foreign affairs were more important. "The women differ strikingly from the men in being much less ready or able to answer. Men rarely say they don't know or don't care; women commonly say so."[19] From this raw data Mass-Observation concluded that "People are BEWILDERED in our foreign policy, or just ignorant.

The women are especially ignorant or (often) absolutely disinterested except in so far as they are themselves directly affected." This led Harrisson to believe "that FOREIGN affairs, on which anyway Labour cannot at present offer any drastically distinct foreign policy which people will easily understand, is NOT THE ONLY MAIN ISSUE SUITABLE FOR THIS ELECTION [capitalization in original]."[20]

Whether it was because she listened to her constituent who did not 'believe in foreigners' and took Mass-Observation's conclusions to heart, Summerskill's strategy could not have contrasted more with that later adopted by the Duchess of Atholl, even when they had in common their passionate opposition to appeasement. Later we will see how the duchess would lose the by-election because she identified herself almost exclusively with foreign policy and thus, by extension, with war, further alienating the voters in the rural Scottish constituency by being bagpiped in to her meetings and taking a map of Europe and pointer. Hawkishness was seen as unbecoming of a woman politician, while schoolmarmism was just as off-putting. In the end Summerskill's strategy was effective, winning the seat for Labour with a narrow majority, 16,583 votes against 15,162 for the Conservative Busby. The Fulham result was considered remarkable on many counts, not least because, as the *Manchester Guardian* put it, "the Labour candidate was a woman, and women have usually more difficulty in fighting tough seats than men."[21] In a complex formula, Summerskill's chemistry provided the right medicine on election day. She was a woman candidate with expertise in health and social care who was ready to suppress her internationalist credentials, while representing a staunchly anti-Government position on the nation's foreign policy. She gave rhetorical expression to this intersectional identity in her speeches where she used domestic tropes and metaphors to try to explain complex diplomatic problems. For example, she explained to voters the importance of protecting the freedom of small nations and why an international police force would solve international problems:

> If you are angry with your neighbour because she hangs the washing where it flaps across your yard, or inconveniences you in some way, you don't lean across the fence and throw a brick at her. You go to the local court and arrange for a summons to be issued. We can, if we try, do just the same among the nations. We of the Labour Party believe that collective security is the only real way of stopping war.[22]

She admitted later that a woman speaker "rarely burns much midnight oil on inventing aphorisms or flights of oratory" and hypothesized that "her biological structure may have something to do with this approach to speech-making,"[23] yet the Fulham electorate was evidently appeased by an anti-appeaser who brought the issues 'home' to them.

Waiting to congratulate Summerskill on her victory was Ellen Wilkinson. With her win there were now three Labour women MPs: Wilkinson herself, Agnes Hirdie, and Summerskill.[24] She supported Republican Spain against the uprising of General Franco, and visited Spain with Wilkinson in 1938, soon after which she embarked on a tour of the USA to advocate the Republican cause.[25] However, what was picked up on as distinctive about Summerskill was not so much her record as a feminist, nor her engagement with international relief work, nor even that her win represented a victory for Labour's foreign policy in defiance of still current pacifist tendencies within the Labour Party, but rather her "notable style and sense of dress."[26] We can speculate that women voters supported the anti-Chamberlain candidate not because of her anti-Government stance but rather because of her appeal to bread and butter issues, further enhanced by her attractive and fashionable appearance.

Just a couple of weeks later at the Litchfield by-election, the question of the important influence of women voters and their presumed support for the Government were again raised. The Conservative National Government candidate Mr Craddock was counting on women's support, his wife carrying on a campaign among women electors "whose uppermost thoughts these days, she knows, 'is the longing for peace and security.'"[27] And yet it was C.C. Poole who won Litchfield for Labour by a majority of 826, the ninth gain by Labour in the 16th by-elections up to that point since the 1935 General Election.

In June in West Derbyshire the by-election win of the Conservative Henry Hunloke was put down to support for the Government's foreign policy, but also to the young candidate's film-star good looks, a suspicion further aroused by the fact that in that constituency there were 2,000 more women than men. It was predicted that "women will just LOVE to have their laws made by him!"[28] Consistent with the discourses aroused by the Flapper's Vote in 1928-1929, here again we hear that women's voting patterns and political decision-making are based on the frivolous and the superficial, even when there are the very weightiest issues to decide.[29] "Now that women have the vote, for some reason, a symmetrical set of features is not unhelpful to a candidate."[30]

'The problem of this election is the female vote:' gender trouble at Oxford City

Oxford City was perhaps the most famous of the post-Munich by-elections due to the candidacy of Alexander Dunlop Lindsay (Independent Progressive), Master of Balliol College and long-standing member of the Labour Party. In the case of both Oxford and Bridgwater the conventional opposition parties withdrew in order to give the best chance to the anti-government candidate. Oxford was also a ground-breaking by-election as it saw the first constituency opinion poll ever conducted in Britain, while the newly launched *Picture Post* published a generously illustrated feature article. Further, it was in the fight for this seat that the Popular Front was its most united, exemplifying not only the possibilities of collaboration between Labourites and Communists, but more crucially between Labour and Liberals.[31] As Pugh has shown, Lib-Lab collaboration was actually far more effective in giving some coherence to the Popular Front and far more pro-active in the wider fight against fascism than has otherwise been acknowledged, with too much attention having been conferred on Labour-Communist squabbling and resultant anti-fascist strategies.[32]

Oxford City also functioned as a thermometer measuring the temperature of the battle of the sexes over national policy. Here too the ambivalence about the power of the female electorate was very much in evidence. To start off with, the motivation for Lindsay's candidature was attributed to a woman's influence: while he had thus far lacked any parliamentary ambitions, he had an 'enthusiastic' wife.[33] Both Lindsay and his opponent Quintin Hogg (Con.) were reported to be "wooing the women voters of the constituency by every means at their disposal, by personal canvassing, and by loudspeaker vans which have made electors listen willy-nilly to the claims of either side." Hogg was even better equipped than his opponent as he was "admirably supported by Mrs Hogg and a host of women workers."[34] Lindsay, on the other hand, had cross-party support, including that of some of the most vociferous of the women anti-appeasers. Those who happily identified themselves with his united Progressive front and came to speak on his behalf were Mrs Corbett Ashby, Lady Rhondda, Lady Layton, Megan Lloyd George, and Miss Ellen Wilkinson. In addition, the daughter of the late Liberal PM Herbert Asquith, Lady Violet Bonham-Carter, campaigned vigorously for Lindsay, while Asquith's widow, the Countess of Oxford and Asquith, announced that she would vote for Hogg in "this craziest of by-elections" where "party lines have become unrecognizable."[35] In the end, there was much speculation about what could account for Lindsay's loss, and a recurring explanation was that there, "almost in the centre of England, a large proportion of women were still obsessed by gratitude to Mr Chamberlain for momentarily averting war."[36]

From the Right there was a sense of reassurance that the women's vote would buoy Chamberlainite candidates, and in mid-October when Michael Harmsworth, son of the *Daily Mail's* proprietor, wanted to be considered as the National Conservative candidate in Duff Cooper's St. George constituency if a by-election was to be forced there, it was "in the belief that the women's vote will go against all anti-Chamberlain war-mongers."[37] Coming from the other side of the political spectrum, Mass-Observation's founder Tom Harrisson conducted a snap poll in Oxford on the eve of the by-election, and what struck him most was the splintering of opinion along gender lines, his report exuding resentment that women were likely to vote against Lindsay. Harrisson pondered a number of bridges over this gender gap, the most pragmatic he felt was to focus more on home affairs and the 'home aspects of war' in the campaign. He remained hopeful that even if women's opinion was Pro-Chamberlain, many would ultimately be swayed by their husbands in the end, as it remained the case that the 'man of the house is most important.' Mass Observers found that there was respect for Lindsay and that he was regarded as an outstanding candidate, but that this view prevailed mainly among those within academic circles. When asked 'WHAT do you think about Lindsay as a candidate?' "Women are undoubtedly far more Pro-Chamberlain than men. I think that the problem of this election is the female vote. Leave the men to vote according to their powerful tradition of that obscure 'fair play.'" In this snap sample conducted over a two-hour period "MEN who were favourable to Lindsay equalled in number those against and doubtful. Women for Lindsay were outnumbered by against and doubtful by five to one." These results led Harrisson to make a number of suggestions that might help Lindsay's campaign along.

> Deal all the time with women. In this connection, do NOT forget that women have reacted violently against the crisis, via gas masks, and that the line of approach to them is not likely to work if Anti-Chamberlain, for they feel he saved us from war, and it is impracticable to argue that in this short campaign.

Under these circumstances he insisted that "the line can only be Home Affairs. And the crisis reaction has swung women back onto that with a woosh." Harrisson allowed his own impressions to intrude, much more in keeping with the remit of Mass-Observation diarists than with the 'objective' social scientist. Throwing academic caution to the wind with his free use of expletives, he remarked:

> I personally feel that this election must be fought simply on foreign affairs, and peace policy, but Above All on home aspects of war. On ARP, evacuation, gas, food, trenches, the government unpreparedness. Here is a line that women CAN and DO get ... And that the difference between men and women is vital in that, perhaps for the first time in any recent election. The general feeling of men: Fuck Hitler. And we ought to have stood up to him before. The general feeling of women: Anything for peace. Chamberlain did his best. He's a good gent.[38]

His view was a fair prediction of the result, and on 27 October, with a 76.3% turnout, Hogg polled 15,797 against Lindsay's 12,363 votes. But where Harrisson and others were mistaken was that all these closely-timed by-elections would go the same way.

Mrs Adamson and the Dartford by-election

In Dartford the Conservative candidate Mr Godfrey W. Mitchell (Conservative), who asked voters to support him as a mark of gratitude and confidence in Chamberlain, was running against Mrs Jennie L. Adamson (Labour) in what was considered to be the tightest race of the lot. Adamson had contested this seat in the 1935 General Election, narrowly losing to the Conservative.[39] Adamson's race was widely regarded as a referendum on the recent Munich agreement, and in an open letter Labour leader Clement Attlee highlighted its significance insofar as:

> [t]his Government has now been in power for nearly seven years and has brought us to the brink of war. It had no constructive policy for peace and had shown gross incompetence in providing for the defence of the country. The only hope for humanity is that there should be a change in the policy of Great Britain, and to effect this there must be a change of Government.[40]

There was no attempt to deemphasize foreign policy even though the anti-Government candidate was female. She too had cross-party support in the shape of the Council of Action. Further, the centrality of foreign policy was illustrated by the "unusual incident" of the LNU holding a meeting at the Town Hall in Crayford on the subject of 'Which way to world peace?,' where both candidates appeared on the platform to answer questions on a questionnaire.[41]

Even as the post-Munich euphoria was fading, there remained serious concern that this by-election would go the way of Oxford City. Women's 'obsession' with gratitude for the PM was reckoned to be even stronger in a largely working-class division that extended along the south bank of the Thames almost from Woolwich to Gravesend, and was thus particularly vulnerable to air attack in the event of war. While there was some evidence "that a certain number of Conservative male voters will abstain through disgust either at the Government's weak foreign policy or at its rearmament and ARP failures," it was still expected that "the extra women's vote will more than compensate for those defections."[42] Of all the by-elections, Dartford was considered the most difficult to forecast because "opinion three weeks ago had swung over to predict the return of the Government candidate through the votes for women offered in thankfulness to Mr Chamberlain. Since then shock of the crisis has lifted and criticism has been poured out by opponents of the Government."[43] Were women voters still so enamoured with Chamberlain the peace maker?

In the final reckoning, Adamson won with a 4,238 majority.[44] She had been able to rely on the support of ten Labour Women's Sections in the constituency and in adjoining ones to rally to help the campaign.[45] The result was seen as "a curious commentary on the instability of public opinion" and had the election "been held three weeks ago Mr Godfrey Mitchell would have been returned through the votes of women offered in thankfulness to Mr Chamberlain." But "the shock of the crisis" had since passed, and as one of the results was that "46,5000 of Dartford's 130,000 voters condemn[ed] what was done at Munich."[46] Adamson herself declared it a victory against the foreign policy of the Government and the betrayal of Czechoslovakia and democracy, and she asserted that it showed "Mr Chamberlain that he had not got the people of this country behind him and he must go."[47] Further, there was another curiosity about Adamson's election—for the fourth time in the history of the House of Commons a husband and wife sat together as MPs, her husband W.M. Adamson representing the Cannock Division of Staffordshire for Labour.[48]

Regardless of the marital accord in Parliament represented by the Adamsons, all was not well in the relationship between the sexes projected onto the national level. It was against the background of these by-election campaigns that National Labour MP Harold Nicolson had levelled his charges against the women of Britain when he addressed the National Council of Women, his own 'J'Accuse' in which he argued that "while men had been resolute women had only been afraid."[49] British women, as a collective, and women voters, as a bloc, were being held responsible for national suicide.

From Dartford to Walsall and Bridgwater

In some respects the Dartford result provided the necessary counter-evidence to Nicolson's sexist allegations. The Dartford result proved that not only could a woman fight successfully on a foreign policy ticket, but also that women voters were not as reliably wedded to Chamberlain's policy as it may at first have appeared. The lesson to be drawn from Dartford, according to Labour campaigners in the upcoming by-election in Walsall, was the instability of the assumption that women would support the Conservatives out of gratitude for Chamberlain's peace. In Walsall the Labour organisers were drawing one conclusion from the Dartford result:

> they regard it as disproving completely the theory that women electors are strongly disposed to cast votes of gratitude for Mr Chamberlain for having saved them from the perils of war a few weeks ago. This theory was confidently held by Conservative officials, many of whom believed that women's votes would be the decisive factor in keeping Dartford for the Government. Dartford provides no evidence to support it, and Walsall, whatever the result here may be, should finally explode it.[50]

In the same light, commentators argued that "the Dartford result, following on the Oxford poll, exhibits convincingly the untruth of the common Conservative statement (repeated every other day as a sort of devotional incantation by *The Times*) that the 'overwhelming mass of British opinion' is 'wholeheartedly' with Mr Chamberlain." More to the point:

> such an absurd statement is, of course, contrary to the personal experience of every one of us but it is useful to have it shown up in black and white. It is useful also to see the explosion of the legend, fostered by fond Government hopes, that if a statesman can be labelled 'peacemaker' the women will be certain to follow him; they did not at Dartford. Why women should be supposed to be less capable of an intelligent critical judgement than men always seemed a little obscure.[51]

However, the lesson to be learned from Dartford was not entirely unambiguous, as the Conservatives held Walsall, and in this case women voters might well have buttressed a peace bloc.[52] Further, notwithstanding the apparent success of her vehement critique of appeasement on the hustings, when Adamson delivered her maiden speech on 15 November the topic was economics, maternal and infant mortality, and the impact of indirect taxation on women.

Speculation about how women would vote carried through all these by-elections. In the Bridgwater Division of Somerset the Conservative P.G. Heathcote-Amory was running against the broadcaster and *News Chronicle* journalist Vernon Bartlett, standing as an Independent Progressive. Bartlett received the endorsement of the Council of Action, as well as letters of support from Eleanor Rathbone and Ellen Wilkinson, among others, support for which he was very worthy considering the consistent vehemence of anti-fascism in his journalism. Wilkinson was enlisted to rouse women voters, sending a letter of appeal to the women to vote for Bartlett as a vote 'for a policy of constructive peace.' She wrote:

> True peace can only be secured by removing the causes of war while at the same time insisting on the observance of international law ... Mr Chamberlain gave way instead, and he has gone on giving way. Can this bring peace? Every sensible woman knows it will only lead to further demands and eventually to war.[53]

Wilkinson's profile, as a woman and a staunch anti-Chamberlainite, with a past as a member of the PPU, rendered her support invaluable in trying to convince women voters. While Bartlett did not receive official support from Labour, he had the strong support of the Liberals, with several Liberal bigwigs coming down to take part in a big demonstration on his behalf, including Megan Lloyd George MP, Wickham Steed, Sir Charles Hobhouse, Lady Violet Bonham-Carter and Richard Acland.

The Bridgwater result was one of the more unpredictable. The constituency was a Tory stronghold. Further, the new register contained 44,653 electors, and there were about 4,000 more women than men. Yet, in the end,

Bartlett won, which was considered 'a by-election sensation,' and a notable victory for the Popular Front. On 17 November 1938 with a turnout of 82.3%, Bartlett polled 19,540 and Heathcote-Amory 17,208 votes.

The Doncaster, West Lewisham, and Fylde by-elections

In Doncaster it was the wife of the National Liberal candidate, Mrs Monteith, who dug the trench that divided male and female over the rectitude of the policy of appeasement.[54] She had taken an active part in her husband's campaign, emphasizing that it was the men who wanted war for all the wrong reasons, while women wanted peace. She argued, "if we had fought in the recent crisis when we were bound by no treaty it would have been a fight to please men who did not like another nation's politics. She asks the women electors to devote themselves to the task of making peace secure."[55] *The Times* was confident that Alexander Montieth could turn the Labour majority of 8,000 into a Government victory due to the large element of Liberal Nonconformists among the railways workers and engineers in the town, as well as "the support of a large proportion of the vote of the women who support Mr Chamberlain's peace policy."[56] (Doncaster was, in fact, a win for Labour's John Morgan.) So, too, in West Lewisham, the sixth by-election after Munich, it was predicated that gender would play a decisive role, with an electorate where there were 30,501 men and 37,140 women. Here in West Lewisham the Government candidate did win.

There was another woman Labour candidate in the by-election in Fylde. Occasioned by the death of Lord Stanley, it was contested by Captain Claud Granville Lancaster as the National Government candidate, and Labour's Dr Mabel Tylecote, a teacher of history to the Workers' Education Association, and wife of a prominent Manchester doctor. It was hoped she would be able to "rally a useful section of middle-class opinion."[57] Tylecote had hitherto been involved in local affairs and social service, but the mounting danger of the international situation drew her to national politics. She was also fighting on an anti-Munich pro-League platform, explaining:

'I suppose I shall be asked what I would have done at Munich. My answer to that question is, 'I should never have been at Munich; I should have been at Geneva.' ... I do not acquit Lord Baldwin of responsibility for the present situation. I say that he and, later, Mr Chamberlain have been guilty of dishonesty in the matter of our foreign policy ... We are suffering from the surrender of pledges and principles. In these days people think a good deal about the risks of war. I think, however, we should not overlook the risks of continued surrender.'[58]

However sound her arguments, despite the fact she "was said to be one of the best non-Conservative candidates offered to the constituency in years,"[59] and notwithstanding her rehearsal here of the 'Guilty Men' thesis that would hold sway for generations to come, she lost to the Government candidate in Fylde. Further, while anti-appeasers had anticipated that Kristallnacht (9–10 November) would have turned voters against the Chamberlainites, this was not the case.[60]

The Duchess of Atholl gambles it all

The by-election that most effectively illustrates the complex and tense interplay between gender and support for appeasement was the one in Kinross and West Perthshire, Scotland, a by-election that was brought on by the sitting member herself, Katherine the Duchess of Atholl (1874–1960). Possible to view as a feminist in practice—she was the first woman Scottish MP and the first Conservative woman to become a minister as Parliamentary Secretary at the Board of Education from 1924–1929—but certainly not in ideology—she had been opposed to the pre-war women's suffrage movement—the duchess was hardly the most predictable of committed anti-fascists. A Conservative from the Right of the party on so many other issues, she was not the most likely candidate for anti-Chamberlain scourge either.

The Duchess had gained her nick-name the 'Red' Duchess for her passionate commitment to the Republican cause in Spain, which also led to her acute awareness of and public campaigns to draw attention to the Nazi menace by seeing to it that an unexpurgated translation of *Mein Kampf* was published. She had already worked untiringly for the relief of refugees, especially Basque children, leading an all-party national joint committee on the issue. With Eleanor Rathbone she had visited Spain, demonstrating considerable personal courage when addressing at least one meeting during an air raid. She wrote the bestselling *Searchlight on Spain*, which sold 47,000 copies in the first week and was in its third edition by the time of her by-election, selling some 300,000 copies overall. She had also visited Roumania, Czechoslovakia, and Yugoslavia with Rathbone and Lady Layton, addressing public meetings where she advocated collective security under the League of Nations. For her efforts she attracted the hostility of many of her Catholic constituents, as well as the attention of Mosley's BU: throughout 1937–1938 she had received offensive letters from members of her constituency association, and a series of Blackshirt meetings were held in her constituency at Crieff, at Aberfeldy, and at Auchterarder.[61]

Although she had emerged as a national figure by becoming an outspoken critic of the Government's foreign policy, she was a personality of contrasts. She puzzled many with her inconsistencies, and in 1931–1932 she was vociferously anti-Russian, but two years later she was eager for Russian admission to the League. "She annoyed her party by opposing the Government of India Bill, though she does not now criticise its administration. She is a strong Imperialist, and her desire for the prosperity of the Empire is combined with an equally ardent desire that it should be faithful to its manifold responsibilities."[62] Her apparent political promiscuity led to a falling out with her own party, and already she had been threatened with loss of the party whip for supporting the candidature of Randolph Churchill in the Wavertree by-election of February 1935. For the 1935 General Election her constituency Conservative association had agreed to respect her independence in foreign affairs, but her doggedness to defy her own party strained this relationship to breaking point. While she returned to the party fold for a short time after the Italian invasion of Abyssinia, soon after this she was again in conflict with her own party over Spain. She lost the party whip in April 1938 because of her persistent protests to the Prime Minister, after which she sat as an Independent. Indeed, along with a small group of fellow back-bench Conservative dissenters on matters of foreign policy, the duchess regularly abstained from foreign policy votes throughout 1938. However, she was not part of the inner circle of anti-appeasers, and never a recognized member of the Edenites or so-called 'glamour boys,' as will be explored in the next chapter. She resigned from Parliament in November 1938 in order to force a by-election on the issue of foreign policy.

The by-election turned into a two-way race after Mrs Coll Macdonald, the Liberal candidate for West Perth and Kinross, stood down because of "the supreme importance of the issues connected with foreign policy, on which this by-election will be fought,"[63] and due to legitimate concern that they might split the anti-Government vote. However, MacDonald's withdrawal did not meet without resistance from the Liberal candidate herself. Meanwhile the duchess stood as an Independent because, as she explained:

> the foreign policy for which I stand is not only the policy of Mr Eden, Mr Churchill and most of the Unionist Members of Parliament who have devoted time to foreign affairs, but also the official policy of the Liberal and Labour parties. I am standing in this election as an Independent, so the Unionists, Liberals and Socialists may be able to support me without voting against their several parties. It is through co-operation of this kind that I believe we can best attain the national unity that we all desire in this time of danger.[64]

She received the tacit support of Winston Churchill and Robert Boothby, even if both decided against campaigning for her in order not to land in the same hot water with their own constituency associations as she had with hers.[65] While the press dubbed her a 'glamour girl,' and as such the only female figure identified with the Edenite 'Glamour boys,' she did not, in fact, get any active support from any of them, nor did she ever attend any of their boys-only meetings.[66] They offered her as a sacrificial lamb to the electorate.

Her disloyalty to party won her the consideration of some members of other parties.[67] With her old party having turned its back on her, the duchess was enmeshed in a politician's nightmare, and "found herself in the strangest company, in a political sense, that any Parliamentary candidate could ever expect."[68] The anti-fascist front supported her, recognizing that "courage is the dominant characteristic of this rather frail-looking woman."[69] It was also seen as good timing that only a couple of weeks before her by-election the Labour Party Executive had decided for more tolerance to anti-Government independent candidates. While they could not be further apart on most women's issues, Lady Rhondda was deeply moved by the Atholl's courage, appreciating that "she has burned her boats and challenged public opinion. If there were more courage like hers this country might be saved," and Rhondda launched an appeal for funds to support Atholl's campaign in *Time and Tide*.[70] Others who came to campaign on her behalf were Eleanor Rathbone, Lord Cecil, Josiah Wedgwood (who suffered a heart attack during the campaign at his hotel in Dunkeld), Vernon Bartlett, Dr Lindsay, Lord Lloyd, Dingle Foot, Richard Acland and Shiela Grant Duff.[71] Lord Cecil supported her rebellion against the Conservative Party, speaking of her in the most glowing of terms: "She is a woman of great ability, energy and courage. I believe it is essential that there should be members of the House of Commons capable of thinking for themselves on a great issue and acting on their convictions."[72] She had the support of Unionists who followed her out of a sense of personal loyalty; the Liberals who would agree with nothing else in her politics up to this point in her career; Lloyd George and his Council of Action; the Socialist who have agreed upon a policy of non-intervention in the election; the Secretary to the Kinross and West Perth divisional Labour party from 1923–1931 who appealed to all his old colleagues to support her; even the Communists were ready to support her, but she told them she did not want their company. In short, she had a motley coalition behind her, more part of the problem rather than a recipe for electoral success. Her gleeful opponents deemed this "another of those anti-Government combinations who see so little to admire in Mr Chamberlain and his policy that they would prefer almost anything else."[73]

In contrast, her Conservative opponent benefitted from concerted Government support, which included some 50 MPs travelling to the constituency on his behalf. Among these was Miss Horsburgh, the Duchess's fellow Scottish woman Conservative MP (Dundee) who remarked: "'I believe it is a tragedy that your Member was not in London or in the House of Commons on September 28 when Mr Chamberlain received the vital summons to Munich or she would not be doing what she is doing now.'"[74] We will recall that while the Tory Party was rejoicing in Parliament and in private at the terms of the Munich Agreement, the duchess was in North America on anti-Franco lecture tour.

In the end, the duchess lost her bid. There was fair voter turnout at 67%, but W.M. Snadden (Con.) won with 11,809 votes to her 10,495, with speculation that the proximity of Christmas and adverse weather conditions in the dispersed largely rural constituency may have contributed to her loss. Others have attributed her defeat to her unpopularity locally, compounded by her evasion of local issues in this campaign, and her ineptitude as a politician, exploited by the Conservative who ably recast her as a warmonger. And yet the Duchess did not sulk for long after what must have been a humiliating turning point in her political career. Already in early January, 1939, she joined forces with Duncan Sandys to form a new political group, launched at a meeting at Caxton Hall and attended by 300 people.[75]

Gendering the Duchess of Atholl's by-election

The Duchess of Atholl defied the political taxonomies of her time, and both the gender factor and the dynamic of anti-fascist commitment played themselves out differently in this by-election story. Stuart Ball's detailed study provides a meticulous blow-by-blow account of the progress of the duchess's political career, and the events leading up to and including the by-election itself.[76] Ball's concern is the administration and functioning of the party, and here in particular that of the relationship between the local Associations, their MP, and Central Office. However, he only shows a passing interest in the gender dimension, noting both that the duchess was not invested in feminist politics in any ideological sense, to be sure, as well as drawing some attention to the gender differentials in support of appeasement in this as in other constituencies at like moments of crisis.

The duchess defied gender stereotypes by caring far less about local issues and more about foreign affairs, travelling a great deal to the world's trouble spots on various missions, and publishing on these topics. Indeed, "the underlying tension in the relationship between the lesser landowners and the ducal house was reinforced by the problem of the duchess's femininity—or lack of it—for she no longer seemed to be conforming to the acceptable model."[77] Her election posters left little doubt as to the prominent and, in fact, sole issue of her campaign. Posters outside the duchess's committee rooms read:

1) Let Your Empire Greetings read Duchess Victorious
2) Only a Strong Britain can Secure Peace
3) PEACE NEWS Country before Party/Vote for the Duchess/Help Fight for Peace/Apply Within
4) Duchess Policy—Peace with Honour
5) Country before Party

Outside the Duchess's Committee Rooms, December 16, the following bills in black letter on a white ground with a Union Jack border were stuck up in the windows:

1) Vote for the Duchess and Honesty and Courage
2) Forewarned is Forearmed! Vote for the Duchess
3) Country before Party: Vote for the Duchess

4) Vote for the Duchess: the Dictators are Watching
5) Send Hitler your Answer: Vote for the Duchess.[78]

She ran a negative campaign, arguing that "Munich has brought us no sign of the appeasement for which our Government had hoped. On the contrary, both Herr Hitler's speeches and the officially-controlled German Press have become increasingly aggressive. And there has been a persecution of the Jews in German of unparalleled brutality."[79] She continued that the attendant danger was of Franco's victory in Spain, which would make Hitler's domination of Europe complete.

While other women candidates in these by-elections either played down international affairs or shrouded their anti-appeasement in the cloak of the opposition's 'peace' discourse, a vote for the duchess was widely regarded as a vote for war. One of the duchess's sub-agents later reported how "the slogan, vote for the duchess and you vote for war, often took this form: you are a supporter of the duchess? Yes! Then you want your son to be killed."[80] There were more women than men on the electoral roll, and "women were genuinely afraid—as had been so carefully explained to them on the doorsteps—that a vote for Kitty meant a vote for war and that their husbands and sons would be off to the army and dead within the year."[81] Indeed, she stated publically that "I blame my defeat on the votes of the women. During the past three days certain unfair speeches were made which indicated to women that if they voted for me they would be voting for war. This had a great effect on women, especially those with sons."[82] She came to understand that women, who made up 55% of the electorate, were not her natural supporters, especially in this campaign, further undermining any sense she may have had about sex solidarity.

By adopting the role of hawk she allowed herself to appear both unladylike by antiquated Victorian standards, and unfashionable as set against the modish pacifism of many feminists and younger people, which was only compounded by her dour dress and appearance. Nor did it help that due to a sudden bout of illness her husband, the duke, was unable to take an active part in her campaign, only adding emphasis to her loneliness and her distance from more acceptable models of women's political behaviour. The duchess's by-election campaign asked voters to take many positions that were counter-intuitive. First, to place country before party and to transcend their allegiances to parties; second, to accept the tantamount importance of foreign affairs in this largely rural and agriculturally-based constituency; and third, to accept a woman candidate who took on the role of belligerent against a local male candidate who could appear to be a dove by riding the coat tails of the ashen-faced PM who had very recently declared that he had achieved 'peace in our time' at Munich.

How should we explain the nature of the duchess's anti-fascist political belief? So many of the anti-fascist women that figure in this study came to their political position organically either via the Liberal party, from feminist politics, or from Leftist politics. In contrast, the duchess's spirit of resistance emanated from her humanitarianism, and it is interesting that the most outspoken and ultimately the most courageous of women anti-appeasers was a self-avowed non-feminist, emerging from a tradition of feminine political endeavours in an auxiliary capacity and respecting the rigid demarcation between the separate spheres. In this sense she would have more in common with those women on the Right and Far Right who harped on about women's duties and were more than a bit dubious about campaigns for women's rights. Thus the duchess did not object to fascism from a particularly female perspective, avoiding the jargon of providing 'a woman's point of view' or a 'woman's perspective,' but instead arrived at her anti-fascism via her conservatism about the appropriate sphere of interest for women, namely philanthropic work. Williams believes that her moniker 'Red Duchess' is misrepresentative: "she was nothing of the sort: she was simply doing what she felt to be morally necessary in the face of injustice."[83] That time in the orbit of anti-fascist liberals and leftists in the late 1930s did not tempt her to cross the floor is well exemplified by her choice of post-war causes when she remerged as a Cold Warrior campaigning against Communist brutality—as before the war she had against fascist outrages—in Poland, Czechoslovakia, and Hungary. She was back to the more familiar terrain of right-wing politics, earning herself the unfortunate and unfair new nickname 'Fascist Beast.' Helpfully, Olechnowicz has provided us with the conceptual framework we need to situate the duchess's anti-fascism, arguing as he does for "the significance of a 'liberal' anti-fascism, which brought together many Liberal, Conservative and Labour politicians and intellectuals in cross-party pressure groups." What united this diverse cohort was "resistance to the ideological challenge to English parliamentary democracy represented by continental 'totalitarian' movements."[84] She certainly proved that one could be an effective anti-fascist from the Right.

Expectations of women electors in later by-elections

The Duchess of Atholl's spectacular loss would have only added substance to the perception that women remained the best friends of the policy of appeasement. Therefore in East Norfolk, the campaign literature of the National Liberal candidate, Mr F. Medlicott contained messages directed to women voters, with the candidate's wife appealing "to them to support and encourage Mr Chamberlain and his Government in the task of consolidating the work of negotiation and appeasement."[85] Indeed, Tories were still trying to capitalize on women's inordinate support for appeasement in early 1939.[86] It remained the assumption that women constituents would be the more receptive to the underlying message of appeasement, which included trying to convince them that they had allies in their overwhelming desire for peace in the populations of the dictatorships.

Another by-election was necessitated in Holderness, Yorkshire, by the death of the sitting Conservative MP, Sir Servington Savery, early in 1939. Again there was a woman candidate, Miss Aline Mackinnon standing for the Liberals, and asking the electorate to decide "whether they were prepared to support the policy of Mr Chamberlain or the policy of the League of Nations and standing by our allies."[87] She had contested the 1935 General Election in the same constituency, and this time she was ready to step down if the Labour candidate would do the same in order to make way for an Independent Progressive candidate. However, Labour refused to do so, and Mackinnon decided not to withdraw. Behind her was organized the support of prominent Liberals, including Richard Acland MP, Lady Gladstone, president of the Women's Liberal Federation, and Mrs Wintringham, vice-chairman of the federation and prospective Liberal candidate for Gainsborough. Mrs Corbett Ashby was also active in the campaign, herself prospective Liberal candidate for Scarborough and Whitby. The Conservative candidate, Mr Brathwaite, repeated a by now familiar assumption that would serve in his favour: "women electors, who outnumber the men by over 3,000 [in the constituency] are definitely behind the Prime Minister in his efforts to secure appeasement, and an exceptionally large number of women, from Hull to Buckrose as well as from inside the division, are working for him."[88] In the end it was, apparently, women's support rather than the candidacy of a woman that decided the election, as the Conservative candidate was victorious, Mackinnon coming second in the four-corned race.

In Batley and Morley, which had seen a Labour victory in the last election, the contest was between Mr W.D. Willis (Conservative) and Mr H. Beaumont (Labour). Here too women *en bloc* were seen as the decisive factor in winning the election. While Beaumont was concentrating on cultivating the Liberal vote, evoking the legacy of Gladstone and asking what he "would have said about the foreign policy of the Government and the tyrannies and cruelties in Germany and Italy to-day," he also pointed out "that the women of the division have it in their power to decide the election, and as the Labour majority in 1935 was under 3,000 and the women voters outnumbered the men by nearly 4,500 this may well be true." In any case, "both sides are making determined efforts to secure the support of the women electors. Mr Willis believes a big proportion will be for him because he represents the man whose efforts averted war last autumn."[89] Willis received enthusiastic help from a large band of women workers, and held special meetings for women, one addressed by Miss Irene Ward MP. His opponent too organized women's meetings where Mrs J Adamson MP, Mrs Ayrton Gould, and Miss Mary Sutherland, as well as Mrs Beaumont, made star turns. As on other occasions, visible backing by women MPs was considered an important part of by-election strategies.

There was another flurry of by-elections in the winter of 1939. Within 12 days in March alone the House of Commons lost six of its members by death, and another two by-elections were made necessary by the appointment of the Conservative MP for Kincardine and Western as Governor of South Australia, and that of the Conservative MP for Birmingham Aston as Governor of Madras, resulting in eight by-elections pending. In these by-elections there were no women candidates, nor was gender seen as particularly relevant in deciding the results. What may account for this change or these variables?

There was a perceptible decline in interest in international affairs across the board, and Labour's victory in North Southwark on 18 May, 1939, was attributed by the successful candidate, Mr Isaacs, to the profound dissatisfaction of the people of the constituency with the conduct of the Government. The voters there "would not permit international questions to side-track home questions." Herbert Morrison MP, secretary of the London Labour Party, drew a similar conclusion, namely that "North Southwark demand greater attention to our economic and social problems at home and a courageous clear-cut policy for the collective organisation of peace abroad, including a sincere willingness to co-operate with the Soviet Union to this end."[90] That same day the Government won the two other seats being contested, the Abbey Division of Westminster, and Aston, Birmingham. These results were understood to signify neither great enthusiasm for Chamberlain nor that Labour was making headway, but rather electoral apathy as there was a 30% drop in voter turnout. What was considered startling about these by-elections was "their uniform tribute of indifference to party politics," with only three electors out of ten even troubling themselves to go to the polls, "a slump probably without precedent." A two-pronged explanation was proffered:

> that the Government does not fully represent the dominant forces of public opinion, and therefore evokes no enthusiasm, apart from what may be still left of Munich-hysteria. And the other half is that the Labour Party, in its eagerness to stand up to the dictators and its reluctance to accept the necessary measures to that end, sheds a large proportion of its bewildered following.[91]

Nonetheless, in the Abbey Division of Westminster where the very young Gabriel Carritt, formerly secretary of the LNU youth groups, was standing as the anti-Government and anti-appeasement candidate, there remained a concern about how women would sway the vote, and Mass-Observation surveys found that women were still expressing their support for Chamberlain.[92] By the time the Kennington by-election was approaching later that month, candidates were "faced with the difficulty of finding really live issues,"[93] in the lull before the storm of war. (Shortly after war broke out it was agreed between the chief whips of the political parties in the House of Commons to avoid war-time by-elections, and that the party holding a seat was to nominate a successor when a vacancy occurred.)[94] What is noteworthy of these explanations is that women are no longer figured as accountable for political inertia or for unconditional admiration for a notional peace maker. There was a unique set of circumstances in 1938, a perfect storm of sorts, that made women, imagined collectively, a minority whose power and influence was seen as both decisive and dangerous.

Certainly by the summer of 1939 the significance of the female franchise factor was seen to have diminished. When the anti-appeasement, Popular Front Liberal candidate, Mr Horabin, was victorious over the pro-Chamberlain Conservative Mr Whitehouse in North Cornwall, the argument made was that women voters had finally been brought around.[95] The conservative press tried to stress that:

> the 'peace or war' issue of the North Cornwall by-election is one which will probably influence the minds of women electors of the division more than anything else. Realizing this, the National Conservatives are pressing home at women's meetings all over the division the debt of gratitude of women of the country owe to Mr Chamberlain for saving their homes and families by his Munich intervention.[96]

Special efforts were being made by local party organizations to target women voters, and Miss Irene Ward MP came to support the Tory candidate. However, this was to little avail and despite the progress Conservatism had been making in North Cornwall in recent years "the people in the constituency have in the main understood the case against the Government. Despite the natural fears of war entertained by the women voters, they have appreciated Mr Horabin's point that the Chamberlain foreign policy created the danger of war."[97] Women had ceased to be the electoral 'problem' that they had been only a few months earlier.

Conclusion: the problem of women's elections in post-enfranchisement Britain

In the discourses surrounding these by-elections we can discern many of the leitmotivs in the metanarrative of women's post-enfranchisement citizenship. On the more positive side, the Munich by-elections marked the progress women had made in the political sphere. The number of women candidates and the victory of two Labour women, Summerskill and Adamson, stand out. In 1922 the three major parties nominated only 33 women for the 615 seats. The total rose to 69 by 1929, but this was still only 4% of the total number of candidates, and by 1935 it was just 5%.[98] Women were also more successful winning their seats at by-elections, and at least ten of the women to become MPs between the wars won their seats at by-elections.[99] Further, considering that the powerful assumption was that women were the strongest supporters of appeasement, of the women by-election candidates only one stood on a pro-Chamberlain National Government platform.[100] While some of these women candidates made an effort to emphasize their traditional gender roles and woman-centred political interests, such as Summerskill, others did not shy away from playing the foreign policy card, which would lead to success in the case of Adamson, and disappointing failure in the case of the Duchess of Atholl. In addition, public women filled prominent supporting roles in many of the by-election campaigns, and all parties mobilized their 'star' women politicians alongside women party workers and the wives of candidates in bids to influence the presumed decisive women's vote. All this together speaks for the elevated status of women in the formal political process.

That being said, there was a clear binary between the projection of women Parliamentary candidates and the imaginative construction of a female voting bloc. The story of these by-elections reveals deep-seated processes of gender bifurcation in British political culture at a rate of hyperactivity. These by-elections are a piece of a larger discursive tapestry. The 1929 General Election fought under the slogan 'Safety First' was designated the 'Women's Election,'[101] with women identified as a peace bloc, representing a new element in the electorate that "led to the question of Peace becoming a dominant issue throughout the election."[102] The 1935 General Election was again described as the 'women's election' because candidates across the board appealed to the female instinct for peace. [103] And so to the recent past, as the 2010 UK General Election was dubbed the 'Mumsnet Election.' While empirical evidence shows that women do not vote on gendered lines, it is true to this day that we hear about the women's vote, women's issues, and women's political priorities, conflations not "paralleled by debates about political men."[104] The result of all these attempts to 'woo' women voters was ambiguous, as there were constituencies that were identified to have a surplus of women, and majorities of women who were still possessed by feelings of gratitude to Chamberlain, which nonetheless returned the anti-Government candidate, and *vice versa*. In practice women voters consistently belied expectations, but in imagination the bogey of the woman voter, the female franchise factor, continued to play a part in candidates' electoral strategies, in the choices of their political technology, and in the analysis of the result after the fact. In the end, by-elections are an instructive measuring device of *representations* of a gendered public opinion as they reveal not so much how women voted, but how politicians, the media, and pollsters thought women would vote.

While gender may have played less of a part in the *outcome* of these by-elections than the media had prophesized, nonetheless the notion of women's power, and the allegation that they held power without responsibility, left an indelible impression on politicians and public alike. It contributed to a mood of distrust between the sexes, or more one-sidedly, men's irritation that women voters, this still new and untried political force, could influence the course of foreign policy and thus world events. Indeed, the inter-war years were obsessed by a series of 'Questions' and 'Problems'—the 'Jewish Question.' the 'German Question,' the 'Sudeten Problem,' etc.,—and it is clear that 20 years after enfranchisement the 'Women Question' was not much nearer resolution.

Certainly women voters were seen to have the tendency for passivity, iso-lationism, and wilful ignorance about foreign affairs. They were also under-stood to be predominately both conservative and Conservative.[105] These were causes for deep concern and disappointment, not just for the often sensationalizing media, but also for women politicians, especially those who had made such great strides in their own careers by breaking through into once male-only spheres. At a meeting in Kingsway Hall, Manchester, Mrs Corbett Ashby spoke of "the responsibility of enfranchised women in international affairs and said that efforts should be made to inter-est and inform home-keeping women who seldom attend public meet-ings."[106] Rather than wait for others to practice what she preached, Corbett Ashby was unanimously adopted as prospective Liberal candidate for the Scarborough and Whitby Division for the next general election. She pre-dicted that the election would come in the early part of the new year, and it would be fought on foreign policy. "Mr Chamberlain would go to Mussolini in January in order to stage another spectacular surrender in the guise of peace. This time having given away the mainland of Europe to Hitler, he would try to hand over the peninsula of Spain to Mussolini."[107] Antipathy for Chamberlain and his foreign policy only grew deeper with Corbett Ashby. That there were a number of women MPs and prospective women candidates who staked their political futures on foreign policy is a bold indicator of the considerable distance travelled in only two decades from women's fixation on local and national politics—and more in the final chapter on these women who defied the notion that their sex did not believe in foreigners.

9
The Women Churchillians and the Politics of Shame

As one of only a handful of women MPs, Labour's Edith Summerskill worked closely with the other women in the House, including Conservatives such as Mavis Tate and Lady Nancy Astor. In her memoirs Summerskill recalled that Astor never tired of telling her fellow women MPs "what a very unpleasant time she endured as the first woman in the House," accusing Winston Churchill of snubbing her because she was a woman in what he considered a Man's House, an attitude consistent with his opposition to women's suffrage. Indeed, Astor's favourite story was how after many years she asked Churchill why he had cut her, to which he retorted: "When you came into the House I felt that you had entered my bathroom and I had no sponge with which to defend myself.' She replied, 'You're not handsome enough to have worries of that kind.'"[1] Of course, there was much else besides different views on women's rights that nourished Churchill and Lady Astor's enmity. They were vigorously opposed on questions of foreign policy (at least up to 1940), she the hostess of the Cliveden Set, he the arch anti-appeaser who never quite managed to lead his own set from the political wilderness he occupied in the 1930s while he would, in due course, lead the nation and become the figurehead of the anti-Nazi war. Their adversarial positions were dramatically illustrated by Astor's interruptions during Churchill's speech repudiating the Munich Agreement in the House of Commons on 5 October, 1938. She cried out "nonsense" after he called the Munich agreement "a total and unmitigated defeat." A few minutes later into his speech when he parodied Chamberlain by talking about Eastern European "countries which are a long way off and of which, as the Prime Minister might say, we know nothing," Astor again took loud exception, crying out "Rude." In turn, Churchill wondered: "She must very recently have been receiving her finishing course in manners," which was met by loud and prolonged laughter.[2] As amusing as Astor and Churchill's verbal sparring may be, fixating on these personal antipathies does risk camouflaging the effective working partnerships between Winston Churchill and a host of women in his immediate social and in the wider political sphere. Astor was one of the very few women who challenged Churchill so often and so publically, while many others were his champions and collaborators in the years between 1936 and 1939 that Brendan Bracken identified as "the best chapter" in Churchill's "crowded public life," dominated by "his long, lonely struggle to expose the dangers of dictatorships."[3]

Were women really the best friends of Neville Chamberlain's policy, and, if so, were they intuitively opposed to the hawkish and pro-rearmament alternative that Churchill represented? The mobilization of women for anti-fascist campaigns, women's own searching confessions and expressions, and the results of the Munich by-elections which failed to make a clear case that the 'women's vote' was a bloc vote for Chamberlain together go a long way towards contesting the press-fuelled notion that women *qua* women supported appeasement. And what of those women who defied Richard Baxter's type-casting of their sex in *Guilty Women*, the ones who were ideologically, tactically, morally, and emotionally opposed to appeasement? For obvious reasons they cannot be subsumed within the Anthony Eden-led 'Glamour Boys,' and they were explicitly excluded from events where the leading anti-Chamberlain figures congregated, like the "dinner-party for men only" made up of MPs, newspaper proprietors, and prominent journalists who came together to commiserate about the agreement signed at Munich in those last days of September 1938.[4] But the culture of male exclusivity in the Foreign Office milieu, and male-domination within the concentric circles of foreign-policy 'dissentients,' should not blind us to the significant contributions women made to anti-appeasement politics. Women built up the anti-appeasement bloc as politicians and campaigners inside and outside parliament, as public intellectuals, as journalists, and as the intimate partners of the anti-appeasers.

A group without a ready-made name, it makes sense to call them and claim them as the 'women Churchillians.' Included here are those who worked in close proximity to Churchill in a number of campaigns; those who shared his outlook, admired his vision, and identified him as the heroic alternative to Chamberlain; and women from across the political spectrum who became Churchill's 'fellow travellers'. In that liminal space between the private and the public sphere, women also ventilated their opposition to the Munich Agreement and their shame at the betrayal of worthy allies by inundating Chamberlain's critics with an abundance of letters. It was not the Prime Minister alone who was in receipt of letters from ordinary British women filled with gratitude and congratulatory sentiments. Letters from women added substantially to Duff Cooper's, Leo Amery's, and Winston Churchill's postbags in the late 1930s, their numbers peaking during the Munich crisis. It is true that some of these letters were desperate pleas for peace and attacks on their recipients as warmongers, but the majority went against our expectations of women's irenic instinct, revealing a powerful strain of female public opinion that balked at the politics of peace at any price.

Giving a collective label to these women should not imply that they were a homogenous group. Even more so than the feminist anti-fascists of the first chapters of this book, their collaboration was inconsistent and they had nothing resembling an organizational base. Of course, from the end of September 1939 when Churchill was appointed First Lord of the Admiralty there were plenty of women Churchillians in Parliament, among the political classes, and in the public at large. His public approval ratings skyrocketed during his Premiership from May 1940 to 1945. Gallup polls found that Chamberlain's public approval ratings fluctuated between 33% and 68%. In December 1939 only 30% of those polled would have opted for Churchill to take over as PM, and 52% thought Chamberlain should stay in the job. When Churchill did succeed as PM his approval ratings went through the roof, and the lowest ever was 82%, the highest 93%.[5] This investigation will not, however, be extended into the war years when the tables were turned and only a small minority agitated for a negotiated peace, while the majority of men and women were mobilized under Churchill's leadership and inspired by his acclaimed patriotic appeals. Rather, what it is important to attempt here is, on the one hand, the restoration of women to the history of high politics and foreign policy dissent in the crisis-ridden years from 1936 to the summer of 1939, and, on the other, resituating gender in the reigning anti-appeasement narrative. Further, only a small part of this chapter is about Churchill or an interrogation of his sexual politics which, incidentally, is a much understudied aspect of an otherwise meticulously scrutinized political life. Churchill has long occupied the spotlight in modern history, and the intention here is to shed light on the women in the shadows of the shadowy world of anti-appeasement politics.

Where are the 'not-guilty' women in appeasement scholarship?

The historiography of anti-appeasement provides a mirror image to that of the 'Guilty Men,' with the very same neglect of women actors, and the failure to take gender seriously as an analytical category. Starting with Richard Baxter, he only credited the efforts of one woman among the 'non-guilty.' He dedicated the last chapter of *Guilty Women* (1941), 'A Woman's Voice Cried out in the Wilderness,' to Ellen Wilkinson, in recognition of her most rousing parliamentary speeches attacking Chamberlain. (By 1941 she was Parliamentary Secretary at the Ministry of Pensions in the wartime coalition government.) Wilkinson was a persistent critic of Chamberlain; in the months after the Munich Crisis she identified him as the leader of a government that was on the road to becoming fascist itself; she was one of the only leaders of the Labour party to support Stafford Cripps's Popular Front campaign; and she was a great advocate for the victims of fascist aggression in Germany, Spain, and Czechoslovakia. She was Baxter's heroine because, speaking at a meeting in Hull on 2 October, 1938, she had exposed the behind-the-scenes machinations of the appeasement conspirators: "There are people in this country in high official positions, some of whom were in Nuremberg, of whom it can be said that their spiritual home is in Germany."[6] She was always outspoken in debates on the international situation, but it was her scorching denunciation of appeasement in the debate on 24 August, 1939, in the wake of the Nazi-Soviet Pact, that has been deemed "the most impressive speech by a woman MP on foreign policy to date."[7] Wilkinson summarized the failures of Chamberlain's foreign policy this way:

> I cannot enter into this general atmosphere of forgive and forget as regards the present Prime Minister ... If the Prime Minister will forgive me for saying so, I think this nation would be much more united if he were not the Prime Minister. I, for one, should find it extremely difficult to be united with those behind him. We all admit the sincerity and high purpose of the Prime Minister, but what in fact did he do? When he came into office, as he made it perfectly clear, he made it his business to torpedo the system of collective security and refuse to pay the premiums that collective security under the League of Nations meant. That has been so from the moment he made his Midsummer madness speech about sanctions until to-day, or, rather, until the situation became so terrible that even he realised the utter bankruptcy of that policy ... I do not want to say, 'We told you so,' when a man is facing such an utter collapse of his policy as the Prime Minister is facing to-day, but we have to realise that that is the fact.

Anticipating the war to come, she charged that "the greatest crime of the Prime Minister of this country is that never once has he really managed to rise to the point of giving the country something worth fighting for."[8] Despite this anti-appeasement *tour de force*, she was not much more approving of Churchill, Eden, and Duff Cooper whom she portrayed as still believing "in the old school tie and what they were told at Eton,"[9] differentiating her Leftist and class-based interpretation of fascism from theirs. It follows that, until quite recently, Wilkinson has hardly featured in the constructed memory of the dissenters.

Unsurprisingly perhaps, Churchill's own *The Gathering Storm*, the keystone of anti-appeasement historiography and a canonical work of 'great man' history writing, barely acknowledged women's presence. There is no mention of the Duchess of Atholl, Eleanor Rathbone, Violet Bonham-Carter, Shiela Grant Duff, or Ellen Wilkinson, and even his beloved wife Clementine makes infrequent appearances. In his portrayal of the Munich Crisis Churchill did record the heightened emotions and deep divisions within Conservative circles as "men and women, long bound together by party ties, social enmities and family connections, glared upon one another in scorn and anger," before moving on to what was for him the climax of this epic tale when Duff Cooper "thrust his way through the exulting throng to declare his total disagreement with its leader."[10] Churchill's rhetoric was infused with gender bifurcated metaphors, his version of the events leading up to the Second World War conveyed through hyper-masculine, heroic, and imperial language, anchored by his definition of honour, while still expressing a depth of feeling and passionate commitment to principle. For example, using mammaric imagery, Churchill described the state of the British and French Cabinets in mid-September 1938 as "a front of two over-ripe melons crushed together; whereas what was needed was a gleam of steel."[11] He implied throughout that his judgement had been clear and right, in contrast to the Men of Munich whose reason was clouded by the hysteria of the crowds. Churchill feminized and emotionalized the nation under the spell of appeasement. In an exchange of polite blows with the pro-German Lord Londonderry, Churchill wrote how "I doubt very much whether Chamberlain will carry the country with him. He is certainly dividing it on vital matters as it has never been split before." He was especially "ashamed to see the great Conservative Party looking forward to an Election where they will exploit the psychosis of fear, and hope that the old women of both sexes will give a renewal of the present incompetent regime."[12] National defence was a man's business, to be spoken about in a diction of virility.[13]

Gradually, some women have been recognized as players in opposition to Chamberlain's appeasement politics. In early classic in the scholarship, *The Anti-Appeasers*, Thompson improves on Churchill's version by giving brief mention to Atholl, Wilkinson, and Rathbone. Indeed, Rathbone is credited with transforming the meaning and the charge of the very term 'appeasement' when she defined it as "a clever plan of selling your friends in order to buy off your enemies—which has the danger that a time comes when you have no friends left, and then you find you need them, and then it is too late to buy them back."[14] Women are only ever represented as backstage players in Churchill's social life in Gilbert's biographical tome and, similarly, Parker does little more than acknowledge that some women attended meetings, giving no thought to the significance of their presence and the obstacles they faced as a function of their sex.[15] In supporting his thesis that "Chamberlain's policies were less universally acclaimed by the [Conservative] party than is commonly supposed," Crowson gives credit where it is due to Conservative women MPs such as Mavis Tate, Thelma Cazalet, Irene Ward, and especially Atholl, for taking their stands in heated foreign policy debates.[16] However, Crowson only names one woman in his classification of anti-appeasement cohorts. Atholl is listed among the Foreign Policy Sceptics Fellow-Travellers group, but there are no women in either the Eden/Amery Group or the Churchill Group.[17] This speaks both for the real paucity of women from these virtually all-male dissenting conclaves within the Parliamentary Tory party, as well as for the lack of historical detective work into sources where women's presence might be more discernible. For instance, women's engagement with foreign policy is revealed in the patchy but still indispensable records of the Conservative Women's Associations, the generous coverage by the local press of Tory women's activities, private papers, and memoirs, and by a trawl through the postbags of leading anti-appeasement politicians.

Although this is the first gender analysis to be attempted, the study of anti-appeasement politics has been reopened in other ways. Much work has been done to deflate the narcissistic accounts of would-be doomsayers, many of these peddled in the post-war memoirs and diaries of the players themselves. Other work has queried the cohesiveness, concreteness, and effectiveness of these anti-Chamberlain political groupings, and questioned the accuracy of various versions of events. More recent interventions into the never-ending revisions/counter-revisionist polemic include Carr's argument that the young 'Glamour Boys' did not oppose Chamberlain "with any degree of clarity." He takes a prosopographical approach to debunk the myth that politicians who were also First World War veterans stood up to Hitler on principle.[18] Although his study focuses on the war years, Toye's masterful analysis of Churchill's rhetoric makes a similar point to Carr, namely that Churchill was less of a rebel within his own party than his later autobiographical writing asserted. Further, Toye argues that in his pro-rearmament speeches in the 1930s Churchill's "rhetoric was calibrated to appeal to progressive and not just traditionalist national security advocates."[19] Churchill's "virile, athletic, English,"[20] reached receptive audiences, and he was never entirely lost in the wilderness in terms of his popularity with the British public. Toye's interest in the reception of Churchill's speeches also begs the question of their appeal to female audiences—were women swept away by Churchill's populist appeal or repelled by his hyper-masculine armour? (Evidence from the immediate pre-war phase would suggest that while women were far more inclined towards Chamberlain, they did not articulate their suspicion of Churchill on the grounds of his virile approach.)

Within women's history scholarship, the neglect of women anti-appeasers has not been as glaring. Whereas the mostly Tory women appeasers have been unloved by feminist historians, and unnoticed by international and diplomatic historians, the more heroic life narratives, the more sympathetic natures, and the fact that history proved that they had right on their side has meant that women antis are the subjects of a number of biographical studies. Pedersen's definitive biography of Eleanor Rathbone provides a highly nuanced account of her subject's shift from feminist, social welfare, and imperial concerns to foreign policy, triggered by the Abyssinia crisis in 1935. Henceforth, Rathbone "would mount her own 'foreign policy,' defending states and peoples vulnerable to fascist aggression."[21] Female protagonists have also been written back into the narrative in both public-facing and behind-the-scenes roles in Olson's well-researched and lively popular history of the pro-Churchill 'conspiracy.'[22] While Olson is not a women's history *per se*, she does bring figures like Violet Bonham-Carter, the Duchess of Atholl, Barbara Cartland (sister of Edenite Ronald Cartland), and Dorothy Macmillan (wife of Edenite Harold Macmillan and lover of Churchillite Bob Boothby) to life in a story that is part political conspiracy and part upper-class soap opera in which social interaction, romance, and emotional entanglements explain political choices.

Churchill's sexual politics

Feminist reclamation efforts can only achieve so much, however, especially when the figure at the nucleus of the circle was not embracing of women's post-enfranchisement potential in the political arena. In fact, as Churchill's biographers have noted, other than the select few women who made a deep impact on the personal level, women did not play much part in Churchill's political career. In what is one of the few if not a very imaginative consideration of Churchill's relationships with women, Addison catalogues all the female figures who nurtured and supported him from cradle to grave, and makes the unassailable point that "politics and war were Churchill's passions: intensely masculine spheres in which his most intimate friends, like his enemies and rivals, were male."[23] Churchill's ambivalence in this regard was matched by his anti-appeasement protégée the incorrigible womanizer Duff Cooper, who also felt that the "House was fashioned by men" and thus "there is no place for women, and women cannot excel there any more than they can on the football field."[24] Churchill's own loose-cannon of a son, Randolph, was no more progressive on this point, openly stating that women had no place in politics, that their presence in the House created a certain lack of dignity, and that they were "unfitted for Parliament."[25] Cooper also damned Chamberlain with faint and feminizing praise in his famous resignation speech, accusing the PM of believing he could address "Herr Hitler through the language of sweet reasonableness (cheers). I have believed that he was more open to the language of the mailed fist."[26] It was among the pro-defence and anti-appeasement lobby that the fear of national emasculation and being engulfed by women was strongest.

Many of the other rebels exhibited less-than-progressive ideas about the opposite sex. Although Eden benefitted from his good looks and sex appeal, addressed the CWA, and was allegedly very popular with women voters, he was hardly more enlightened, as exemplified by his reluctance to take the necessary steps to admit women to the consular service. This despite that fact that, in Mass-Observation's estimation, "Eden's general popularity, especially with women, helped to make a sensational story of his resignation, and it reached through to sections of the population not usually touched by political happenings."[27] We have already provided a platform for Harold Nicolson's misogynist rant at women for their putative cowardly behaviour during the Munich Crisis. Nicolson was just as hostile to elite women for their meddling in diplomatic affairs, believing that "the harm which these silly selfish hostesses do is really immense," and that Lady Astor and Mrs Ronnie Greville in particular "have a subversive influence."[28] Harold Macmillan was a product of homo-social patrician spheres, and he was only at ease in the company of men—"his was a masculine world, a 'society made for men and run for men,' in which women almost always felt like outsiders."[29] Indeed, all these figures were from that markedly male-centred elite that Simon Haxey described as the 'cousinhood,' as the vast majority of Tory MPs were one of the wealthiest (mainly titled) 10,000 of the population, had taken the same routes through education (mainly Eton and Harrow, followed by usually undistinguished Oxbridge degrees), and shared common interests in business, politics, and international affairs.[30] Would women's influence in these elite anti-appeasement conclaves have been greater had they not been dominated by men who were so dismissive of women's political abilities? We could easily speculate that under the leadership of politicians who rated women more highly, the gender make-up of the anti-appeasement coterie may have been more diverse.

This picture of Churchill as a man's-man-politician is complicated by one unusual article in his substantial journalistic output. Written for *Strand* magazine—its publication just happening to coincide with Eden's resignation—Churchill considered the role of women in history and in modern war from the air. His main points, however, were in keeping with his anti-feminist politics, and he took some evident pleasure in ribbing Adam's Rib in the discussion of the women's suffrage movement. What concerned him most profoundly though was the role of women in modern warfare in which the distinction between civilian and combatant had been erased. He argued strenuously against women making incursions into the armed forces, opined that women aviators fell "into the category of women impersonating men and acting as men," regarded as perfectly sensible how the Germans had implemented a stark sexual division of labour in war preparation, and placed great value on women in their supporting roles as the makers of munitions but never as fighters. He remained equivocal about Britain's lead in the world by the measure of feminist achievements, where:

it is the tendency to treat men and women generally on an equal footing. This is due to the fact that we enjoy peace, are highly civilised, and on an island. The tests of war would very soon show that the stronger sex would have to do the fighting and the weaker the suffering and weeping.[31]

In his one serious reflection on women in history, Churchill confirmed that he was a firm supporter of the sexual status quo.

The variances in Chamberlain's and Churchill's political relationships with women are illuminating. Neville Chamberlain worked hard to court the woman's vote. He went out of his way to enter into relationships of some intimacy with women in Britain and around the world, flattering women by addressing them directly in his most game-changing speeches. He recognized the importance of securing the support of the CWA. He responded to women's deepest anxieties by appearing to them as the angel of peace, and he was ably supported in these efforts by his sisters and his wife. In contrast, Churchill made very little effort with women in his party or in the general population. He and Sir Edward Grey had been the two Liberal politicians whose refusal to engage with WSPU hecklers Christabel Pankhurst and Annie Kenney at a Manchester meeting in 1905 unleashed the militant phase of the suffragette campaign, and he again stood against women's equal suffrage in 1927. He does not seem to have placed any particular importance in the CWA, and did not address women's meetings in his constituency, or at national level, in this period. In one instance Churchill did build his case for the urgent preparation for a war against Germany by citing Nazi brutality towards women. In a speech in 1935 he expressed his deep discomfort at "the hideous medieval spectacle a few days ago of the decapitation of two women."[32] But otherwise he did not make common cause with the feminist anti-fascists. It was fitting that Churchill should have been one of the star contributors to the newly launched monthly *Men Only* in 1936, a magazine devoted entirely to men's interests, and proudly proclaimed that "it doesn't want Women Readers ... [ellipses in original] Won't have them."[33] Unlike Chamberlain, Churchill does not appear to have placed great store in the letters from women that fell into his constituency postbag. Further, he acted as a lone wolf for much of the 1930s, suspicious of internationalism, and sceptical of the political technologies and rituals of protest relied upon by so many peace and women's organizations. He was averse to signing petitions, round robin letters, and penning letters to the editor, and by the late 1930s he even wondered how effective his public meetings were, especially as they failed to get press coverage. When asked to sign a letter to demonstrate British support for Czechoslovakia, he confided to Lord Cecil: "I am always rather doubtful about these 'round robin' letters, in which the same people trot out time after time, and no one seems to pay much attention to what they say."[34]

Most crucially, Churchill's pro-rearmament, pro-defence, and jingo politics and public persona were never geared to make a special appeal to the female electorate. Churchill's stubborn determination and 'stand up to the bully' position registered well with men. While there was not much mention of Churchill by name in September and October, 1938—which is significant in itself—Mass-Observation's investigation of the impact of the crisis in mainly working-class communities revealed an unmistakable pattern whereby women were overwhelmed with relief and gratitude, whereas, and with remarkable speed, "men turned against [Chamberlain] when his terms became known, and their readiness to fight Hitler rather sooner than later, are in themselves striking enough examples of the rapidity with which popular feeling remoulds itself."[35] Male affinity with Churchill was also illustrated well by this response from a Bolton man, aged 40, to a Mass-Observation questionnaire in 1940 about whether it was time for Churchill to replace Chamberlain as Prime Minister: "I've nowt against him, but Churchill's more the man for times like these, or Duff Cooper, not Chamberlain. He's too soft and he's too old. No, Chamberlain isn't the man and it's time he gave way."[36] As already discussed, it was Churchill's manly qualities that were emphasized in public discourse and exaggerated in political cartoons. Iconographically, he was the direct descendent of Colonel Blimp and the personification of British bull-dog determination. A reductive claim is not being made here that women will refuse to support a manly man as a war leader who arouses the nation with his virile rhetoric and nationalist resolve—time and again throughout history the truth is to the contrary. However, in the specific historical context of the last nervous years before the outbreak of war, the cigar-chomping imperious Churchill was not likely to be able to steal many mother's hearts away from Chamberlain, the umbrella-yielding peaceable gentleman who, as so many were convinced, had saved their sons, their husbands, and their homes from inevitable annihilation.

The glamour girls: leading women anti-appeasers

Churchill did not, of course, have to be a feminist for women to side with him in their opposition to the National Government's foreign policy. By focusing on a handful of high-profile women Churchillians we will see that their influence was not nearly as negligible as either their male counterparts or historians have led us to believe. We will start with the women in direct contact and collaboration with Churchill. These were the Liberal Violet Bonham-Carter, with whom Churchill's personal and political relationship was already very well established by the 1930s; the Conservative Katherine, the Duchess of Atholl, with whom he carried on a regular and mutually respectful if not very intimate correspondence; Eleanor Rathbone, the Independent MP who reached out to him on numerous occasions in search of a true leader; and Shiela Grant Duff, a young journalist related by blood to his wife Clemmie, who was a press correspondent in Czechoslovakia in the lead up to the Crisis. In their relentless critique of Chamberlain's foreign policy, these women were of like mind with other women of influence, such as the Liberal feminist internationalist and Popular Fronter Margery Corbett Ashby; the well-connected LNU leader, passionate Zionist, and once-Conservative then National Labour activist Blanche 'Baffy' Dugdale; Labour's Ellen Wilkinson; the right-wing feminist Flora Drummond; *Time and Tide* editor Lady Rhondda; and the pro-national defence editor of the Radical Right *National Review* Violet Milner. Of course, protest at the Munich

Agreement was strong on the Left and far-Left too, in the Labour Party, the ILP, the CPGB, and among more independent-minded veteran critics like Sylvia Pankhurst. The ever widening personal and political gulf between sisters Christabel and Sylvia was exposed in bold relief as the former wrote a warm letter of support to the Chamberlains, while the latter regarded "the Munich peace as a triumph for the mailed fist."[37] The Agreement was described in the darkest funerary terms in the *New Times and Ethiopian News*, of which she was editor, and on whose advisory board of six sat Nancy Cunard, Rosika Schwimmer, and Isabel Fry:

> The flowers piled before 10, Downing Street are very fitting for a funeral of British honour and, it may be, of the British Empire ... [W]hat he returns from saving our skins from a blackmailer at the price of other people's flesh, and waves, laughing with glee, a piece of paper with Herr Hitler's name on it, if it were not ghastly, it would be grotesque.[38]

While these women did not join in any one political organization, their paths often crossed and their similar views on foreign policy often transcended party divisions. Had anyone at the time been of the mind to give them a moniker, they might well have been called the 'Glamour Girls'— although 'Glamour Women' would be more apt as most were well into middle-age, and seasoned veterans of party, feminist, and internationalist politics.

The preeminent woman Churchillian: Violet Bonham-Carter

Of all the women Churchillians it was Violet Bonham-Carter, daughter of former Prime Minister H.H. Asquith, who was on terms of intimacy with Churchill, and she was probably the only political woman he truly respected. In the immediate post-war years she reflected the progressive opinions of the majority about the promise of the League of Nations, the punitive terms of the Treaty of Versailles, and women's role as peacemakers. But she was an early convert to a militant anti-Nazism that by the end of the decade developed into a relentless critique of the National Government's foreign policy. Already in April 1933 she wrote to Gilbert Murray: "The German atrocities make me feel quite ill with rage & shame. They also make me feel foolish at having been so steadfast a Pro-German even since they became under-dogs."[39] The plight of the Jews in Germany was the prompt for her anti-Nazism, and she built on her considerable social connections to support an array of charitable endeavours and rescue work with refugees.

Although they were divided on many issues, Churchill and Bonham-Carter's shared alarm at the rise of Nazi Germany and Britain's unpreparedness for war drew them close together again. Indeed, during a walk through the woods at a mutual friend's country-house weekend it was she who urged

Churchill to be "the awakener." She entreated him to "rouse public opinion. You alone can do it." When he expressed his concerns that he could hardly take the lead without a following or press support, she answered "we must recruit a following for you, and we must create a springboard."[40] From the mid-1930s they worked together to this end in a number of multi-partisan and pro-rearmament groups. She urged him to become involved in the cross-party Anti-Nazi Council, founded in March 1936 to enlighten public opinion about Germany's large-scale war preparations, with leading figures Commander Locker-Lampson MO and Mr Vyvyan Adams MP. Reluctant to throw in his lot with the Council, Churchill finally agreed to attend a strictly private luncheon on 19 May, 1936, with the various figures who were associating themselves with the manifesto and the campaign.[41] The seating plan for this luncheon shows Churchill next to Bonham-Carter and across the table from Labour's Margaret Bondfield, the only two women out of a dozen in attendance. The transcripts of their speeches have been preserved, and every attempt was made to find common ground within the group. Bonham-Carter was most concerned about how to deal with Italy in all this, and she wrote to Churchill to this effect a few days after the luncheon meeting. He replied with a defined set of strategic points, in the end encouraging her to continue with the Anti-Nazi Council but with a touch of condescension about its idealistic approach to the problem. He concluded this letter to her with affection, but also as only a man might address a woman, and never another man:

> There my dear Violet, I have set forth my thought with every feeling of humility before such grievous and giant events. Now see how far with your friends you can formulate the more general principles which might form the basis, not necessarily of 'articles of association' to which eventually many men and women of courage and good-will might pledge their faith and hope.[42]

When the Council met again on 15 October, they agreed to set up the 'Defence of Freedom and Peace' movement, also called 'Focus.' It was Churchill's special request that Bonham-Carter should be included and identified as one of the movement's most prominent representatives.[43] Finally, on 3 December Churchill spoke on the Anti-Nazi Council platform at the Albert Hall.

With their connections in high places and their distrust of the government's foreign policy, both Bonham-Carter and Megan Lloyd George MP were prominent supporters of the Popular Front from its launch by Richard Acland, John Strachey, G.D.H. Cole, and Robert Boothby in December 1936. Close to both the Liberal leader Sir Archibald Sinclair and Winston Churchill, together they participated in the launch of Churchill's 'Arms and the Covenant' movement in December 1936, another cross-party anti-appeasement movement. Bonham-Carter eased Churchill's way with the League of Nations Union, which was not his natural ideological home. It was considered a great achievement that the relatives of at least five Prime Ministers were leaders of the LNU. These were Violet Bonham-Carter, Lord Cecil, Sir Austen Chamberlain, Megan Lloyd George, and Mrs Dugdale, niece of Lord Balfour.[44] Indeed, the LNU became a magnet for dissenting foreign policy opinion in the late 1930s, and, in addition to the aforementioned women, MPs Eleanor Rathbone and the Duchess of Atholl, and well-known public personalities Margery Corbett Ashby, Kathleen Courtney, Viscountess Gladstone, Lady Hall, and Lady Layton were all active members.

Predictably, Bonham-Carter reacted angrily to the Munich agreement. She had real and personal links with Czechoslovakia since her visit in 1935, and on the morning after the Munich conference a depressed Jan Masaryk, Czech Ambassador in London, came to visit her. She was grateful to Churchill for his public opposition to Munich, and wrote to him: "Dearest Winston, 1,000 congratulations and thanks—for a marvellous speech—(will it pierce the shell of those drowsy tortoises—? digging us to our doom) All thanks and love—Violet."[45] What we hear in her public pronouncements on Munich, and certainly this would have been echoed in her more private encounters (while she was a prolific diary writer, she did not keep one for the years of the late 1930s), was a feeling of mortification for betraying worthy allies. Speaking at a Liberal Party lecture on Collective Security on 20 October, 1938, she condemned the Munich agreement:

> We meet in a very dark hour. The events of the last three weeks have shattered what remained of that new world-order which some of us have hoped & worked & striven to build for 20 years. They have done more. They have broken a great & honourable tradition of English foreign policy to which this country has adhered through changing Governments & changing parties for centuries. The keystone of that policy has been the refusal to truckle to the strong at the expense of the weak .... When the Prime Minister signed the Munich Agreement he renounced us all claims to moral leadership. We ceased to be trustees of a standard of justice and decency in international relationships ... All this is hailed as a triumph by its supporters. I do not believe than any Peace worthy of the name can be built upon an act of flagrant injustice backed by Force.[46]

Soon after Kristallnacht, she was again overcome with shame in her address to the 'National Demonstration Against Religious and Racial Persecution' at the Albert Hall. She said:

> I speak only as an English woman—of no importance—one of the many thousands in this country who to-day are stricken with horror, and who long to hold out a hand to those who are enduring suffering, which is

outside our own experience and perhaps beyond the reach of our imagination. ... But there is one thing you cannot share with us, our shame—shame that the government of a nation which for centuries has at least called itself a Christian nation, should outrage justice, gentleness and mercy, should violate every cannon of Christian faith.[47]

Here she downplayed her own significance, evoking her feelings of powerlessness as a woman. Indeed, the feeling of shame is a leitmotif in Bonham-Carter's correspondence and public speaking from the rise of the Nazis in 1933 to the outbreak of the war.[48]

Soon after this she joined Stafford Cripps' campaign for a Popular Front, trying to persuade the Liberal Party to come on board.[49] There was no divided loyalty here, as Cripps was one of a growing number who urged Churchill's inclusion in the Cabinet. When war broke out she was more desperate than ever for Chamberlain to go and for a man like Churchill to provide leadership, writing how "I long for the great ghosts to come back & lead us—instead of these small men."[50] She stands out as one of the leading woman anti-appeasers, and not only because she was one of very few women who actually had the ear of Winston Churchill. Her achievements in arming Britain for an anti-Nazi war, tangible and moral, should not be measured only by Churchill's.

Bonham-Carter was in sync with her party and with other leading figures in the Women's National Liberal Federation in her anti-appeasement ideals and practices. Margery Corbett Ashby and Lady Gladstone, both leaders of the WNLF, were vocal critics of appeasement. Further, by the late 1930s the LNU's Women's Advisory Council became more and more dominated by women with a Liberal pedigree, and these women took it upon themselves to reach out to the women of Czechoslovakia in the aftermath of Munich. In a 'Message from British Women to the Women of Czechoslovakia,' the undersigned, representing millions of British women, wanted the women of Czechoslovakia to know the sacrifices they had made to avert a European war were appreciated, they expressed sorrow at the suffering of her people, and they offered help in every kind. There was some regret, however, that the message "had contained no mention of the shame which was the predominant feeling of many people."[51] This solidarity campaign carried on into 1939 when figures like Lady Gladstone and Margery Corbett Ashby made every effort to keep the plight of the Czechs in the news and lead relief efforts on their behalf.[52]

Like Bonham-Carter, Baffy Dugdale was another of the handful of women anti-appeasers from the finest political pedigree to have the same sort of access to powerful figures, her closest confidant the pro-appeasement Minister of Agriculture Walter Elliott. Although born and bred a Conservative, it was her opposition to the National Government's foreign policy that led her to join National Labour in 1937, and it was at her initiative that leading

National Labourites, among them Harold Nicolson and Sir Alfred Zimmern, were brought together to form a Foreign Policy Group in 1937. That her sex was no great barrier at this point was exemplified by the fact that she was content that this group begin to emerge as 'Anthony's men,' i.e., Eden's fellow travellers.[53] Her connection with the Edenites became more tenuous, however, and she had little trust in Eden himself who she felt 'ratted' during the Munich crisis. Her disgust at the Munich Agreement was absolute, and she confided her very physical revulsion to Nicolson, namely that "she had been sick twice in the night over England's shame." After reading *The Times* leader that demonstrated little sympathy for the poor Czechs, "she dashed to the lavatory and was sick a third time."[54] The content of her stomach now evacuated, she proceeded to clear her conscience and wrote her letter of resignation from National Labour. In public too she aligned herself with the anti-Municheers, and on the evening of 30 September, 1938, she shared a platform with Eleanor Rathbone and Tory renegade Bob Boothby at a meeting on the Czech-German Crisis, under the auspices of the National Committee of Peace and Friendship with the USSR, at Friends House, London. Her diaries also reveal how she was overcome by shame, describing the Agreement as 'the utmost humiliation,' 'black shame,' and the moment 'honour died.'

Forewarned and forewarned by women of courage and conscience

Presumably, Churchill set aside his objection to women's presence in what he reckoned should have remained a man's chamber, and he also collaborated with MPs Katherine, the Duchess of Atholl (Con., Kinross) and Eleanor Rathbone (Ind., Combined Universities). While Atholl came from an anti-suffrage background and never identified with feminism, she wanted to guide women as they matured into citizens, and she had a reputation for being outspoken and an imposing heckler in parliament. She was also prominently identified with the unexpected trend among women MPs to be preoccupied with foreign affairs, going against "the accepted idea that women's interests were chiefly domestic."[55] From imperial affairs she turned her attention to Europe and fascist aggression in Abyssinia, in Spain, in Czechoslovakia, and in Germany itself.

Atholl's political collaboration with Churchill began with their shared opposition to the Indian constitutional reform. Atholl supported Winston's son Randolph when he contested the Wavertree by-election in January 1935 as an Independent Conservative against a National Conservative candidate, and she addressed a number of meetings of women devoted entirely to the India question. This must have ingratiated her with the father, and she and Winston naturally moved on to sharing confidences concerning deteriorating European affairs. Her association with Churchill was both publically known and privately mutually beneficial. Already in 1936 *Time and Tide* identified her as a Churchillian, "a lady whose beaver-like persistency can produce surprising results as her work on the India bill showed," and one who was "attracted by Mr Churchill's bitter anti-Germanism."[56] They also carried on a business-like and not very personal private correspondence that demonstrated their mutual trust and joint commitment to expose Germany's increasing military and political potency. She wrote to him fairly frequently, sending intelligence she had obtained through meetings with foreign dignitaries or via other anti-Nazis, and from her foreign trips. She also kept him in the loop about the mistranslation of *Mein Kampf,* and her campaign to publish an unexpurgated edition. Further, both she and Rathbone were involved with Focus, and in March 1938 Churchill invited Atholl to join the National Committee of Focus, which she accepted on the proviso that it discuss what could be done to prevent an insurgent victory in Spain. Churchill reassured her that Spain was one of the topics that concerned the group. Of course her focus throughout these years was on the Spanish Civil War, and although a Tory through and through in her anti-Communism, she was nicknamed the 'Red' Duchess for her unstinting efforts. Atholl's rather confusing intersectional identity and apparent political promiscuity did not endear her to many, and Leftist dissident George Orwell understood that the war in Spain "has had a catalytic effect upon English opinion, bringing into being combinations which no one could have foreseen a few years ago." At the time of writing in the summer of 1938, he felt that much is "not yet clear, but I do not see how patriotic Communists and communistic duchesses can be explained except on the supposition that the ranks are being closed for war."[57]

Atholl unintentionally sat out the Czech Crisis in America, on a lecture tour on behalf of the Republican cause in Spain. Indeed, it is remarkable how British elite women were able to conduct informal and semi-official diplomacy, especially along the Anglo-American axis. This kind of activity was a vital component of women's anti-fascist resistance, and a crucial complement to male-dominated diplomacy. But Atholl was clearly disappointed not to be in Britain at the climax of the crisis, sounding her alarm and her readiness to join any opposition that may emerge by telegramming Churchill on 20 September: "WILL SUPPORT ANY PROTEST AGAINST SURRENDER SUDETENLAND TOO DANGEROUS FOR US ALL= K ATHOLL."[58] She was eager to see him immediately upon her return to Britain on 24 October, and again she wrote to him for guidance as she contemplated resigning from the party and standing as an Independent. Considering their history as anti-appeasement comrades, one wonders how disappointed she must have been that Churchill did not come to speak on her behalf when she was fighting for her political life on an anti-Chamberlain platform in the by-election in December, 1938. He did send both private and public statements of support, and he recognized the danger were she to lose: "It would be widely accepted as another sign that Great Britain is sinking under the weight of her cares, and no longer has the spirit and will-power to confront the tyrannies and cruel persecutions which have darkened this age."[59] His belief in her cause notwithstanding, he decided against making an appearance in her constituency because he was in trouble with his own constituency organization for his continuous defiance of the Tory party line. The very different status of a woman foreign policy dissenter is vividly illustrated by Atholl's story, as she ran "political risks that no male anti-appeaser would run. Churchill admired her grit, but never found her another parliamentary seat."[60]

Eleanor Rathbone's connection with Churchill was somewhat more distant.[61] From 1936 she had regular contact with Churchill, and she had marked him out as the next PM. She wrote to him a number of times along these lines. For example, Churchill was impressed that she had adopted his figures on German air strength in one of her letters to the editor to the *Manchester Guardian*, hoped she would stand to her guns, and warned this Cassandra that "we are really in great danger."[62] By September 1938 she was in no doubt that Churchill represented the great white hope, and she begged him and Eden to rally opinion in the country because "there is a great longing for leadership."[63] She made the same plea in public for their inclusion in the Cabinet.[64] But despite their political compatibility, as Pedersen emphasizes, no place was made for either Rathbone or Atholl in the anti-appeasement cabal.[65] The two women had been disapprovingly dubbed the "feminine United Front"[66] by William Waldorf Astor (Con.) during a debate on the importance of propaganda in Spain and the Little Entente countries, and their sex remained a significant liability. Unswerving and unclubbable, both Rathbone and Atholl lacked the easy access to Churchill and his fellow sceptics in the autumn of 1938, and both were excluded from meetings where these men conspired. Consistent with his misogynist assumptions about British women's putative cowardice in the face of the crisis, Glamour-Boy Harold Nicolson ventilated his justifications for Rathbone's exclusion from the all-male charmed circle of foreign policy rebels. While the rebels all knew how to play the homo-social game of politics, Rathbone was like "Vishnu, with four arms," and given to "emotional or self-advertising revolt." Nicolson could not bear her sanctimony, and while claiming to admire her motives, he apprised that she "tilts at her windmills with wholly altruistic fervour."[67] Just as before, Rathbone and Atholl were left to voice their dissent on public platforms, at open meetings, and through the press.

As we can see, in this phase of their lives Atholl and Rathbone's political careers were closely intertwined. Both were high-profile and admired (rather than popular) women MPs. Rathbone's demeanour was that of "the headmistress of an expensive and prosperous girls' college. Furiously angry with Mussolini; Haile Selassie is her hero. When members shout 'Order!' in response to her innumerable supplementary questions on Abyssinia, she beams."[68] Similarly, Atholl was depicted as a "frail-looking lady" who "can develop astonishing energy when her conscience is aroused, as it has been on Spain. She has a technique of gathering people around her, of always speaking for a group rather than as a lone fighter." Wilkinson supposed this was "the hostess instinct of a great lady, and it is amazing how effective it has been among her own Party."[69] Both Rathbone and Atholl began from a position of support for collective security through the League of Nations, both were critics of the strong pacifist tendency, and both eventually gave up on the League and the LNU by the time of the Munich Crisis. Rathbone worked closely with the LNU and wrote *War Can Be Averted* (1937) under its auspices. Atholl addressed the LNU's Women's Advisory Council on the European Crisis on 8 April, 1938, differentiating herself from so many other women by confessing these:

> seem to me days in which the policy of all peace-loving nations should stand together, not merely talking and passing resolutions, but looking to their arms and showing that they are ready to use their arms in defence of any country that is the victim of unprovoked aggression, anyhow in Europe.[70]

They were two of a trio at the core of the 'Glamour Girls,' and Atholl, Rathbone, and Wilkinson shared numerous platforms, experienced trans-formative fascist encounters together, and embarked on relief and fact-finding missions. With Dorothea Layton, wife of *The Economist* editor and *News Chronicle* proprietor Walter Layton, Atholl, and Rathbone took an unofficial but well publicized tour of the Little Entente countries—Yugoslavia, Roumania, and Czechoslovakia—in February, 1937. Building on the success of that visit, together with Ellen Wilkinson and Dame Rachel Crowdy, Atholl and Rathbone embarked on an eminent fact-finding and relief mission to Spain in the spring of 1937. In mid-September, 1938, Wilkinson and Rathbone were key speakers at a Trafalgar Square rally in support of the Czech people, an assembly that included a large proportion of women, and finished with a march to the Czechoslovakian Legation to deliver a resolution.[71] The only reason Atholl was not there was because she was on a tour of Canada and the USA campaigning on behalf of the Spanish government.[72] After the crisis Rathbone went again to Czechoslovakia to organize relief and rescue for refugees, the cause of the victims of Nazism thereon becoming the focus of her political work.[73]

On the one hand, the humanitarian aspects of these women's engagement with foreign affairs was very much in keeping with the pervasive construc-tions of gender-based citizenship and women's place in civic life as social mothers. On the other, when these same women became identified with war, their political problems became acute. Atholl's Kinross by-election cam-paign posters all displayed slogans that were meant to exonerate her of the charge of warmonger, including "Only a Strong Britain/Can Secure Peace;"

"Duchess Policy/ Peace with Honour;" "Forewarned is forearmed! Vote for the Duchess" and "Vote for the Duchess: The Dictators are Watching."[74] If what the anti-appeasers felt was shame at Britain's foreign policy, what they demanded now was courage, to be exercised by men and women. As editor of *Time and Tide* —which had declared itself the 'Unofficial Journal of the Centre' at the end of October, 1938—Lady Rhondda was among many who came out in support of Atholl during the by-election, describing her as 'courageous' no less than seven times in the same short article. For Rhondda, at this time of national emergency, "we can support courage unreservedly whenever a spark of it shines. The Duchess of Atholl is undoubtedly displaying courage. What she has done and what she is now attempting require very unusual moral courage and initiative ... If there were more courage like hers this country might be saved."[75] Not enough of the electors were convinced, and Atholl lost the by-election by 1,313 votes—those of a superstitious bent saw this as especially significant. Nonetheless, the band of women Churchillians continued to grow, and in May, 1939, *Time and Tide* declared "We Need Churchill," and reported that "everywhere—in the clubs, in the pubs, in the cafes and in the streets, people are talking about Mr Churchill. In the press, too, the demand grows apace."[76]

With Atholl out of Parliament, Rathbone carried on the struggle, and entertained the idea of joining forces with Cripps' Popular Front, because, from the vantage point of the beginning of 1939, the past year "has been the worst year I have ever lived through. One disaster has followed another, and I think we all feel that in each disaster our country has played a part of which, whatever the excuses you can make for it, none of us can feel proud."[77] For her part Atholl, who was not yet convinced that her political career was at an end, and Duncan Sandys, Churchill's son-in-law, co-founded the dissenting Hundred Thousand Crusade in January, 1939. At its inaugural private meeting of 300 people at the Caxton Hall, one third were women.[78] Within a few weeks Sandys dropped out and Atholl assumed the leadership of the ginger group, supported in her endeavours by Rathbone.[79]

Atholl is an exemplar of a distinct albeit less dominant type in British women's political history, that of the 'woman defencist.' She was joined in this group by other women during the 1930s, although she stands out as the only one with such a direct connection to Churchill. Had she not died in 1936, the eccentric Baldwin-scourge Lady Lucy Houston, owner of the *Saturday Review*, would very likely have joined forces with the anti-appeasers to insist on rapid air rearmament. Likewise coming from the Right of the spectrum, the prolific anti-Nazi historian and current affairs writer E.O. Lorimer was another Cassandra figure. Lorimer was favourably inclined to eugenics, betrayed signs of anti-Semitism, and Stone classifies her as a "conservative anti-fascist."[80] She had wanted to dedicate her *What Hitler Wants* (Penguin, January 1939) to Edvard Benes, who was soon to become the President of the Czechoslovak Government-in-Exile in London, but he had turned down her request. Lorimer joined Robert Vansittart's Never Again Association, which was pledged to preventing Germany from ever acquiring the capacity to wage war again. Then there were the pro-defence patriotic feminists like Flora Drummond, president of the Women's Guild of Empire. 'General' Drummond joined forces with Leo Amery in the Universal Service campaign and the Citizens Service League in 1939, placing all her efforts to prepare women to perform their national service in wartime. All members of Drummond's Guild joined up for service of some kind as soon as war broke out in September, 1939.This was entirely consistent with the 'Right to Serve' ethos of the Right-veering Emmeline and Christabel Pankhurst as they developed a strain of nationalist feminism during the First World War. Indeed, the Munich Crisis was a spur for the growth of women's patriotic organizations and, for example, in Devon the WI, the Mother's Union, and Devon's Women's British Legion all increased their membership.[81] On the national level, two national women's organizations were the legacy of the drawn-out international crisis, the Women's Voluntary Service (formed four months before Munich), and the female counterpart to the Territorial Army, the Women's Auxiliary Territorial Service (WATS).

Another woman defencist was Violet Milner, sister of *National Review* editor Leopold Maxse. Her first marriage was to former-PM Lord Salisbury's son Edward Cecil, and after his death she married Sir Alfred Milner, with whom she had conducted a longstanding love affair. When her brother fell ill in 1929 she took over editorship of the Radical-right *National Review*. Under her tight editorial control the *'Nat'* was consistently anti-German, calling for massive rearmament and preparation for war from 1933, suspicious of the whole League of Nations machinery, and it took a highly critical line against Chamberlain's foreign policy.[82] She also used the *'Nat'* to publish excerpts from the unexpurgated edition of *Mein Kampf*. The journal described the emotional cycle of the Munich crisis as one "[f]rom grave anxiety to relief, from relief to dismay, from dismay to a conviction that things are very seriously wrong."[83] Yet despite this very Churchillian line, Violet Milner did not ally herself with Churchill, having hated him since he had made a vitriolic attack on Lord Milner in his capacity as under-secretary of state for the colonies.[84] Finally, in August 1939, she put personal rancour aside and came out in support of Churchill whom she now acknowledged had "played the part of Demosthenes in our State during these critical years."[85] There were, therefore, women of influence and affluence who put a feminine twist on the most masculinized of all policy positions: arming for war. Arguably, it is this tendency within Tory gender politics that culminated in the policies and persona of Margaret Thatcher.

The Czech mate: Shiela Grant Duff

The women Churchillians were politically eclectic, and so far we have only considered those who were part of an older generation and well established by dint of elevated social position or personal achievement in the political sphere. The Labour-leaning Oxford-educated freelance foreign correspondent Shiela Grant Duff was another woman who had access to Churchill, and stands out from the others in terms of her youth and her chosen profession. She was a cousin of Clementine Churchill, but quite the opposite in terms of her position in Anglo-German relations to another of Clementine's cousins, Unity Mitford. Despite the blood ties, the first time Grant Duff met the Churchills and went to Chartwell was when she requested an appointment to discuss Czech politics. If the prelude to world war was sex war then women were the war correspondents of the domestic front. Indeed, Britain stood apart from America and France for not producing many women for their foreign press corps between the wars. France had the redoubtable Madame Tabouis, and America produced famous foreign and war correspondents such as Martha Gellhorn, Virginia Cowles, Helen Kirkpatrick, and Dorothy Thompson, all four anti-isolationist and anti-fascist. The latter was convinced that National Socialism "cannot be appeased; it can only be opposed."[86] In contrast, British women journalists had a hard time scooping the foreign news, well exemplified by Grant Duff's first experience when she approached the Foreign Editor, Ralph Deakin, of the *Times* looking for an assignment. Deakin explained to her that it was quite impossible for a woman to work on the editorial side as it meant she would be working alongside men. However, he suggested to her if "I was going to Paris anyways, perhaps I would like to send them some fashion notes. I was deeply incensed."[87] This sexism extends to the scholarship as neither she nor Elizabeth Wiskemann are mentioned in Churchill's *The Gathering Storm* or later in Cockett's *Twilight of Truth*, a study of the press and appeasement.

Grant Duff's memoir can be seen as a *bildungsroman* of a woman anti-appeaser, and it is significantly subtitled 'a personal account of the Thirties.' It was due to her aristocratic status and connections in high places that she was able to become a player in Anglo-German and Anglo-Czech relations, her sex less of a handicap because of these privileges. Only going up to 3 September, 1939, her memoir details her education in the new branch of social science, International Relations, at Oxford in the early 1930s; chronicles her journey from pacifism to a post-pacifism and then to an active anti-fascism; and comes to its climax as she embarks on her career as a self-employed journalist (mentored by American foreign correspondent in Nazi Germany Edgar Mowrer), and experiences transformative European encounters in the Little Entente countries. She had a unique vantage point during the Munich crisis as one of the very few English journalists who had been *in situ* in Prague from 1936, and she enjoyed profound friendships with leading Czech politicians such as Hubert Ripka, and she had acquired expert knowledge of the history of the young nation. As such her detailed recollections of those tense ten days in September 1938 provide both an alternative diplomatic history and an emotional history of the crisis, punctuated by the public mass hysteria she observed and her personal sense of shame.

Her recollections are also framed by her romantic friendship with Adam von Trott, whom she first met when they were students together in Oxford, and who was a regular guest at the Astor's Cliveden estate in the late 1930s— he was executed in 1944 for his role in the failed plot to assassinate Hitler. The fluctuations between their intimacy and distancing ran parallel to the stresses, strains, and breakdowns in Anglo-German relations, exacerbated by their polarized views of appeasement. As she put it "war broke out between us even before it broke out between our two countries."[88] Presumably, she would not have been pleased but not very surprised to hear how von Trott described her to Nancy Astor:

> There is also, I confess, an English girl called Shiela Grant Duff ... who upset me a good deal by having turned violently anti-'German'—which surely is an unforgiveable thing after all—and also by thinking that political is all that women must be good at nowadays. Apparently hating seems an important part of that job. It would be excellent if you would set her head right about it all one day. You may have read her book.[89]

It was ironic that he should express these views about women's political participation to Nancy Astor.

Grant Duff became a devout Churchillian despite her leftist political sympathies and her belief that his views on India were anarchic. Churchill did not have much to say about her in his autobiographical writings, but her contact with him in a 14 month period starting in July 1937 was absolutely fundamental to her mission to "save Czechoslovakia from destruction and Europe from war."[90] She quickly came to see him as "a great Englishman, someone who actually made one proud to be English and set a standard to live up to."[91] She was proud to be able to be a conduit for intelligence on Czech affairs, and wrote to him from Prague in October, 1938, with eye-witness accounts and drawing relevant articles to his attention. But as important as these private exchanges were, her real impact can be measured by her work as a self-appointed whistle-blower. What shocked her most was the "ignorance of ordinary people about what was going on in Europe" and even worse "their attitude that this could all be left in the hands of the Government and the Foreign Office who were perfectly entitled to keep their activities secret."[92] She found that even those in official positions were terribly misinformed, believing Czechoslovakia and not Germany was the threat, and not realizing that the former was a democracy with no concentration camps. She sought to enlighten the British with her Penguin special *Europe and the Czechs* (1938). However, its publication was untimely, appearing on bookstalls just as the newspapers announced the terms of the Munich Agreement, rendering it almost immediately a "useless book."[93] She carried on in her role as Cassandra with her contribution to another Penguin special, *Germany: What Next?* and, at Churchill's advice, joined the Liberal Party. Further, she went to stay with the Haldanes at their Perthshire home so that she could help in Atholl's by-election campaign. However, she chose not to use her newfound reputation as an expert on German-Czech relations to elevate her public standing, and instead she retreated to private life in a Kentish farmhouse in the 11 months between Munich and the outbreak of war. Indeed, her political and professional ambitions peaked with the crisis of 1938, and after the war she devoted herself to marriage and raising her four children.

Masses of missives from misses and Mrs: an epistolary democracy

Grant Duff's decision to disengage from politics was clearly motivated by her deep sense of "terrible shame for what my Government had done."[94] In her telegram congratulating Duff Cooper upon his resignation, she reiterated this: "Gratitude and respect your courageous action this most shameful page British history."[95] What runs through all these texts, both immediate responses and later reflections, is the visceral and very personal sense of shame. Violet Bonham-Carter felt only "shame and humiliation" and "betrayals," and confessed that "no public event has ever filled me with such horror and real <u>fear</u> [emphasis in the original] for the future."[96] Many British women certainly experienced profound feelings of guilt, in the exact opposite sense to Richard Baxter's indictment against the female sex in *Guilty Women*. Writers and life-partners Sylvia Townsend Warner and Valentine Ackland refused to applaud Chamberlain who:

> has released us temporarily from a fear we could have faced courageously, and given us instead the burden of a guilt too heavy to bear. Even if only a small section of your readers reacts like this, will you not record it as a fact that some people in England today are most bitterly ashamed.[97]

The second stanza of Theresa Hooley's poem, written to mark an especially poignant Armistice Day in 1938, likewise conveyed the depth of personal shame for those betrayed by Chamberlain's policy:

> Let there be no reminders,
> no evocation of those proud and shining spirits,
> lest, drawing near,
> they behold their country
> treacherous,
> dishonoured and despised,
> and driven by anguish and despair
> lose their guerdon of rest for evermore.[98]

On political platforms too it was women's voices that cried 'shame' at the National Government's betrayal of the Abyssinians, Republican Spain, the Czechs, and European Jewry. Was shame a more feminine emotion? Did its expression come more naturally to women, socially and psychologically conditioned to feel shame about their bodies, their sexuality, and for any failure to fulfil their biologically-determined roles? Certainly there was a feminine ethics at play here, and women endured acute psychic pain at the suffering of women, children, the persecuted, and the vulnerable.

This current of cringing mortification was also communicated by women to Churchill and other Tory foreign policy non-conformists in an outpouring of missives. It is interesting to read the correspondence Churchill received in the autumn of 1938 (and preserved), as there were hundreds of women who wrote to him to voice their outrage at the Munich Agreement and to call on him to reverse a disastrous and dishonourable policy. There are important differences between the Crisis Letters sent to the Chamberlains and collected in many folios and the thinner files of Churchill correspondence. The first point of contrast is scale, and because Churchill was not the Prime Minister, he received significantly fewer letters. Nevertheless, as the recognized figurehead of the anti-Chamberlain position and after giving wide public exposure to his protestations—such as his broadcast to America on 16 October, 1938[99]—Churchill's postbags did fill up with letters, not only from his Epping constituents but from much further afield. In terms of the gender distribution, less than half of Churchill 'Crisis Letters' were from women, a lower proportion than the Chamberlain fan mail. Further, unlike the Chamberlain folios, many of the letters Churchill received, especially from his own constituents, were hostile to his stance, and entreated him to prevent war at all costs. But the most important difference between the Chamberlain and Churchill crisis letters would seem to be in their reception. We have ample evidence to show that Chamberlain was inspired by the tens of thousands of messages of support, and uniquely moved by those sent by women, whereas Churchill does not appear to have been inordinately flattered by women's adulation or moved to action by their entreaties.

Consistent with the thrust of the Chamberlain Crisis Letters, Churchill did receive some scolding from women. This was the first time Amy Bewick had written to someone in power, and she did so with a sense of urgency and to speak for the mothers: "We want peace & all I speak to want peace—why should we be involved in a war when all we want is to live quietly and peaceably—we are not asked & how helpless—utterly helpless we feel." Bewick wanted to know if Churchill had "given one thought to the intolerable anguish to which we quiet Mothers of England—are subjected while you discuss Pacts which should not concern us and when nothing should provoke war."[100] Representing the PPU, Miss Gowers asked Churchill to see this as a time for "sacrifice and repentance" when "Britain must be prepared to give up some of her territories and to disarm."[101] Two sisters among his constituents betrayed pro-German sympathy, and called for all and any sacrifices to be made for peace. They believed "our plain duty, as a nation, is to join with the Czechs in giving, to the point of great economic sacrifice."[102] Another constituent wanted to let him know how impressed she had been by Chamberlain's speech over the wireless on 27 September, and that "nothing justifies War."[103] [understrike in original] Similarly, a member for Chingford, Hettie Brazier, entreated him to sue for peace as "we women of this country do not wish our menfolk to be involved in another terrible war."[104] There were certainly plenty of women Chamberlainites in and around Epping, and it helps to explain the many difficulties Churchill encountered with his own Conservative association.

However, most of the letters, written in grieving tones, were sympathetic to Churchill's critique of British foreign policy, and "sickened by the pretence that this Peace at Any Price is 'Peace with Honour.'"[105] Their reigning themes are the shame and dishonour of the Munich terms, the immorality and un-Christian character of the agreement, the yearning for real and virile leadership, and the bankruptcy of the National Government. Two women from Loughton pleaded with him to "insist on saving this country from lasting dishonour, future war and crippling militarism. The Premier's tyranny has aroused seething indignation."[106] Mrs Streeton feared that "our Union Jack will be little more than Hitler's doormat, unless a firm stand can be taken by our present Prime Minister," and she was looking to Churchill to "uphold your reputation and our good name. My neighbours and acquaintances are all dismayed at the price of peace, and fear the aggressor will triumph. The Czechs have been betrayed—shamefully, in Britain's name may you restore our prestige. Good luck."[107] Constance Reavey wrote to both Chamberlain and Churchill, telling the latter that she "grieved to think that so gallant a people should be sacrificed to the butchers to provide Mr Chamberlain with the Wings of the Dove ... Never in all my life have I done such things for I am not a collector of autographs."[108] Marjorie Stephenson supposed "you are as ashamed of our foreign policy as I am. This mass hysteria cannot last, but meanwhile it obscures the shameful betrayal of democracy and the surrender to brute force .... I wish you had been in charge of our Foreign Policy."[109] Women wrote to Churchill to express their approval and their desperation too, a very different kind of desperation from that conveyed in the letters to Chamberlain. These women felt only humiliation at the loss of British prestige and honour, and in this vein Dorothy Bolton looked to Churchill "to give forcible utterance" to the people's "shame and dismay at the betrayal of Czechoslovakia and the real interests of this country by Mr Chamberlain."[110] Correspondingly, Mrs Spitzer felt "a deep sense of disgust and shame at our capitulation to bullying threats" and begged him to lead the nation "by reason of your uncompromising standards ... and your deep regard for England's honour."[111] Women correspondents also shared with him their diagnosis of the national mood as a moment of mass pathology and hysteria. While Dorothy Womersly was relieved that war had been averted, this was counter-balanced by being "very sore at the price paid, and very apprehensive for the future. And I found many people the same, when they got the news on Friday night—gloomy, depressed, apprehensive."[112]

While fewer of these mass women Churchillians drew attention to their primary identities as wives and mothers than did Chamberlain's admirers, some did explicitly evoke their motherhood to make the case for standing up to bullies and dictators. In this way Mrs Marshall was full of frustration that

> even our children have lost confidence in us. We have brought them up to believe sincerely those ideals which have passed down to us through the generations. That a Briton will never strike another when he is down. That a Briton will never strike another who is smaller or weaker than himself. That a Briton's word is his Bond. These same children can hear today the noble and pathetic speeches from Prague and also the vulgar campaigns from Berlin to crush the smaller states.[113]

Daisy Drewitt had lost her husband in the war and her only son was serving with the army in India, but this only hardened her anti-appeasement stand: "I have in the past been proud to be a British woman, but now I am ashamed for what my country has done. My heart bleeds for the Czecho-Slovakian People; I must be giving voice to the wish of thousands of my fellow-country men."[114] Similarly, Beatrice Macdonald, who had single-handedly raised and schooled two sons now on the threshold of manhood, felt that as a mother she had to stand up for honour: "I would give my life and theirs without a murmur for the honour and future security of Britain. 'Peace with Honour!' Honour in pieces, more correctly."[115] Others feared that the Munich Agreement had prevented a short and quick war, and that a much more horrific war was now inevitable. Mrs Aldous spoke on behalf of "mothers of British sons" disgusted by "the crowds who cheered [Chamberlain] on Friday evening—overcome with emotion at the removal of the threat of immediate war—were blind to the danger and horror, which they will hand down to their children, if this infamous pact is allowed to pass into statute!"[116] These Churchillian mothers were the 'security mums' of their day. Belying the potent stereotype of maternal pacifism, they were rehearsing the heart-wrenching choices mothers would have to make between the protection of their loved ones and national defence.

As moving as these messages must have been, Churchill made no special references to women's support in his speeches or in private correspondence. Further, women's letters are dispersed throughout the Churchill papers. In contrast, there is reason to believe that Duff Copper was more sensitive to gender differentials in public opinion and to the separate significance of women's letters of support. I suspect this was the case because of the way his papers have been catalogued, and among the files of letters received upon his dramatic resignation as First Lord of the Admiralty on 1 October, 1938, there is one reserved for women only. Cooper clearly enjoyed a big fan mail, and more letters, telegrams, and postcards from women also appear in other files—telegrams were the Twitter feeds of their day, spontaneously fired-off short, abrupt, affecting communiques. The motifs in these letters are consistent with those sent by the women Churchillians, congratulating Cooper on his honourable and brave act, some identifying him as an alternative Prime Minister, and others voicing their shame at the betrayal of Czechoslovakia.

The correspondents' war: women and the politics of shame

There was the suggestion that even if the Munich Agreement had averted war, it had sparked a battle of the letters. Because Londoner Yvonne Moyse failed to "see why the Prime Minister should be the only politician in England to enjoy a fan mail, I am writing to express to you my sincere thanks for voicing in the House of Commons not only my feelings, but those of many of my friends."[117] Similarly, Mrs Cocks was impelled to write because:

> Mr Chamberlain has had many letters from women, but I believe numbers of Englishwomen will not be found in the ranks of his admirers and I, for one, would like to thank you warmly for the protest you have made against a policy which has brought such terrible dishonour upon our country.

Even though Mrs Cocks had suffered great loss in the Great War, she could not countenance "England allowing her ships to be bombed, her strategic position handed over, and now, she has deserted a small nation that trusted her!"[118] Georgina Aitken was "stunned and mortified" by "the emotion of rejoicing displayed by the British Public because a temporary peace truce had been secured at the expense of our national honour and security ... I felt sorry I was British."[119] This shame was only slightly relieved by Cooper's resignation that had made her cry for joy. Cooper was also in receipt of letters from mothers whose shame at Munich overruled their fear of war, and Gladys Wood from Stafford, mother of two young children, explained how "I would gladly have borne my share of the suffering through war rather than contemplate, as we now must, the miseries which millions of the Czech peoples must undergo."[120] Had Bertolt Brecht not subverted the meaning of courageous motherhood in his powerful anti-Nazi play "Mother Courage" (1939) only a year later, such a moniker would have been suitable for these anti-appeasement mothers.

On the same night as Chamberlain returned from Munich, Leo Amery had a longstanding commitment to speak to his constituents, counteracting their delirious enthusiasm with his admission of "a deep sense of shame that such a fate should have befallen a gallant little people."[121] He reiterated these sentiments in the House of Commons debate only days later. As a prominent anti-appeaser, Amery was also in receipt of a flood of letters during the fallout of the crisis, including some telling examples from women.[122] Indeed, it is interesting to observe that women rapidly understood that as a collective they were being represented as the champions of appeasement. Many women took exception. Nine women wrote to Amery how:

> we note that you were among those who voted against the Government in the debate yesterday on Mr Chamberlain's lamentable decision, and as strenuous efforts are being made to show that the women of the country support this decision, we wish to find a means of protesting against such an indictment.

They wished Amery to know that whoever would come to assume the leadership of the dissidents would be "assured of a volume of support and an army of active workers."[123] With the help of Flora Drummond in mobilizing women for his Citizens Service League (launched January, 1939) in the months that followed he was, in fact, able to tap this source of female service.

Letter writing was a vital means of civic expression for women who otherwise had little access to power, revealing the subjective impact of the crisis on the individual and the collective levels. Both women's pro-Chamberlain and anti-appeasement letters give us insight into an 'epistolary democracy' where public opinion and responses to national events were conveyed from one intimate space to another. It is remarkable how many of the women correspondents were self-reflexive about the whole process, especially when it was the first time that they had availed themselves of the opportunity to share their views with a political figure. This form of (gendered) political engagement has been overlooked in the study of appeasement, but these sources vividly illuminate the broader spectrum of women's anti-appeasement activism and opinion, and are key to understanding how the British people were gradually coming to intellectual, moral, and psychological terms with what would be their 'People's War.'

Conclusion and final reckoning

There was a much wider swath of heretical opinion among women at the National Government's foreign policy than the either the Chamberlainite narrative of women's championship of appeasement or the gender-blind historiography of the anti-appeasers have allowed. Nor has it helped that prominent women were too often absent in the autobiographical writings of the 'Glamour Boys.' Certainly partisan and class differences remained highly divisive factors, and most politically active women toed the party line. The vast majority of Labour women resisted the Popular Front movement and were as suspicious of the class enemy Churchill as of the allegedly fascistic PM Chamberlain. Conservative women embraced Chamberlain as a national saviour, and there is little evidence of a pro-Churchill lobby within the women-dominated party organizations. Liberal women balanced their acceptance of the necessity for rapid rearmament with the collective security mantra, and probably came closest to the Churchillian formula during the Munich Crisis. Consequently, in the later 1930s Winston Churchill attracted to his side women who took a more active or independent approach to European affairs, and we have seen that a loosely constituted group of formidable anti-fascist Cassandra figures worked within the concentric circles of the Churchillian foreign-policy apostasy. They shared his position on vital questions of foreign policy, they amplified the chorus of national shame for the betrayal of Britain's allies, and they contributed to the growing support for Churchill to take what they felt was his rightful place at the helm of the nation. In their rhetoric, their reasoning, and in their efforts to mobilize the nation's resources, they represented the vanguard of the war effort. However, it is not enough merely to write a prosopography of these women as an exercise in feminist rehabilitation. Rather, it is important to see how gender mattered, how sex constrained the conduct of foreign policy, and how particular renderings of femininity and masculinity framed the discourse of British national identity and conscience.

Throughout this study I have avoided a teleological reading of women's post-enfranchisement progress in the political sphere. In fact, I have provided myriad examples of the persistence of sex-based prejudices, illustrated further setbacks as women had to make their claims to citizenship rights against the backdrop of the reactionary sexual politics of the fascists and Nazis at home and abroad, and explored the many challenges women faced when attempting to advance their political emancipation in the spheres of domestic and international politics. Yet the story of the women Churchillians irradiates the significant distances, literal and figurative, that British women had travelled between the wars. Even in the inhospitable circles surrounding the feminist-unfriendly Winston Churchill, women emerged as among the most vociferous and probably the most *affective* anti-appeasers. They cried out for the victims of the Nazis, ventilated the nation's shame, and exposed the moral lapses of 'save-our-own-skin' appeasement. From the parliament-based trio of Atholl, Rathbone, and Wilkinson (with the support of Dr Edith Summerskill who, appropriate to her profession, depicted Chamberlain going to Munich "as a world obstetrician complete with gamp," producing "a monstrosity of which we were asked to be foster parents"[124]); to those exercising extra-parliamentary pressure such as Bonham Carter, Corbett Ashby, and Baffy Dugdale; to Rhondda, Wiskemann, Lorimer, and Grant Duff honing their expertise in IR to influence government and public opinion, these and many more women put paid to the view that the female sphere, in private and public, was the domestic one. Each of the aforementioned demonstrated by their personal example what women were capable of in post-suffrage Britain, and it is noteworthy too that all were fiercely independent women, either unmarried or if married then the spouse with the higher public profile.

Two steps forward, one step back. The Munich Crisis and its fallout was also experienced and expressed as a crisis in the relationship between the sexes. For its part, the inter-war feminist movement was not an absolute failure, but many feminists were on the retreat. In the post-enfranchisement period British feminists tempered their militancy, some, like Rathbone and Rhondda, redirecting their energies into foreign policy debate, many others, like Royden, Swanwick, and Brittain leading the absolute pacifist cause. Women had every reason to and did object to the regressive sexual politics of the Italian Fascists, Britain's Blackshirts, and the German National Socialists, but they defused the feminist charge of their arguments in favour of universalist, humanist, and humanitarian triggers. It was in this context of a restrained feminist movement, where younger women were conspicuously underrepresented, that the newsworthy but rather low-key commemorative celebrations of the 21st anniversary of women's suffrage were held in February, March, and April of 1939. Sharply divided in their views about foreign policy, Royden, Corbett Ashby, Summerskill, Brittain, and Mrs Eva Hubback could nonetheless all come together to speak at the 21st anniversary celebration hosted by the National Council for Equal Citizenship on 17 March, 1939—importantly, this was two days after Hitler's troops marched into Bohemia and Moravia. But it was the keynote speaker, Eleanor Rathbone, whose speech provided the most apt epithet for inter-war feminism. She said that on 21st birthdays "one usually looked forward, but in their case it was perhaps safer to dwell on the past. They could say that they were now better equipped to face difficult times by their past stern struggles." It was true that "everybody now had a share in choosing their rulers, and also a share in the responsibility for the choice." The women's movement as a whole "had achievements to their credit, in the cause of peace and wider humanity, disregarding national boundaries." Great things had also been achieved in the sphere of international politics and "the charter of the League of Nations provided that all appointments under the League should be open to both sexes equally, but this was not more effective than some other of the League's provisions." The greatest achievement, however was that "women cared most for the opportunities their citizenship gave them for taking full part in the life of the nation,"[125] vividly illustrating the shift from a separatist woman-centred struggle to the exercise of women's citizenship in all spheres.

Even if feminist militancy had been considerably neutralized, the discord between the sexes had been building up over the 1930s, and many social diagnosticians had observed a virulent woman-hating strain throughout the decade. For his part the uncompromisingly anti-German Robert Vansittart, Undersecretary of State for Foreign Affairs from 1930 to early 1938 whom Chamberlain then 'kicked upstairs,' came to understand Britain's interwar 'degeneracy' and her 'lost instinct of self-preservation' as the result of the shortcomings of the English gentleman-type, and of the public's distraction from world events by "lots of other things—sex, money, pleasure, comfort ... (No generation has ever *talked* more about sex!)."[126] Equally accomplished as a detective writer and a theologian, Dorothy L. Sayers recognized that "everybody has his own particular bogey on which he likes to put the blame for all subsequent disorders," with the "emancipation of women" coming top of the list of bugbears that followed.[127]

This disorder was multi-causal. The primary socio-economic causes were feelings of male demoralization during the Great Depression and emasculation with the ascendency of the woman worker, while the demographic imbalance of a generation with a superfluity of demonized single women widened the gulf. Women scoring 'firsts' in politics, education, culture, and leisure were met with an equal measure of side-show curiosity and male defensiveness. Some men were so overcome by a nervous misogyny that a small band grouped together to unleash a wave of anti-woman militancy. However lamentable an enterprise, the National Men's Defence League, formed in Bristol in 1937 and holding its first meeting in London in 1939, roughly coinciding with the 21st anniversary events as detailed above, was part of the zeitgeist.[128] Mounting the avant-garde of the 'Revolt of Man' to counteract the 'feminine invasion,' the danger these men professed to fear was "the complete domination of males by females and the league is out to fight for the rights of man as distinct from those of women. Its members claim women are overrunning the professions."[129] Much of the angst expressed by the NMDL was shared by others in the realms of politics and journalism, and boldly projected onto the nation during the international crises that precipitated the Second World War. At the height of the Munich Crisis, far-Right, pro-defence Rothermere journalist Collin Brooks could feel an unmistakable sea change in the tone and mood of the nation: "It is as if the soft, sordid years have gone, and the hard refreshing years are coming back."[130] Harold Nicolson identified a direct causality between the emancipation of women and the dishonourable policy of appeasement, and, more broadly, accused women of hastening national decline. Less than a fortnight after the Munich Agreement Nicolson confessed in his diary: "Go up to Leicester. Bertie Jarvis says I have put the women's vote against me by abusing Munich. I expect that the historians of our decline and fall will say that we were done the moment we gave the women the vote."[131] According to Richard Baxter, the 'guilty' women "lowered the dignity and prestige of Great Britain and the Empire,"[132] they trusted Hitler and allowed him to lull them all into a false sense of security, and in the months after Munich "they would keep the war spirit down in England even though a few bold politicians dared attempt to foster it."[133] In spite of the efforts of a good many forthright women, appeasement was constructed as an effete policy that crowned a decade of intertwining sexual and international crisis.

Notes

Introduction—Guilty Women? Gendering Appeasement

1. Baxter was on a mission to reveal the female powers behind Nazi tyranny and atrocities. He also wrote *Women of the Gestapo* (London, 1943), as well as sensationalist eye-witness accounts of Nazi atrocities. See Jean de Vos (as Related to Richard Baxter), *I was Hitler's Slave* (London, 1942), and Richard Baxter, *Hitler's Darkest Secret: What He Has in Store for Britain* (London, 1941). However, despite my efforts, I have not been able to find out much about him, and it is highly likely that this was a *nom de plume*, and that he was somehow associated with the Vansittartists, those who followed Robert Vansittart's (Permanent Under-Secretary at the Foreign Office 1930–1938) line that militarism was innate to the German character. Baxter's publisher, the Quality Press, was in business from 1937 to 1949. 16,000 copies of *Guilty Women* had been sold by the summer of 1941.
2. Richard Baxter, *Guilty Women* (London, 1941), p. 9.
3. See Joanna Alberti, "British Feminists and Anti-Fascism in the 1930s," in Sybil Oldfield (ed.), *This Working-Day World: Women's Lives and Cultures in Britain, 1914–1945* (London, 1994), pp. 112–124; Julie Gottlieb, "Varieties of Feminist Anti-Fascism," in Nigel Copsey and Andrzej Olechnowicz (eds), *Varieties of Anti-Fascism: Britain in the Inter-war Period* (Basingstoke, 2010), pp. 101–118, and Julie Gottlieb, "Feminism and Anti-Fascism in Britain between the Wars: Militancy Revived?" in Nigel Copsey and Dave Renton (eds), *British Fascism, the Labour Movement and the State* (Basingstoke, 2006), pp. 68–94.
4. See Claudia Koonz, *Mothers of the Fatherland: Women, the Family and Nazi Politics* (New York, 1987), and Gisela Bock, "Antinatalism, Maternity and Paternity in National Socialist Racism," in D.F. Crew (ed.) *Nazism and German Society, 1933–1945* (London, 1994), pp. 110–140.
5. Baxter, *Guilty Women*, p. 9.
6. See Jim Wilson, *Nazi Princess: Hitler, Lord Rothermere and Princess Stephanie von Holenlohe* (London, 2011).
7. The figure of Unity Mitford is as popular as ever, fictionalized in the 2011 remake of *Upstairs, Downstairs* (BBC One) as Lady Persephone, the sexually wanton Hitler-obsessed traitor passing on secrets to the Germans. See also Kathryn Steinhaus, *Valkyrie: Gender, Class, European Relations, & Unity Mitford's Passion for Fascism* (unpublished PhD, McGill University, 2012).
8. Baxter, *Guilty Women*, p. 9.
9. Ibid., p. 10.
10. Ibid., p. 11.
11. Cato's *Guilty Men* was republished as a Penguin Twentieth Century Classic in 1998.
12. See David Reynolds, *Summits: Six Meetings that Shaped the Twentieth Century* (London, 2007), p. 37.
13. Graham Stanford, "Cabinet Leads The Crowd in Whoops of Joy," *Daily Mail*, 1 October, 1938.

14. Even in quite recent studies Norman Rose's *The Cliveden Set: Portrait of an Exclusive Fraternity* (London, 2001) and David Faber's *Munich: The 1938 Appeasement Crisis* (London, 2008), a popular history, there is little divergence from the top-down perspective.
15. "Our London Correspondent," *Manchester Guardian*, 19 March, 1938.
16. "Women Can Make Premier Change his Policy," *Daily Mirror*, 21 March, 1938.
17. "Issue of 'Peace or War:' Appeal to Women of N. Cornwall," *The Western Morning News and Daily Gazette*, 8 July, 1939.
18. "Survey Finds British Behind Chamberlain," *New York Times*, 19 October, 1938.
19. Oxford by-Election, First Day of Campaign, 18 October [1938], report from Tom Harrisson, Mass-Observation Archive, File 2/G.
20. Stephen Moulton. "News and Views," *The Cornishman*, 16 February, 1939.
21. Monday 17 October, 1938, Nicholas J. Crowson (ed.), *Fleet Street, Press Barons and Politics: The Journals of Collin Brooks, 1931–1940* (London, 1998), p. 227.
22. "MP's Appeal to Women," *Aberdeen Journal*, 28 October, 1938.
23. Scott argues that because "war, diplomacy, and high politics have not been explicitly about [sexual] relationships, gender seems not concerned with issues of politics and power." Joan W. Scott, "Gender: A Useful Category of Historical Analysis," *American Historical Review*, 91(5), December, 1986, pp. 1053–1075.
24. See Helen McCarthy, *The British People and the League of Nations: Democracy, Citizenship and Internationalism, c. 1918–45* (Manchester, 2011).
25. "Pale Cast of Thought," *Manchester Guardian*, 4 November, 1938.
26. E.M. Forster, "Post-Munich" [1939] in *Two Cheers for Democracy* (London, 1951), p. 36.
27. *Britain by Mass-Observation* (London, 1939), pp. 24–25.
28. Blackwell, I 3568, "Comments on the Crisis," 28 September, 1938, M-OA: Directive Replies 1938, Box 11 of 13, Munich Crisis, September–October—Women, Mass-Observation Archive.
29. Letter from E.A. Russell to Mr Prime Minister, 19 February, 1939, Neville Chamberlain Papers, Cadbury Research Centre, University of Birmingham, NC 13/9/19.
30. Letter from May Yale to Sir and Madame Chamberlain, 30 September, 1938, NC 13/11/517.
31. Tuesday 13 September, 1938, Anne Olivier Bell (ed.), *The Diary of Virginia Woolf, Vol. Five, 1936–1941* (San Diego, 1984), p. 170.
32. Friday 30 September, 1938, Bell (ed.), *The Diary of Virginia Woolf, Vol. Five, 1936–1941*, p. 177.
33. Sunday 2 October, 1938, Bell (ed.), *The Diary of Virginia Woolf, Vol. Five, 1936–1941*, p. 178.
34. Robert Graves and Alan Hodge, *The Long Weekend: The Living Story of the Twenties and Thirties* (London, 1940), p. 440.
35. See John Charmley, *Chamberlain and the Lost Peace* (London, 1991); Martin Gilbert and Richard Gott, *The Appeasers* (London, 1963); and A.J.P Taylor, *The Origins of the Second World War* (London, 1961).
36. Mikkel Vedby Rasmussen, "The History of a Lesson: Versailles, Munich and the Social Construction of the Past," *Review of International Studies* 29, 2003, pp. 499–519.
37. See Sidney Aster, "Appeasement: Before and After Revisionism," *Diplomacy & Statecraft*, 19(3), 2008, pp. 443–480; John Charmley, "'Reassessments of Winston Churchill:' A Reply," *International History Review*, 18(2), 1996, pp. 371–375; Daniel Huckner, "The Unending Debate: Appeasement, Chamberlain and the Origins of

the Second World War," *Intelligence and National Security*, 23(4), 2008, pp. 536–551; Norrin M. Ripsman and Jack S. Levy, "Wishful Thinking or Buying Time? The Logic of British Appeasement in the 1930s," *International Security*, 33(2), Fall, 2008, pp. 148–181; Paul W. Schroeder, "Munich and the British Tradition," *Historical Journal*, 19(1), March, 1976, pp. 223–243; G. Bruce Strang, "The Spirit of Ulysses? Ideology and British Appeasement in the 1930s," *Diplomacy & Statecraft*, 19(3), 2008, pp. 481-526; Wesley Wark, "Review Article: Appeasement Revisited," *International History Review*, 17(3), 1995, pp. 545–562; Gerhard L. Weinberg et al. "Essay and Reflection: The Munich Crisis Revisited," *International History Review*, 11(4), 1989, pp. 668-688; Special Issue: The Munich Crisis, 1938 Prelude to World War II, *Diplomacy & Statecraft*, 10(2-3), 1999.

38. R.J. Q. Adams, *British Politics and Foreign Policy in the Age of Appeasement, 1935–39* (Stanford, 1993), p. 160.

39. Sidney Aster, "Appeasement: Before and After Revisionism," *Diplomacy & Statecraft*, 19(3), 2008, pp. 443–480. Aster cites my first book *Feminine Fascism: Women in Britain's Fascist Movement, 1923–1945* (London, 2000) as one such attempt.

40. Patrick Finney, "The Romance of Decline: The Historiography of Appeasement and British National Identity," *Electronic Journal of International History* (June, 2000); Dan Stone, *Responses to Nazism in Britain, 1933–1939* (Basingstoke, 2003); Kate McLouglin, "Voices of the Munich Pact," Critical Inquiry, 34(3), Spring, 2008, pp. 543–562; Daniel Hucker, *Public Opinion and the End of Appeasement* (Farnham, 2011).

41. Richard Overy, *The Morbid Age: Britain and the Crisis of Civilization, 1919–1939* (London, 2010), p. 361.

42. Juliet Gardiner, *The Thirties: An Intimate History* (London, 2011), p. 727.

43. See Susan Grayzel, *At Home and Under Fire: Air Raids and Culture in Britain from the Great War to the Blitz* (Cambridge, 2012); Susan Pedersen, *Eleanor Rathbone and the Politics of Conscience* (New Haven NJ, 2004); Susan Pennybacker, *From Scottsboro to Munich: Race and Political Culture in 1930s Britain* (Princeton, 2009). The conceptual cross roads where gender, cultural and the new political history meet have been charted in Nicoletta Gullace, '*The Blood of Our Sons:*' *Men, Women, and the Regeneration of British Citizenship During the Great War* (Basingstoke, 2002); Susan Kingsley Kent, *Making Peace: The Reconstruction of Gender in Interwar Britain* (Princeton, 1993) and her *Aftershocks: Politics and Trauma in Britain, 1918–1931* (Basingstoke, 2009); Sonya Rose, *Which People's War? National Identity and Citizenship in Wartime Britain 1939–1945* (Oxford, 2003). *Guilty Women* wedges itself between Grayzel and Rose, both conceptually and in its chronological focus and concentration on the Munich Crisis.

44. Zara Steiner, "On Writing International History: Chaps, Maps and Much More," *International Affairs*, 73(3), July, 1997, pp. 531–546.

45. Susan Pedersen, "The Future of Feminist History," *Perspectives*, October, 2000. For a recent collaborative contribution to this sub-field, see Julie V. Gottlieb and Richard Toye (eds), *The Aftermath of Suffrage: Women, Gender, and Politics in Britain, 1918–1945* (Basingstoke, 2013).

46. Stefan Dudnik, Karen Hagemann, and John Tosh (eds) *Masculinities in Politics and War* (Manchester, 2004) p. xvi.

47. J. Ann Tickner and Laura Sjoberg (eds.), *Feminism and International Relations: Conversations About Past, Present and Future* (New York, 2011).

48. Robert Gilbert Vansittart, *Lessons of My Life* (London, 1943), p. 76.

49. "Keep mum—she's not so dumb!" [1942], NA INF 3/229.

1 British Women and the Three Encounters: International, European, and Fascist

1. British Committee of Women's International Congress, Preliminary Agenda of a Conference to be held at Caxton Hall, Westminster on Thursday 30 September, and Friday, 1 October, 1915, International Women's Suffrage Alliance Papers, John Rylands Library, University of Manchester.

2. It was first named the International Committee of Women for Permanent Peace, changing its name to the WILPF in 1919. Membership of the WIL was approximately 5,000.

3. Second Yearly Report, October 1916–October 1917, Women's International League (British Section of the International Committee of Women for Permanent Peace), Catherine Marshall Papers, Cumbria Record Office.

4. "Transnationalism has been defined as a school of thought that takes the interconnectivity of people around the globe and the flow of people and ideas across national boundaries and its starting point, in the process, its adherents re-examine ties that continue to bind humans to citizenship and to the nation." Erika Kuhlman, *Reconstructing Patriarchy after the Great War: Women, Gender, and Post-war Reconciliation between Nations* (New York, 2008), p. 4.

5. See Antoinette Burton, *Burdens of History: British Feminists, Indian Women and Imperial Culture, 1865–1915* (North Carolina, 1994); Nurpur Chauhuri and Margaret Strobel (eds), *Western Women and Imperialism: Complicity and Resistance* (Indiana, 1992); and Barbara Bush, *Imperialism and Postcolonialism* (Harlow, 2006).

6. Christine Bolt, *Sisterhood Questioned? Race, Class and Internationalism in the American and British Women's Movements, c. 1880s–1970s* (London, 2004), p. 53. See also Barbara Bush, *Imperialism, Race and Resistance: Africa and Britain 1919–1945* (London, 1999).

7. Leila J Rupp, *Worlds of Women: The Making of the International Women's Movement* (Princeton NJ, 1997), p. 129.

8. "Women in Conference," *Manchester Guardian*, 26 May 1935.

9. Review articles are particularly helpful at mapping the direction of the debates on inter-war feminism. See Adrian Bingham, "An Era of Domesticity? Histories of Women and Gender in Interwar Britain," *Cultural and Social History*, 1(2), 2004, pp. 225–233; Julie Gottlieb "'Flour Power' and Feminism between the Waves," Special Issue: Feminism and Feminists after Suffrage, *Women's History Review*, 23(3), June, 2014, pp. 325–329; Pat Thane, "What Difference did the Vote Make?" *Historical Research*, 76(192), May 2003, pp. 268–285.

10. See Pamela M. Graves, *Labour Women: Women in British Working-class Politics, 1918–1939* (Cambridge, 1994); Helen Jones, *Women in British Public Life, 1914–1950* (London, 2000); G.E. Maguire, *Conservative Women: A History of Women in the Conservative Party, 1874–1997* (Basingstoke, 1998); Martin Pugh, *Women and the Women's Movement, 1914–1959* (Basingstoke, 1992).

11. Brian Harrison, *Prudent Revolutionaries: Portraits of British Feminists between the Wars* (Oxford, 1987), p. 7.

12. The literature on the roles women played at the League of Nations has considerably expanded. See Helen McCarthy, *Women of the World: The Rise of the Female Diplomat* (London, 2014); Carol Miller, "'Geneva-the key to Equality': Inter-war Feminists and the League of Nations," *Women's History Review*, 3 (2) 1994, pp. 219–245; Susan Pedersen, "Metaphors of the Schoolroom: Women Working the Mandates System of the League of Nations," *History Workshop Journal* 66(1),

2008, pp. 188–207; Glenda Sluga, "Female and National Self-Determination: A Gender Re-reading of 'The Apogee of Nationalism,'" *Nations and Nationalism*, 6 (4), October, 2000, pp. 495–521.

13. See M. Sinha, D. Guy and A. Woollacott (eds), *Feminism and Internationalism* (Oxford, 1999).

14. V. Spike Peterson, "Feminism and International Relations," *Gender & History*, 10 (3) November, 1998, pp. 581–589. See also Eric M. Blanchard, "Gender, International Relations, and the Development of Feminist Security Theory," *Signs*, 28 (4), Summer, 2003, pp. 1289–1312; Cynthia Enloe, *Bananas, Beaches and Bases: Making Feminist Sense of International Politics* (Berkeley, 1990); Adam Jones, "Does 'Gender' Make the World Go Round? Feminist Critiques of International Relations," *Review of International Studies*, 22 (4), October, 1996, pp. 405–429; Judith Squires and Jutta Weldes, "Beyond Being Marginal: Gender and International Relations in Britain," *BJPIR*, 9(2), 2007, pp. 185–203.

15. See Jane Addams, Emily Balch, and Alice Hamilton, *Women at the Hague: The International Congress of Women and Its Results* (Urbana, 2003); Mineke Bosch (ed.), *Politics and Friendship: Letters from the International Woman Suffrage Alliance, 1902–1942* (Columbus, 1990); Gertrude Bussey and Margaret Tims, *Pioneers for Peace: WILPF 1915–1965* (London, 1980); Jill Liddington, *The Long Road to Greenham Common: Feminism and Anti-Militarism in Britain since 1820* (Syracuse, 1989); Sybil Oldfield, *Women against the Iron Fist: Alternatives to Militarism 1900–1989* (Oxford, 1989).

16. Verta Taylor and Leila J. Rupp, "Loving Internationalism: The Emotion Culture of Transnational Women's Organizations, 1888–1945," *Mobilization*, 7(2), 2002, pp. 141–158.

17. Christine Bolt, *Sisterhood Questioned?* (London, 2004), p. 74.

18. Martin Pugh, *Women and the Women's Movement in Britain* (Basingstoke, 2000), p. 107.

19. Deborah E. Van Seters, "Women's Foreign Policy Advocacy in 1930s Britain," PhD, 1999, University of Toronto, p. 382.

20. See Paula Bartley, *Ellen Wilkinson from Red Suffragist to Government Minister* (London, 2014); Deborah Gorham, *Vera Brittain: A Feminist Life* (London, 1996); Susan Pedersen, *Eleanor Rathbone and the Politics of Conscience* (New Haven, 2004); Matt Perry, "In Search of 'Red Ellen' Wilkinson Beyond Frontiers and Beyond the Nation State," *IRSH* 58(2), 2013, pp. 219–246; Jo Vellacott, *From Liberal to Labour with Women's Suffrage: The Story of Catherine Marshall* (Montreal, 1993).

21. Sonya Rose, *Which People's War? National Identity and Citizenship in Britain 1939–1945* (Oxford, 2003), p. 149.

22. "Women Voters and the Red Flag," by Evelyn Sharpe [c. December, 1918][WIL pamphlet], Catherine Marshall Papers, Cumbria Archives, D/MAR/4/80.

23. Eleanor Rathbone, "Changes in Public Life," in Ray Strachey (ed.), *Our Freedom and Its Results* (London, 1936), p. 40.

24. "Women and War Horrors: Fascist Aggression," *Manchester Guardian*, 17 June, 1938.

25. Vera Brittain, "Peace and the Public Mind," in Philip Noel Baker et al. (eds), *Challenge to Death* (London, 1934), p. 59.

26. Home or Foreign Affairs, 26 March, 1938, M-O, File 2/C.

27. See Susan Kingsley Kent, *Aftershocks: Politics and Trauma in Britain, 1918–1931* (Basingstoke, 2009).

28. Virginia Woolf, *A Room of One's Own* (London, 1929), p. 92.

29. Winifred Holtby, *Woman and a Changing Civilization* (London, 1934), p. 2.
30. There were also significant schisms in the international women's movement that were extensions of the growing gulf between Old/egalitarian Feminists and the New/protectionist Feminists at the national level. Becker argues that this schism helps to explain the movement's inability "to resist the impact of the deepening worldwide depression and the rise of fascism." (Quoted in C. Bolt, p. 60).
31. See June Purvis, "The Pankhursts and the Great War," in A.S. Fell and I. Sharp (eds), *The Women's Movement in Wartime* (Basingstoke, 2007), pp. 141–157, and Nicoletta F. Gullace, "Christabel Pankhurst and the Smethwick Election: Right-wing Feminism, the Great War and the Ideology of Consumption," *Women's History Review*, 23 (3), June, 2014, pp. 330–346. We should also note that both these efforts were led by women of the Right, highlighting one often overlooked tendency of post-war feminism.
32. See Mary Hilson, "Women Voters and the Rhetoric of Patriotism in the British General Election of 1918," *Women's History Review*, 10(2), 2001, pp. 325–347.
33. Quoted in Jo Vellacott, "Feminism as if All People Mattered: Working to Remove the Causes of War, 1919–1929," *Contemporary European History*, 10(3), 2001, pp. 375–394.
34. "House of Commons," *The Times*, 20 June 1917.
35. Glenda Sluga, *Internationalism in the Age of Nationalism* (Philadelphia, 2013), pp. 5–6.
36. See Daniel Laqua (ed.), *Internationalism Reconfigured: Transnational Ideas and Movements between the Wars* (London, 2011); Susan Pedersen, "Review Essay: Back to the League of Nations," *American Historical Review*, (October, 2007), pp. 1091–1117.
37. Catherine E. Marshall, "The Future of Women in Politics," in M. Kamester and J. Vellacott (eds), *Militarism Versus Feminism: Writing on Women and War* (London, 1987), p. 47.
38. "Women Voters and the Red Flag," by Evelyn Sharpe [c. Dec., 1918][WIL pamphlet], D/MAR/4/80.
39. See Carol Miller, "'Geneva—the Key to Equality': Inter-war Feminists and the League of Nations," *Women's History Review*, 3(2) 1994, pp. 219–245; and Helen McCarthy, *The British People and the League of Nations: Democracy, Citizenship and Internationalism, c. 1918–1945* (Manchester, 2011); Susan Pedersen, "Metaphors of the Schoolroom: Women Working the Mandates System of the League of Nations," *HWJ*, 66(1), 2008, pp. 188–207.
40. Bolt, *Sisterhood Questioned?* (London, 2004), p. 43.
41. "Equality for Women," *Gloucester Journal*, 27 October, 1928.
42. Winifred Holtby, "Where We Could Excel: From a Woman's Angel," *News Chronicle*, 22 January, 1934.
43. Letter from V.B. to W.H., 20 August 1935, in Vera Brittain and Geoffrey Handley-Taylor (eds), *Selected Letters of Winifred Holtby and Vera Brittain (1920–1935)* (London, 1960).
44. Leila J. Rupp, *Worlds of Women*, (Princeton, 1997), pp. 38–40.
45. "World Peace Campaign: Women's Manifesto," *Manchester Guardian*, 20 July, 1936.
46. See Christine von Oertzen, *Science, Gender and Internationalism: Women's Academic Networks, 1917–1955* (Basingstoke, 2014).
47. Minutes of Executive Committee Meeting, 16 October, 1934, LSE Library, WILPF 1/10.
48. G. Bussey and M. Tims, *Pioneers of Peace*, WILPF (The Hague, 1915), p. 132.

49. The Congress of Peace and Freedom with the USSR included many of the same members as the WWCAWAF.
50. Julie Gottlieb and Matthew Stibbe, "When Hitler's perfect woman came to call," *BBC History Magazine,* March, 2014, pp. 51–54.
51. Malcolm Muggeridge, *The Thirties* (London, 1940), p. 26.
52. Verta Taylor and Leila J. Rupp, "Loving Internationalism: The Emotion Culture of Transnational Women's Organizations, 1888–1945," *Mobilization,* 7(2), 2002, pp. 141–158.
53. Open Door Council, Eighth Annual Report, March 1934, Women's Library, 5/ODC/ A7.
54. Open Door International, Report of Third Conference, Prague, 24–28 July, 1933, 5/ODI/B1-8.
55. Letter from Flora Drummond to Mrs Archdale, 13 June 1932, Women's Library, 5/ERI, Box 331.
56. Winifred Holtby, *Women and a Changing Civilization* (London, 1934), p. 152.
57. "Women's Position in Europe," *Manchester Guardian,* 3 June 1935.
58. Ethel Mannin, *Women and the Revolution* (London, 1939), p. 196.
59. Mannin, *Women and the Revolution,* p. 200.
60. See Mineke Bosch (ed.), *Politics and Friendship: Letters from the International Woman Suffrage Alliance, 1902–1942* (Columbus, 1990).
61. Jo Vellacott, "Feminism as if All People Mattered: Working to Remove the Causes of War, 1919–1929," *Contemporary European History,* 10(3), 2001, pp. 375–394.
62. Mary Sheepshanks, Mss of Memoir [n.d., unpublished] p. 21, Women's Library, 7/MSH, Box 642
63. Rose Macaulay, *Non Combatants and Others* (London, 1986), p. 148. First published in 1916.
64. Macaulay, *Non Combatant and Others,* pp. 176–177.
65. "A dismal group of Peacettes are waiting at Tilsbury for a boat to take them to Holland for the International chirrup with the German fraus." "Hopeless Dawn at Tilbury," *Daily Express,* 26 April, 1915.
66. Pocket diaries etc., Kathleen Courtney Papers, Women's Library, KDC/KI, Box 457.
67. Letter from K. Courtney to Mrs Laura Duffer Morgan, 25 September, 1940, KDC I1/36-54.
68. Letter from Kathleen Courtney to Laura Duffer Morgan, 14 March, 1941, KDC/I1/77-10.
69. See Jo Vellacott, *From Liberal to Labour with Women's Suffrage: The Story of Catherine Marshall* (Montreal, 1993).
70. Women were also active in the Czechoslovak–British Friendship Club established in 1938, of whose patrons half were women: Margery Corbett Ashby, Miss Lilian Bowes-Lyon, Miss Elizabeth Denby, Mrs F.M. Lloyd, and Dame Sybil Thorndike.
71. "Berlin Congress, 1904," Box 483 International MICA/C, Margery Corbett Ashby Papers. First constituted as the International Woman Suffrage Alliance in Berlin in 1904, in 1926 the title was changed to International Alliance of Women for Suffrage and Equal Citizenship. Its organ was the monthly *International Women's News.* Founded in 1906 "the paper has survived two world wars and continues to give news of women and the women's movement and of international questions of a more general kind." International Alliance of Women, 14th Congress, Interlaken, 10–17 August, 1946.
72. "Mrs Corbett Ashby Elected President of the WNLF," *Ninth Annual Report of the Women's National Liberal Federation,* May 1927–May 1928.

73. Women's Peace Crusade, "Women and Disarmament," Margery Corbett Ashby Papers, 6B/106/7/MCA/CA, Box 484

74. "Our London Correspondent," *Manchester Guardian*, 8 March, 1935.

75. Quoted in Deborah Van Seters, "Women's Foreign Policy Advocacy in 1930s Britain" (1999), [Margery Corbett Ashby to Marie Corbett, 25 January, 1932, MCA Papers].

76. Quoted in Deborah Van Seters, "Women's Foreign Policy Advocacy in 1930s Britain" (1999), p. 7. [MCA to Brian Ashby, 8 February, 1933, MCA Papers].

77. Disarmament Conference in Geneva 1932/33, Women's Library, MICA/C.

78. "The Use of War to Stop War: Mrs Corbett Ashby and Pacifists' Dilemma," *Manchester Guardian*, 9 March, 1934.

79. "Democracy and Peace: Women's Campaign," *Manchester Guardian*, 19 May, 1936.

80. "Congress 39 (July 1939) Copenhagen again," Women's Library, International MICA/C.

81. *Evening Angus*, 24 October, 1961.

82. "Congress 39 (July, 1939)", Margery Corbett Ashby Papers, Box 483 International MICA/C.

83. Letter from Rosa Manus to Carrie Chapman Catt [Amsterdam] 31 July, 1939, M. Bosch (ed.), *Politics and Friendship*, p. 247.

84. In fact, the European encounter ran in parallel with the colonial encounter, and especially in that Liberal Party members remained intimately engaged in the affairs and the position of women in the colonies. The WNLF attended the 'Mother India' conference in 1927, "organized to enquire into the conditions of life of Indian women—as the result of the publication of Miss Mayo's book on Mother India ... [as well as the] Conference on Native Labour (represented by Lady Horsley and Lady Simon), organized by the Anti-Slavery and Aborigines Protection Society to abolish or reduce child labour in the mines of Southern Rhodesia." "Conferences," *Ninth Annual Report of the Women's National Liberal Federation*, May 1927–May 1928.

85. "Deputations and Conferences," Women's National Liberal Federation, 1926–1927: *Seventh Annual Report*, October, 1926.

86. "Prominent Liberal Women: The Viscountess Gladstone," *Liberal Women's News*, October, 1925.

87. Margery Corbett Ashby, "Women in Many Lands," *Women's Liberal News*, January, 1927.

88. "During the year communication has been opened with groups of women of Liberal opinion in Germany and America. Points under discussion have been the admission of Germany, Russia, and America to the League of Nations, Conditions in the Ruhr, and Equal Franchise." "Intercourse with the Liberal Women of Other Nationalities," Women's National Liberal Federation, *Fifth Annual Report*, September, 1924.

89. See Helen McCarthy, *The British People and the League of Nations* (Manchester, 2011), pp. 49–50.

90. Lady Barlow, "Germany, August 1926," *Liberal Women's News*, October, 1926.

91. Lady Barlow, "A Short Visit to Germany," *Liberal Women's News*, November, 1933. There were also many reports of Liberal women who travelled to Soviet Russia (see Mrs Wedgwood Benn, "Factory Life in Soviet Russia," *Women's Liberal News*, February, 1927; "Miss Mackinnon's Visit to Russia, *Liberal Women's News*, October, 1931; and "Mrs Wintringham's Visit to Russia," *Liberal Women's News*, June, 1934). See also Mrs Corbett Ashby, "Glimpses at Four Countries," *Liberal Women's News*, May, 1934.

92. Hilda M.A. Buckmaster, "The Rapid Changes in the 'Family Life' of States," *Liberal Women's News*, June, 1933.
93. "Report of the Council Meetings of the WNLF, Scarborough, May 16–17, 1933," *Liberal Women's News*, May, 1933.
94. "Things in Germany: First-Hand Impressions (By Miss Hilda Buckmaster)," *Chelmsford Chronicle*, 11 August, 1933.
95. Enid Lapthorn, "What Germans are Thinking about Peace and War," *Liberal Women's News*, April, 1935.
96. "Liberty and the Danger of Dictatorship," *Liberal Women News*, June, 1935.
97. "International Affairs," *Women's Liberal Federation: Eighteenth Annual Report*, October, 1937.
98. See *Women's Liberal Federation: Eighteenth Annual Report*, October, 1937.
99. See *Women's Liberal Federation: Nineteenth Annual Report*, May, 1938.
100. See Martin Francis, "Labour and Gender," in D. Tanner et al. (eds), *Labour's First Century* (Cambridge, 2001), pp. 191–220; David Thackeray, "From Prudent Housewife to Empire Shopper: Party Appeals to the Female Voter, 1918–1928," in J. V. Gottlieb and R. Toye (eds), *The Aftermath of Suffrage* (Basingstoke, 2013), pp. 37–53.
101. International Study Week, International Committee of the LSI, Belgian Labour College, Brussels, 22–29 August, 1936, LSI papers, Labour History Archive, Manchester.
102. Minutes of Meeting held 9 November, 1932, Manchester Labour Women's Advisory Council (Minutes), M449/1, Manchester Public Library.
103. Minutes of Meeting held 5 December, 1932, Manchester Labour Women's Advisory Council (Minutes), M449/1, Manchester Public Library.
104. "Dictatorship, Right or Left," *Manchester Guardian*, 6 October, 1933.
105. "United Front: Labour Women Divided: Heated Debate," *Manchester Guardian*, 28 April, 1937
106. "The Editor's Monthly Letter, Mary E. Sutherland," *Labour Woman*, June, 1938.
107. Minutes of Meeting held 5 December, 1938, M449/1.
108. Minutes of Meeting held 6 February, 1939, M449/1.
109. "The Popular Front," by the Editor, *Labour Woman*, May, 1939.
110. "Mr Lloyd George at Albert Hall: Appeal to Women," *Manchester Guardian*, 10 May, 1929.
111. "Women's Part in Public Life," *Manchester Guardian*, 8 March, 1930.
112. "Support the Charter for Peace and Social Justice" [n.d] WILPF 1/15, LSE.
113. "Why Current Events Matter to Us," Halifax Luncheon Club, 30 November 1932, Vera Brittain Papers, McMaster University, F10.
114. "Importance of Foreign Affairs in Everyday Life," [handwritten notes, c. 1933], Vera Brittain Papers, F11.

2 Women's War on Fascism

1. Ethel Mannin, *Young in the Twenties* (London, 1971), p. 165.
2. Storm Jameson, "The Twilight of Reason," in Philip Noel Baker (ed.), *A Challenge to Death* (London, 1934), p. 6.
3. "Women's War on Fascism," *News Chronicle*, 17 December, 1937.
4. Richard Overy, *The Morbid Age: Britain and the Crisis of Civilization, 1919–1939* (London, 2009), p. 370.
5. Mary Agnes Hamilton, *Remembering My Good Friends* (London, 1944), p. 288.

6. Michele Haapanki, "Writers in Arms and the Just War: The Spanish Civil War, Literary Activism and Leftist Masculinity," *Left History*, 10(2), 2005, pp. 33–52.
7. *Authors Take Sides on the Spanish War (Left Review,* 1937).
8. See Julie V. Gottlieb, "'The Women's Movement Took the Wrong Turning:' British Feminists, Pacifism and the Politics of Appeasement," *Women's History Review*, 23(3), June, 2014, pp. 441–462.
9. The WILPF also convoked a purely private consultative conference of women's international organizations for the defence of women against Fascism for 18–19 November, 1933. This was mired in controversy as the different women's organizations could not find common ground. As a result the conference concluded by holding the women's movement itself partly responsible for the rise of fascism, as women had not done enough to protest against war from 1914 to 1918, and fascism was the child of the war.
10. "Women under Hitlerism," *Manchester Guardian*, 19 May, 1933.
11. Annual Report of Six Point Group, 1938–1939, Women's Library, SPG/B6-13.
12. See Julie V. Gottlieb, "Varieties of Feminist Anti-Fascism," in Nigel Copsey and Andrzej Olechnowicz (eds), *Varieties of Anti-Fascism: Britain in the Inter-war Period* (Basingstoke, 2010), pp. 101–118.
13. See M. Ceadel, "Pacifism versus Pacificism," in Nigel J. Young (ed.), *The Oxford International Encyclopaedia of Peace* (New York, 2010), pp. 323–325.
14. "Crisis of the Left" [n.d], I36 Unpublished Articles, Vera Brittain Papers.
15. "Nazi Victims: Manchester Relief Committee," *Manchester Guardian*, 31 July, 1933.
16. "The Peace Pledge Union," *Manchester Guardian*, 1 July, 1936.
17. "Spreading 'Peace Area,'" *Manchester Guardian*, 8 March, 1938.
18. Matt Perry, "In Search of 'Red Ellen' Wilkinson Beyond Frontiers and Beyond the Nation State," International Review of Social History 58(2), 2013, pp. 219–246.
19. Monica Whately, Honorary Secretary, Six Point Group, "The Status of Women," *Time and Tide*, 28 October, 1937.
20. Letter from Elizabeth Bibesco to V. Woolf, 1 January, 1935, Virginia Woolf Papers, University of Sussex, B 16 f 2.
21. (Sunday, 6 January 1935) in Anne Olivier Bell (ed.), *The Diary of Virginia Woolf: Vol. IV: 1931–1935* (London, 1982), p. 273.
22. See Julie V. Gottlieb, "Feminism and Anti-fascism in Britain: Militancy Revived," in N. Copsey and D. Renton (eds), *British Fascism, the Labour Movement and the State* (Basingstoke: Palgrave, 2005), pp. 68–94.
23. Annual Report of the Six Point Group, November, 1935–November, 1936, SPG/B6-13.
24. Referring to a range of sources, rather cynically, Conze asserted that "the best atrocity stories have as much sex appeal as the girl who is schoolgirl complexion all over," and they were craved "as a source of vicarious satisfaction for suppressed, and repressed instincts." Edward Conze, "Atrocity Propaganda," *Left Forum*, No. 31, April, 1939, pp. 68–71.
25. Letter from Monica Whately, SPG, to Virginia Woolf, 7 June, 1935, Virginia Woolf Papers, B 16 f 3.
26. "In Defence of Individual Women," Annual Report of the Six Point Group, November, 1935–November, 1936, SPG/B6-13
27. Six Point Group, Annual Report, November, 1933–November, 1934, SPG/ B1-5.
28. Monica Whately, "Elsie Evert and Olga Prestes," *Time and Tide*, 21 November, 1936.
29. Annual Report of the Six Point Group, November, 1935–November, 1936, SPG/B6-13.

30. 27 February, 1937, statement signed by Monica Whately, CPGB archive, Labour History Museum, CP/CENT/SUBJ/04/04.
31. Monica Whately, Honorary Secretary, Six Point Group, *Manchester Guardian*, 3 September, 1937.
32. Letter from Monica Whately, SPG, to Nancy Astor, 24 May, 1935, Nancy Astor Papers, University of Reading, MS 1416/1/1/1221.
33. Letter from Nancy Astor to Monica Whately, 4 July, 1935, MS 1416/1/1/1221.
34. Monica Whately, "Liselotte Herrmann," *Time and Tide*, 25 June, 1938.
35. Letter from Monica Whately to Nancy Astor, 19 March, 1937, MS 1416/1/1/1483.
36. Linda Walker, "Whately, Monica (1889–1960)," *ODNB* (2004) http://www.oxforddnb.com/view/article/63900.
37. Susan Pedersen, *Eleanor Rathbone and the Politics of Conscience*, (Newhaven and London, 2004) p. 271.
38. Rathbone was vice-president of the Emperor of Ethiopia Fund.
39. See Petra Rau, "The Fascist Body Beautiful and the Imperial Crisis in 1930s British Writing," *Journal of European Studies*, 39(1), March, 2009, pp. 5–35.
40. Hamilton, *Remembering my Good Friends*, p. 193.
41. Letter from Eleanor Rathbone on House of Commons note paper, 11 August, 1933, Eleanor Rathbone Papers, Liverpool University Library, XIV.2.6 (5).
42. Letter from Eleanor Rathbone to Mr Franklin, Wayfarers Travel Agency, 5 February, 1936, XIV 2.6 (16).
43. See David Caute, *Fellow Travellers: Intellectual Friends of Communism* (London, 1973); Paul Fussell, *Abroad: Literary Travelling Between the Wars* (New York, 1980); Richard Griffiths, *Fellow Travellers of the Right: British Enthusiasts for Nazi Germany, 1933–1939* (London, 1980).
44. Norman Angell, "Holidays Under the Volcano," *Foreign Affairs*, Incorporated into *Time and Tide*, 7 August, 1937.
45. Bernard Schweizer, *Radicals on the Road: The Politics of English Travel Writing in the 1930s* (Virginia, 2001), p. 2.
46. See Helen McCarthy, "Petticoat Diplomacy: The Admission of Women to the British Foreign Service, c. 1919–1946," *Twentieth Century British History*, 20(3), 2009, pp. 285–321.
47. D/MAR/4/86
48. "Victims of Nazism," *Manchester Guardian*, 16 October, 1933.
49. Shirley Harrison, *Sylvia Pankhurst: A Crusading Life, 1882–1960* (London, 2003), p. 242.
50. Katherine Atholl, Rachel Crowdy, Eleanor Rathbone, and Ellen Wilkinson, "Report of Our Visit to Spain (April, 1937).
51. "Spain Needs Your Help," Edith M. Gow, *The Labour Woman*, February, 1938.
52. Women's Advisory Council, 29 April, 1938, LSE, LNU 5/3.
53. The Editor's Monthly News Letter, Mary E. Sutherland, *Labour Woman*, February, 1938.
54. See Helen Jones, "National, Community and Personal Priorities: British Women's Responses to Refugees from the Nazis, from the Mid-1930s to the Early 1940s," *Women's History Review*, 21(1), 2012, pp. 121–151.
55. "Miss Bergner's New Film," *Manchester Guardian*, 19 January, 1939.
56. Letter from Vera Brittain to Winifred Holtby, 19 May, 1934, in Vera Brittain and Geoffrey Handley-Taylor (eds), *Selected Letters of Winifred Holtby and Vera Brittain* (London, 1960).
57. "Woman Author Risks £1,000," *Daily Mirror*, 19 April, 1937.

58. Evelyn Sharpe, "The Panoply of Peace: Unimaginative Pacifism," *Manchester Guardian*, 22 March, 1933.
59. Winifred Holtby, "A Woman Looks at the News," *News Chronicle*, 26 May, 1934.
60. Executive Committee of the Six Point Group, 28 April, 1936, SPG A1-9.
61. Executive Committee of the Six Point Group, 12 December, 1935, SPG A1-9.
62. See Maroula Joannou, *'Ladies, Please Don't Smash These Windows:' Women's Writing, Feminist Consciousness and Social Change 1918–1938* (Oxford, 1995); Phyllis Lassner, *British Women Writers of World War II: Battlegrounds of Their Own* (New York, 1998).
63. Letter from Helena Swanwick to Winifred Holtby, 24 December, 1934, Winifred Holtby Papers, Hull History Centre, WH/ 5/5.21/05/01a-01g.
64. Winifred Holtby, "Black Words for Women Only," *Clarion*, 24 May, 1934.
65. BBC Director of Television to Vera Brittain, 29 July, 1938, Correspondence, Vera Brittain Papers.
66. Thelma Cazalet Keir, *From the Wings* (London, 1967), p. 134.
67. Bosley Crowther, "The Screen: 'The Mortal Storm,' a deeply tragic Anti-Nazi Film," *New York Times*, 21 June, 1940.
68. Alexis Pogorelskin, "Phyllis Bottome's *The Mortal Storm*: Film and Controversy," *The Space Between*, 6(1), 2010, pp. 39–58. See also Pam Hirsch, "Authorship and Propaganda: Phyllis Bottome and the Making of *The Mortal Storm*, (1940)," *Historical Journal of Film, Radio and Television*, 32(1), March, 2012, pp. 57–72.
69. Winifred Holtby, *Woman and a Changing Civilization* (London, 1934), p. 4.
70. "Jew Baiting in Germany: The Duty of Writers," to the editor from Storm Jameson, *Manchester Guardian*, 13 December, 1938.
71. Helen McCarthy, *The British People and the League of Nations* (Manchester, 2011), p. 190.
72. Ibid., p. 118
73. Vera Brittain, "Peace and the Public Mind," Noel Baker (eds), *Challenge to Death* (London, 1934), p. 46.
74. See Zara Steiner, "On Writing International History: Chaps, Maps and Much More," *International Affairs*, 73 (3), July, 1997, pp. 531–546.
75. Jeremy Lewis, *Penguin Special: The Life and Times of Allen Lane* (London, 2006), p. 135.
76. Shiela Grant Duff, *The Parting of Ways: A Personal Account of the Thirties* (London, 1982), p. 96.
77. Elizabeth Wiskemann, *The Europe I Saw* (London, 1968), p. 84.
78. Ibid., p. 139.
79. Grant Duff admits to meeting Wiskemann when in the Saar to cover the plebiscite in 1935. Grant Duff, *The Parting of Ways*, p. 79.
80. Dan Stone, "The 'Mein Kampf Ramp:' Emily Overend Lorimer and Hitler Translations in Britain," *German History*, 26 (4), 2008, pp. 504–519.
81. Letter from Katherine, Duchess of Atholl, to WSC, 10 March, 1936, Churchill Papers, CHAR 2/275/4.
82. See, for example, "Women Fight at Fascist Meeting," *Morning Post*, 23 October, 1936; "Cars Fired: Girl Hurled into Window," *Daily Mail*, 12 October, 1936.
83. Quoted in Ethel Mannin, *Women and the Revolution* (London, 1938), p. 203. Mannin also explains: "All that the long-drawn-out fight of the Suffrage Movement achieved for women, all that the Great War made possible for them, at its own bitter price, will be swept away in a few months if Fascism comes to this country, and women will have no say in the matter, and allowed no protest." (pp. 201–202).

84. *Report of the National Conference of Labour Women*, Brighton, 14, 15, and 16 June 1932, p. 26.
85. Anti-Fascist Special: Facts Against Fascist Fancies [n.d], CP/CENT/SUBJ/04/09.
86. "Saturday Competition: The Lipstick Era," *Manchester Guardian*, 16 August, 1933.
87. "Defence of Women Against Fascism," *Pax International*, No. 10, December, 1933.
88. Oliver Baldwin, "A Farewell to Liberty," *Daily Herald*, 14 June, 1933.
89. "Fascism—Is it for Peace? Opposing Views at Oxford Discussion," *Oxford Mail*, 22 February, 1934.
90. "Women and Fascism," *Manchester Guardian*, 30 July, 1934.
91. Naomi Mitchison, *Home and a Changing Civilization* (London, 1934), pp. 104–105.
92. Rebecca West, "The Necessity and Grandeur of the International Idea," in Philip Noel Baker (ed.), *A Challenge to Death* (London, 1934), p.251.
93. Virginia Woolf, *Three Guineas* (London, 1938), p. 102.
94. Ray Strachey, "Changes in Employment," in Ray Strachey (ed.), *Our Freedom and its Results* (London, 1936), p. 153.
95. "Women in War: Demand for Training Now," *Manchester Guardian*, 24 April, 1939.
96. "Many women finally took their resistance to Fascism into practical activities which were anti-fascist, but not necessarily feminist. Fascism disrupted and muted the impact of such powerful discourses as were provided by Rhondda, Holtby, Wilkinson, Mitchison, and Woolf." Joanna Alberti, "British Feminists and Anti-Fascism in (ed.) Sybil Oldfield the 1930s," in *This Working-Day World: Women's Lives and Culture(s) in Britain, 1914–1945*, p. 123.
97. On the cleavages in anti-fascist mobilization on the left see Nigel Copsey, *Anti-Fascism in Britain* (Basingstoke, 2000); N. Copsey and A. Olechnowicz (eds.), *Varieties of Anti-Fascism: Britain in the Inter-war Period* (Basingstoke, 2010); Geoff Eley, *Forging Democracy: The History of the Left in Europe, 1850–2000* (Oxford, 2002), especially Chapter 12, "The Politics of Gender;" Kevin Morgan, *Against Fascism and War: Ruptures and Continuities in British Communist Politics, 1935–1941* (Manchester, 1989), Andrew Thorpe, *The British Communist Party and Moscow* (Manchester, 2000).
98. See Martin Ceadel, *Semi-detached Idealists: The British Peace Movement and International Relations, 1854–1945*(Oxford, 2000); David Cortright, *Peace: A History of Movements and Ideas* (Cambridge, 2008).
99. Women's pre-emptive war on fascism mirrored that of World Jewry in 1933. See "Judea Declares War on Germany: Jews of all the World Unite in Action," *Daily Express*, 24 March, 1933.

3 'Guilty Women:' Conspiracy and Collusion

1. "This is Hitler's Perfect Nazi Woman," *Daily Mirror*, 8 March, 1939. In fact, she had visited London before in her official capacity in July 1936 to take part in an International Conference of Social Work. See "She Leads 11,000,000 Nazi Women— And Claims to be Freest in the World," *Nottingham Evening Post*, 15 July, 1936.
2. "Women Leaders Meet "Perfect Nazi Woman," *Daily Telegraph*, 8 March, 1939.
3. Richard Baxter, *Guilty Women* (London, 1941), p. 43. There were a series of articles that made similar allegations of a German spy ring made up of well-educated and well-groomed German women placed in domestic service in Britain. See "Nazi Spy Headquarters: Regular Meetings at Sutton Railway Station," *Croydon Advert*, 7 July, 1939.

4. "'Perfect Nazi' Protest," *Daily Mirror*, 10 March, 1938.
5. "Nazi Woman's Visit: Lady Astor has no Sympathy with her Activities," *Western Morning News*, 9 March, 1939.
6. Annual Report of Six Point Group 1938–1939, Women's Library, SPG/B6-13.
7. Baxter, *Guilty Women*, pp. 42–43.
8. Anne De Courcey, *1939: The Last Season* (London, 1989), p. 16.
9. There is, of course, a contingent of officially 'guilty women,' actual fifth column-ists, sympathisers with the enemy and subversives. See "A Letter from Hitler," *Jewish Chronicle*, 14 June, 1940; "Nazi Society Dupes," *Daily Mirror*, 21 August, 1940; and the KV 2 Security Service: Personal Files in the National Archives detail-ing intelligence on pro-Soviet and pro-Nazi individuals.
10. See "Perfect Nazi Woman in London," *Sydney Morning Herald*, 9 March, 1939; and S.L. Solon and Albert Brandt, "Sex under the Swastika," *American Mercury*, XLVII(188), August, 1939, pp. 425–432.
11. Baxter, *Guilty Women*, p. 123. I am grateful to Richard Toye for bringing to my attention this reference: "There is a book called Guilty Women—Edda Mussolini is said to be one. Mrs South and I want to read it." [entry for 2.8.1943] in Vera Hodgson, *Few Eggs and No Oranges: A Diary Showing How Unimportant People in London and Birmingham Lived Through the War Years* (London, 1976).
12. Baxter, *Guilty Women*, p. 119.
13. See Julie Gottlieb, *Feminine Fascism: Women in Britain's Fascist Movement, 1923–1945* (London, 2000), and Richard Thurlow, "The Evolution of the Mythical British Fifth Column, 1939–1946," *Twentieth Century British History* 10(4), 1999, pp. 477–498.
14. "Three in Five," *The Times*, 8 January, 1937.
15. 'Cato,' *Guilty Men* (New York, 1940), p. 15.
16. Ibid., p. 17.
17. Sunday, 25 September, 1938, John Julius Norwich (ed.), *The Duff Cooper Diaries* (London, 2005), p. 266.
18. Baxter, *Guilty Women*, p. 13.
19. "Princess's Part in the Munich Pact," *Aberdeen Journal*, 11 November, 1939.
20. See Jim Wilson, *Nazi Princess: Hitler, Lord Rothermere and Princess Stephanie Von Hohenlohe* (Stroud, 2011).
21. See Helen McCarthy, *Women of the World: The Rise of the Female Diplomat* (London, 2014), p. 32.
22. Letter from Emerald Cunard to Mrs Chamberlain, 30 September, 1938, Chamberlain Papers, Cadbury Research Centre, University of Birmingham, NC 13/12/165.
23. Mrs Chamberlain's Broadcast to the Women of France, 31 December, 1939, NC 11/11/2.
24. For Information Only: Mrs Neville Chamberlain (June, 1940) With the Compliments of the Conservative Central Office Press Department, NC 11/16/5.
25. NC to Hilda Chamberlain, 30 May, 1937, in Robert Self (ed.), *The Neville Chamberlain Diary Letters: Volume 4: The Downing Street Years, 1934–1940* (Aldershot, 2005), p. 253.
26. See entry for 29 June, 1938, Gordon Martel (ed.), *The Times and Appeasement: The Journals of A.L. Kennedy 1932–1939* (Cambridge, 2000), p. 276.
27. *Daily Mirror*, 29 September, 1938.
28. The Chamberlains were the first commoners to appear on the balcony of Buckingham Palace, which was the source of some controversy after the fact. However, the images were plastered all over the press and newsreel. See "Munich Crisis: Special Number," *London Illustrated News*, 8 October, 1938.
29. Mrs Neville Chamberlain—Notebooks and Diaries, NC 11/2/1A/ (3).

30. "God Bless You," *Daily Mirror*, 1 October, 1938.
31. Letter from NC to Hilda, 2 October, 1938, in R. Self (ed.), p. 349.
32. "Mrs Chamberlain Must be Very Worried Now," *Daily Mirror*, 31 March, 1939.
33. "Mrs Chamberlain on Shaken Policy of Peace," *Western Daily Press*, 23 November, 1938.
34. Letter from NC to Hilda, 6 November, 1938, R. Self (ed.), p. 359.
35. "Premier's Optimistic View of 1939," *Western Gazette*, 24 February, 1939.
36. Letter from NC to Hilda, 19 March, 1939, R. Self (ed.), p. 394.
37. "Good Health," *Nottingham Evening Post*, 18 April, 1940
38. Diana Cooper, *The Light of Common Day* (Harmsworth, 1959), p. 84.
39. Letter from Lucy Baldwin of Bewdley to Mrs Chamberlain, 20 September, 1938, NC 13/12/40. There was a rivalry between the two, and when Annie had taken over No. 10 Downing Street and made certain renovations, the only one not to be charmed was Countess Baldwin, "who refuses to come near it but says to her acquaintances 'I hear they've spoiled No 10'!" (Letter from NC to Ida, 18 June, 1938, R. Self (ed.), p. 327.)
40. Philip Williamson and Edward Baldwin (eds.), *Baldwin Papers: A Conservative Statesmen 1908–1947* (Cambridge, 2004), p. 460.
41. Sidney Aster, "Appeasement: Before and After Revisionism," *Diplomacy & Statecraft*, 19(3), 2008, pp. 443–480.
42. Diary entry for 2 May, 1939, in Robert Rhodes James (ed.), *'Chips:' The Diaries of Sir Henry Channon* (London, 1999), p. 196.
43. Nick Smart, *Neville Chamberlain* (London, 2010), p. 228.
44. Other pro-Italian women Muriel Currey OBE, journalist, contributor to the BUF press, and author of *A Woman at the Abyssinian War* (London, 1936).
45. Quoted in Peter T. Marsh, *The Chamberlain Litany: Letters Within a Government Family from Empire to Appeasement* (London, 2010), p. 294.
46. Anthony Eden, *The Eden Memoirs: Facing the Dictators* (London, 1962), p. 573.
47. Ibid., p. 295.
48. "Lady Chamberlain, Widow of Austen: Noted Political Hostess Who Wielded Influence in Affairs of Europe Dies in London," *New York Times*, 14 February, 1941. See also David Low, "Low's Topical Budget," *Evening Standard*, 5 March, 1938.
49. Letter from N.C. to Ida Chamberlain, 11 September, 1938, in R. Self (ed.), p. 345.
50. "'Oh Dear'' Said the Premier, by Peter Snoop," *Reynolds News*, 5 March, 1939.
51. Baxter, *Guilty Women*, p. 119.
52. "Lady Chamberlain, Widow of Austen: Noted Political Hostess Who Wielded Influence in Affairs of Europe Dies in London," *New York Times*, 14 February, 1941.
53. Letter from NC to Hilda, 27 March, 1938, in R. Self (ed.), p. 312.
54. Ibid., p. 299.
55. Ibid., p. 300.
56. Quoted in Ibid., p. 305.
57. Smart, *Neville Chamberlain*, p. 243.
58. Quoted in Ibid., p. 312.
59. Dorothy Dunbar Bromley, "Pro-Nazi Sympathies of Britons Puzzling: It is Easier to Understand Friendship of Lady Chamberlain for Mussolini than Attitude of Lady Astor's Set,"[n.d.], Lady Nancy Astor Papers, Special Collections, University of Reading, MS 1416/1/1/1587.
60. "Men and Women of Mystery," *John Bull*, 16 April, 1938.
61. See the most recent, Adrian Fort, *Nancy: The Story of Lady Astor* (London, 2012).
62. *Daily Mirror*, 17 March, 1939.

63. Margaret George, *The Hollow Men: An Examination of British Foreign Policy Between the Years 1933 and 1939* (London, 1967), p. 153. See also Norman Rose, *The Cliveden Set: Portrait of an Exclusive Fraternity* (London, 2001) in which Nancy Astor is given her due as a key actor in this mostly mythical band of conspirators.
64. Rose, *The Cliveden Set*, p. 152.
65. Alex May, "Cliveden Set (act. 1937–1939)" *Oxford Dictionary of National Biography* (Oxford, 2004–2013)
66. "Lady Astor writes: I Abominate Fascism," *The Tribune*, 23 December, 1938, and "My Hope for Peace Does not Mean that I'm a Fascist: Munich and the Cliveden Set by Lady Astor" *News Chronicle*, 12 March, 1939.
67. [No date and unsigned], Lady Nancy Astor Papers, Special Collections, University of Reading, MS 1416/1/1/1588.
68. Patricia Cockburn, *The Years of the Week* (Harmondsworth, 1968), p. 236.
69. Quoted in J.P. Wearing (ed.), *Bernard Shaw and Nancy Astor* (Toronto, 2005), p. xx.
70. "A Changed Policy" *Manchester Guardian*, 10 November, 1938.
71. "Lady Astor Gives a Manless Dinner," *New York Times*, 3 December, 1930.
72. Letter from Nancy Astor to Ruth [Legation of the USA], 12 July, 1934, MS 1416/1/1/1434.
73. "The Sex Bar in Diplomacy," *Manchester Guardian*, 30 April, 1936.
74. See Bee Wilson, "Musical Chairs with Ribbentrop," *London Review of Books*, 34(24), 20 December, 2012.
75. Correspondence, *Manchester Guardian*, 29 October, 1921.
76. "Women's Peace Crusade," *Manchester Guardian*, 26 July, 1928.
77. Quoted in Brian Harrison, "Women in a Men's House: The Women MPs, 1919–1945," *Historical Journal*, 29(3), September, 1986, pp. 632–654.
78. "Bigger Air Force," *Manchester Guardian*, 11 May, 1934.
79. Letter from N.C. to Hilda Chamberlain, 25 June, 1938, in R. Self (ed.), p. 330.
80. "Lady Astor and Peace," *Western Morning News*, 24 February, 1938.
81. "Women Must Work for Peace," *Western Morning News*, 26 February, 1938.
82. Brian Harrison, "Women in a Men's House: The Women MPs, 1919–1945," *Historical Journal*, 29(3), September, 1986, pp. 632–654.
83. Draft of Istanbul Speech: Position of Women under Different Forms Draft of Istanbul Speech: Position of Women Under Different Forms of Government (1935), MS 1416/1/1/1435.
84. "Congress 39 (July, 1939) Copenhagen again," International, Women's Library, MICA/C.
85. Dictated 21.XII.38 [An interview with Nancy Astor], MS 1416/1/1/1591.
86. "At Last! Lady Astor Tells the Truth About the Cliveden Set, by Lady Astor," *Sunday Chronicle*, 5 March, 1939.
87. Executive Committee of Six Point Group, 17 July, 1939, Women's Library, SPG/A19-28.
88. See Germany in Nancy Astor Papers, MS 1416/1/1/1483.
89. "Lady Astor MP," *Western Morning News*, 4 February, 1937.
90. Quoted in Maurice Hollis, *Nancy Astor* (London, 1960), pp. 184–185.
91. David Low, "Low's Topical Budget," *Evening Standard*, 2 April, 1938.
92. Chamberlain did not have a very good press in the USA, and the Astors arranged a luncheon for him to meet dozens of American journalists and address them on the situation on Europe. Letter from NC to Ida Chamberlain, 10 May, 1938, in ed. R. Self (ed.), p. 320.
93. "That 'Cliveden Set Leader'" *Western Morning News*, 17 February, 1939.

4 'Guilty Women:' Powers behind Thrones

1. *Hansard*, HC Deb, 14 February, 1939, Vol. 343 cc 1545–1546.
2. "The Rights of Women," *Dundee Courier*, 15 February, 1939.
3. Richard Griffiths, *Fellow Travellers of the Right* (London, 1981).
4. Martin Pugh, *'Hurrah for the Blackshirts!' Fascists and Fascism in Britain Between the Wars* (London, 2005), p. 271.
5. See Nicoletta Gullace, *The Blood of our Sons: Men, Women and the Renegotiation of British Citizenship During the Great War* (Basingstoke, 2004); June Purvis, "Emmeline Pankhurst in the Aftermath of Suffrage, 1918–1928," in Julie V. Gottlieb and Richard Toye (eds), *The Aftermath of Suffrage* (Basingstoke, 2013), pp. 19–36; Barbara Storm Farr, *The Development and Impact of Right-Wing Politics in Britain, 1903–1932* (New York, 1987).
6. The Marchioness of Londonderry, *Retrospect* (London, 1938), p. 145.
7. Ian Kershaw, *Making Friends with Hitler: Lord Londonderry, the Nazis and the Road to War* (New York, 2004), p. 23.
8. See A. Susan Williams, *Ladies of Influence: Women of the Elite in Interwar Britain* (London, 2000), pp. 13–38.
9. Anne De Courcy, *Society's Queen: The Life of Edith, Marchioness of Londonderry* (London, 2004), p. 329.
10. Kershaw, *Making Friends with Hitler*, p. 11.
11. N.C. Fleming, *The Marquess of Londonderry: Aristocracy, Power and Politics in Britain and Ireland* (London, 2005).
12. Kershaw, *Making Friends with Hitler*, p. 139.
13. Quoted in Ibid., p. 140.
14. Ibid., p. 145.
15. Quoted in Anne De Courcy, *Society's Queen* (London, 1992), p. 322.
16. Ibid., p. 333.
17. Kershaw, *Making Friends with Hitler*, p. 155.
18. Ibid., p. 156.
19. The Chamberlains had already been houseguests of the Londonderrys at Mt Stewart in January 1935, when Chamberlain was Chancellor.
20. Letter from Lord Londonderry to NC, 21 July, 1937, NC 8/21/3.
21. "Westcountry Guests: Lady Londonderry's 'At Home'," *Western Morning News*, 26 October, 1937.
22. "War Minister in Ulster, *Western Daily Press*, 13 January, 1938.
23. Lady Londonderry to Neville, 17 September, 1938, NC 13/11/711.
24. The Marchioness of Londonderry, *Retrospect* (London, 1938), pp. 255–256.
25. De Courcy, p. 350.
26. They both objected to their daughter's marriage to a Jewish man. For helpful taxonomies of anti-Semitism in the British context see Tony Kushner, *The Persistence of Prejudice: Antisemitism in British Society During the Second World War* (Manchester, 1989), and more specifically women's anti-Semitism, Julie V. Gottlieb, "'Motherly Hate:' Gendering Anti-Semitism in the British Union of Fascists, Gender & History, 14(2), August, 2002, pp. 294–320.
27. Jeremy A. Crang, "The Revival of the British Women's Auxiliary Services in the Late Nineteen Thirties," *Historical Research* 83(220), May, 2010, pp. 343–357.
28. See R.M. Douglas, *Feminist Freikorps: The British Voluntary Women Police, 1914–1940* (Westport CT, 1999).
29. Duff Cooper, *Old Men Forget* (London, 1953), p. 251.

30. Diana Cooper, *The Light of Common Day* (London, 1959), p. 197.
31. 14 September, 1938, John Julius Norwich (ed.), *The Duff Cooper Diaries* (London, 2005), p. 260.
32. Duff Cooper, *The Light of Common Day*, pp. 202–203.
33. Duff Cooper, *Old Men Forget*, p. 241.
34. Duff Cooper, *The Light of Common Day*, p. 206.
35. 3 September, 1939, J.J. Norwich (ed.), *The Duff Cooper Diaries*, pp. 273–274.
36. Ibid., p. 275.
37. Ibid., p. 277.
38. [Kathleen, Duchess of Rutland, his mother-in-law] Belvoir Castle, Grantham, to Duff Cooper, Sunday [October, 1938], Churchill Archive, Churchill College, Cambridge, DUFC 2/15.
39. Duff Cooper, *Old Men Forget*, p. 251.
40. Ibid, p. 251.
41. 17 September, 1938, J.J. Norwich (ed.), *The Duff Cooper Diaries*, p. 260.
42. Duff Cooper, *Old Men Forget*, p. 249.
43. Diary of Florence Amery, Churchill Archive Centre, Churchill College, Cambridge, AMEL 6/3/12. Leo Amery was Jewish on his mother's side, but he kept this secret. See David Faber, *Speaking for England: Leo, Julian and John Amery—The Tragedy of a Political Family* (London, 2007).
44. Diary of Florence Amery, AMEL 6/3/12.
45. Ibid.
46. Ibid.
47. "Memoirs: Munich 1938," Leo Amery's note to self, AMEL 1/5/55.
48. L.S. Amery, *My Political Life, Vol. 3: The Unforgiving Years 1929–1940* (London, 1955).
49. Andrew Roberts, *'The Holy Fox:' The Life of Lord Halifax* (London, 1997) p. 8.
50. The Earl of Halifax, *Fullness of Days* (London, 1957).
51. Martha Dodd, *My Years in Germany* (London, 1939), p. 287.
52. See Letter from NC to Ida, 19 September, 1938, in Robert Self (ed.), *The Neville Chamberlain Diary Letters: Volume 4: The Downing Street Years, 1934–1940* (Aldershot, 2005), p. 347.
53. Nevile Henderson, *Failure of a Mission: Berlin 1937–1939* (London, 1940), p. 22.
54. Henderson, p. 166.
55. Ibid., p. 166.
56. See "In Westminster Abbey: Prayers at the Unknown Warrior's Grave," and "In Westminster Cathedral: Thousands Join in Prayer for Peace," part of "Record Number: The Crisis and the Agreement," *Illustrated London News*, 8 October, 1938.
57. Letter from N.C. to Hilda, 2 Oct., 1938, in R. Self (ed.), p. 349.
58. Richard Griffiths, *Fellow Travellers of the Right* (London, 1980); Richard Griffiths, *Patriotism Perverted* (London, 1998). Public fascination with this story was fed by recent documentaries: "Churchill and the Fascist Plot" (Channel 4, UK, broadcast 16 March, 2013).
59. See "Diana Mosley Taught Children Nazi Salute, MI5 Files Reveal," *Times*, 14 November, 2003.
60. See David Pryce-Jones, *Unity Mitford: A Quest* (London: 1976); Paul Fussell, *Abroad: British Literary Travelling Between the Wars* (Oxford, 1980); Angela Schwartz, "British Visitors to National Socialist Germany: In a Familiar or a Foreign Country?" *Journal of Contemporary History*, 28(3), July, 1993, pp. 487–509; Kathryn Steinhaus, "Valkyrie: Gender, Class, European Relations and Unity

Mitford's Passion for Fascism," unpublished PhD Thesis (McGill, 2011); Petra Rau, "The Fascist Body Beautiful and the Imperial Crisis in 1930s British Writing," *Journal of European Studies*, 39(1), March, 2009, pp. 5–35.

61. See Rosita Forbes, "Hitler—as a Woman Know Him," *Sunday Dispatch*, 19 March, 1939.

62. Mary Allen's *Lady in Blue* (London, 1936) details her meetings with the top brass in Nazi Germany in 1936.

63. There were letters to the editor of *Time and Tide* about a letter "In Germany Today" written to the *Sunday Times* of 6 November, 1938 by Miss Enid Bagnold. See "Time-Tide Diary," *Time and Tide*, 12 November, 1938, accompanied by a cartoon of Bagnold in her car driving past swastika waving Aryan children while behind her and out of sight soldiers are marching stooped men to the concentration camp. Bagnold was the author of *National Velvet* (1935) and *The Chalk Garden*. She was a journalist, and married Sir Roderick Jones, head of Reuters. In the 1930s she openly supported Hitler, despite her love for an anti-Nazi diplomat. Her great-great granddaughter is Samantha Cameron, wife of the PM.

64. "'Lady Douglas Hamilton,' spoke of Chamberlain as a traitor who had sold out to the Jews," at a Nordic League meeting in 1939. (Griffiths, *Patriotism Perverted*, p. 46.) This may have been Stack's mother-in-law rather than the newly married Stack herself.

65. Nesta Webster, "Germany and England: I. The Volte Face," *The Patriot*, 13 October, 1938 CHAR 2/322 [The editors of *The Patriot* sent this edition of the magazine to Churchill, in which he is severely attacked. His secretary send back a biting note]

66. Baxter, *Guilty Women*, p. 36.

67. Dame Christabel Pankhurst to Mrs Chamberlain, 23 September, 1938, NC 13/11/747.

68. Maude Royden to the Rt. Hon. Neville Chamberlain, 12 October, 1938, NC 13/11/397.

69. NC to Hilda, 15 October, 1938, in R. Self (ed.), p. 354.

70. Griffiths, *Patriotism Perverted*, pp. 56–57.

71. Cicely Hamilton, *Time and Tide*, 15 October, 1938.

72. Ethel Smyth, "A Recantation," *Time and Tide*, 5 November, 1938.

73. See Susan Grayzel, *At Home and Under Fire: Air Raids and Culture in Britain from the Great War to the Blitz* (Cambridge, 2012).

74. Luciana Ashworth, "Feminism, War and the Prospects of International Government: Helena Swanwick and the Lost Feminists of Interwar International Relations," *International Feminist Journal of Politics*, 13(1), March, 2011, pp. 25–43.

75. Beryl Haslam, *From Suffrage to Internationalism: The Political Evolution of Three British Feminists, 1908–1939* (New York, 1999).

76. Letter from HMS [Helena Swanwick] to Winifred Holtby, 29 July, 1933, Winifred Holtby Papers WH/5/5.21/04/01a—01q.

77. "Pacifists and the Fascist Regime: The Cost of International Non-Resistance," *Manchester Guardian*, 7 November, 1938.

78. Ellen Wilkinson, "Techniques of Peace-Keeping," *Time and Tide*, 25 December, 1937.

79. "I Hate Fascism: A Letter to the Editor from Viscountess Nancy Astor," *The Forum*, p. 237 [no date shown, 1939] MS1416/1/1/1592.

80. Swanwick, *Time and Tide*, 22 October, 1938.

81. "My pacifism is no passive creed, nor ever has been. I believe that wrongs, if unredressed, fester and produce revolutions and wars; therefore it is our duty to know

of the wrongs we have helped to inflict, so that we may right them before it is too late. If they are allowed to fester, the task of righting them becomes infinitely harder, for violence leads not to reason and toleration but to answering violence and to the disastrous worship of the dictator who will lead men in the indulgence of their violent passions..." (H.M. Swanwick, *Manchester Guardian*, 21 September, 1938).

82. H.M. Swanwick, Maidenhead, February 11, *Manchester Guardian*, 15 February, 1939.
83. Deborah E. Van Seters, "Women's Foreign Policy Advocacy in 1930s Britain," unpublished PhD, University of Toronto, 1999, p. 369.
84. However, the Astor family owned *The Times* (editor Geoffrey Dawson), and the *Observer* (editor J.L. Garvin), both papers that were deemed to be at the heart of the Cliveden Set conspiracy. Lady Rhondda was the founder and editor of *Time and Tide*.

5 'To Speak a Few Words of Comfort to Them:' Conservative Women's Support for Chamberlain and Appeasement

1. By 'women worthies' I mean notable women who are remembered because they made something of themselves in a man's world or achieved something ground-breaking as women. See June Purvis's definition of women worthies in June Purvis (ed.), *Women's History: Britain, 1850–1945* (London, 1997).
2. Daniel Hucker, *Public Opinion and the End of Appeasement in Britain and France* (Farnham, 2011); Nick J. Crowson, *Facing Fascism: The Conservative Party and the European Dictators, 1935–1940* (London, 1997).
3. Martin Pugh, *Women and the Women's Movement in Britain*, 2nd Edition (London, 2000), p. 127.
4. Neal R. McCrillis, *The British Conservative Party in the Age of Universal Suffrage: Popular Conservatism, 1918–1929* (Columbus, 1998), p. 47.
5. David Jarvis, "Mrs Maggs and Betty: The Conservative Appeal to Women Voters in the 1920s," *Twentieth Century British History*, 5(2), 1994, pp. 129–152; David Thackeray, "From Prudent Housewife to Empire Shopper: Party Appeals to the Female Voter, 1918–1928," in J. Gottlieb and R. Toye (eds), *The Aftermath of Suffrage* (Basingstoke, 2013), pp. 37–53.
6. Matthew Hendley, "Citizens or Consumers? British Conservative Political Propaganda Towards Women in the Two World Wars," in Ho Hon Leung, Matthew Hendley, Robert W. Compton, and Brian D. Haley (eds), *Imagining Globalization: Language, Identities and Boundaries* (New York, 2009), p. 127.
7. Ibid., p. 128.
8. McCrillis, *The British Conservative Party in the Age of Universal Suffrage*, p. 47.
9. Christine K. Erikson, "So Much for Men. Conservative Women and National Defence in the 1920s and 1930s," *American Studies*, 45(1), Spring, 2004, pp. 85–102. For earlier in the century there is coverage of Conservative women and nationalist causes. See Barbara Storm Farr, *The Development and Impact of Right-Wing Politics in Britain, 1903–1932* (New York, 1987); Matthew Hendley, *Organised Patriotism and the Crucible of War: Popular Imperialism in Britain, 1914–1932* (Montreal, 2012); Julia Bush, *Edwardian Ladies and Imperial Power* (London and New York, 2000).
10. "Our Nine Women MPs are Good Champions of their Sex," *Daily Mirror*, 18 May, 1936.

11. Clair Price, "A Dozen Daughters of Parliament," *New York Times*, 5 June, 1938.
12. "Women in the Election: Losses for the Cause of Peace," *Manchester Guardian*, 28 October, 1931.
13. Brian Harrison, "Women in a Men's House: The Women MPs, 1919–1945," *Historical Journal*, 29(3), September, 1986, pp. 632–654.
14. "These Women MPs—the Questions they Ask," *Daily Mirror*, 4 September, 1935.
15. "What They Tell Me," *Gloucestershire Echo*, 29 July, 1936.
16. "Lectures on Politics," *Western Morning News*, 19 November, 1936.
17. "Political School Opened in Bristol," *Western Daily Press*, 18 November, 1936.
18. "Women Conservatives," *Western Gazette*, 11 June, 1937.
19. Mark Pottle, "Graves, (Frances) Marjorie (1884–1961)," *Oxford Dictionary of National Biography*.
20. "Woman MP Lauds British System," *New York Times*, 18 November, 1936.
21. "International Debut," *Gloucester Echo*, 26 August, 1937.
22. "Issue of 'Peace or War:' Appeal to Women of N. Cornwall," *The Western Morning News and Daily Gazette*, 8 July, 1939.
23. Martin Pugh, "Tate, Mavis Constance (1893–1947), *Oxford Dictionary of National Biography* (Oxford, 2004).
24. "The Only Woman MP Air Champion," *Hull Daily Mail*, 13 July, 1935. Both she and the Duchess of Atholl were members of the Ladies Carlton Club, and she was cousin of Lord Halisham.
25. "Frome Lady MP," *Western Daily Press*, 29 March, 1937.
26. Wednesday 1 June, 1938, Neal J. Crowson (ed.), *Fleet Street, Press Barons and Politics: The Journals of Collin Brooks, 1932–1940* (London, 1998), p. 209.
27. Mary Allen and Lady Londonderry were in competition for a certain type of nationalist feminism, and when Allen established the Women's Reserve in the 1930s, it was seen to be in direct competition with Lady Londonderry's Women's Legion, and they came to blows in *The Times*.
28. Mary Allen, *Lady in Blue* (London, 1936), p. 86.
29. Mary S. Allen and Julie Heynemann, *Woman at the Cross Roads* (London, 1934), p. 160.
30. J Wentworth Day, *Lady Houston DBE: The Woman Who Won the War* (London, 1958).
31. See Liz Millward, *Women in British Imperial Airspace, 1922–1937* (Montreal, 2008). For continued fascination with these women pioneers in the air see Karen Bush Gibson, *Women Aviators: 26 Stories of Pioneer Flights* (Chicago, 2013).
32. Letter from Mavis Tate to Duff Cooper, 2.15 p.m. 3 October [1938], Churchill Archive, Churchill College, Cambridge, DUFC 2/14.
33. "Rival Election Appeals," *The Times*, 17 December, 1938.
34. "'Rebels' Meeting," *Dundee Courier*, 10 May, 1940. After the war Tate visited German concentration camps with other MPs in 1945, which contributed her deteriorating health. She committed suicide in June 1947.
35. By-Election Addresses, 1937–39, Hemel Hempstead Bye-Election (Tuesday, 22 June, 1937), Oxford, Bodleian Library, Conservative Party Archive, PUB229/1/8.
36. "Britain's Part in World Affairs," *Western Morning News*, 20 June, 1938.
37. Brian Harrison, "Women in a Men's House: The Women MPs, 1919–1945," *Historical Journal*, 29(3), September, 1986, pp. 632–654.
38. This deputation was led by Thelma Cazalet-Keir and included Lady Davidson, Eleanor Rathbone, and Nancy Astor.
39. "I Shall Work Hard," *Dundee Courier*, 15 July, 1939.

40. "Miss Horsbrugh on Danger to Britain," *Dundee Courier*, 7 March, 1936.
41. "'Branches' of the League of Nations," *Dundee Courier*, 28 March, 1936.
42. From Florence Horsbrugh (London) to Mrs Chamberlain, 28 September, 1938, Chamberlain Papers, University of Birmingham, NC 13/11/686.
43. "Miss Horsbrugh on New Leaf in Foreign Policy," *Dundee Courier*, 18 October, 1938.
44. "'Europe Saved from Armageddon:' Prime Minister's Reply to his Critics," *The Times*, 7 October, 1938.
45. "Candidates Toe the Line at Crieff," *Perthshire Constitutional and Journal*, 16 December, 1938.
46. "Turning Point for Peace," *Dundee Courier*, 13 March, 1939.
47. "Support Premier to Secure Peace," *Western Morning News*, 5 July, 1939.
48. "What They Tell Me," *Gloucestershire Echo*, 30 June, 1938.
49. For the Parliamentary session from October 21, 1937 to April 14, 1938 "women MPs are well represented in the official report of the debates. Miss Rathbone's speeches occupy 29 columns; Miss Wilkinson's 26; Miss Horsbrugh's 22; and the Duchess of Atholl, 21." "Women's Part in Commons Debates," *Dundee Courier*, 14 May, 1938.
50. "Donald Duck—MP," *Evening Telegraph*, 25 November, 1938.
51. Thelma Cazalet-Keir, *From the Wings* (London, 1967), pp. 137–138.
52. Ibid., pp. 102–103.
53. Ibid., pp. 133–134.
54. Ibid., pp. 138–139.
55. Ibid., p. 139.
56. Ibid., p. 147.
57. Letter from Violet Bonham Carter to WSC, 1 June, 1945, CHAR 20/196/61.
58. "Bigger Air Force," *Manchester Guardian*, 11 May, 1934.
59. "Conservative Women: A Christchurch School," *Western Gazette*, 16 November, 1934.
60. Eastern Provincial Area (Women's Advisory Committee), Political School, 18–21 October, 1935, Bonar Law College, Ashridge, Berkhamsted, Herts, Oxford, Bodleian Library, Conservative Party Archive, ARE 7/11/2.
61. Clarisse Berthezene, "Creating Conservative Fabians and the Founding of Ashridge College," *Past and Present*, No. 1982 (February, 2004), pp. 211–240.
62. "Classes for Speakers," *Manchester Guardian*, 8 September, 1935.
63. "Political School for Women," *Manchester Guardian*, 24 September, 1936.
64. Minutes of a meeting of the Cornwall County Committee of the Women's Advisory Council, 28 July, 1937, Oxford, Bodleian Library, Conservative Party Archive, ARE 11/11/3.
65. National Union of Conservative and Unionist Associations, Central Women's Advisory Committee, 18th Annual Conference, Queen's Hall, London, 10 May, 1939, p. 38, CCO 170/3/1-2.
66. Monday, 29 November, 1937, in Stuart Ball (ed.), *Parliament and Politics in the Age of Churchill and Attlee: The Headlam Diaries, 1935–1951* (Cambridge, 1999), p. 119.
67. Wednesday 1 December, 1937, in Ball (ed.), *Parliament and Politics in the Age of Churchill and Attlee*, p. 119.
68. Tuesday 14 June, 1938 in Ball (ed.), *Parliament and Politics in the Age of Churchill and Attlee*, p. 131.
69. These annual conference did grow over the years from 2,000 participants in the 1920s and early 1930s.

70. "Mr Baldwin on the League," *Manchester Guardian*, 15 May, 1936.
71. "Dual Peace Policy," *The Times*, 13 May, 1938.
72. Letter from NC to Ida, 10 [15?] May 1938, in Robert Self (ed.), *The Neville Chamberlain Diary Letters: Volume 4: The Downing Street Years, 1934–1940* (Aldershot, 2005), p. 321.
73. Beatrix Campbell, *The Iron Ladies: Why Do Women Vote Tory?* (London, 1987), pp. 66–67.
74. Quoted in "Scenes in Tory Women's Debate on Flogging," *Manchester Guardian*, 11 May, 1939.
75. Letter from NC to Hilda, 14 May, 1939, in Self (ed.), p. 415.
76. "Bringing up a Conservative: Lady Maureen Stanley Expounds her Faith," *Manchester Guardian*, 16 January, 1935.
77. Lady Oliver Stanley, wife of the British Minister of Labour, and Lady Margaret Stewart, daughter of Lord Londonderry, left Berlin in October 1934. "Lady Stanley, it is stated, took a special interest in the Labour Service camps, and was conducted through two of these camps in the neighbourhood of Berlin by Colonel Muller. According to the German Press, Lady Stanley had regarded these camps as a method of dealing with the unemployment problem ... Lady Stanley was also able to have interviews with Dr Goebbels and General Göring." ("Lady Oliver Stanley," *Observer*, 7 October, 1934).
78. The Primrose League made an urgent request for guidance on the subject of British Fascism in 1934. Martin Pugh, *The Tories and the People 1880–1935* (Oxford, 1985), p. 191. See also Matthew Hendley, "Anti-Alienism and the Primrose League: The Externalization of the Postwar Crisis in Great Britain, 1918–32", *Albion*, 33(2), Summer, 2001, pp. 243–2469.
79. "Conservative Women's Meeting at Exmouth," *Exeter and Plymouth Gazette*, 2 March, 1934.
80. Minutes of a Meeting of the Somerset County Committee of the Women's Advisory Council, 29 May, 1934, ARE 11/11/3.
81. "Mr Baldwin on Fascism: Danger of Class War," [Osmaston, 16 July, 1934], Oxford, Bodleian Library, Conservative Party Archive, 1934/27. See also P. Williamson, "The Conservative Party, Fascism and anti-Fascism 1918–1939," in Nigel Copsey and Andrzej Olechnowicz (eds), *Varieties of Anti-Fascism in the Inter-war Period* (Basingstoke, 2010), pp. 73–97.
82. See LP/FAS/34, 'Labour Party Questionnaire on Fascist Activity, National Museum of Labour History, Manchester. See also Julie V. Gottlieb, "Femmes, Conservatisme et Fascisme en Grand-Bretagne: Comparisons et Convergences" in P. Varvaecke (ed.), *Radical Rights in France and Britain in the 20th Century: Comparison, Transfers and Crossed Perspectives* [translated from the English] (Paris, 2012), pp. 387–424.
83. Report of the Women's Advisory Committee for June, 1933 to May, 1934 (Lancashire, Cheshire and Westmorland Provincial Area, ARE 3/11/1.
84. Stanley Baldwin MP, "Our Heritage of Freedom: The Menace of Dictatorship" [speech broadcast 6 March, 1934], 1934/19.
85. Report of the Women's Advisory Committee for June, 1934 to May, 1935 (Lancashire, Cheshire and Westmorland Provincial Area, ARE 3/11/1.
86. Dan Stone, *Responses to Nazism in Britain, 1933–1939* (Basingstoke, 2003), p. 143.
87. Women's Advisory Committee, North-Western Provincial Area, Annual Report (June, 1942), ARE 3/11/2.
88. "Why You Should Join the Women's Branch of Your Local Conservative and Unionist Party," 1938/ 133.

89. Marchioness of Londonderry, *Retrospect* (London, 1938), pp. 255–256.
90. Martin Pugh, *Women and the Women's Movement in Britain* (London, 1992), p. 106.
91. General Meeting, 30 September, 1936, Minutes of the National Society of Women Organisers, Oxford, Bodleian Library, Conservative Party Archive, CCO 170/2/1/1.
92. Minutes, 25 November, 1937, Women's Advisory Committee for the North-Western Provincial Area, ARE 3/11/1.
93. Minutes of the Central Women's Advisory Committee, 22 March, 1937, CCO 170/1/1/1-CCO170/1/1/2.
94. "Peace Weeks: Report for Administrative Committee" 14.10.37, LNU-3/3, London School of Economics Library.
95. Minutes, 21 February, 1938, ARE 3/11/3.
96. Minutes of the Central Women's Advisory Committee, 28 June, 1939, CCO 170/1/1/1-CCO 170/1/1/2.
97. When the United Nations Association was set up in 1946, local CWAs welcomed its formation. See Minutes of Central Women's Advisory Committee, 9 May, 1946, CCO 170/1/1/1-CCO170/1/1/2. In 1952 the first British woman appointed as a full delegate to the General Assembly of the UN was Alderman Evelyn Emmet, JP, of West Sussex County Council and chairman of the Women's National Advisory Committee of the Conservative Party.
98. Quoted in Sybil Oldfield, *Women Against the Iron Fist: Alternatives to Militarism 1900–1989* (Oxford, 1989), p. 208.
99. Ladies Grand Council, Primrose League, to Mrs Chamberlain, 30 September, 1938, Neville Chamberlain Papers, NC 13/12/700.
100. Minutes, 24 November, 1938, Women's Advisory Committee for the North-Western Provincial Area, ARE 3/11/1.
101. "Scenes in Tory Women's Debate on Flogging," *Manchester Guardian*, 11 May, 1939.
102. "Women: Their Political Activities Increasing", *Exeter and Plymouth Gazette*, 6 November, 1928.
103. "Cabinet on Trial in 7 By-elections," *Daily Mirror*, 19 October, 1938.
104. Letter from NC to Ida, 12 February, 1939, in Self (ed.), p. 381.
105. Letter from R. Cyril Yates (Birmingham) to Mr Chamberlain, 4 October, 1938, NC 13/11/518.
106. "Tamworth Women Unionists," *Tamworth Herald*, 26 November, 1938.
107. "Why Sudeten Germans Were Willing Pawns," *Hull Daily Mail*, 19 October, 1938.
108. "Twyning Women Conservatives: Crisis Resolution Sent to Mr Morrison," *Cheltenham Chronicle*, 29 October, 1938.
109. "Appeasement the Only Way to Peace," *Western Times*, 13 January, 1939.
110. "Sent to Prime Minister," *Western Daily Press*, 21 March, 1939.
111. "Support by Winchcombe Conservatives," *Gloucestershire Echo*, 22 March 1939.
112. "Dover Borough Women's Conservative Association," *Dover Express*, 19 May, 1939.
113. "Poulton Conservatives," *Cheltenham Chronicle*, 19 March, 1938.
114. "Mr Eden's 'Unwise' Decision," *Western Morning News and Daily Gazette*, 26 February, 1938.
115. "'Not True I Wanted War'—Lord Cranborne," *Daily Mail*, 13 October, 1938.
116. "A News Miscellany," *The Essex Chronicle*, Friday 21 October, 1938.

117. Diary of Florence Amery, Churchill Archive, Churchill College, Cambridge, AMEL 6/3/12.
118. "Darn Those Socks," *Derby Daily Telegraph*, 11 May, 1938.
119. The National Union of Conservative and Unionist Associations: Central Women's Advisory Committee, 18th Annual Conference, London, 10 May, 1939, CCO 170/3/1.
120. "Correspondence: 1. LNU Women's Advisory Council: The Chairman reported that a letter was received (13 October) concerning a message of sympathy to the Women of Czechoslovakia, and that she had agreed, in consultation with Lady Falmouth, that no action be taken. The Committee endorsed the Chairman's decision." (Minutes of the Central Women's Advisory Committee, 9 November, 1938, National Union of Conservative and Unionist Associations, Central Women's Advisory Committee, CCO 170/1/1/1-CCO170/1/1/2.)
121. Anne Brock Griggs, "British Mothers Demonstrate," *Action*, No. 138, 8 October, 1938.
122. Letter from Daisy di Mobilant to Mrs Chamberlain, 15 September, 1938, Neville Chamberlain Papers, NC 13/12/471.
123. Anne Brock Griggs, "Organise for Peace: Democracy's War Measures," *Action*, No. 124, 2 July, 1938.
124. F.E. Hayes, "How Unnecessary it was: A Woman's View of the Crisis," *Action*, 15 October, 1938.
125. "Candid Commentary by Olive Hawks," *Action*, No. 139, 15 October, 1938.
126. See Julie Gottlieb, *Feminine Fascism: Women in Britain's Fascist Movement, 1923–1945* (London, 2000), and A.W. Brian Simpson, *In the Highest Degree Odious: Detention without Trial in Wartime Britain* (Oxford, 1994).
127. Richard Baxter, *Guilty Women* (London, 1941), p. 109.
128. Griffiths, *Patriotism Perverted*, p. 40.
129. Ibid., p. 126.
130. *Evening Standard*, 27 July, 1939.
131. Lord Boothby, *Recollections of a Rebel* (London, 1938), p. 133.

6   'Women are the Best Friends of Mr Chamberlain's Policy:' Gendered Representations of Public Opinion

1. Michael Barsely, "Mess Observation," *Time and Tide*, 28 January, 1939. Barsely was author of *Grabberwocky and Other Flights of Fancy* (London, 1939), an adaptation of Lewis Carroll's nonsense poem parodying the Nazi threat.
2. By agents of civil society I mean press, politicians, commentators, and opinion makers.
3. Harold Nicolson, "Modern Diplomacy and British Public Opinion," *International Affairs*, 14(5), September–October, 1935, pp. 599–618 complained about the insularity of the British public and its lack of knowledge of or interest in international matters, the press's incorrect reporting on news from abroad, and the many misunderstandings about the responsibility of the Treaty of Versailles for the current situation, presenting a characteristically pompous account of the superiority of those with experience in the diplomatic profession as opposed to the ignorant 'peace'-fixated public. Kenneth Younger, "Public Opinion and British Foreign Affairs," *International Affairs*, 40(1), Jauary, 1964, pp. 22–33, includes reflection on the lessons to be learned from the Munich Crisis. Robbins' chapter on "Public

Opinion: War and Peace" is a bit of a misnomer, offering a panoramic view of inter-war popular pacifism, with no reference to polling or even claims made by the Press to speak for public opinion. Keith Robbins, *Appeasement*, 2nd Edition (Oxford, 2001). More recently Jon Lawrence has argued that "the public meeting, as much as the political crowd, began to lose its legitimacy within British politics. Long before the dawn of opinion polling in Britain, politicians had begun to talk of 'the silent majority' and to dismiss meetings and demonstrations as the clamour of an unrepresentative and often dangerous 'active minority.'" (Jon Lawrence, "Forging a Peaceable Kingdom: War, Violence, and Fear of Brutalization in Post-First World War Britain," *Journal of Modern History*, 75(3), September, 2003, pp. 557–589).

4. More attention has been paid to the relationship between public opinion and foreign policy post-war. See Thomas Risse-Kappen, "Public Opinion, Domestic Structure, and Foreign Policy in Liberal Democracies," *World Politics*, 43(4), July, 1991), pp. 479–512. He does not consider gender, but he does offer an interesting way of breaking down public opinion: "One should at least distinguish between (1) mass public opinion, (2) the attentive public, which has a general interest in politics, and (3) issue publics, which are particularly attentive to specific questions."

5. David N. Dilks, "Public Opinion and Foreign Policy: Great Britain," in *Opinion publique et politique exterieure en Europe. II 1915–1940: Actes du Colloque de Rome* (1981), p. 58.

6. D.G. Boyce, "Public Opinion and Historians," *History*, 63(208), June, 1978), pp. 214–228.

7. Nicholas Pronay, "Rearmament and the British Public: Policy and Propaganda," in James Curran, Anthony Smith, and Pauline Wingate (eds.), *Impacts and Influences: Essays on Media Power in the Twentieth Century* (London, 1987), p. 57.

8. Martin Ceadel, "The First British Referendum: The Peace Ballot, 1934–5," *English History Review*, 95(377), October, 1980), pp. 810–839, and J.A. Thomson, "The Peace Ballot and he People," *Albion*, 13(4), Winter, 1981), pp. 381–392. While there exists no gendered study of appeasement, Helen McCarthy has offered a gendered study of the Peace Ballot. See Helen McCarthy, *The British People and the League of Nations: Democracy, citizenship and internationalism, c. 1918–1945* (Manchester, 2011), pp. 199–202, and "Democratizing British Foreign Policy: Rethinking the Peace Ballot, 1934–1935," *Journal of British Studies*, 49(2), April, 2010, pp. 358–387.

9. Frank Mort, "Love in a Cold Climate: Letters, Public Opinion and Monarchy in the 1936 Abdication Crisis," *Twentieth Century British History* (Advanced Access publication 7 June, 2013)

10. Roger Eatwell, "Munich, Public Opinion, and the Popular Front," *Journal of Contemporary History*, 6(4), 1971, pp. 122–139.

11. Daniel Hucker, *Public Opinion and the End of Appeasement in Britain and France* (Farnham, 2011), p. 12.

12. Ibid., pp. 12–13.

13. See Review of Hucker's book by Mona Siegel, *French History*, 26(3), 2012, pp. 421–422.

14. See Julie V. Gottlieb and Richard Toye (eds), *The Aftermath of Suffrage: Women, Gender, and Politics in Britain 1918–1945* (Basingstoke, 2013); Nicoletta Gullace, *'The Blood of Our Sons:' Men, Women, and the Renegotiation of British Citizenship During the Great War* (New York, 2002); Glenda Sluga, "Masculinities, Nations, and the New World Order: Peacemaking and Nationality in Britain, France, and the United States After the First World War," in Stefan Dudnik, Karen Hagemann

and John Tosh (eds.), *Masculinities in Politics and War* (Manchester, 2004); Susan Kingsley Kent, *Making Peace: The Reconstruction of Gender in Interwar Britain* (Princeton, 1993); and *Aftershock: Politics and Trauma in Britain, 1918–1931* (Basingstoke, 2009); Sonya Rose, *Which People's War? National Identity and Citizenship in Wartime Britain, 1939–1945* (Oxford, 2003).

15. Stefan Dudnik, Karen Hagemann, and John Tosh (eds.), *Masculinities in Politics and War* (Manchester, 2004) p. xvi.
16. Anthony King (ed.), *British Political Opinion: 1937–2000, The Gallup Polls* (London, 2001), p. ix.
17. "Our London Correspondent," *Manchester Guardian*, 19 March, 1938.
18. British Institute of Public Opinion, "Public Opinion Survey," *Public Opinion Quarterly*, 4(1), March, 1940, pp. 75–82.
19. "If you HAD to choose between Fascism and Communism, which would you choose? (May 37') Fascism 49%; Communism 51%, No. answer 46." Less than two years later the shift was significant with 26% opting for Fascism, 74% Communism, and 16 No answer. British Institute of Public Opinion, "Public Opinion Survey," *Public Opinion Quarterly*, 4(1), March, 1940), pp. 75–82.
20. Laura Drummond Beers, "Whose Opinion? Changing Attitudes Towards Opinion Polling in British Politics, 1937–1964," *Twentieth Century British History*, 17(2), 2006, pp. 177–205. Eleanor Rathbone made reference to polls during her incursions into foreign policy debates in the House.
21. "The Crisis 'Fever' Chart," *Illustrated London News*, 8 October, 1938. This appeared in a special issue "Record Number. The Crisis and the Agreement," with presentation plate of Mr Neville Chamberlain.
22. Helen McCarthy, *The British People and the League of Nations: Democracy, Citizenship and Internationalism, c. 1918–1945* (Manchester, 2011), p. 8.
23. Harold Nicolson, "British Public Opinion and Foreign Policy," *The Public Opinion Quarterly*, 1(1), January, 1937), pp. 53–63.
24. "The By-Elections," *Manchester Guardian*, 14 November, 1938.
25. Dorothy Sheridan (ed.), *Wartime Women: A Mass-Observation Anthology* (London, 2000), p. 29.
26. 31 January, 1938, Stuart Ball (ed.), *Parliament and Politics in the Age of Churchill and Attlee: The Headlam Diaries 1935–1951* (Cambridge, 1999), p. 122.
27. 18 May, 1937, in Gordon Martel (ed.), *The Times and Appeasement: The Journals of A.L. Kennedy, 1932–1939* (Cambridge, 2000), p. 247.
28. Simon Haxey, *Tory MP* (London, 1939), p. 240.
29. Ibid., p. 238.
30. Adrian Bingham, *Gender, Modernity and the Popular Press in Inter-war Britain* (Oxford, 2004), p. 187.
31. "The Thoughtful Shopper Makes Her Gift List," *Manchester Guardian*, 13 November, 1938.
32. See Maggie Andrews, *Domesticating the Airwaves: Broadcasting, Domesticity and Femininity* (London, 2012).
33. "'Flash Folks! World News …' The American Radio and the Crisis," *Manchester Guardian*, 18 October, 1938.
34. *Daily Mirror*, 20 September, 1938.
35. Adrian Bingham, *Gender, Modernity and the Popular Press in Inter-war Britain*, (Oxford, 2004) p. 211.
36. 2 December, 1936, John Julius Norwich (ed.), *The Duff Cooper Diaries* (London, 2005), p. 236.

37. In 1938 PEP published a *Report on the British Press,* an investigation motivated by the fact that country after country was losing its press freedom. In 1936 the estimated average circulation of daily newspapers was 19.05 million, and that of the 12 national Sunday papers was 14.44 million. There were 52 morning, 86 evening, and 18 Sunday papers, of which 20, four, and ten, respectively, were published in London.
38. Richard Cockett, *Twilight of Truth: Chamberlain, Appeasement & the Manipulation of the Press* (London, 1989), p. 65.
39. The first edition of the American-based *Public Opinion Quarterly* provided this definition:

> The term public opinion is given its meaning with reference to a multi-individual situation in which individuals are expressing themselves, or can be called upon to express themselves, as favouring or supporting (or else disfavouring or opposing) some definite condition, person, or proposal of widespread importance, in such a proportion of number, intensity, and constancy, as to give rise to the probability of affecting action, directly or indirectly, towards the object concerned.

Floyd H. Allport, "Towards a Science of Public Opinion," *Public Opinion Quarterly,* 1(1), January, 1937, pp. 7–23.
40. Susan Grayzel, *At Home and Under Fire: Air Raids and Culture in Britain from the Great War to the Blitz* (Cambridge, 2012), pp. 2–3. See also Brett Holman, *The Next War in the Air: Britain's Fear of the Bomber, 1908–1941* (Farnham, 2014).
41. "Thou Shalt Not ... " *Daily Mirror,* 29 September, 1938.
42. "Democracy and Defence," *The Times,* 12 January, 1938.
43. Winifred Peck, "The Cheated: Women and War," *Manchester Guardian,* 9 December, 1938.
44. Public opinion personified as a nurse in David Low, "Bedside Manner," *Evening Standard,* 24 September, 1943.
45. "Winifred Davies Asks What's Wrong with Women?" *The Tribune,* 23 December, 1937.
46. Helen Fletcher, "Notes on the Way," *Time and Tide,* 4 September, 1937.
47. "In the Press Now," *Western Morning News,* 1 October, 1938.
48. Friday 30 September, [1938], Anne Olivier Bell (ed.), *The Diary of Virginia Woolf, Vol. Five, 1936–1941* (San Diego, 1984), p. 177.
49. "Under the Franchise Soon to be Passed Women Will Outnumber the Men Voters by 2,000,000—New-Won Rights Bring Large Responsibilities," *New York Times,* 24 April, 1927.
50. Anne Petersen, "World Survey Spurs Drive to Put More Women in Public Office, *New York Times,* 13 February, 1938.
51. S.C. Leslie, "How the Public Thinks," *The Spectator,* 28 October, 1938.
52. "How Peace was Saved: The Story of the Great Crisis" (Essex, October, 1938), p. 18.
53. See Susan Sontag, 'Fascinating Fascism' in *Under the Sign of Saturn* (New York, 1980), pp. 73–105.
54. "The Issues at Stake," *Time and Tide,* 1 October, 1938. Winston Churchill's chapter on the Anschluss was titled "The Rape of Austria, February 1938" in *The Gathering Storm* (London, 1948).
55. "The Rape and After," *The Spectator,* 17 March, 1939.
56. 24 September, 1938, in John Julius Norwich (ed.), *The Duff Cooper Diaries,* p. 265.

57. Law to Emrys-Evans, 30 December, 1939, quoted in Stuart Ball, *Portrait of a Party: The Conservative Party in Britain 1918–1945* (Oxford, 2013), p. 53.

58. Letter from Neville to Hilda, 5 March, 1939, in Robert Self (ed.), *The Neville Chamberlain Diary Letters: Volume 4: The Downing Street Years, 1934–1940* (Farnham, 2005), p. 388. See Gilbert Murray to the Editor of *The Times*, 1 March, 1939.

59. "Our London Correspondence," *Manchester Guardian*, 19 March, 1938.

60. "Survey Finds British Behind Chamberlain," *New York Times*, 19 October, 1938. See also "Widespread demand for National Register in Public Opinion Survey: 57 per cent for Chamberlain: 43 per cent Against: More Women than Men are in his Favour," *News Chronicle*, 19 October, 1938.

61. Dr Henry Durant, Director, British Institute of Public Opinion, "British Back War, New Survey Shows," *New York Times*, 29 July, 1940.

62. From Dino Grandi, Italian Embassy, 4 Grosvenor Square, to N. Chamberlain, 16 September, 1938, Neville Chamberlain Papers, Cadbury Research Centre, University of Birmingham, NC 13/11/661.

63. From Nevile Henderson, British Embassy, Berlin, to Neville Chamberlain, 30 September, 1938, NC 13/11/678.

64. Kennedy heard that this is what Chamberlain had said, 17 January, 1939 in Gordon Martel (ed.), *The Times and Appeasement: The Journals of A.L. Kennedy, 1932–1939*, p. 284.

65. Quoted in William W. Hadley, *Munich Before and After* (London, 1944), p. 99.

66. Ladies Grand Council, Primrose League, to Mrs Chamberlain, 30 September, 1938, NC 13/12/700.

67. "Anxious Times for Women," *Derby Daily Telegraph*, 14 October, 1938.

68. "Premier's Wonderful Work," *Exeter and Plymouth Gazette*, 14 October, 1938.

69. "A Diary: For Women Only," *Headway*, November, 1938, p. 32.

70. "A German's View of England," *Gloucester Citizen*, 14 October, 1938.

71. 3 November, 1938, in Gordon Martel (ed.), *The Times and Appeasement: The Journals of A.L. Kennedy, 1932–1939* (Cambridge, 2000), p. 280. Conwell-Evans was Professor of English, University of Konigsberg 1932–1934; Joint Secretary, Anglo-German Fellowship 1934–1949; interpreted for Lloyd George during visit to Hitler in 1936. His popularity with the Germans was important to Chamberlain: "I hear I am the most popular man in Germany! 'He came to save us from a war.'" Letter from Neville to Ida, 19 September, 1938, in Self (ed.), p. 349.

72. *Observer*, 16 October, 1938.

73. Letter from Neville Chamberlain to Hilda, 6 November, 1938 in Self (ed.), p. 361.

74. "Paris Crowds Cheer Chamberlain," *Dundee Courier*, 24 November, 1938.

75. Letter from Nancy Astor to Mrs Neville Chamberlain, 24 October, 1938, Nancy Astor Papers, Special Collections, University of Reading, MS 1416/1/2/181.

76. "ARP Problem of Evacuation," *Manchester Guardian*, 15 October, 1938.

77. "Now," *Daily Mirror*, 29 September, 1938.

78. See R. Gerald Hughes, *The Postwar Legacy of Appeasement: British Foreign Policy Since 1945* (London, 2014).

79. Speech, "International Crisis," October, 1938, MS 1416/1/1/1689.

80. A Sir Neville Chamberlain: Reconaissance Francaise, La Baule—1938 (2 October, 1938), NC 13/6/1.

81. "The Lighter Side," *Nottingham Evening Post*, 11 February, 1939.

82. Letter from Neville to Hilda, 13 November, 1938, in Self (ed.), pp. 362–363.

83. An interesting postscript to this is the Denby series of table wear launched in 2011–2012 in partnership with the IWM, with mugs, serving trays, coasters, and cutting boards emblazoned with iconic images of gas-mask-wearing working-class housewives chatting in the front yard.
84. Letter from Neville to Hilda, 15 October, 1938 in Self (ed.), p. 355.
85. Quoted in Cockett, *Twilight of Truth*, p. 89.
86. I found this Loving Cup on e-Bay, currently asking £245 (September, 2013).
87. Available on bid or buy.co.za for £400 in December, 2013.
88. Edward Shanks, "No, Hero-Worship is Not Really Dying Out," *Aberdeen Press and Journal*, 23 November, 1938.
89. "Time-Tide Diary," *Time and Tide*, 5 November, 1938.
90. Virginia Cowles, *Looking for Trouble* (London, 1941), p. 197.
91. "Hogtied with a ribbon: The etiquette of giving gifts to sovereign countries requires updating," *The Economist*, 13 July, 2013.
92. Cinema-going boomed in Britain in the 1930s. From the already high admission figures of 903 million for 1934, the figure climbed to 990 million admissions for 1939. It was estimated that half of cinema-goers were children and young people, and of the adults about 75% were women.

    The evidence from a survey conducted in the early 1940s shows that the women who were regular (at least once a week) cinema-goers were young, working-class and educated to a low standard: 81% of women in the 14–17 age group and 45% of women in the 18–40 age group, compared to 76% and 38% of men, said that they went to the cinema at least once a week. (Deirdre Beddoe, *Back to Home and Duty: Women Between the Wars 1918–1939* (London, 1989), p. 116).

93. Max Everest-Phillips, *Neville Chamberlain and the Art of Appeasement* (London, 2013).
94. "Reflexions by Reflex," *Essex Newsman*, 8 October, 1938.
95. "'Umbrella' Cocktail Attacked by Broughty Lady," *Dundee Courier*, 29 March, 1939.
96. "Women and their Ways: Letter from Paris," *Nottingham Evening Post*, 30 March, 1939.
97. Cowles, *Looking for Trouble*, p. 188.
98. A Chamberlain mask head jug from c. 1938 can be purchased for £95 at time of publication.
99. Richard Overy, *The Morbid Age: Britain and the Crisis of Civilization* (London, 2010), p. 381.
100. See Jeffrey Richards, *The Age of the Dream Palace: Cinema and Society in 1930s Britain* (London, 2010).
101. David Low, "Low's Topical Budget," *Evening Standard*, 9 October, 1937.
102. "Chamberlain in 1938 Glamour King—And Here's the Queen," *Daily Mirror*, 31 December, 1938.
103. "What Smart Women are Wearing," *Aberdeen Journal*, 11 February, 1939.
104. "A Diary: For Women Only," *Headway*, November, 1938, p. 31.
105. "God Bless Neville," Getty Images, editorial image # 2658480, dated 01 October, 1938.
106. "The Influence of Public Opinion," *The Times*, 12 July, 1938.
107. Overy, *The Morbid Age*, p. 345

296 *Notes*

108. Chapter 10: Responding to Air War's Return: The Militarized Domestic Sphere from September '38 to the Blitz, in Susan Grayzel (ed.), *At Home and Under Fire: Air Raids and Culture in Britain from the Great War to the Blitz* (Cambridge, 2012), pp. 251–294.
109. Ibid., p. 257.
110. Cockett, *Twilight of Truth*, p. 75.
111. See Ian Hislop, "Stiff Upper Lip: An Emotional History of Britain," BBC One, broadcast 22 November, 2012.
112. 'Affable Hawk,' "The Intellectual Status of Women," in Virginia Woolf (ed.), *Killing the Angel in the House: Seven Essays* (London, 1993), pp. 23–24.
113. J.B. Priestley, "Notes on the Way," *Time and Tide*, 12 November, 1938.
114. E.H. Carr, "Public Opinion as a Safeguard of Peace," *International Affairs*, 15(6), November–December, 1936, pp. 846–862.
115. Letter from Betty, Manor House, Cranborne, Dorset, to Duff Cooper, Sunday [n.d.], Duff Cooper Papers, Churchill Archive Centre, University of Cambridge, DUFC 2/15.
116. Letter from Delia Macdonald (M.B.B.S) to WSC, 2 October, 1938, Churchill Papers, Churchill Archive Centre, University of Cambridge, CHAR 2/607 A-C.
117. Letter from Marjorie Stephenson to WSC, 2 October, 1938, CHAR 2/607 A-C.
118. 'Cato,' *Guilty Men* (London, 1940), pp. 51–52.
119. While public expression of emotion was regarded as undignified for an imperial power, in private many of the key players confessed to the strain on their bodies and psyches, 'couched' in the same popular psychology terms. Chamberlain himself, who suffered from terrible gout, was brought close to a nervous breakdown by the beginning of October, and his letters exhibit how attuned he was to the personal and mass psychology of the Crisis. Duff Cooper awoke every morning "with a feeling of sickening anxiety which gradually gives way to the excitement of the day," (20 September, 1938, in Norwich (ed.), p. 262) and when he heard that news that the agreement had been met at Munich, he was "extremely depressed." (29 September, 1938, in Norwich (ed.), p. 269).
120. Harold Nicolson, "British Public Opinion and Foreign Policy," *The Public Opinion Quarterly*, 1(1), January, 1937, pp. 53–63.
121. "Pale Cast of Thought," *Manchester Guardian*, 4 November, 1938.
122. A member of the NCW, *Time and Tide*, 22 October, 1938.
123. He was guest of honour at the Home Counties Women's Liberal Federation luncheon in late November, 1938. See THRS II 66/10, Churchill Archive, Churchill College, University of Cambridge.
124. See Dale Spender, *Time and Tide Wait for No Man* (London, 1984).
125. P.Y. Betts, "Public Opinion in our Suburb," *Time and Tide*, 2 January, 1937.
126. "Miss Dartle's Diary," *Time and Tide*, 26 June, 1937.
127. Rose Dartle, "Miss Dartle Wants to Know," *Time and Tide*, 19 March, 1938.
128. "Miss Dartle Wants to Know," *Time and Tide*, 8 October, 1938.
129. Jan Struther, "The Truth About Mrs Miniver," *English*, 2(12), 1939, pp. 347–355.
130. "Sunday in London," *The Times*, 31 March, 1938.
131. "The Miniver's and Gas Masks: Thoughts in a Queue," *The Times*, 28 September, 1938.
132. "Back to Normal: The Afterthoughts of Mrs Miniver," *The Times*, 6 October, 1938.
133. "Mrs Miniver in November: A Wild Day," *The Times*, 29 November, 1938.

134. A photo of people sorting the parcels of clothes, books, and toys, sent in response to Mrs Miniver's appeal on behalf of Jewish refugees appeared on 22 December, 1938 in *The Times*.
135. "London in August: Mrs Miniver and the Other Children," *The Times*, 21 August, 1939.
136. Fred M. Leventhal, "British Writers, American Readers: Women's Voices in Wartime," *Albion*, 32(1), Spring, 2000), pp. 1–18.
137. See Penny Summerfield, "Dunkirk and the Popular Memory of Britain at War, 1940–1958," *Journal of Contemporary History*, 45(4), October, 2010, pp. 788–811.
138. See Joanna Bourke, *Dismembering the Male: Men's Bodies, Britain and the Great War* (London, 1996); Susan Kingsley Kent, *Making Peace: The Reconstruction of Gender in Interwar Britain* (Princeton, 1993); Nicollette Gullace, *The Blood of Our Sons: Men, Women and the Renegotiation of British Citizenship During the Great War* (Basingstoke, 2002).
139. Marcus Collins, "The Fall of the English Gentleman: The National Character in Decline, c. 1918–1970," *Historical Research*, 75(187), February, 2002, pp. 90–110.
140. See Stanley Baldwin, 'The Englishman' (1940). Quoted in Marcus Collins.
141. S. Haxey, *Tory MP*, p. 243. Arthur and Margaret Wynn (married in 1938) were "a latter-day Sydney and Beatrice Webb" ("Arthur Wynn Obituary," *Guardian*, 29 September, 2001) and their collaboration began with this study, first titled *England's Money Lords*. She died in February 2010. Arthur Wynn was revealed to have recruited a network of communist spies at Oxford before and during the war. See "Civil Servant Arthur Wynn Revealed as Recruiter of Oxford Spies," *The Times*, 13 May, 2009.
142. Ibid., p. 13.
143. Emmeline Pethick Lawrence, *My Part in a Changing World* (London, 1938), p. 347.
144. Beverly Nichols, *News of England/or A Country Without a Hero* (London, 1938), p. 14.
145. See Gerwin Strobl, *The Germanic Isle: Nazi Perceptions of Britain* (Cambridge, 2000).
146. "A Letter from London by Our Own Correspondent," *Devon and Exeter Gazette*, 7 October, 1938.
147. A.K. Chesterton, "Return to Manhood: Regiment of Old Women Routed," *Action*, 21, 9 July, 1936.
148. G. Strube, *Daily Express*, 27 May, 1937.
149. On the other hand, in the LNU's *Headway* "peace" was embodied in female form, and in general the League of Nations was consistently symbolized by a female figure. As the post-war years wore on her body and her visage showed ever more visible signs of physical and mental abuse, and a spirit betrayed. Indeed, one could trace the public's deepening remorse at the failures of the League through the ever more sickly representations of the iconic angel of peace in political cartoons. Internationalism was a female-identified political ideal, ideals of international citizenship coalesced with feminine idealism, while national citizenship remained male-identified.
150. "Session 1937," by Ellen Wilkinson, *Time and Tide*, 31 July, 1937.
151. "Hastily Returned," *Time and Tide*, 15 April, 1939.
152. *New Times and Ethiopian News*, 12 March, 1938.
153. Ibid., 20 July, 1938.

154. David Low, "Foreign Policy Vaudeville Act," *Evening Standard*, 10 December, 1937.
155. "The Dashing Young Men and the Flying Trapeze," David Low, *Evening Standard*, 2 March, 1938.
156. David Low, "Shiver Sisters Celebrate," *Evening Standard*, 23 March, 1938.
157. David Low, "Low's Topical Budget," *Evening Standard*, 2 April, 1938.
158. Rose, *The Cliveden Set*, p. 179.
159. Cowles, *Looking for Trouble*, p. 139.
160. David Low, *Evening Standard*, 24 December, 1938.
161. "Mr Chamberlain's Umbrella," *Yorkshire Post and Leeds Intelligencer*, 14 October, 1938.
162. Winston Churchill, *The Second World War: The Gathering Storm* (London, 1948), p. 268.
163. See Churchill, *The Gathering Storm*, pp. 265–266, where he makes the case that appeasement represented the lapse of honour.
164. *Picture Post*, 29 June, 1940. Quoted in Sonya O. Rose, *Which People's War? National Identity and Citizenship in Wartime Britain, 1939–1945* (Oxford, 2002), pp. 168–169.
165. A.C.C., "Peace with Honour," October, 1938, Papers of Leo Amery, Churchill Archive Centre, University of Cambridge, AMEL 1/5/55.
166. See Peter Mandler, *The English National Character: The History of an Idea from Edmund Burke to Tony Blair* (New Haven, 2006), p. 181.
167. Alison Light, *Forever England: Femininity, Literature and Conservatism Between the Wars* (London, 1991), pp. 8–9.

7 'Anyway Let's Have Peace:' Women's Expressions of Opinion on Appeasement

1. See Murray Goot, "Mass-Observation and Modern Public Opinion Research," in Wolfgang Donsbach and Michael Traugott (eds.), *The SAGE Handbook of Public Opinion Research* (London, 2008), pp. 93–103, for a comparative study of the ethos, methods, and definition of 'public opinion' of Gallup and Mass-Observation.
2. Annebella Pollen, "Research Methodology in Mass Observation Past and Present," *History Workshop Journal*, 75(1), Spring, 2013, pp. 213–235.
3. James Hinton, *Nine Wartime Lives: Mass Observation and the Making of the Modern Self* (Oxford, 2010), p. 2.
4. Robert Graves and Alan Hodge, *The Long Weekend: The Living Story of the Twenties and Thirties* (London, 1940), p. 397.
5. Tony Kushner, *We Europeans? Mass-Observation, 'Race' and British Identity in the Twentieth Century* (Farnham, 2005), p. 23.
6. Hinton, *Nine Wartime Lives*, p. 7.
7. For studies of wartime women that rely heavily on Mass-Observation material, see Lucy Noakes, *War and the British: Gender and National Identity, 1939–1991* (London, 1998); Sonya Rose, 'Sex, Citizenship, and the Nation in World War II Britain,' *American Historical Review*, 103(4), October, 1998), pp. 1147–1176; Penny Summerfield, *Women Workers in the Second World War: Production and Patriarchy in Conflict* (London, 1984); and Penny Summerfield, *Reconstructing Women's Wartime Lives: Discourse and Subjectivity in Oral Histories of the Second World War* (Manchester, 1998).

8. I asked Helen Fisher, Archivist, Chamberlain Collection, University of Birmingham, whether it was known if these files were weeded. She reckoned:

> it is likely that Chamberlain and his secretary made efforts to keep the positive and congratulatory letters and may well have disposed of those opposing the Munich Agreement, but the volume of letters does indicate that many people were relieved that an agreement had been reached, and this reflects public responses reported elsewhere, though I know that reaction was obviously not wholly favourable.

Email from Helen Fisher to the author, 8 February, 2013.
9. Charles Madge and Tom Harrisson, *Britain by Mass-Observation* (Harmsworth, 1939) first published January, 1939, reprinted February and April, 1939, p. 66.
10. Ibid., p. 101.
11. Ibid., p. 99.
12. James Hinton, *The Mass-Observers: A History, 1937–1949* (Oxford, 2013), p. 14.
13. Dorothy Sheridan (ed.), *Wartime Women: A Mass-Observation Anthology* (London, 2000), p. 4.
14. Ibid., p. 10.
15. Robert Malcolmson (ed.), *Love & War in London: The Mass Observation Diary of Olivia Cockett* (London, 2009), p. 12.
16. Mass-Observation, September 1938, Miss Muriel Barker, Barker 3567, M-OA: Directive Replies 1938, Box 11 of 13, Munich Crisis, September-October—Women.
17. Dawson 1016, "After the Crisis," 3 October, 1938, M-OA: Directive Replies 1938, Box 11 of 13, Munich Crisis, September–October—Women.
18. W. Thompson 2053, 3 October, 1938, M-OA: Directive Replies 1938, Box 11 of 13, Munich Crisis, September–October—Women.
19. Winifred F. Peck, "Hospitality: Christmas Cards and the Crisis," *Manchester Guardian*, 15 November, 1938.
20. Her wartime diaries have been published, but the volume does not include her work for Mass-Observation pre-September 1939. See Dorothy Sheridan (ed.), *Among you Taking Notes ... The Wartime Diary of Naomi Mitchison 1939–1945* (London, 2000).
21. Naomi Mitchison 1534 [September–October, 1938] M-OA: Directive Replies 1938, Box 11 of 13, Munich Crisis, September–October—Women.
22. Sheridan (ed.), *Wartime Women*, p. 30.
23. Friday 20 May, 1938 in Anne Olivier Bell (ed.), *The Diary of Virginia Woolf, Vol. Five 1936–1941* (San Diego, 1984), p. 142.
24. Brand, Dorothy 1068, "Personal Impressions", 13 September, 1938, M-OA: Directive Replies 1938, Box 11 of 13, Munich Crisis, September–October—Women.
25. Muriel Bennett 1072, M-OA: Directive Replies 1938, Box 11 of 13, Munich Crisis, September–October—Women.
26. Margot Jones 1071, "The Crisis," M-OA: Directive Replies 1938, Box 11 of 13, Munich Crisis, September–October—Women.
27. Mrs Phyllis Perlow (housewife), "Crisis" 1081, M-OA: Directive Replies 1938, Box 11 of 13, Munich Crisis, September–October—Women.
28. Sheridan (ed.), *Wartime Women*, p. 34
29. See Penny Summerfield, *Reconstructing Women's Wartime Lives* (Manchester, 1998):

> In the context of the Second World War, the contradictory character of the discourses constituting 'woman' is particularly visible. This 'total' war stimulated a rhetoric concerning 'the people,' all of those whose efforts had

to be mobilised. Within this process, contradictory demands were placed on women ... They were represented both as loyal citizens and as treacherous subversives.

(p. 14)

Of oral history, "Personal narratives draw on the generalised subject available in discourse to construct the particular personal subject." On women as wartime subversives see Antonia Lant, *Blackout: Reinventing Women for Wartime British Cinema* (Princeton, 1991), Chapter 2.

30. Blackwell, I. 3568, "Comments on the Crisis," 28 September, 1938, M-OA: Directive Replies 1938, Box 11 of 13, Munich Crisis, September–October—Women.
31. M.E. Grant 2251, September, 1938, Ramsgate, M-OA: Directive Replies 1938, Box 11 of 13, Munich Crisis, September–October—Women.
32. Sheridan (ed.), *Wartime Women*, p. 41.
33. Ibid., p. 41.
34. Woman, 25 [no number], M-OA: Directive Replies 1938, Box 11 of 13, Munich Crisis, September–October—Women.
35. Margot Edgelow 1033, Mass-Observation Report, 28 September, 1938, M-OA: Directive Replies 1938, Box 11 of 13, Munich Crisis, September–October—Women.
36. Richard Overy, The *Morbid Age: Britain and the Crisis of Civilization, 1919–1939* (London, 2010), p. 347.
37. Miss Edith Oakley 1085 [aged 36, Glasgow], 1-2 October, 1938, M-OA: Directive Replies 1938, Box 11 of 13, Munich Crisis, September–October—Women.
38. Tuesday 4 October, 1938 in Neal J. Crowson (ed.), *Fleet Street, Press Barons and Politics: The Journals of Collin Brooks, 1931–1940* (London, 1998), p. 221.
39. Tom Harrisson, "What is Public Opinion?" *The Political Quarterly*, 11(4) October, 1940, pp. 368–383.
40. Norman Rose, "The Resignation of Anthony Eden," *Historical Journal*, 25(4), 1982, pp. 911–931.
41. See Martel (ed.), A.L. Kennedy journals, p. 270. In his memoirs, *Facing the Dictators*, Eden does mention the high level of public support and the high volume of letters he received "many thousands of messages" (p. 598) but otherwise gives short shrift to public opinion—it is merely background music to the set piece of parliamentary politics and the intrigues of diplomacy in which a handful of men decide the fate of the world.
42. Martin Pugh, *Women and the Women's Movement in Britain* (Basingstoke, 2000), p. 107.
43. "Women Revolt for Eden: 200 Ejected from House," *Daily Mirror*, 22 February, 1938.
44. See Chapter 5, "Mosley's Women and Mosley's Woman: The Leader's Sexual Politics," in Julie V. Gottlieb (ed.), *Feminine Fascism: Women in Britain's Fascist Movement 1923–1945* (London, 2000).
45. "No Intentional Backsliding," *Manchester Guardian*, 21 December, 1935.
46. Martin Francis, "Tears, Tantrums, and Bared Teeth: The Emotional Economy of Three Conservative Prime Ministers, 1951–1963," *Journal of British Studies*, 41(3), July 2002, pp. 354–387.
47. Robert Self, *Neville Chamberlain: A Biography* (Aldershot, 2006), p. 328.
48. "Dual Peace Policy," *The Times*, 13 May, 1938.
49. Neville Chamberlain, *In Search of Peace: Speeches, 1937–1938* (London, 1939), pp. 274–276.
50. "Mr Chamberlain's Foreign Policy: St Andrews Professors Who Admire It," *Manchester Guardian*, 21 November, 1938.

51. "Scenes in Tory Women's Debate on Flogging," *Manchester Guardian*, 11 May, 1939.
52. 1939/7 The Prime Minister's Great Speech: Peace through Strength: Mr Chamberlain's Great Speech delivered at the mass meeting of women Conservatives at the Royal Albert Hall, London, on Thursday 11 May, 1939, Oxford, Bodleian Library, Conservative Party Archive.
53. Letter from Neville Chamberlain to Ida, 19 September, 1938, in Robert Self (ed.), *The Neville Chamberlain Diary Letters: Volume 4: The Downing Street Years, 1934–1940* (Aldershot, 2005), p. 348.
54. Letter from Neville Chamberlain to Ida, 9 October, 1938, in Self (ed.), p. 353.
55. Ibid., 17 December, 1938, in Self (ed.), p. 371.
56. Ibid., 17 December, 1938, in Self (ed.), p. 371.
57. Letter from Neville Chamberlain to Hilda, 15 January, 1939, in Self (ed.), p. 374.
58. Ibid., 5 February, 1939, in Self (ed.), p. 377.
59. Letter from Neville Chamberlain to Ida, 12 March, 1939, in Self (ed.), p. 392.
60. Letter from Neville Chamberlain to Hilda, 15 April, 1939, in Self (ed.), p. 405.
61. Virginia Cowles, *Looking for Trouble* (London, 1941), p. 192.
62. See Jill Liddington, *The Road to Greenham Common: Feminism and Anti-Militarism in Britain Since 1820* (Syracuse, 1989).
63. Anonymous to Mrs Chamberlain, 30 September, 1938, Neville Chamberlain Papers, Cadbury Research Centre, University of Birmingham, NC 13/12/778.
64. Letter from Julie Aves to Mr Chamberlain, 5 October, 1938, NC 13/7/55.
65. Letter from Mrs Helen Allison to Mr and Mrs Chamberlain, 25 October, 1938, NC 13/7/21.
66. Letter from E.A. Russell to Mr Prime Minister, 19 February, 1939, NC 13/9/19.
67. From Alice Pralt, Birmingham Central Advisory Women's Council, Birmingham Unionist Association, to PM, 10 July, 1939, NC 13/9/20.
68. Letter from Lady Claire Templemore to Mr Chamberlain, 30 September, 1938, NC 13/11/782.
69. Letter from Gladys H. Turner to Mr Neville Chamberlain, March, 1939, NC 13/9/110.
70. Letter from Ellen L. Llowelin to Mr Neville Chamberlain, 17 December, 1938, NC 13/9/87.
71. From Mrs Driver to Mr Chamberlain, 17 September, 1938, NC 13/11/136.
72. From Hilda M. Kent to 'My dear Noble Gentleman, 10 October, 1938, NC 13/11/234.
73. From anonymous to Mr Chamberlain, [n.d], NC 13/11/606.
74. Letter from Mrs H.T. Collett, Chairman of the Broadway Ward Women's Unionist Association to Mrs Chamberlain, 1 October, 1938, NC 13/12/147.
75. From R. Cyril Yates (Birmingham) to Mr Chamberlain, 4 October, 1938, NC 13/11/518.
76. Letter from Marion Phillmore to Mrs Chamberlain, 25 September, 1938, NC 13/12/518.
77. Frank Mort, "Love in a Cold Climate: Letters, Public Opinion and Monarchy in the 1936 Abdication Crisis," *Twentieth Century British History* 25(1), 2014, pp. 30–62.
78. Letter from Osbert Sitwell to Mrs Chamberlain, 23 September, 1938, NC 13/11/770.
79. "Neville Chamberlain" by Enid Blyton [1938], NC13/7/154.
80. Lord Londonderry (Charley) to My dear Neville, 3 September, 1938, NC 13/11/709.
81. Lady Londonderry to Neville, 17 September, 1938, NC 13/11/711.
82. Lady Ethel Desborough (Norfolk) to My dear PM, 30 September, 1938, NC 13/11/645.
83. Post Office Telegram, 17 September, 1938, NC 13/11/68.

84. Letter from Daisy di Mobilant to Mrs Chamberlain, 15 September, 1938, NC 13/12/471.
85. "Rumours in London: Cheering Crowds," *Manchester Guardian*, 30 September, 1938.
86. Letter from Richard Wilson to Mrs N. Chamberlain, 10 October, 1938, NC 13/ 4/37.
87. Letter from Beatrice Johnson to Mrs Chamberlain, 27 September, 1938, NC 12/12/360.
88. From Florence Horsbrugh (London) to Mrs Chamberlain, 28 September, 1938, NC 13/11/686.
89. Letter from Eileen (Hastings) Anderson, Ladies Carlton Club, to Mrs Chamberlain, 30 September, 1938, NC 13/12/23.
90. Letter from 'A few Nurses' (Manchester) to Mrs. N. Chamberlain, 19 September, 1938, NC 13/12/717.
91. Letter from 'A Mother' to Mrs Chamberlain, 23 September, 1938, NC 13/12/726.
92. Letter from Kathleen M (Newcastle on Tyne) to Mrs Chamberlain, 28 September, 1938, NC 13/12/731.
93. Letter from 'A father and husband' to Mrs Chamberlain, 29 September, 1938, NC 13/12/745.
94. Letter from A.M.D to Mrs Chamberlain, 28 September, 1938, NC 13/12/739.
95. Frank Mort, "Love in a Cold Climate: Letters, Public Opinion and Monarchy in the 1936 Abdication Crisis," *Twentieth Century British History* 25(1), 2014, pp. 30–62.
96. One exception was this rather farcical letter:

> A cat is an independent and private animal and you have no right to pub-licise the black cat living at 10 Downing Street as you do; or accept for him presents of Dover sole from people who haven't the guts to stand up to the Germans, as though he were an endorser of your husband's policy. This is not a joke.
>
> (Letter from Beryl Pritchard to Mrs Chamberlain, 13 December,1938, NC 13/12/530.)

97. T.M. Rannie (Winchester) to the Editor[?], NC 13/12/537.
98. "Campaign for Peace to be Won," *Aberdeen Journal*, 28 October, 1938.
99. The Chamberlains received a plethora of letters from abroad, with a high con-centration sent from France (French-language letters were the only ones that were not translated as the Chamberlains were proficient in the language), some from Germany, many from the British Empire, others from South America and the United States, all praising Chamberlain for preserving the peace.
100. Letter from Mary V. Angel (journalist, Surrey) to Mr N. Chamberlain, 3 September, 1939, NC 13/13/7.
101. "Are you satisfied with Mr Neville Chamberlain as Prime Minister?

	Yes	No	No Op.
Oct. 38	57%	43%	10%
Dec. 38	56	44	9
Mar. 38	58	42	10
May 39	55	45	4
Jul. 39	59	41	7
Oct. 39	65	29	6."

British Institute of Public Opinion, "Public Opinion Survey," *Public Opinion Quarterly*, 4(1), March, 1940, pp. 75–82.

8 'Don't Believe in Foreigners:' The Female Franchise Factor and the Munich By-elections

1. "The Election Speculations," *Manchester Guardian*, 5 October, 1938.
2. Stuart Ball, "The Politics of Appeasement: the Fall of the Duchess of Atholl and the Kinross and West Perth By-election, December 1938," *Scottish Historical Review*, LXIX(187), April, 1990, pp. 49–83.
3. See Chris Cook and John Ramsden (eds), *By-Elections in British Politics* (London, 1997), p. 5.
4. "Women Can Make Premier Change his Policy," *Daily Mirror*, 21 March, 1938.
5. John Cunningham Sparks, "British By-Elections: What Do They Prove?" *American Political Science Review*, 34(1), February, 1940, pp. 97–104.
6. Roger Eatwell, "Munich, Public Opinion, and Popular Front," *Journal of Contemporary History*, 6(4), 1971, pp. 122–139.
7. Iain McLean, "Oxford and Bridgwater," in Chris Cook and John Ramsden (eds), *By-elections in British Politics* (London, 1997), pp. 130–150.
8. Martin Ceadel, "Interpreting East Fulham," in Chris Cook and John Ramsden (eds), *By-elections in British Politics* (London, 1997), pp. 94–111.
9. Martin Ceadel, "The First British Referendum: The Peace Ballot, 1934–1935," *English Historical Review*, 95(377), October, 1980, pp. 810–839.
10. Norman Rose, "The Resignation of Anthony Eden," *Historical Journal*, 25(4), 1982, pp. 911–931.
11. Central Women's Electoral Committee: Woman Candidate in West Fulham by-Election, 26 March, 1938, Mass-Observation Archive, University of Sussex, M-0, File 2/B.
12. Edith Summerskill, *A Woman's World: Her Memoirs* (London, 1967), p. 59.
13. Conservative Meeting, 30 March, 1938, 3 p.m. West Fulham, Box 1 By-Elections—297, M-O, File 1/B.
14. Sir Archibald Sinclair, a formidable anti-appeaser himself, was leader of the non-National Liberals, while Lloyd George had detached himself from the Liberal Party since 1931 and formed his own Council of Action for Peace and Reconstruction. It was a significant player in all Popular Front campaigns. Though Liberal in its composition, it had the support from across party lines, including Eleanor Rathbone and Labour's Margaret Bondfield. See Martin Pugh, "The Liberal Party and the Popular Front," *English Historical Review*, CXXI(494), December, 2006), pp. 1328–1350.
15. Conservative Meeting, 30 March, 1938, 3 p.m. West Fulham, Box 1 By-Elections—297, M-O, File 1/B.
16. Subject Matter of Speeches, West Fulham, Box 1 By-Elections—297, M-O, File 1/B.
17. "Keen Fight in West Fulham," *Observer*, 3 April, 1938.
18. Home or Foreign Affairs, 26 March, 1938, M-O, File 2/C.
19. Ibid.
20. Second Series of questions, relevant to interest and attitude on foreign policy and world affairs: Work done by Harrisson and Mass-Observers, Stoneham's publicity group, etc., West Fulham, M-O, File 2/C.
21. "West Fulham," *Manchester Guardian*, 7 April, 1938.
22. Speech by Dr Summerskill, File 2/A West Fulham by-election, 1938, By-Elections, Box 2, M-O, 29/3 1938.
23. Summerskill, *A Woman's World*, p. 62.
24. Summerskill's Fulham win was the beginning of a very successful parliamentary career, and she held the Fulham West seat for Labour from 1938 to 1955, before serving as MP for Warrington from 1955 to 1961.

25. See Penny Summerfield, "'Our Amazonian Colleague:' Edith Summerskill's Problematic Reputation," in R. Toye and J. Gottlieb (eds), *Making Reputations* (London, 2005), pp. 135–150. "Summerskill's medical background was seen as defining not only the political causes she took up, but also the way she performed her role as an MP. Use of 'medi-speak' and the deployment of the persona of the doctor were characteristic of her style." (p. 140)
26. Summerskill, p. 61.
27. "The Litchfield Election: Poll on Thursday," *Manchester Guardian*, 1 May, 1938.
28. "New MP is the Handsomest," *Daily Mirror*, 4 June, 1938.
29. See Adrian Bingham, "'Stop the Flapper Folly:' Lord Rothermere, the *Daily Mail* and the equalization of the franchise, 1927–1928," *Twentieth Century British History*, 13(1), 2002, pp. 17–37.
30. K.R.G. Browne is all for Youth at the Helm and putting our House (of Commons) in order," *The Hull Daily Mail*, 5 February, 1938.
31. Lindsay approached Churchill to come to Oxford to support his by-election bid, but Churchill, in trouble with his own constituency association in Epping, was understandably cautious about supporting candidates who were fighting a Unionist candidate. Letter from WSC to Lindsay, 19 October, 1938, CHAR 2/322.
32. Martin Pugh, "The Liberal Party and the Popular Front," *English Historical Review*, CXXI(494), December, 2006, pp. 1327–1350.
33. Roger Eatwell, "Munich, Public Opinion, and Popular Front," *Journal of Contemporary History*, 6(4), 1971, pp. 122–139.
34. "By-Election at Oxford," *Manchester Guardian*, 23 October, 1938.
35. "Oxford Poll Today Will Test Opinion," *New York Times*, 27 October, 1938.
36. "Dartford By-Election Campaign," *Manchester Guardian*, 3 November, 1938
37. Monday 17 October, Nicholas J. Crowson (ed.), *Fleet Street, Press Barons and Politics: The Journals of Collin Brooks, 1931–1940* (London, 1998), p. 227.
38. Oxford by-Election, First Day of Campaign, 18 October, report from Tom Harrisson, M-O File 2/G.
39. In 1935 there was a Conservative majority of 2,646; in 1929 Labour had won the seat with a 10,000 strong majority.
40. "The Dartford By-Election: Mr Attlee's Message," *Manchester Guardian*, 27 October, 1938.
41. "Our London Correspondent," *Manchester Guardian*, 28 October, 1938.
42. "Dartford By-Election Campaign," *Manchester Guardian*, 3 November, 1938.
43. "Voting To-day in Dartford," *The Times*, 7 November, 1938.
44. Adamson (Lab.) 46,514; Mitchell (Con.) 42,276.
45. "The Bye-Elections: Another Working Woman, MP?," *Labour Woman*, September, 1938.
46. "A Socialist Gain," *Western Morning News*, 8 November, 1938.
47. "Labour Majority of 4,200," *Manchester Guardian*, 8 November, 1938.
48. The first three husband and wife teams were Lord and Lady Runciman, Sir Oswald and Lady Cynthia Mosley, and Dr and Mrs Hugh Dalton.
49. "Pale Cast of Thought," *Manchester Guardian*, 4 November, 1938.
50. "Nominations at Walsall," *Manchester Guardian*, 9 November, 1938.
51. "The King's Speech," *Manchester Guardian*, 9 November, 1938.
52. In Walsall it was a National Government win, with the National Liberal candidate, Sir G. Schuster, elected with 28,720 votes, and Labour's G. Jeger with 21,562.
53. "The By-Elections: Mr Bartlett Making Headway at Bridgwater," *Manchester Guardian*, 11 November, 1938.

54. Labour retained Doncaster with an 11,708 majority, announced 18 November, 1938.
55. "Two By-Elections To-day," *The Times*, 17 November, 1938. N.B. Doncaster was, in fact, a win for Labour.
56. "Nominations at Doncaster," *The Times*, 8 November, 1938.
57. "The Coming By-Elections," *Time and Tide*, 12 November, 1938.
58. "The By-Elections," *Manchester Guardian*, 18 November, 1938.
59. John Cunningham Sparks, "British By-Elections: What Do They Prove?" *American Political Science Review*, 34(1), February, 1940, pp. 97–104.
60. "Quem Deus vult perdere … ?" *Time and Tide*, 19 November, 1938.
61. A. Susan Williams, *Ladies of Influence* (London, 2000), p. 125.
62. "The Duchess of Atholl: Outspoken Critic of the Premier's Foreign Policy," *Manchester Guardian*, 25 November, 1938.
63. "Duchess's Rival Stands Down," *Daily Mirror*, 9 December, 1938.
64. Parliamentary Bye-Election, 1938, Kinross and West Pertshire Division: Vote for the Duchess of Atholl, Independent Candidate, 13 December, 1938, M-O File 2/D.
65. "Mr Winston Churchill Supports the Duchess … [in an open letter to her] ' … You stand for the effective rearmament of our country and for an end to the procrastination, half measures, and mismanagement which have led us from a safe position into a state of woeful unpreparedness and danger. The creation of a Ministry of Supply, which you have advocated, is an essential step in our rearmament, but besides that it would be a welcome symbol of earnestness and energy, which could not fail to make an impression upon the foreign countries, many of whom are beginning to think, some with pleasure, others with dismay, that British democracy is losing its will to live. You are, no doubt, opposed by many Conservatives as loyal and patriotic as yourself, but the fact remains that outside our island your defeat at this moment would be relished by the enemies of Britain, and of freedom in every part of the world. It would be widely accepted as another sign that Great Britain is sinking under the weight of her cares, and no longer has the spirit and the will-power to confront the tyrannies and cruel persecutions which have darkened this age.'" ("Candidates Toe the Line at Crieff," *Pertshire Constitutional and Journal*, 16 December, 1938.)
66. Nicholas J. Crowson, "Conservative Parliamentary Dissent over Foreign Policy during the Premiership of Neville Chamberlain: Myth or Reality?" *Parliamentary History*, 14(3), 1995, pp. 315–336.
67. She did not, however, win over the ILP who were warned not to:

    have any illusion about the Duchess's regard for the workers of this county … Tory 'democrats' and Liberal 'humanists' are still Capitalist defenders and are a menace to the working-class movement. It is a thousand pities that no section of the movement is strong enough in that part of Scotland to contest the election.

    ("—And the 'Popular Front' Duchess's," *New Leader*, 9 December, 1938.)

68. "West Perth Electors' Chance to Preserve Peace," *The People's Journal*, 17 December, 1938.
69. "Time-Tide Diary," *Time and Tide*, 3 December, 1938.
70. Rhondda, "Courage: The Duchess of Atholl's Fight," *Time and Tide*, 10 December, 1938.
71. S.J. Hetherington, *Katherine Atholl (1874–1960): Against the Tide* (Aberdeen, 1989), p. 212.
72. "Viscount Cecil Campaigns for Duchess," *News Chronicle*, 10 December, 1938.

73. "West Perth Electors' Chance to Preserve Peace," *The People's Journal*, 17 December, 1938.
74. "Candidates Toe the Line at Crieff," *Perthshire Constitutional and Journal*, 16 December, 1938.
75. "New Group Fight 'Weak' Cabinet," *Daily Mirror*, 5 January, 1939.
76. Stuart Ball, "The Politics of Appeasement: the Fall of the Duchess of Atholl and the Kinross and West Perth By-election, December 1938," *Scottish Historical Review*, LXIX(187), April, 1990), pp. 49–83.
77. Ibid.
78. "Posters," Kinross by-election, 15 December, 1938, M-O File 2/D.
79. Parliamentary Bye-Election, 1938, Kinross and West Perthshire Division: Vote for the Duchess of Atholl, Independent Candidate, 13 December, 1938, M-O File 2/D.
80. Quoted in Stuart Ball, "The Politics of Appeasement: the Fall of the Duchess of Atholl and the Kinross and West Perth By-election, December 1938," *Scottish Historical Review*, LXIX(187), April, 1990, pp. 49–83.
81. Hetherington, *Katherine Atholl*, p. 216.
82. "Premier to New MP—'Splendid Victory,'" *Daily Mail*, 23 December, 1938.
83. Williams, *Ladies of Influence*, p. 128.
84. Andrzej Olechnowicz, "Liberal Anti-Fascism in the 1930s: The Case of Sir Ernest Baker," *Albion*, 36(4), Winter, 2004, pp. 636–660.
85. "East Norfolk Contest Appeals to Women Electors," *The Times*, 12 January, 1939.
86. See "Solicitor-General and 'Noisy People,'" *The Times*, 17 January, 1939.
87. "Rates Policy," *Hull Daily Mail*, 8 February, 1939.
88. "Complications at Holderness," *The Times*, 9 February, 1939.
89. "The Liberals at Batley," *The Times*, 2 March, 1939.
90. "Labour Winds Southwark," *Manchester Guardian*, 18 May, 1939.
91. "The World: Week by Week," *Observer*, 21 May, 1939.
92. Again we see that female support for Chamberlain remains high, with 36.1% identifying themselves as pro-Chamberlain; only 8.3% pro-pamphlet, i.e., for Carritt; 13.9% who give no answer; 11.1% who do not understand; 2.8% who are vague, 13.9% who are either not bothered or not interested, and 13.9% who leave it to the men-folk. In contrast, 25% of the men are pro-pamphlet; 8.3% pro-Chamberlain; 8.3% give no answer; 8.3% don't understand; 25% are vague; 16.7% either not bothered or not interested; and 8.3% Fascist.

    "Question One: of the 46 people who answered Questions One, 71.7% did NOT know that there was an election on.

    Question Two: Of the 48 people interviewed, 12 were male and 36 female."
    (Westminster 14/4, M-O survey, M-O File 2/F)

93. "Our London Correspondent," *Manchester Guardian*, 23 May, 1939.
94. In the Silvertown by-election it was clear that the war had not mended the divisions between the sexes, and they were not unified in their support for the war effort. Mass-Observation discovered that the main issue of this by-election was the undesirability of the war, and "It is evident in this case, as in many others, women are openly more against the war, more ready to stop it at once, vaguer about it. One third of women adopt the view of the Government, as compared with over half the men."(Silvertown By-Election (Report from Mass-Observation), 28.2.40 TH, File 4/A.)

95. See Garry Tregidga, "Turning of the Tide? A Case Study of the Liberal Party in Provincial Britain in the Late 1930s," *History*, 307, July, 2007, pp. 347–366.

96. "Issue of 'Peace or War:' Appeal to Women of N. Cornwall," *The Western Morning News and Daily Gazette*, 8 July, 1939.

97. "A Clear Verdict," *Manchester Guardian*, 15 July, 1939.

98. Martin Pugh, "The Impact of Women's Enfranchisement in Britain," in Caroline Daley and Melanie Nolan (eds), *Suffrage and Beyond* (New York, 1994), p. 318.

99. Between 1918 and 1939, 31 women contested by-elections for the three main parties, a tactic especially favoured by Labour which provided 18 of them.

> The explanation for this is that for the parties rather less was at stake at a by-election than at a general election. The by-election was also a useful test of electors' reactions since it was tempting to focus attention upon the individual candidates, especially if they were women. That women polled very well on these occasions when placed under the limelight makes the parties' reservations about them seem irrational even in this period.
>
> Martin Pugh, *Women and the Women's Movement in Britain* (Basingstoke, 2000), p. 162.

100. The only pro-appeasement woman candidate was Dr Catherine Gavin standing in the South Ayrshire by-election.

101. Mrs Baldwin said the election would "go down to history as a women's election." "A Women's Election," Cornishman, 16 May, 1929.

102. Women's International League, Fourteenth Yearly Report, 1929, Catherine Marshall Papers, Cumbria Records Office, D/MAR/4/84.

103. *Daily Mirror*, 14 November, 1935. Quoted in Adrian Bingham, *Gender, Modernity and the Popular Press in Inter-war Britain* (Oxford, 2004), p. 207.

104. Krista Cowman, *Women in British Politics, c. 1689–1979* (Basingstoke, 2010), p. 170.

105. Pat Thane, "What Difference did the Vote Make? Women in Public and Private Life in Britain since 1918," *Historical Research*, 79(192), May, 2003, pp. 268–285.

106. "Women and War Horrors: Fascist Aggression," *Manchester Guardian*, 17 June, 1938.

107. "Mrs Corbett Ashby: Adoption as Candidate for Scarborough," *Manchester Guardian*, 1 December, 1938.

9   The Women Churchillians and the Politics of Shame

1. Edith Summerskill, *A Woman's World* (London, 1967), p. 60.

2. "Parliament," *The Times*, 6 October, 1938.

3. Quoted in Martin Gilbert, *Churchill: A Life* (London, 1991), p. 613.

4. Duff Cooper, *Old Men Forget*, (London, 1953), p. 241.

5. (ed.) George H. Gallup, *The Gallup International Public Opinion Polls: Great Britain 1937–1975, Vol. 1 1937–1964* (New York, 1976).

6. Richard Baxter, *Guilty Women* (London, 1941), p. 120.

7. Brian Harrison, "Women in a Men's House: The Women MPs, 1919–1945," *Historical Journal*, 29(3), September, 1986, pp. 632–654.

8. *Hansard*, HC Deb 24 August, 1939 vol. 351 cc48–52.

9. "Big Business and its Puppets: The Threat of Fascism," *Manchester Guardian*, 13 February, 1939.

10. Winston Churchill, *The Gathering Storm* (London, 1948), p. 268.

11. Ibid., p. 251.
12. Letter from Winston Churchill to Charley, Lord Londonderry, 18 November, 1938, CHAR 2/333.
13. It is interesting to note that the historical telefilm *The Gathering Storm* (2002), starring Albert Finney and Vanessa Redgrave, is all about the overlapping of private and political life. See also Mary Soames (ed.), *Speaking for Themselves: The Personal Letters of Winston and Clementine Churchill* (London, 1999).
14. *Manchester Guardian*, 25 February, 1939. Quoted in Neville Thompson, *The Anti-Appeasers: Conservative Opposition to Appeasement in the 1930s* (Oxford, 1971), p. 27.
15. See R.A.C. Parker, *Churchill and Appeasement* (Basingstoke, 2000).
16. Nicholas J. Crowson, *Facing Fascism: The Conservative Party and the European Dictators 1935–1940* (London, 1997), p. 82.
17. See Appendix in Crowson, *Facing Fascism*, pp. 205–209.
18. See Richard Carr, "Veterans of the First World War and Conservative Anti-Appeasement," *Twentieth Century British History*, 22(1), 2011, pp. 28–51. See also Richard Grayson, "Leo Amery's Imperialist Alternative to Appeasement in the 1930s," *Twentieth Century British History*, 17(4), 2006, pp. 489–515.
19. Richard Toye, *The Roar of the Lion: The Untold Story of Churchill's World War II Speeches* (Oxford, 2013), p. 26.
20. Quoted in Ibid., p. 30.
21. Susan Pedersen, *Eleanor Rathbone and the Politics of Conscience* (New Haven, 2004), p. 283.There are a number of biographies of Rathbone, focusing on various parts of her career, but Pedersen's is the most compelling and comprehensive. See also Laura Beers, "A Model MP? Ellen Wilkinson, Gender, Politics and Celebrity Culture in Interwar Britain," *Cultural and Social History*, 10(2), June, 2013, pp. 231–250; and Matt Perry, *'Red Ellen' Wilkinson: Her Ideas, Movements and World* (Manchester, 2014).
22. Lynne Olson, Troublesome *Young Men: The Churchill Conspiracy of 1940* (London, 2007).
23. Paul Addison, "Churchill and Women," Churchill Archive online, 2012.
24. Duff Copper, *Old Men Forget*, p. 251.
25. Randolph made these remarks in 1929 when he was accompanying his father on a trip to Canada. Quoted in Letter from Gertrude Lucas, Liverpool Women's Unionist Federation, to Lady Astor, 2 February, 1935, Lady Astor Papers, MS 1416/1/1/1435.
26. "Parliament," *The Times*, 4 October, 1938.
27. *Britain by Mass-Observation* (London, 1939), p. 42.
28. 10 April, 1939, Nigel Nicolson (ed.), *Harold Nicolson: Diaries and Letters 1930–1939* (London, 1966), p. 396.
29. Olson, *Troublesome Young Men*, p. 51.
30. See Simon Haxey, *Tory MP* (London, 1939).
31. Winston Churchill, "Women in War," *Strand Magazine*, February, 1938. His views here did not stand out as Neanderthal, and when in November 1941 Gallup asked 'Would you approve or disapprove if women were allowed to become fighting members of the forces?' 25% approved, 65% disapproved, and 10 % had no opinion. George H. Gallup (ed.), *The Gallup International Public Opinion Polls*, p. 50.
32. "Conservatives and the Next Election: Mr Churchill and the Leadership" *The Times*, 23 February, 1935.
33. "Men Only," *The Times*, 22 May, 1936.
34. Letter from WSC Churchill to Lord Cecil, 23 October, 1938 CHAR 2/322.

35. Charles Madge and Tom Harrisson, *Britain by Mass-Observation* (London, 1939), pp. 77–78.
36. "Re: Chamberlain, Bolton," 7/3/40, Worktown Collection, Churchill and Chamberlain, Mass-Observation Archive, University of Sussex, Box 50, W 50/A.
37. "Miss Sylvia Pankhurst at Whitby," *NTEN*, 15 October, 1938.
38. F.L. Lucas, "The Basest Day in British History," *NTEN*, 8 October, 1938.
39. VCB to Gilbert Murray, 4 April, 1933 in Mark Pottle (ed.), *Champion Redoubtable: The Diaries and Letters of Violet Bonham-Carter 1914–1945* (London, 1998), p. 181.
40. Quoted in Olson, *Troublesome Young Men*, p. 77.
41. The luncheon was attended by leading figures representing all points on the political compass: Winston Churchill, Randolph Churchill, Walter Citrine, Violet Bonham-Carter, Philip Guedalla, Norman Angell, Locker Lampson, Hugh Dalton, Julian Huxley, Victor Cofman, A.H. Richards, Margaret Bondfield, Lord Melchett, Wickham Steed, Dr F.W. Norwood, Duncan Sandys, George Lathan, I. Abrahams, and P. Horowitz.
42. Letter from WSC to Violet Bonham-Carter, 25 May, 1936, CHAR 2/282.
43. "Defence of Freedom and Peace," *The Times*, 24 November, 1936.
44. Geoffrey Mander, MP, *We Were Not All Wrong* (London, 1944), p. 97.
45. Letter from Violet [Bonham-Carter], 5 October, 1938, CHAR 2/332.
46. Pottle (ed.), *Champion Redoubtable*, p. 192. For the importance of religious imagery in the appeasement debate, see and P. Williamson, "Christian Conservatives and the Totalitarian Challenge, 1933–1940," *English History Review*, 115(462), 2000, pp. 607–642.
47. Pottle (ed.), *Champion Redoubtable*, p. 193.
48. Shame was also the operative word in Churchill's private correspondence, vividly illustrated by his letter to Lord Moyne after he understood that Chamberlain and Halifax had no intention to stand by the Czechs:

> Owing to the neglect of our defences and the mishandling of the German problem in the last five years, we seem to be very near the bleak choice between War and Shame. My feeling is that we shall choose Shame, and then have War thrown in a little later, on even more adverse terms than at present.
> (Quoted in Gilbert, *Churchill*, p. 595.)

49. "Asquith's Daughter Speaks Out," *Manchester Guardian*, 23 February, 1939.
50. VBC to Desmond McCarthy, Friday 8 September, 1939 in Pottle (ed.), *Champion Redoubtable*, pp. 204–205.
51. "To Societies represented on the Women's Advisory Council," 13 October, 1938, LNU- 5/73, League of Nations Union Papers, London School of Economics.
52. See "Message to Women of Czechoslovakia," LNU, 3 January, 1939, LNU-5/73.
53. 9 November, 1937, (ed.) Norman A. Rose, *Baffy: The Diaries of Blanche Dugdale 1936–1947* (London, 1973), p. 65.
54. 20 September, 1938, in Nicolson (ed.), *Harold Nicolson Diaries and Letters 1930–1939*, p. 362.
55. "These Women MPs—the Questions they Ask," *Daily Mirror*, 4 September, 1935.
56. "Churchill," *Time and Tide*, No. 48, 28 November, 1936.
57. George Orwell, Review of *Searchlight on Spain*, *New English Weekly*, 21 July, 1938, in Sonia Orwell and Ian Angus (eds.), *The Collected Essays, Journalism and Letters of George Orwell, Vol. 1 An Age Like This, 1920–1940* (Harmsworth, 1970), pp. 383–384.
58. Telegram from K. Atholl to WSC, 20 September, 1938, CHAR 2/331.

59. Letter from Mr Churchill to the Duchess of Atholl, Chartwell, 12 November, 1938, CHAR 2/333/41.
60. Pedersen, *Eleanor Rathbone and the Politics of Conscience*, p. 294.
61. "During the Second World War, Rathbone and Astor became alert champions of Churchill, that old anti-feminist bogey: 'my admiration for him is such, that I hate to differ from him on anything,' said Rathbone in August 1945, 'because I believe that he will go down in history as the man to whom not only this country, but the whole world, owes more than to any other British statesman who ever lived.'" Brian Harrison, "Women in a Men's House: The Women MPs, 1919–1945," *Historical Journal*, 29(3), September, 1986, pp. 632–654.
62. Letter from Winston Churchill to Eleanor Rathbone, 13 April, 1936, Eleanor Rathbone Papers, University of Liverpool, RP XIV.4.1–8.
63. Letter from E. Rathbone to Winston Churchill, September, 1938, RP XIV.4.1–8.
64. "A Reconstructed Government," *Manchester Guardian*, 30 June, 1939.
65. Pedersen, *Eleanor Rathbone and the Politics of Conscience*, pp. 292–293.
66. 321, HC Deb, 25 March, 1937, col.3136.
67. Harold Nicolson, "People and Things," *Spectator*, 20 January, 1939.
68. "Our 9 Women MPs are Good Champions of their Sex," *Daily Mirror*, 18 May, 1936.
69. "Session 1937," by Ellen Wilkinson, *Time and Tide*, 31 July, 1937.
70. "The European Crisis: Address by the Duchess of Atholl to the Women's Advisory Council, 8 April, 1938," 12.5.38, LNU-5/7.
71. "Our London Correspondence," *Manchester Guardian*, 19 September, 1938.
72. "Fund Given for Spain at Dinner to Duchess: Farewell for Atholl's Wife Aids Loyalist Relief," *New York Times*, 18 October, 1938.
73. See "Notes on Visit to Prague: 14–20 January, 1939," Eleanor Rathbone Papers, XIV.2.15(12). See also Susan Cohen, *Rescue the Perishing: Eleanor Rathbone and the Refugees* (London, 2010).
74. "Posters," 15 December, 1938, File 2/D Kinross By-election, M-O Archive.
75. Rhondda, "Courage: The Duchess of Atholl's Fight," *Time and Tide*, 10 December, 1938.
76. "We Need Churchill," *Time and Tide*, 6 May, 1939.
77. "Miss Eleanor Rathbone: A Common Front," *Manchester Guardian*, 25 February, 1939.
78. "Critics of the Government," *The Times*, 5 January, 1939.
79. "Duchess to Lead Ginger Group," *Daily Mirror*, 8 March, 1939.
80. Dan Stone, "The 'Mein Kampf Ramp:' Emily Overend Lorimer and Hitler Translations in Britain," *German History*, 26(4), 2008, pp. 504–519.
81. "Crisis Left Indelible Mark on Women's Organisations," *Western Morning News*, 28 December, 1938.
82. Eliza Riedi, "Imperialist Women and Conservative Activism in Early-Twentieth-Century Britain: the political world of Violet Milner," *Women's History Review*, 22(6), 2013, pp. 930–953.
83. "Episodes of the Month," *The National Review*, No. 669, November, 1938.
84. See Richard Toye, *Churchill's Empire* (Basingstoke, 2010), p. 149.
85. Quoted in A. Susan Williams, *Ladies of Influence* (London, 2000), p. 82.
86. Dorothy Thompson, *Let the Record Speak* (Boston, 1939), p. 3.
87. Shiela Grant Duff, *The Parting of Ways: A Personal Account of the Thirties* (London, 1982), p. 67.
88. Ibid., p. 211.

89. Letter from Adam Trott (Berlin) to Lady Astor, 5 March, 1939, Lady Nancy Astor Papers, Special Collections, University of Reading, MS 1416/1/1/1585.
90. Grant Duff, *The Parting of Ways*, p. 157.
91. Ibid., p. 160.
92. Ibid., p. 168.
93. Ibid., p. 188.
94. Ibid., p. 197.
95. Telegram from [Shiela?] Grant Duff to Duff Cooper, 1 October, 1938, Duff Cooper Papers, Churchill Archive Centre, Churchill College, Cambridge, DUFC 2/20.
96. Letter from Violet Bonham-Carter to Duff Cooper, 13 October, [1938], DUFC 2/15.
97. Sylvia Townsend Warner and Valentine Ackland, *Time and Tide*, 8 October, 1938.
98. Teresa Hooley, "1918–1938," *Time and Tide*, 12 November, 1938.
99. "The Defence of Freedom and Peace: An Address by the Rt. Hon. Winston S. Churchill to the People of the United States of America, broadcast 16 October, 1938, by the National Broadcasting Corporation, was published as a Supplement to *Headway*, November, 1938.
100. Letter to Rt. Hon. Winston Churchill from Amy M. Bewick, 27 September, 1938 CHAR 7/107/A/49-52.
101. Letter from Miss M.S. Gowers, PPU, to Winston Churchill, 27 September, 1938, CHAR 7/107/A/57.
102. Letter to the Rt. Hon. Winston Churchill from Miss M. Akhurst, 27 September, 1938, CHAR 7/107/A/46-48.
103. Letter from Mary Mugridge to WSC, 27 September, 1938, CHAR 7/107/A/59.
104. Letter to Rt. Hon. Winston Churchill, from Hettie Brazier, 28 September, 1938, CHAR 7/107/A/67-68.
105. Letter from Mrs E. Boyden to WSC, 2 October, 1938, CHAR 2/607 A-C.
106. Letter from Jessie C Robinson and Mabel E. Robinson to Winston Churchill, 22 September, 1938, CHAR 7/107/A/26.
107. Postcard from Mrs Constance A. Streeton to Winston Churchill, 3 October, 1938 CHAR 7/107 A/115.
108. Letter from Constance M. Reavey to WSC, 2 October, 1938, CHAR 2/607 A-C.
109. Letter from Marjorie Stephenson to WSC, 2 October, 1938, CHAR 2/607 A-C.
110. Letter from Dorothy Bolton to WSC, 2 October 1938, CHAR 2/607 A-C.
111. Letter from Mrs Winifred Spitzer to WSC, [n.d] CHAR 2/607 A-C.
112. Letter from Dorothy H. Womersly, 2 October, 1938, CHAR 2/607 A-C.
113. Letter from Mrs E. Marshall to WSC, 2 October, 1938, CHAR 2/607 A-C.
114. Letter from Daisy M. Drewitt, 2 October, 1938, CHAR 2/607 A-C.
115. Letter from Beatrice Macdonald (Australia and New Zealand) to WSC, 2 October, 1938, CHAR 2/607 A-C.
116. Letter from Mrs Margaret Aldous to WSC, 2 October, 1938, CHAR 2/607 A-C.
117. Letter from Yvonne Moyse, London WC1, to Duff Cooper, 3 October, 1938,DUFC 2/28.
118. Letter from Mrs R.L. Cocks, Bridport, Dorset, to Duff Cooper, Saturday 1 October, 1938, DUFC 2/28.
119. Letter from Georgina Aitken, Glasgow, to Duff Cooper, 2 October 1938, DUFC 2/28.
120. Letter from Gladys V. Wood, Staffs, to Duff Cooper, 4 October, 1938, DUFC 2/28.
121. Leo S. Amery, *My Political Life, Vol. 3: The Unforgiving Years 1929–1940* (London, 1955), p. 284.

122. See David Faber, *Speaking for England: Leo, Julian and John Amery—The Tragedy of a Political Family* (London, 2007).
123. Letter from A.D.S. Large et. al [nine women signed], 78 Chandos House, Palmer Street, London SWI, to Leo Amery, 7 October, 1938, Leo Amery Papers, Churchill Archive Centre, Churchill College, Cambridge, AMEL 1/5/55.
124. "Anglo-Italian Agreement Debate," *Manchester Guardian*, 3 November, 1938.
125. "Women's Suffrage Comes of Age," *Manchester Guardian*, 18 March, 1939.
126. Robert Gilbert Vansittart, *Lessons of My Life* (London, 1943), p. 9.
127. Dorothy L. Sayers, *Being Here* (London, 1940), p. 15.
128. See Julie V. Gottlieb, "Introduction: 'Flour Power' and Feminism Between the Waves," *Women's History Review*, 23(3), June, 2014, pp. 325–329.
129. "The Rights of Man," *Evening Telegraph*, 8 April, 1939.
130. Saturday 17 September, 1938 in Nicholas J. Crowson (ed.), *Fleet Street, Press Barons and Politics: The Journals of Collin Brooks, 1932–1940* (London, 1998), p. 217.
131. 8 October, 1938, Nigel Nicolson (ed.), *Harold Nicolson* (London, 1966), p. 376. He remained cynical about women's political influence. While in March 1939, before Hitler marched into Prague, he met his constituency's chair wish that he would give public endorsement to the government's present policy, in a letter to his wife he "revealed that he had few illusions about why the 'ladies of Leicester' needed such a statement. They were worried about the world situation and eager to trust in Chamberlain who 'had rendered cowardice and treachery respectable.'" John W. Young, "Harold Nicolson and Appeasement," in Malcolm Murfett (ed.), *Shaping British Foreign and Defence Policy in the Twentieth Century* (Basingstoke, 2014), pp. 136–158.
132. Baxter, *Guilty Women*, p. 119.
133. Ibid., pp. 122–123.

Bibliography

Archives and collections

Papers of individuals

Leo Amery Papers, Churchill Archive Centre, Churchill College, University of Cambridge.
Nancy Astor Papers, Special Collections, University of Reading.
Don Bateman Collection, University of Bristol Library.
Teresa Billington Greig Papers, Women's Library, LSE.
Vera Brittain Papers, Mills Memorial Library, McMaster University.
Neville Chamberlain Papers, Cadbury Research Centre, University of Birmingham.
Winston Churchill Papers, Churchill Archive Centre, Churchill College, University of Cambridge.
Duff Cooper Papers, Churchill Archive Centre, Churchill College, University of Cambridge.
Margery Corbett Ashby Papers, Women's Library, LSE.
Kathleen Courtney Papers, Women's Library, LSE.
Winifred Holtby Papers, Hull History Centre.
Catherine Marshall Papers, Cumbria Record Office.
Hannah Maria Mitchell, Manchester Central Library.
Eleanor Rathbone Papers, Liverpool University Library.
Maude Royden Papers, Women's Library, LSE.
Mary Sheepshanks Papers, Women's Library, LSE.
Archibald Henry Macdonald Sinclair Papers, Churchill Archive Centre, Churchill College, University of Cambridge.
Virginia Woolf Papers, University of Sussex.

Papers of organizations

British Union Collection, Special Collections, University of Sheffield Library.
Communist Party of Great Britain Papers, Labour History Archive and Study Centre, Manchester.
Conservative Party Archive, Bodleian Library, Oxford.
Equal Rights International Papers, Women's Library, LSE.
International Women's Suffrage Alliance Papers, John Rylands Library, University of Manchester.
League of Nations Union Papers, British Library of Political and Economic Sciences, LSE.
Labour Party Papers, Labour History Archive and Study Centre, Manchester.
Liberal Party Collection, University of Bristol Library.
Mass-Observation Archive, University of Sussex.
National Council of Women, Manchester and Salford Branch, Manchester Central Library.
National Joint Committee of Working Women's Organisations, Labour Party Archive and Study Centre, Manchester.
Open Door Council, Women's Library, LSE.
Open Door International, Women's Library, LSE.

313

Penguin Books Archive, University of Bristol Library.
Security Service Files, KV2, National Archives, Kew.
Six Point Group Papers, Women's Library, LSE.
Standing Joint Committee of Industrial Women's Organisations, Labour History Archive and Study Centre, Manchester.
Women of the Labour and Socialist International, Labour History Archive and Study Centre, Manchester.
Women's International League of Peace and Freedom—WIL British Section—Papers, British Library of Political and Economic Sciences, LSE.

Reference works

Hansard
Oxford Dictionary of National Biography

Newspapers and newspaper collections

Action
The Blackshirt
British Cartoon Archive, University of Kent (online).
British Library British Newspapers Archive (online).
British Universities Film and Video Council (online)
Daily Mail
Daily Mirror
Illustrated London News
Jewish Chronicle
Liberal Women's News
Labour Woman
Manchester Guardian
The National Review
New Leader
New Times and Ethiopian News
New York Times
Picture Post
Spectator
Time and Tide
The Times

Unpublished PhDs

Steinhaus, Kathryn, "Valkyrie: Gender, Class, European Relations, & Unity Mitford's Passion for Fascism," PhD, McGill University, 2012.
Van Seters, Deborah E., "Women's Foreign Policy Advocacy in 1930s Britain," PhD, University of Toronto, 1999.

Printed primary sources

Addams, Jane, Balch, Emily, and Hamilton, Alice, *Women at The Hague: The International Congress of Women and Its Results*. Urbana: University of Illinois Press, 2003.
Allen, Mary S., *Lady in Blue*. London: Stanley Paul, 1936.
Allen, Mary S. and Heynemann, Julie, *Woman at the Cross Roads*. London: Unicorn, 1934.

Allport, Floyd H., "Towards a Science of Public Opinion," *Public Opinion Quarterly*, Vol. 1, No. 1 (Jan., 1937), pp. 7–23.

Amery, L.S., *My Political Life, Vol. 3: The Unforgiving Years 1929–1940*. London: Hutchinson, 1955.

Atholl, Duchess of, *Searchlight on Spain*. Harmsworth: Penguin, 1938.

Atholl, Katherine, Crowdy, Rachel, Rathbone, Eleanor, and Wilkinson, Ellen, *Report on Our Visit to Spain* (April, 1937).

Authors Take Sides on the Spanish War. Left Review, 1937.

Baker, Philip Noel (eds.), *Challenge to Death*. London: Constable, 1934.

Ball, Stuart (ed.), *Parliament and Politics in the Age of Churchill and Attlee: The Headlam Diaries, 1935–1951*. Cambridge: CUP, 1999.

Barsely, Michael, *Grabberwocky and Other Flights of Fancy*. London: John Murray, 1939.

Baxter, Richard, *Guilty Women*. London: Quality Press, 1941.

——, *Hitler's Darkest Secret: What He Has in Store for Britain*. London: Quality Press, 1941.

——, *Women of the Gestapo*. London: Quality Press, 1943.

Beattie, Allan, Dilks, David and Pronay, Nicholas, "Neville Chamberlain," British Inter-University History Film Consortium, Archive Series 1, 1975.

Bell, Anne Olivier (ed.), *The Diary of Virginia Woolf, Vol. Five, 1936–1941*. San Diego: Harcourt Brace Jovanich, 1984.

Birmingham, George, *Appeasement: A Novel*. London: Methuen, 1939.

Boothby, Robert, *Recollections of a Rebel*. London: Hutchinson, 1978.

Bosch, Mineke (ed.), *Politics and Friendship: Letters from the International Woman Suffrage Alliance, 1902–1942*. Columbus: Ohio UP, 1990.

British Institute of Public Opinion, "Public Opinion Survey," *Public Opinion Quarterly*, Vol. 4, No. 1 (Mar. 1940), pp. 75–82.

Brittain, Vera, *Diary of the Thirties 1932–1939: Chronicle of Friendship*. London: Victor Gollancz, 1986.

——, *Testament of Experience: An Autobiographical Story of the Years 1925–1950*. London: Victor Gollancz, 1957.

Brittain, Vera and Handley-Taylor, Geoffrey (eds.), *Selected Letters of Winifred Holtby and Vera Brittain (1920–1935)*. London: A Brown & Sons, 1960.

Brooks, Robert C., *Deliver Us From Dictators!* Philadelphia: University of Philadelphia Press, 1935.

Burdekin, Katherine, *Swastika Night*. London: Victor Gollancz, 1940.

Carr, E.H., "Public Opinion as a Safeguard of Peace," *International Affairs*, Vol. 15, No. 6 (Nov.–Dec., 1936), pp. 846–862.

Castle, Barbara, *Fighting All the Way*. London: Macmillan, 1993.

"Cato," *Guilty Men*. New York: Frederick A. Stokes, 1940.

Cazalet-Keir, Thelma, *From the Wings*. London, The Bodley Head, 1967.

Chamberlain, Neville, *In Search of Peace: Speeches, 1937–1938*. London: Hutchinson, 1939.

Churchill, Winston, *The Second World War: The Gathering Storm*. London: Cassell, 1948.

Cockburn, Patricia, *The Years of the Week*. Harmsworth: Penguin, 1968.

Cooper, Diana, *The Light of Common Day*. Harmsworth: Penguin, 1959.

Cooper, Duff, *Old Men Forget*. London: Rupert Harris-Davis, 1953.

Cowles, Virginia, *Looking for Trouble*. London: Hamish Hamilton, 1941.

Crowson, N.J. (ed.), *Fleet Street, Press Barons and Politics: The Journals of Collin Brooks, 1931–1940*. London: RHS, 1998.

Currey, Muriel, *A Woman at the Abyssinian War*. London: Hutchinson, 1936.

Dodd, Martha, *My Years in Germany*. London: Victor Gollancz, 1939.

Eden, Anthony, *The Eden Memoirs: Facing the Dictators*. London: Cassell, 1962.

Fascist War on Women: Facts from Italian Goals. [pamphlet] London: Martin Lawrence, 1934.

Forster, E.M., *Two Cheers for Democracy*. London: Edward Arnold, 1951.

Gallup, George H. (ed.), *The Gallup International Public Opinion Polls: Great Britain 1937–1975, Vol. 1 1937–1964*. New York: Random House, 1976.

Gibbs, Philip, *This Nettle, Danger*. London: Hutchinson Universal Book Club, 1939.

Gilbert, Martin, *Winston S. Churchill, Vol. V Companion Pt. 3, Documents: The Coming of War 1936–1939*. London: Heineman, 1982.

Grant Duff, Shiela, *Europe and the Czechs*. Harmsworth: Penguin, 1938.

———, *The Parting of Ways: A Personal Account of the Thirties*. London: Peter Owen, 1982.

Graves, Robert, and Hodge, Alan, *The Long Weekend: The Living Story of the Twenties and Thirties*. London: Faber & Faber, 1940.

Hadley, W.W., *Munich Before and After*. London: Cassell, 1944.

Halifax, the Earl of, *Fullness of Days*. London: Collins, 1957.

Hamilton, Cicely, *Modern England and Seen by an Englishwoman*. London: J.M. Dent, 1938.

Hamilton, Mary Agnes, *Remembering My Good Friends*. London: Jonathan Cape, 1944.

Harrisson, Tom, "What is Public Opinion?" *The Political Quarterly*, Vol. 11, No. 4 (Oct., 1940), pp. 368–383.

Haxey, Simon, *Tory MP*. London: Victor Gollancz, 1939.

Henderson, Nevile, *Failure of a Mission: Berlin 1937–1939*. London: Hodder and Stoughton, 1940.

Hellman, Lilian, *The Searching Wind*. New York: Viking, 1944.

Hodgson, Vera, *Few Eggs and No Oranges: A Diary showing how Unimportant People in London and Birmingham Lived through the War Years*. London: Persephone, 1976.

Holtby, Winifred, *Take Back Your Freedom*. London: Jonathan Cape, 1939.

———, *Woman and a Changing Civilization*. London: John Lane the Bodley Head, 1934.

"How Peace was Saved: The Story of the Great Crisis." Essex: Anchor Press, Oct., 1938.

James, Robert Rhodes (ed.), *"Chips": The Diaries of Sir Henry Channon*. London: Phoenix, 1999.

Jones, Elwyn, *The Attack from Within*. Harmsworth: Penguin, 1939.

Kamester M. and Vellacott, J. (eds), *Militarism Versus Feminism: Writing on Women and War*. London: Virago, 1987.

Keir, Thelma Cazalet, *From the Wings*. London: The Bodley Head, 1967.

King, Anthony (ed.), *British Political Opinion: 1937–2000, The Gallup Polls*. London: Politico's, 2001.

Landau, Rom, *Love for a Country: Contemplations and Conversations*. London: Nicolson & Watson, 1939.

Londonderry, the Marchioness of, *Retrospect*. London: Frederic Muller, 1938.

Londonderry, Marquess of, *Ourselves and Germany*. Harmsworth: Penguin, 1939.

Lorimer, E.O., *What Germany Needs*. London: George Allen & Unwin, 1942.

———, *What Hitler Wants*. Harmsworth: Penguin, 1939.

Macaulay, Rose, *Non Combatants and Others*. London: Hodder & Stoughton, 1916.

Madge, Charles and Harrisson, Tom, *Britain by Mass-Observation*. Harmsworth: Penguin, 1939.

Malcolmson, Robert (ed.), *Love & War in London: The Mass Observation Diary of Olivia Cockett*. London: History Press, 2009.

Mander, Geoffrey, *We Were Not All Wrong*. London: Gollancz, 1944.

Mannin, Ethel, *Women and the Revolution*. London: Secker & Warburg, 1939.

———, *Young in the Twenties*. London: Hutchinson, 1971.

Martel, Gordon (ed.), *The Times and Appeasement: The Journals of A.L. Kennedy 1932–1939*. Cambridge: Cambridge University Press, 2000.

Mitchison, Naomi, *Home and a Changing Civilization*. London: John Lane the Bodley Head, 1934.

Muggeridge, Malcolm, *The Thirties*. London: Hamish Hamilton, 1940.

Neumann, Sigmund, "Europe before and after Munich: Random Notes on Recent Publications," *Review of Politics*, Vol. 1, No. 2 (Mar., 1939), pp. 212–228.

Newitt, Hilary, *Women Must Choose: The Position of Women in Europe To-day*. London: Victor Gollancz, 1937.

Nichols, Beverly, *News of England/or A Country Without a Hero*. London: Jonathan Cape, 1938.

Nicolson, Harold, "Modern Diplomacy and British Public Opinion," *International Affairs*, Vol. 14, No. 5 (Sept.–Oct. 1935), pp. 599–618.

———, *Why Britain is at War*. Harmsworth: Penguin, 1939.

Nicolson, Nigel (ed.), *Harold Nicolson: Diaries and Letters 1930–1939*. London: Collins, 1966.

Norwich, John Julius (ed.), *The Duff Cooper Diaries*. London: Orion, 2005.

Orwell, Sonia, and Angus, Ian (eds.), *The Collected Essays, Journalism and Letters of George Orwell, Vol. 1 An Age Like This, 1920–1940*. Hamondsworth: Penguin 1970.

Pethick Lawrence, Emmeline, *My Part in a Changing World*. London: Victor Gollancz, 1938.

Pollack, James K., "British By-Elections Between the Wars," *American Political Science Review*, Vol. 35, No. 3 (Jun., 1941), pp. 519–528.

Pottle, Mark (ed.), *Champion Redoubtable: The Diaries and Letters of Violet Bonham Carter 1914–1945*. London: Weidenfeld & Nicholson, 1998.

Rathbone, Eleanor, *War Can Be Averted: The Achievability of Collective Security*. London: Victor Gollancz, 1938.

Rose, N.A (ed.), *Baffy: The Diaries of Blanche Dugdale 1936–1947*. London: Valetine Mitchell, 1973.

Sayers, Dorothy L., *Being There*. London: Victor Gollancz, 1940.

Self, Robert (ed.), *The Neville Chamberlain Diary Letters: Volume 4: The Downing Street Years, 1934–1940*. Aldershot: Ashgate, 2005.

Sheridan, Dorothy (ed.), *Among you Taking Notes … The Wartime Diary of Naomi Mitchison 1939–1945*. London: Phoenix, 2000.

———, *Wartime Women: A Mass-Observation Anthology*. London: Phoenix, 2000.

Sidelights on the Cliveden Set: Hitler's Friends in Britain. London: Marston [Communist Party of Great Britain], 29/3/38.

Soames, Mary (ed.), *Speaking for Themselves: The Personal Letters of Winston and Clementine Churchill*. London: Black Swan, 1999.

Sparks, John Cunningham, "British By-Elections: What Do They Prove?" *American Political Science Review*, Vol. 34, No. 1 (Feb., 1940), pp. 97–104.

Strachey, Ray (ed.), *Our Freedom and Its Results*. London: Hogarth, 1936.

Struther, Jan, "The Truth About Mrs Miniver," *English*, (1939) 2 (12), pp. 347–355.

Summerskill, Edith, *A Woman's World: Her Memoirs*. London: Heinemann, 1967.

Swanwick, H.M, *Collective Insecurity*. London: Jonathan Cape, 1937.

————, *The Roots of Peace: A Sequel to Collective Insecurity*. London: Jonathan Cape, 1938.

Tabouis, Geneviev, *Blackmail or War*. Harmsworth: Penguin, 1938.

Thompson, Dorothy, *Let the Record Speak*. Boston: Houghton Mifflin, 1939.

Vansittart, Robert Gilbert, *Lessons of My Life*. London: Hutchinson, 1943.

Wagner, M. Seaton, *Germany in my Time*. London: Rich & Cowman, 1935.

Wearing, J.P. (ed.), *Bernard Shaw and Nancy Astor*. Toronto: U of Toronto Press, 2005.

Wilkinson, Ellen & Conze, Edward, *Why Fascism*. London: Selwyn and Blount, 1934.

Williamson, Philip, and Baldwin, Edward (eds.), *Baldwin Papers: A Conservative Statesmen 1908–1947*. Cambridge: Cambridge University Press, 2004.

Wiskemann, Elizabeth, "Czechs and Germans After Munich," *Foreign Affairs* (Jan., 1939).

————, *Czechs and Germans*. London: Oxford University Press, 1938.

————, *The Europe I Saw*. London: Collins, 1968.

————, *Undeclared War*. London: Constable, 1939.

Woolf, Virginia, *A Room of One's Own*. London: Hogarth, 1929.

————, *Three Guineas*. London: Hogarth, 1938.

Secondary sources (books)

Adams, R. J. Q., *British Politics and Foreign Policy in the Age of Appeasement, 1935–39*. Stanford: Stanford U.P., 1993.

Andrews, Maggie, *Domesticating the Airwaves: Broadcasting, Domesticity and Femininity*. London: Continuum, 2012.

Ball, Stuart, *Portrait of a Party: The Conservative Party in Britain 1918–1945*. Oxford: OUP, 2013.

Bartley, Paula, *Ellen Wilkinson from Red Suffragist to Government Minister*. London: Pluto, 2014.

Beddoe, Deirdre, *Back to Home and Duty: Women between the Wars 1918–1939*. London: Pandora, 1989.

Bingham, Adrian, *Gender, Modernity and the Popular Press in Inter-war Britain*. Oxford: Clarendon Press, 2004.

Bolt, Christine, *Sisterhood Questioned? Race, Class and Internationalism in the American and British Women's Movements, c. 1880s–1970s*. London: Routledge, 2004.

Bourke, Joanna, *Dismembering the Male: Men's Bodies, Britain and the Great War*. London: Reaktion, 1996.

Bullock, Ian, and Pankhurst, Richard (eds.), *Sylvia Pankhurst: From Artist to Anti-Fascist*. London: Macmillan, 1992.

Burton, Antoinette, *Burdens of History: British Feminists, Indian Women and Imperial Culture, 1865–1915*. University of North Carolina Press, 1994.

Bussey, Gertrude, and Tims, Margaret, *Pioneers for Peace: WILPF 1915–1965*. London: George Allen, 1980.

Campbell, Beatrix, *The Iron Ladies: Why Do Women Vote Tory?* London: Virago, 1987.

Caute, David, *Fellow Travellers: Intellectual Friends of Communism*. London: Weidenfeld & Nicolson 1973.

Ceadel, Martin, *Semi-detached Idealists: The British Peace Movement and International Relations, 1854–1945*. Oxford: Oxford University Press, 2000.

Charmley, John, *Chamberlain and the Lost Peace*. London: PaperMac, 1991.

Cockett, Richard, *Twilight of Truth: Chamberlain, Appeasement & the Manipulation of the Press*. London: Weidenfeld & Nicolson, 1989.

Cohen, S., *Rescue the Perishing: Eleanor Rathbone and the Refugees*. London: Valetine Mitchell, 2010.

Cook, Chris, and Ramsden, John (eds.), *By-Elections in British Politics*. London: UCL Press, 1997.

Copsey, Nigel, *Anti-Fascism in Britain*. Basingstoke: Macmillan, 2000.

Cortright, David, *Peace: A History of Movements and Ideas*. Cambridge: Cambridge University Press, 2008.

Cowman, Krista, *Women in British Politics, c. 1689–1979*. Basingstoke: Palgrave, 2010.

Crowson, N.J., *Facing Fascism: The Conservative Party and the European Dictators, 1935–1940*. London: Routledge, 1997.

Daley, C. and Nolan M. (eds.), *Suffrage and Beyond*. New York: New York U.P., 1994.

DeCourcy, Anne, *1939: The Last Season*. London: Phoenix, 1989.

———, *Society's Queen: The Life of Edith, Marchioness of Londonderry*. London: Phoneix, 2004.

Douglas, R.M., *Feminist Freikorps: The British Voluntary Women Police, 1914–1940*. Westport CT: Praeger, 1999.

Dudink, Stefan, Karen Hagemann and John Tosh (eds.) *Masculinities in Politics and War*. Manchester: Manchester UP, 2004.

Eley, Geoff, *Forging Democracy: The History of the Left in Europe, 1850–2000*. Oxford: Oxford University Press, 2002.

Enloe, Cynthia, *Bananas, Beaches and Bases: Making Feminist Sense of International Politics*. Berkeley: University of California Press, 1990.

Everest-Phillips, Max, *Neville Chamberlain and the Art of Appeasement*. London: i2f Publishing, 2013.

Faber, David, *Speaking for England: Leo, Julian and John Amery—The Tragedy of a Political Family*. London: Pocket Books, 2007.

———, *Munich: The 1938 Appeasement Crisis*. London: Pocket Books, 2008.

Farr, Barbara Storm, The *Development and Impact of Right-Wing Politics in Britain, 1903–1932*. New York: Garland, 1987.

Fleming, N.C., *The Marquess of Londonderry: Aristocracy, Power and Politics in Britain and Ireland*. London: I.B. Tauris, 2005.

Fort, Adrian, *Nancy: The Story of Lady Astor*. London: Jonathan Cape, 2012.

Fussell, Paul, *Abroad: Literary Travelling between the Wars*. New York: Oxford University Press, 1980.

Gannon, Franklin Reid, *The British Press and Germany 1936–1939*. Oxford: Clarendon, 1971.

Gardiner, Juliet, *The Thirties: An Intimate History*. London: Harper, 2011.

George, Margaret, *The Hollow Men: An Examination of British Foreign Policy Between the Years 1933 and 1939*. London: Leslie Frewin, 1967.

Gilbert, Martin, *Churchill: A Life*. London: Heinemann, 1991.

Gilbert, M., and Gott, R., *The Appeasers*. London: Weidenfeld & Nicolson, 1963.

Gorham, Deborah, *Vera Brittain: A Feminist Life*. London: Blackwell, 1996.

Gottlieb, Julie V., *Feminine Fascism: Women in Britain's Fascist Movement, 1923–1945*. London: I.B. Tauris, 2000.

Gottlieb, Julie V. and Toye, Richard (eds.), *The Aftermath of Suffrage: Women, Gender, and Politics in Britain, 1918–1945*. Basingstoke: Palgrave, 2013.

Graves, Pamela M., *Labour Women: Women in British Working-class Politics, 1918–1939*. Cambridge: Cambridge University Press, 1994.

Grayzel, Susan, *At Home and Under Fire: Air Raids and Culture in Britain from the Great War to the Blitz*. Cambridge: Cambridge University Press, 2012.

Griffiths, Richard, *Fellow Travellers of the Right: British Enthusiasts for Nazi Germany, 1933–39*. London: Constable, 1980.

———, *Patriotism Perverted: Captain Ramsay, the Right Club and British Anti-Semitism 1939–40*. London: Constable, 1998.

Gullace, Nicoletta, *"The Blood of Our Sons": Men, Women, and the Regeneration of British Citizenship During the Great War*. Basingstoke: Palgrave, 2002.

Harrison, Brian, *Prudent Revolutionaries: Portraits of British Feminists between the wars*. Oxford: Clarendon, 1987.

Harrison, Shirley, *Sylvia Pankhurst: A Crusading Life, 1882–1960*. London: Arum Press, 2003.

Haslam, Beryl, *From Suffrage to Internationalism: The Political Evolution of Three British Feminists, 1908–1939*. New York: American University Studies, 1999.

Hendley, Matthew, *Organised Patriotism and the Crucible of War: Popular Imperialism in Britain, 1914–1932*. Montreal: McGill Queens University Press, 2012.

Hetherington, S.J., *Katherine Atholl (1874–1960): Against the Tide*. Aberdeen: Aberdeen University Press, 1989.

Hinton, James, *Nine Wartime Lives: Mass Observation and the Making of the Modern Self*. Oxford: OUP, 2010.

———, *The Mass-Observers: A History, 1937–1949*. Oxford: OUP, 2013.

Hollis, Maurice, *Nancy Astor*. London: Faber & Faber, 1960.

Holman, Brett, *The Next War in the Air: Britain's Fear of the Bomber, 1908–1941*. Farnham: Ashgate, 2014.

Hucker, Daniel, *Public Opinion and the End of Appeasement*. Farnham: Ashgate, 2011.

Izzard, Molly, *A Heroine in Her Time: A Life of Dame Helen Gwynne-Vaughan 1879–1967*. London: Macmillan, 1969.

Joannou, Maroula, *"Ladies, Please Don't Smash These Windows": Women's Writing, Feminist Consciousness and Social Change 1918–38*. Oxford: Berg, 1995.

Jones, Helen, *Women in British Public Life, 1914–1950*. London: Longman, 2000.

Kent, S. Kingsley, *Aftershocks: Politics and Trauma in Britain, 1918–1931*. Basingstoke: Palgrave, 2009.

———, *Making Peace: The Reconstruction of Gender in Interwar Britain*. Princeton: Princeton University Press, 1993.

Kershaw, Ian, *Making Friends with Hitler: Lord Londonderry, the Nazis and the Road to War*. New York: Penguin, 2004.

Koonz, Claudia, *Mothers of the Fatherland: Women, the Family and Nazi Politics*. New York: St. Martin's Press, 1987.

Kuhlman, Erika, *Reconstructing Patriarchy after the Great War: Women, Gender, and Postwar Reconciliation between Nations*. New York: Palgrave Macmillan, 2008.

Kushner, Tony, *The Persistence of Prejudice: Antisemitism in British Society During the Second World War*. Manchester: Manchester University Press, 1989.

———, *We Europeans? Mass-Observation, "Race" and British Identity in the Twentieth Century*. Farnham: Ashgate, 2005.

Lassner, Phyllis, *British Women Writers of World War II: Battlegrounds of Their Own*. New York: St. Martin's Press, 1998.

Laqua, Daniel (ed.), *Internationalism Reconfigured: Transnational Ideas and Movements Between the Wars*. London: I.B. Tauris, 2011.

Lewis, Jeremy, *Penguin Special: The Life and Times of Allen Lane*. London: Penguin, 2006.

Liddington, Jill, *The Long Road to Greenham Common: Feminism and Anti-Militarism in Britain since 1820*. Syracuse: Syracuse University Press, 1989.

Light, Alison, *Forever England: Femininity, Literature and Conservatism between the Wars*. London: Routledge, 1991.

Lynch, Cecelia, *Beyond Appeasement: Interpreting Interwar Peace Movements in World Politics*. Ithaca: Cornell University Press, 1999.

Maguire, G.E., *Conservative Women: A History of Women in the Conservative Party, 1874–1997*. Basingstoke: Palgrave, 1998.

Mandler, Peter, *The English National Character: The History of an Idea from Edmund Burke to Tony Blair*. New Haven: Yale University Press, 2006.

Marsh, Peter T., *The Chamberlain Litany: Letters within a Government Family from Empire to Appeasement*. London: Haus, 2010.

McCarthy, Helen, *The British People and the League of Nations: Democracy, Citizenship and Internationalism, c. 1918–45*. Manchester: MUP, 2011.

——, *Women of the World: The Rise of the Female Diplomat*. London: Bloomsbury, 2014.

McCrillis, Neal R., *The British Conservative Party in the Age of Universal Suffrage: Popular Conservatism, 1918–1929*. Columbus: Ohio University Press, 1998.

Millward, Liz, *Women in British Imperial Airspace, 1922–1937*. Montreal and Kingston: McGill Queen's University Press, 2008.

Morgan, Kevin, *Against Fascism and War: Ruptures and Continuities in British Communist Politics, 1935–41*. Manchester: Manchester University Press, 1989.

Noakes, Lucy, *War and the British: Gender and National Identity, 1939–91*. London: I.B. Tauris, 1998.

Oldfield, Sybil, *Women Against the Iron Fist: Alternatives to Militarism 1900–1989*. Oxford: Basil Blackwell, 1989.

Olson, Lynne, *Troublesome Young Men: The Churchill Conspiracy of 1940*. London: Bloomsbury, 2007.

Overy, Richard, *The Morbid Age: Britain and the Crisis of Civilization, 1919–1939*. London: Penguin, 2010.

Parker, R.A.C., *Churchill and Appeasement*. Basingstoke: Macmillan, 2000.

Passerini, Luisa, *Europe in Love/Love in Europe: Imagination and Politics in Britain Between the Wars*. London: I.B. Tauris, 1999.

Pedersen, Susan, *Eleanor Rathbone and the Politics of Conscience*. New Haven: Yale University Press, 2004.

Pennybacker, Susan, *From Scottsboro to Munich: Race and Political Culture in 1930s Britain*. Princeton: Princeton University Press, 2009.

Pryce-Jones, David, *Unity Mitford: A Quest*. London: Weidenfeld & Nicolson, 1976.

Pugh, Martin, *"Hurrah for the Blackshirts!" Fascists and Fascism in Britain between the Wars*. London: Jonathan Cape, 2005.

——, *The Tories and the People 1880–1935*. Oxford: Basil Blackwell, 1985.

——, *Women and the Women's Movement, 1914–1999*, 2nd Edition. Basingstoke: Macmillan, 2000.

Purvis, June (ed.), *Women's History: Britain, 1850–1945*. London: UCL Press, 1997.

Reynolds, David, *Summits: Six Meetings that Shaped the Twentieth Century*. London: Basic Books, 2007.

Richards, Jeffrey, *The Age of the Dream Palace: Cinema and Society in 1930s Britain*. London: I.B. Tauris, 2010.

Robbins, Keith, *Appeasement*, 2nd Edition. Oxford: Blackwell, 2001.

Roberts, Andrew, *The Holy Fox': The Life of Lord Halifax*. London: Phoenix, 1997.

Rose, Norman, *The Cliveden Set: Portrait of an Exclusive Fraternity*. London: Pimlico, 2001.

Rose, Sonya, *Which People's War? National Identity and Citizenship in Wartime Britain 1939–1945*. Oxford: OUP, 2003.

Rupp, Leila J., *Worlds of Women: The Making of the International Women's Movement*. Princeton: Princeton University Press, 1997.

Schweizer, Bernard, *Radicals on the Road: The Politics of English Travel Writing in the 1930s*. Virginia: UP of Virginia, 2001.

Self, Robert, *Neville Chamberlain: A Biography*. Aldershot: Ashgate, 2006.

Simpson, A.W. Brian, *In the Highest Degree Odious: Detention without Trial in Wartime Britain*. Oxford: Clarendon Press, 1994.

Sinha, Mrinalini, Donna Guy and Angela Woollacott (eds.), *Feminism and Internationalism*. Oxford: Blackwell, 1999.

Sluga, Glenda, *Internationalism in the Age of Nationalism*. Philadelphia: University of Pennsylvania Press, 2013.

Smart, Nick, *Neville Chamberlain*. London: Routledge, 2010.

Spender, Dale, *Time and Tide Wait for No Man*. London: Pandora, 1984.

Stone, Dan, *Responses to Nazism in Britain, 1933–1939*. Basingstoke: Palgrave, 2003.

Strobl, Gerwin, *The Germanic Isle: Nazi Perceptions of Britain*. Cambridge: Cambridge University Press, 2000.

Summerfield, Penny, *Reconstructing Women's Wartime Lives: Discourse and Subjectivity in Oral Histories of the Second World War*. Manchester: MUP, 1998.

———, *Women Workers in the Second World War: Production and Patriarchy in Conflict*. London: Routledge, 1984.

Taylor, A.J.P., *The Origins of the Second World War*. London: Hamish Hamilton, 1961.

Thompson, Neville, *The Anti-Appeasers: Conservative Opposition to Appeasement in the 1930s*. Oxford: Clarendon Press, 1971.

Thorpe, Andrew, *The British Communist Party and Moscow*. Manchester: Manchester University Press, 2000.

Tickner J. Ann and Sjoberg, Laura (eds.), *Feminism and International Relations: Conversations About Past, Present and Future*. New York: Routledge, 2011.

Toye, Richard, *Churchill's Empire*. Basingstoke: Macmillan, 2010.

———, *The Roar of the Lion: The Untold Story of Churchill's World War II Speeches*. Oxford: Oxford University Press, 2013.

Vellacott, Jo, *From Liberal to Labour with Women's Suffrage: The Story of Catherine Marshall*. Montreal: McGill-Queen's Press, 1993.

Wentworth Day, J., *Lady Houston DBE: The Woman Who Won the War*. London: Allan Wingate, 1958.

Williams, A. Susan, *Ladies of Influence: Women of the Elite in Interwar Britain*. London: Penguin, 2000.

Wilson, Tim, *Nazi Princess: Hitler, Lord Rothermere and Princess Stephanie Von Hohenlohe*. Stroud: History Press, 2011.

Secondary sources (articles and essays)

Addison, Paul, "Churchill and Women," Churchill Archive online, 2012.

Alberti, Joanna, "British Feminists and Anti-Fascism in the 1930s," in Oldfield, Sybil (ed.), *This Working-Day World: Women's Lives and Cultures in Britain, 1914–1945*. London: Taylor & Francis, 1994, pp. 112–124.

Ashworth, Luciana, "Feminism, War and the Prospects of International Government: Helena Swanwick and the Lost Feminists of Interwar International Relations," *International Feminist Journal of Politics*, March 2011, Vol. 13, No. 1, pp. 25–43.

Aster, S., "Appeasement: Before and After Revisionism," *Diplomacy & Statecraft*, Vol. 19, No. 3, (2008), pp. 443–480.

Ball, Stuart, "The Politics of Appeasement: the Fall of the Duchess of Atholl and the Kinross and West Perth By-election, December 1938," *Scottish Historical Review*, Vol. LXIX, No. 187 (Apr., 1990), pp. 49–83.

Beaumont, Caitriona, "Citizens not Feminists: The Boundary Negotiation between Citizenship and Feminism in Mainstream Women's Organisations in England, 1928–39," *Women's History Review*, Vol. 9, No. 2 (2000), pp. 411–429.

Beers, Laura Drummond, "A Model MP? Ellen Wilkinson, Gender, Politics and Celebrity Culture in Interwar Britain," *Cultural and Social History*, Vol. 10, No. 2 (Jun., 2013), pp. 231–250.

——, "Whose Opinion? Changing Attitudes Towards Opinion Polling in British politics, 1937–1964," *Twentieth Century British History*, Vol. 17, No. 2, 2006, pp. 177–205.

Berthezene, Clarisse, "Creating Conservative Fabians and the Founding of Ashbridge College," *Past and Present*, Vol. 182, Issue 1 (Feb. 2004), pp. 211–240.

Bingham, Adrian, "An Era of Domesticity? Histories of Women and Gender in Interwar Britain," *Cultural and Social History*, Vol. 1, No. 2 (2004), pp. 225–233.

——, "'Stop the Flapper Folly': Lord Rothermere, the *Daily Mail* and the Equalization of the Franchise, 1927–8," *Twentieth Century British History*, Vol. 13, No. 1 (2002), pp. 17–37.

Black, Naomi, "The Mother's International: The Women's Co-Operative Guild and Feminist Pacifism," *Women's Studies International Forum*, Vol. 7, No. 6 (1984), pp. 467–476.

Blanchard, Eric M., "Gender, International Relations, and the Development of Feminist Security Theory," *Signs*, Vol. 28, No. 4 (Summer, 2003), pp. 1289–1312.

Bock, Gisela, "Antinatalism, Maternity and Paternity in National Socialist Racism," in Crew, D.F. (ed.), *Nazism and German Society, 1933–1945*. London: Routledge, 1994, pp. 110–140.

Boyce, D.G., "Public Opinion and Historians," *History*, Vol. 63, No. 208 (Jun., 1978), pp. 214–228.

Buchanan, Tom, "Anti-fascism and Democracy in the 1930s," *European History Quarterly*, Vol. 32, No. 2, (2002), pp. 39–57.

Bush, Barbara, "'Britain's Conscience in Africa': White Women, Race and Imperial Politics in Inter-war Britain," in Midgley, Clare (ed.), *Gender and Imperialism*. Manchester: Manchester University Press, 1998, pp. 200–223.

Carr, Richard, "Veterans of the First World War and Conservative Anti-Appeasement," *Twentieth Century British History*, Vol. 22, No. 1 (2011), pp. 28–51.

Ceadel, Martin, "Interpreting East Fulham," in Cook, Chris and Ramsden, John (eds.), *By-elections in British Politics* (London: UCL Press, 1997), pp. 94–111.

——, "The First British Referendum: The Peace Ballot, 1934–5," *English Historical Review*, Vol. 95, No. 377 (Oct., 1980), pp. 810–839.

Cesarani, David, "Mad Dogs and Englishmen: Towards a Taxonomy of Rescuers in a 'Bystander' Country—Britain 1933–45," *British Journal of Holocaust Education*, Vol. 9, No. 2/3 (1999), pp. 28–56.

Charmley, John, "'Reassessments of Winston Churchill': A Reply," *International History Review*, Vol. 18, No. 2 (1996), pp. 371–375.

Collins, Marcus, "The Fall of the English Gentleman: The National Character in Decline, c. 1918–1970," *Historical Research*, Vol. 75, No. 187 (Feb., 2002), pp. 90–110.

Cornwall, Mark, "Elizabeth Wiskemann and the Sudeten Question: A Woman at the 'Essential Hinge' of Europe," *Central Europe*, Vol. 1, No. I (May, 2003), pp. 55–75.

Costin, Lela B., "Feminism, Pacifism, Internationalism and the 1915 International Congress of Women," *Women's Studies International Forum*, Vol. 5, No. 3/4 (1982), pp. 301–315.

Crang, Jeremy A., "The Revival of the British Women's Auxiliary Services in the Late Nineteen Thirties," *Historical Research*, (May, 2010) 83.220, pp. 343–357.

Crowson, N.J., "Conservative Parliamentary Dissent over Foreign Policy During the Premiership of Neville Chamberlain: Myth or Reality?," *Parliamentary History*, Vol. 14, No. 3 (1995), pp. 315–336.

Dilks, David N., "Public Opinion and Foreign Policy: Great Britain," *Opinion publique et politique exterieure en Europe. II 1915–1940: Actes du Colloque de Rome* (1981), pp. 57–79.

Eatwell, Roger, "Munich, Public Opinion, and the Popular Front," *Journal of Contemporary History*, Vol. 6, No. 4 (1971), pp. 122–139.

Erikson, Christine K., "So Much for Men. Conservative Women and National Defence in the 1920s and 1930s," *American Studies*, Vol. 45, No. 1 (Spring, 2004), pp. 85–102.

Finney, Patrick, "The Romance of Decline: The Historiography of Appeasement and British National Identity," *Electronic Journal of International History* (Jun., 2000). http://sas-space.sas.ac.uk/3385/1/Journal_of_International_History_2000-06_Finney.pdf

Francis, Martin, "Labour and Gender," in Duncan Tanner, Pat Thane and Nick Tiratsoo (eds.), *Labour's First Century,* Cambridge: Cambridge University Press, 2001, pp. 191–220.

———, "Tears, Tantrums, and Bared Teeth: The Emotional Economy of Three Conservative Prime Ministers, 1951–1963," *Journal of British Studies*, Vol. 41, No. 3, (Jul., 2002), pp. 354–387.

Gewitz, Sharon, "Anglo-Jewish Responses to Nazi Germany 1933–39: The Anti-Nazi Boycott and the Board of Deputies of British Jews," *Journal of Contemporary History*, Vol. 26, No. 2 (Apr., 1991), pp. 255–276.

Goot, Murray, "Mass-Observation and Modern Public Opinion Research," in Donsbach, W. and Traugott, M. (eds.), *The SAGE Handbook of Public Opinion Research.* London: Sage, 2008, pp. 93–103.

Gottlieb, Julie, "'Broken Friendships and Vanished Loyalties': Gender, Collective (In) Security and Anti-Fascism in Britain in the 1930s," *Politics, Religion & Ideology*, Vol. 13, No. 2 (2012), pp. 197–219.

———, "Feminism and Anti-Fascism in Britain between the Wars: Militancy Revived?" in Copsey, Nigel, and Renton (eds.), Dave, *British Fascism, the Labour Movement and the State.* Basingstoke: Palgrave, 2006, pp. 68–94.

———, "Femmes, Conservatisme et Fascisme en Grand-Bretagne: Comparisons et Convergences" in Varvaecke, P. (ed.), *Radical Rights in France and Britain in the 20th Century: Comparison, Transfers and Crossed Perspectives.* Paris: Presses du Septentrion, pp. 387–424.

———, "'Flour Power' and Feminism between the Waves," Special Issue: Feminism and Feminists after Suffrage, *Women's History Review*, Vol. 23, No. 3 (Jun., 2014), pp. 325–329.

———, "'Motherly Hate': Gendering Anti-Semitism in the British Union of Fascists", *Gender & History*, Vol. 14, No. 2 (Aug., 2002), pp. 294–320.

———, "Varieties of Feminist Anti-Fascism," in Copsey, Nigel and Andrzej Olechnowicz, Andrzej (eds.), *Varieties of Anti-Fascism: Britain in the Inter-war Period.* Basingstoke: Palgrave, 2010, pp. 101–118.

——— and Stibbe, Matthew, "When Hitler's Perfect Woman Came to Call," *BBC History Magazine* (Mar., 2014), pp. 51–54.

———, "'The Women's Movement Took the Wrong Turning': British Feminists, Pacifism and the Politics of Appeasement," *Women's History Review*, Vol. 23, No. 3 (Jun., 2014), pp. 441–462.

Grayson, Richard, "Leo Amery's Imperialist Alternative to Appeasement in the 1930s," *Twentieth Century British History*, Vol. 17, No. 4 (2006), pp. 489–515.

Gullace, Nicoletta F., "Christabel Pankhurst and the Smethwick Election: Right-wing Feminism, the Great War and the Ideology of Consumption," *Women's History Review*, Vol. 23, No. 3 (Jun., 2014), pp. 330–346.

Haapanki, Michele, "Writers in Arms and the Just War: The Spanish Civil war, Literary Activism and Leftist Masculinity," *Left History*, Vol. 10, No. 2 (2005), pp. 33–52.

Harrison, Brian, "Women in a Men's House: The Women MPs, 1919–1945," *Historical Journal*, Vol. 29, No. 3 (Sept., 1986), pp. 632–654.

Hendley, Matthew, "Anti-Alienism and the Primrose League: The Externalization of the Postwar Crisis in Great Britain, 1918–32," *Albion*, Vol. 33, No. 2 (Summer, 2001), pp. 243–269.

———, "Citizens or Consumers? British Conservative Political Propaganda Towards Women in the Two World Wars," in Ho Hon Leung, Matthew Hendley, Robert W. Compton and Brian D. Haley (eds.), *Imagining Globalization: Language, Identities and Boundaries*. New York: Palgrave, 2009.

Hilson, Mary, "Women Voters and the Rhetoric of Patriotism in the British General Election of 1918," *Women's History Review*, Vol. 10, No. 2 (2001), pp. 325–347.

Hirsch, Pam, "Authorship and Propaganda: Phyllis Bottome and the Making of *The Mortal Storm*, (1940)," *Historical Journal of Film, Radio and Television*, No. 32, No. 1 (Mar., 2012), pp. 57–72.

Huckner, Daniel, "The Unending Debate: Appeasement, Chamberlain and the Origins of the Second World War," *Intelligence and National Security*, Vol. 23, No. 4, (2008), pp. 536–551.

Hurtley, Jacqueline and Russell, Elizabeth, "Women Against Fascism: Nancy Cunard and Charlotte Haldane," *Bells: Barcelona English Language and Literature Studies*, Vol. 7 (1996), pp. 43–52.

Jarvis, David, "Mrs Maggs and Betty: The Conservative Appeal to Women Voters in the 1920s," *Twentieth Century British History*, Vol. 5, No. 2 (1994), pp. 129–152.

Jones, Adam, "Does 'gender' Make the World Go Round? Feminist Critiques of International Relations, *Review of International Studies*, Vol. 22, No. 4 (Oct., 1996), pp. 405–429.

Jones, Helen, "National, Community and Personal Priorities: British women's Responses to Refugees from the Nazis, from the Mid-1930s to the Early 1940s," *Women's History Review*," Vol. 21, No. 1 (2012), pp. 121–151.

Lawrence, Jon, "Forging a Peaceable Kingdom: War, Violence, and Fear of Brutalization in Post-First World War Britain," *Journal of Modern History*, Vol. 75, No. 3 (Sept., 2003), pp. 557–589.

Lee, Gerald, "'I See Dead People': Air-Raid Phobia and Britain's Behavior in the Munich Crisis," *Security Studies*, Vol. 13, No. 2 (2003), pp. 230–272.

Leventhal, Fred M., "British Writers, American Readers: Women's Voices in Wartime," *Albion*, Vol. 32, No. 1 (Spring, 2000), pp. 1–18.

Lukowitz, David C., "British Pacifists and Appeasement: The Peace Pledge Union," *Journal of Contemporary History*, Vol. 9, No. 1 (Jan., 1974), pp. 115–127.

McCarthy, Helen, "Democratizing British Foreign Policy: Rethinking the Peace Ballot, 1934–1935," *Journal of British Studies*, Vol. 49, No. 2, (Apr., 2010), pp. 358–387.

———, "Petticoat Diplomacy: The Admission of Women to the British Foreign Service, c. 1919–1946," *Twentieth Century British History*, Vol. 20, No. 3 (2009), pp. 285–321.

McLean, Iain, "Oxford and Bridgwater," in Cook, Chris and Ramsden, John (eds.), *By-elections in British Politics*. London: UCL Press, 1997, pp. 130–150.

Miller, Carol, "'Geneva-the key to equality': Inter-war Feminists and the League of Nations," *Women's History Review*, Vol. 3, No. 2 (1994), pp. 219–245.

Mort, Frank, "Love in a Cold Climate: Letters, Public Opinion and Monarchy in the 1936 Abdication Crisis," *Twentieth Century British History*, Vol. 25, No. 1 (2014), pp. 30–62.

Olechnowicz, Andrzej, "Liberal Anti-Fascism in the 1930s: The Case of Sir Ernest Baker," *Albion*, Vol. 36, No. 4 (Winter, 2004), pp. 636–660.

Pedersen, Susan, "Review Essay: Back to the League of Nations," *American Historical Review*, (Oct. 2007), pp. 1091–1117.

———, "Metaphors of the Schoolroom: Women Working the Mandates System of the League of Nations," *History Workshop Journal*, Vol. 66, No. 1 (2008), pp. 188–207.

———, "The Future of Feminist History," *Perspectives* (Oct., 2000).

Perry, Matt, "In Search of 'Red Ellen' Wilkinson Beyond Frontiers and Beyond the Nation State," *IRSH*, Vol. 58 (2013), pp. 219–246.

Peterson, V. Spike, "Feminism and International Relations," *Gender & History*, Vol. 10, No. 3, (Nov., 1998), pp. 581–589.

Pogorelskin, Alexis, "Phyllis Bottome's *The Mortal Storm*: Film and Controversy," *The Space Between*, Vol. 6, No. 1. (2010), pp. 39–58.

Pollen, Annebella, "Research Methodology in Mass Observation Past and Present," *History Workshop Journal*, Vol. 75, No. 1 (Spring, 2013), pp. 213–235.

Pugh, Martin, "The Liberal Party and the Popular Front," *English Historical Review*, Vol. CXXI, No. 494, (Dec., 2006), pp. 1328–1350.

Pronay, Nicholas, "Rearmament and the British public: policy and propaganda," in Curren, James, Smith, Anthony, Wingate, Pauline (eds.), *Impacts and Influences: Essays on Media Power in the Twentieth Century*. London: Methuen, 1987, pp. 53–96.

Purvis, June, "The Pankhursts and the Great War," in Fell, A.S. and Sharp, I. (eds.), *The Women's Movement in Wartime*. Basingstoke: Palgrave, 2007, pp. 141–157.

Rasmussen, M. Vedby, "The History of a Lesson: Versailles, Munich and the Social Construction of the Past," *Review of International Studies*, Vol. 29 (2003), pp. 499–519.

Rau, Petra, "The Fascist Body Beautiful and the Imperial Crisis in 1930s British Writing," *Journal of European Studies*, Vol. 39, No. 1 (Mar., 2009), pp. 5–35.

Riedi, Eliza, "Imperialist Women and Conservative Activism in Early-Twentieth-Century Britain: the political world of Violet Milner," *Women's History Review*, Vol. 22, No. 6 (2013), pp. 930–953.

Ripsman, Norrin M. and Levy, Jack S., "Wishful Thinking or Buying Time? The Logic of British Appeasement in the 1930s," *International Security*, Vol. 33, No. 2 (Fall, 2008), pp. 148–181.

Risse-Kappen, Thomas, "Public Opinion, Domestic Structure, and Foreign Policy in Liberal Democracies," *World Politics*, Vol. 43, No. 4 (Jul., 1991), pp. 479–512.

Rose, Norman, "The Resignation of Anthony Eden," *Historical Journal*, Vol. 25, No. 4 (1982), pp. 911–931.

Rose, Sonya, "Sex, Citizenship, and the Nation in World War II Britain," *American Historical Review*, Vol. 103, No. 4 (Oct., 1998), pp. 1147–1176.

Rupp, Leila J., "Constructing Internationalism: The Case of Transnational Women's Organizations, 1888–1945," *American Historical Review*, Vol. 99, No. 5 (Dec., 1994), pp. 1571–1600.

Schroeder, Paul W., "Munich and the British Tradition," *Historical Journal*, Vol. 19, No. 1 (Mar., 1976), pp. 223–243.

Schwartz, Angela, "British Visitors to National Socialist Germany: In a Familiar or a Foreign Country?" *Journal of Contemporary History*, Vol. 28, No. 3 (Jul., 1993), pp. 487–509.

Scott, Joan W., "Gender: A Useful Category of Historical Analysis," *American Historical Review*, Vol. 91, No. 5 (Dec., 1986), pp. 1053–1075.

Sluga, Glenda, "Female and National Self-Determination: A Gender Re-reading of 'The Apogee of Nationalism,'" *Nations and Nationalism*, Vol. 6, No. 4. (Oct., 2000), pp. 495–521.

Sontag, Susan, "Fascinating Fascism" in *Under the Sign of Saturn*. New York: Pan, 1980, pp. 73–105.

Strang, G. Bruce, "The Spirit of Ulysses? Ideology and British Appeasement in the 1930s," *Diplomacy & Statecraft*, Vol. 19, No. 3 (2008), pp. 481–526.

Steiner, Zara, "On Writing International History: Chaps, Maps and Much More," *International Affairs*, Vol. 73, No. 3 (Jul., 1997), pp. 531–546.

Stone, Dan, "The 'Mein Kampf Ramp': Emily Overend Lorimer and Hitler Translations in Britain," *German History*, Vol. 26, No. 4 (2008), pp. 504–519.

Squires, Judith and Weldes, Jutta, "Beyond Being Marginal: Gender and International Relations in Britain," *BJPIR*, Vol. 9 (2007), pp. 185–203.

Summerfield, Penny, "Dunkirk and the Popular Memory of Britain at War, 1940–58," *Journal of Contemporary History*, Vol. 45, No. 4 (Oct., 2010), pp. 788–811.

———, "'Our Amazonian Colleague': Edith Summerskill's Problematic Reputation," in Toye, R. and Gottlieb, J. (eds.), *Making Reputations*. London: I.B. Tauris, 2005, pp. 135–150.

Taylor, Verta and Rupp, Leila J., "Loving Internationalism: The Emotion Culture of Transnational Women's Organizations, 1888–1945," *Mobilization*, Vol. 7, No. 2 (2002), pp. 141–158.

Thane, Pat, "What Difference did the Vote Make?," *Historical Research*, Vol. 76, No. 192 (May, 2003), pp. 268–285.

Thomson, J.A., "The Peace Ballot and he People," *Albion*, Vol. 13, No. 4 (Winter, 1981), pp. 381–392.

Thurlow, Richard, "The Evolution of the Mythical British Fifth Column, 1939–46," *Twentieth Century British History*, Vol. 10, No. 4 (1999), pp. 477–498.

Tregidga, Garry, "Turning of the Tide? A Case Study of the Liberal Party in Provincial Britain in the Late 1930s," *History*, Vol. 307 (Jul., 2007), pp. 347–366.

Vellacott, Jo, "Feminism as if All People Mattered: Working to Remove the Causes of War, 1919–1929," *Contemporary European History*, Vol. 10, No. 3 (2001), pp. 375–394.

Wark, Wesley, "Review Article: Appeasement Revisited," *International History Review*, Vol. 17, No. 3 (1995), pp. 545–562.

Weinberg, Gerhard L., Rock, William R. and Cienciala, Anna M. (ed.) "Essay and Reflection: The Munich Crisis Revisited," *International History Review*, Vol. 11, No. 4 (1989), pp. 668–688.

Wilford, R.A., "The PEN Club, 1930–50," *Journal of Contemporary History*, Vol. 14, No. 1 (Jan., 1979), pp. 99–116.

Williamson, Philip, "Christian Conservatives and the Totalitarian Challenge, 1933–1940," *English History Review*, Vol. 115, No. 462 (2000), pp. 607–642.

———, "The Conservative Party, Fascism and anti-Fascism 1918–1939," in Copsey, N. and Olechnowicz, A. (eds.), *Varieties of Anti-Fascism in the Inter-war Period*. Basingstoke: Palgrave, 2010, pp. 73–97.

Workman, Joanne, "Wading Through the Mire: An Historiographical Study of the British Women's Movement between the Wars," *University of Sussex Journal of Contemporary History*, Vol. 2 (2001). https://www.sussex.ac.uk/webteam/gateway/file.php?name=2-workman-wading-through-the-mire&site=15

Young, John W., "Harold Nicolson and Appeasement," in Murfett, Malcolm (ed.), *Shaping British Foreign and Defence Policy in the Twentieth Century*. Basingstoke: Palgrave Macmillan, 2014, pp. 136–158.

Younger, Kenneth, "Public Opinion and British Foreign Affairs," *International Affairs*, Vol. 40, No. 1 (Jan., 1964), pp. 22–33.

Youngs, Gillian, "Feminist International Relations: A Contradiction in Terms? Or: Why Women and Gender are Essential to Understanding the World 'we' Live in," *International Affairs*, Vol. 80, No. I (2004), pp. 75–87.

Zweininger-Bargielowska, Ina, "Building a British Superman: Physical Culture in Interwar Britain," *Journal of Contemporary History*, Vol. 41, No. 4 (2006), pp. 595–561.

Index

A

Abdication crisis 154, 160, 172, 203,
    225, 240
Abyssinia 5, 33, 39–40, 47, 49–50, 249,
    251, 258, 276n38
Ackland, Valentine 257
Acland, Richard 222, 226, 230, 246
Adams, R.J.Q 7
Adams, Vyvyan 246
Adamson, Jennie 220–2, 230, 232–3
Adamson, W.H. 220
Addams, Jane 21
aerial warfare 1, 5, 6, 157, 161, 220, 242
Air Raid Precautions (ARP) 128, 157,
    167, 171, 219
Allen, Mary 48, 105, 128–9, 286n27
Amery, Florence 91–3, 126
Amery, Leo 89, 91–3, 106, 113, 126,
    182–3, 209, 236, 239, 254, 261–2,
    283n43
Anglo-German Fellowship 61–2, 85,
    94, 129, 294n71
Anglo-German relations 4–5, 10, 32,
    61–81, 82–100, 235–65 passim
Anglo-Italian relations *see Italy*
Anschluss *see Austria*
anti-communism 75, 101–2, 117–23,
    224, 250
anti-fascism *see Nazism* and *feminist
    anti-fascism*
anti-militarism *see also pacifism* and
    feminist pacifism 13,16, 30, 38,
    113, 189
Anti-Nazi Council 246
anti-Semitism *see Jews*
anti-slavery 31, 273n84
Appeasement
    anti-appeasers 6, 9, 12, 30, 42,
        48, 126, 155–7, 173–4, 225, 229,
        235–265 passim
    and cartoons 178–84
    and Conservative women 122–30
    definition of 3, 239
    elite women's support for 61–81

historiography of 3, 6–10, 237–8,
    290n3
and the Left 41–2
popular support for 153–184, 188–211
Archdale, Betty 24, 28
Archdale, Helen 28
Arms and the Covenant 246–7
Armistice Day 209, 257
Army Territorial Service (ATS) 53, 61,
    167, 254
Aryton Gould, Barbara 230
Ascroft, Eileen 159
Ashridge College 107, 113
Aster, Sidney 7–8
Astor, Lady Nancy 10, 12, 19, 30, 40–1,
    45–7, 62, 65, 72–7, 83–4, 88, 98,
    103, 106–7, 112–3, 118, 126, 131,
    134, 167, 181, 215, 235–6, 242, 256,
    281n63, 281n92, 286n38
Astor, Lady Violet 61, 125
Astor, Waldorf 74–5, 285n84
Astor, William Waldorf 78, 168, 212, 251
Atholl, Duchess of 12, 35, 49, 55–7,
    103, 106, 109–10, 131, 212, 216,
    224–9, 233, 238–9, 241, 244, 247,
    249–54, 257, 263, 286n24, 287n49,
    305n65, 305n67, 310n61
Attlee, Clement 220
Attolico, Bernardo 94
Asquith, Margo 218
Australia 19
Austria 5, 25–6, 31, 33, 34, 44, 56–7,
    164, 214
aviation 105–6, 242, 286n31

B

Bagnold, Enid 48, 95, 284n63
Balch, Emily 21
Balcon, Michael 170
Baldwin, Lady Lucy 67, 69, 203, 280n39
Baldwin, Oliver 58
Baldwin, Stanley, 48, 64, 69, 84–6, 106,
    111, 114, 118–9, 122, 179–80, 183,
    197, 203–4, 223

Lightning Source UK Ltd.
Milton Keynes UK
UKHW022054270322
400702UK00005B/56

9 780230 304307